LANDSCAPE ASSESSMENT

COMMUNITY DEVELOPMENT SERIES

Series Editor: Richard P. Dober, AIP

Volumes Published and in Preparation

EDRA CONFERENCE PUBLICATIONS

CDS/11

LANDSCAPE ASSESSMENT: VALUES, PERCEPTIONS, AND RESOURCES

Edited by

Ervin H. Zube
Institute for Man and Environment

Robert O. Brush
*Pinchot Institute of Environmental
    Forestry Research*

Julius Gy. Fabos
University of Massachusetts

Dowden, Hutchinson & Ross, Inc.

STROUDSBURG, PENNSYLVANIA

Distributed by
HALSTED
PRESS   A division of
    John Wiley & Sons, Inc.

Copyright © 1975 by **Dowden, Hutchinson & Ross, Inc.**
Community Development Series, Volume 11
Library of Congress Catalog Card Number: 74–13331
ISBN: 0–470–98423–6

77   76   75   5   4   3   2   1
Manufactured in the United States of America.

Library of Congress Cataloging in Publication Data

Zube, Ervin H
    Landscape assessment.

    (Community development series, v. 11)
    1. Landscape protection--United States. 2. Environ-
mental protection--United States. 3. Environmental
policy--United States. I. Brush, Robert O., joint
author. II. Fabos, Julius Gy., joint author.
III. Title.
QH76.Z82   333.7'2'0973   74-13331
ISBN 0-470-98423-6

Exclusive Distributor: **Halsted Press**
A Division of John Wiley & Sons, Inc.

SERIES EDITOR'S FOREWORD

There are many reasons to think that landscape appreciation is a more commonly held cultural value now than it was several decades ago. Among many signs and signals supporting this view are these: consumer preferences in housing location and the strength of the second-home market, both of which are heavily landscape-oriented; significant increases in expenditures for outdoor camping and recreation equipment; the number of popular books and journals published about many facets of the outdoor world; rising membership in clubs and societies that are environmentally based; and political action at every government level to enhance, improve, and use the landscape wisely.

Underlying this phenomenon is the idea that certain landscape elements — such as scenery — are unique, if not scarce, resources. As such, they are amenable to constructive manipulation and management.

As an example of how this might be done, we are pleased to publish this pioneering effort on landscape assessment. It is a fresh conceptualization of a design methodology that is as pragmatic as it is timely. Of particular merit are those techniques that involve the user, including getting responses and feedback that focus on the perceptual landscape, man-made and nature-given. The subject of this book, then, fits in well with the purpose of the Community Development Series — to provide professionals and their clients with technical and reference works that advance the art and science of the built environment.

Richard P. Dober, AIP
Series Editor

v

PREFACE

Within the past 15 years public awareness of the landscape as a scenic resource has expanded from concern with the uniquely beautiful, the Yosemites and Grand Canyons of America, to the uniquely ugly, the strip mines, auto junkyards, and billboard alleys of America, to the everyday nonunique landscapes in which most Americans live, recreate, work, and travel. In other words, what our everyday world looks like is becoming recognized as a matter of some importance by public policy makers. The traditional concerns of designers and planners for visual quality in the environment are being transformed into legislation at the federal, state, and local level.

President Johnson, in his message to Congress on February 8, 1965, stated:

We must not only protect the country-side and save it from destruction, we must restore what has been destroyed and salvage the beauty and charm of our cities. Our conservation must be not just the classic conservation of protection and development, but a creative conservation of restoration and innovation. Its concern is not with nature alone, but with the total relationship between man and the world around him. Its object is not just man's welfare, but the dignity of man's spirit.

In this conservation the protection and enhancement of man's opportunity to be in contact with beauty must play a role.

The Highway Beautification Act of 1965 and the Appalachian Regional Development Acts of 1965 and 1969 are exemplary of this desire to "restore what has been destroyed," to attack the uniquely bad or ugly in the American land-scape.

On January 1, 1970, the National Environmental Policy Act of 1969 was signed into law. Section 102(2)(b) of the act requires that all agencies of the federal government shall

identify and develop methods and procedures, in consultation with the Council on Environmental Quality established by Title II of this Act, which will insure that presently unquantified environmental amenities and values may be given appropriate consideration in decision making along with economic and technical considerations.

The Act requires that all agencies of the federal government predict the impact of major federal actions on the environment — including the aesthetic impact.

The June 1970 report of the Public Land Law Review Commission and the 1970 Special Task Force report of the Water Resources Council on planning guidelines drew attention to the need for the consideration of aesthetic values in resource planning and management programs. The former called for the setting of environmental quality standards and for the classification of public lands for environmental quality enhancement and maintenance such that the importance of visual and aesthetic environmental experiences is included therein. The Special Task Force report set forth as an environmental quality objective in the planning of water and related land resources the "Management, protection, enhancement, or creation of areas of natural beauty and human enjoyment such as open and green space, wild and scenic rivers, lakes, beaches, shores, mountain and wilderness areas and estuaries."

The 1965 White House Conference on Natural Beauty served as a very real stimulus to activity at the state level. Between 1965 and 1968, 34 states held similar conferences on natural beauty. Since then this concern with natural beauty has been subsumed in the broader issue of land-use policy. While legislation is pending at the federal level, a number of states have taken aggressive steps in the development of policy and in the implementation of land-use controls. For example, in 1970 both Maine and Vermont enacted legislation that established state permit systems as a means of controlling large commercial, residential, and industrial developments. The legislation was prompted in both states because of a very real concern for the threat these developments were posing to scenic landscapes and natural resources. The Maine law cites four criteria for the granting of a permit. The first, second, and fourth, respectively, relate to financial capacity, traffic movement, and soil types. The third states that there can be

no adverse effect on natural environments. The proposed development has made adequate provision for fitting itself harmoniously into the existing natural environment and will not adversely affect existing uses, scenic character, natural resources or property values in the municipality or in adjoining municipalities.

The Vermont law cites nine conditions for the granting of a permit. They relate to questions of water and air pollution, water supply, soil, traffic, delivery of municipal, educational, and governmental services, and the relationship to existing plans. The eighth condition states that the proposed development

will not have an undue adverse effect on the scenic or natural beauty of the area, aesthetic, historic sites or rare and irreplaceable natural areas.

In both Maine and Vermont, aesthetics has been a major factor in the review of applications for permits during the first 3 years of operation. In both states, approximately 50 percent of the applications have had conditions attached and have required some modification of the plans because of aesthetic factors. As of March 1, 1974, Vermont had received 1,642 applications of which 1,466 had been acted upon and 196 were pending.

This then is the background of and the impetus for this volume. Increased environmental awareness with attention focused on intangible or amenity values in the landscape has laid down the challenge to planners, designers, and scientists to ensure that these values are identified and entered into the public decision-making process.

The social norms expressed by these public actions and laws clearly suggest that scenic quality — the visual attributes of the landscape — has become a thing of value, a resource. This visual–cultural resource is also being recognized, along with other renewable and non-renewable resources, as something that must be included in the development of environmental plans and management programs. During the past decade, behavioral scientists and environmental designers and planners have begun to undertake the kinds of research and to develop the kinds of assessment techniques required to make such planning and management possible and meaningful.

The editors of this volume believe that a considerable amount of work has been done in landscape perception and in the development of landscape-assessment methods by individuals working collaboratively and individually in a number of disciplines. It is our opinion that both practitioners in the field and researchers in the universities can benefit from a state-of-the-art report. To that end, the authors of the chapters in this volume were invited both to review briefly recent pertinent literature and to report on the current status of their own research and perceptions of the state of the art. In an effort to obtain the broadest possible coverage, authors were invited from the behavioral, social, and natural sciences, from the humanities, and from the planning and design professions.

This book is organized around three major themes: values, perceptions, and resources.

The first theme, landscape values, focuses on the traditional qualitative values associated with the landscape as they are expressed in contemporary culture. The values are considered from the perspectives of history, humanism, design, conservation, and economics. The perception theme draws upon the work of environmental psychologists and designers and focuses on human responses to the visual landscape. It serves as a bridge from the traditionally identified or assumed values to the resource-assessment issues of the third theme. The study of landscape perception provides an element of validation for landscape values and also provides guidance to planners and designers charged with developing and implementing resource-management programs. The resources theme focuses on application, on the models that have been developed for landscape planning and management. It includes both general approaches to landscape assessment and more specific models developed for dealing with the impact of highways and recreation on visual–cultural resources.

Most of the authors of these chapters met in Amherst, Massachusetts, on November 15 and 16, 1973, at a conference on landscape assessment to participate in a series of discussions organized around the three themes of this book. As a result of those discussions, several chapters have been considerably revised or expanded. All the chapters represent original contributions.

We wish to acknowledge the valuable assistance of the several organizations and agencies that cooperated in the development of this publication and provided the support for the conference at which the authors met and discussed their individual and collective contributions. These were the American Society of Landscape Architects Foundation, Washington, D.C.; The Conservation Foundation, Washington, D.C.; Department of Landscape Architecture and Regional Planning, University of Massachusetts, Amherst, Massachusetts; Institute for Man and Environment, University of Massachusetts, Amherst, Massachusetts; Pinchot Institute of Environmental Forestry Research, U.S. Department of Agriculture — Forest Service, Northeastern Forest Experiment Station, Upper Darby, Pennsylvania; University of Massachusetts Landscape Association, Amherst, Massachusetts; Water Resources Institute, Department of the Army, Corps of Engineers, Washington, D.C.

We are indebted to our colleagues Ethan Gluck, R. Jeffrey Riotte, and Gary Robinette, who assisted in planning and organizing the November conference, and to David Aggerholm, Hugh C. Davis, Stanley Moss, Andrew J. W. Scheffey, and Harry Schwarz, who served as moderators of the discussion sessions.

We extend our thanks to William Menke for his work on the graphic material in the book. And finally, we wish to express a special note of gratitude to Helen Swartz for her invaluable assistance on every aspect of the conference and book.

Ervin H. Zube
Robert O. Brush
Julius Gy. Fabos

CONTENTS

LANDSCAPE ASSESSMENT

LANDSCAPE VALUES

The six contributors to this first section articulate some of the qualitative values that are commonly associated with the American landscape. These chapters are intended to provide a context in which to consider the assumptions and results of the quantitative studies reported in the following two sections. These statements of qualitative values were elicited from persons of quite different standpoints and perspectives, yet they are remarkably cohesive. The content of each chapter will be summarized briefly, and several recurring themes will be noted.

John B. Jackson describes two social forces that have not only shaped the American landscape, but have prescribed the standards by which the landscape was to be appreciated. The Puritan ethic prevailing in the eighteenth century fostered small communities of families who husbanded the land with a religious purpose. In those times a landscape was thought to be beautiful when it revealed a moral or ethical truth. The nineteenth century brought a new ethic, that of the engineer, whose visions held human enterprise to the goal of efficiency in the production, use, and conservation of energy. Beauty in the landscape was redefined in terms of efficiency in the flow of energy within the system.

Jackson sees a third social force arising in the pragmatic acceptance of the "dirt and confusion and crowds" of the engineer's world. This contemporary reaction is altering society's evaluation of the natural environment. Landscapes are seen as *settings* for an experience rather than the experience itself, and are deemed beautiful insofar as they contribute to self-awareness and self-knowledge.

Roderick Nash expands upon a thesis of historian Frederick Jackson Turner that the character and culture of a people are shaped by their environment; the rigors of subsisting in a wild and rugged land forged the individuality of American frontiersmen, and influenced the culture of the nation and its democratic institutions. Nash expands upon this theme and cites certain values that wilderness landscapes hold for American society today.

Calvin W. Stillman delves beyond the visual landscape to explore some of the meanings of nature for the individual. He asserts that the fundamental values of nature are peculiar to the individual and are so elusive as to defy analysis and measurement. Since the values we ascribe to nature and to the landscape are subjective, there can be no objective determination of natural beauty that holds for all people. Moreover, any consensus of opinion as to what is natural beauty is no more than a political expression of dominance on the part of a segment of society.

Garrett Eckbo states the necessity for the environmental designer and planner to create new landscapes that sensitively integrate necessary economic development with established cultural and natural landscapes. He reflects upon the cultural values that influence the perception of the physical environment, and how they are developed and transmitted.

Ross S. Whaley traces the development of analytical tools for measuring the monetary values associated with land resources. Benefit–cost analysis and regional analysis were intended to express tangible monetary values,

but failed to adequately incorporate social costs and benefits. Landscape-assessment models compensate for this deficiency to the extent that they reflect social values, but these tools also fail by providing only a partial analysis. He concludes that the need clearly exists to develop a common denominator for comparing all benefits and all costs inherent in the landscape.

Charles E. Little sees in the prospect of a national land-use policy an urgent need to develop goals and standards regarding qualitative values inherent in land. Governmental actions toward preserving landscapes have in the past countered the prevailing materialistic values with rationalizations based upon concepts of environmental determinism, the conservation of natural resources, or the need to provide facilities for outdoor recreation. None of these rationalizations has been altogether successful in its objective of protecting the qualitative values in the landscapes that were reserved. Rationalizations aside, Little proposes that landscape preservation goals be based upon the visceral feeling that people have for the land and the landscape.

Although the authors of these six chapters write of qualitative landscape values from the standpoints of different disciplines and professions, they address several common themes. All seem to agree that the utilitarian values associated with measures of efficiency are not wholly adequate in evaluating landscapes. The economist's benefit–cost analysis, the ecologist's criterion of efficient energy utilization, the maximization of recreational user-days per acre, the optimal intertemporal utilization of fixed natural-resource stocks — all these concepts ignore the subjective meaning of landscapes for sentient human beings. The authors are agreed that the subjective values have so far evaded adequate analysis and measurement.

Another recurring theme is the value attached to the relative permanence of natural environments, which provides a relatively constant frame of reference in the face of urban expansion. The enduring mountains and age-old trees lend comfort and solace when all else seems to be in perpetual flux and imminently subject to change.

In a similar vein is attachment to a particular place — a highly imageable, memorable, familiar, and favorite plot of ground. The sense of place is the only value expressed in this section that refers to a specific piece of land.

Several contributors point out the value of natural settings as a recourse in times of stress. Just knowing that untrammeled natural settings exist provides psychic relief for some, even though they may never experience the settings directly. This suggests that the attraction of green open space and wilderness may not be so much for what it is, but rather for what it is not — the absence of concrete, asphalt, noise, and dirt.

Perhaps the most significant value that land-scapes hold for contemporary urban society is derived from settings which enable urban man to achieve a more complete sense of his own identity. Jackson identifies this value and proposes that new settings, part natural, part artificial, be formulated by environmental designers and planners. Such settings, he feels, should be made to evoke qualities of openness, freedom, and unpredictability.

In all these chapters the concern is not as much with the landscape as with people and how their environment affects them. There is little mention of the composition or content of landscapes as intrinsic values. These chapters suggest that the principal qualitative values of any landscape exist only in the eye and psyche of the beholder. Thus, the proper study of landscapes may not be the landscapes themselves, but rather the people who experience them and the human feelings and meanings evoked by external surroundings. The next section will deal specifically with human responses to the landscape.

The Historic
American Landscape

John B. Jackson

John B. Jackson lectures in the Carpenter Center for the Visual Arts at Harvard University and in the Department of Landscape Architecture at the University of California, Berkeley.

4

How to identify the main visual resources of the landscape, how to create them as well as how to preserve them and know that they have served a good purpose — these are topics of perennial concern to all. Of equal concern is the role that society plays in this kind of judgment. The history of the American landscape is in large measure the history of the social forces that have controlled it. A man-made landscape does not evolve according to some natural law; it changes as our social philosophy changes, sometimes very radically. Yet every landscape, no matter how it has been determined, has a capacity for beauty and for giving joy. It is at a time like the present, when we are becoming aware of the changes taking place, that the vision and skill of the environmental expert become most valuable.

The Connecticut River Valley, for example, is a man-made landscape of exceptional age and beauty. It is one of the classic historic landscapes of the United States. To our generation its towns and villages and farmlands epitomize New England of the eighteenth and early nineteenth centuries. To those who first explored it, almost 350 years ago, the valley offered the first reassuring glimpse of the rich New World they had dreamt of but had failed to find on the shores of Massachusetts Bay. Sixteen years after the landing at Plymouth, settlers had found their way west, and they came in increasing numbers throughout the seventeenth century.

Despite Indian raids and wars, the settlements multiplied and prospered, and as the meadows and areas of cultivation grew closer together the valley became something more than a topographical concept. It became a landscape, perhaps the most extensive and certainly the most clearly defined human landscape in New England.

Throughout the eighteenth century, travelers going by stagecoach between Boston and the Hudson River towns must have welcomed the sight of the fields and the scattering of villages in the valley — doubly welcome after the rough forested stretches of Massachusetts or the hills of western Connecticut. In their letters home or in their published accounts they often described the pattern of settlement, the abundance of sheep and cattle, and the prosperous farms.

The best and most detailed eighteenth-century description was written by Timothy Dwight in 1796. He had shortly before been chosen president of Yale, and had decided to devote his summer vacations to exploring New York State and New England. For the next 10 years he did so, and the four volumes of his *Travels,* recently reissued by the Harvard University Press, constitute one of the most valuable — and one of the most neglected — accounts of the American landscape and its settlement that we have.

Dwight, as a theologian, preacher, and educator, was firmly loyal to the Puritan tradition, and also a very ardent defender of all things American. The two convictions produced an extremely fresh and opinionated appraisal of the environment: although he detested the crude lawlessness of frontier society as he saw it in upper New York State, he had an insatiable interest in every unknown or unexplored aspect of the American landscape and a quick appreciation of scenic beauty, no matter how untamed. The Connecticut Valley, with its vivid memories of Dwight's grandfather, Jonathan Edwards, and with the splendor of its mountains, delighted him; he expressed his approval in long passages of stately prose.

The section describing the view over the Connecticut Valley from the summit of Mt. Holyoke is far too long to quote in full. Dwight starts with the broad river meandering between its tree-grown banks; he then gives a picture of the fields, meadows, and roads, where

a perfect neatness and brilliancy is everywhere diffused, without a neglected spot to tarnish the luster or excite a wish in the mind for a higher finish. When [the eye] marks the sprightly towns which rise upon [the river's] banks, and the numerous churches which gem the whole landscape in its neighborhood; when it explores the lofty forests, wildly contrasted with the rich scene of cultivation . . . and when last of all it fastens upon the Monadnock in the northeast and in the northwest upon Saddle Mountain, ascending each at a distance of fifty miles in dim and misty grandeur, far above all other objects of view; it will be difficult not to say that with these exquisite varieties of beauty and grandeur the relish for landscape is filled, neither a wish for a higher perfection, nor an idea of what it is remaining in the mind.

At least two aspects of this passage are worthy of note. First, in its complete unedited form it constitutes one single sentence, suspended from various semicolons, of more than 250 words. Second, from the pen of an eighteenth-century New England theologian has come one of the clearest and most eloquent statements of the religious humanist point of view toward the environment and the man-made landscape. It is sometimes said that because of his unusual awareness of natural beauty Dwight was the first of America's nature romantics. But there is no trace of romanticism in his unemotional description of the beauty confronting him; there is no melancholy yearning for more, no despairing self-deprecation. "The relish for landscape," he says, "is filled." And he presumably withdrew from Mt. Holyoke, his identity intact.

What was the nature of the scenic beauty that Dwight sought to describe? What were to him the significant landscape values? I think we can say that they were essentially religious. Twice in that one passage he expresses an awareness of having glimpsed completeness, of having glimpsed the highest form of perfection, and the emphasis on "the perfect neatness and brilliancy" of the scene, its jewel-like aspect, reminds us of that mystic vision which Huxley analyzed in "The Doors of Perception" (1954). We could no doubt dismiss that phrase concerning "the idea" of a higher perfection as rhetoric, were it not that the focus of the entire panorama (as Dwight viewed it) was the village in the valley directly below. Here was the heart of the landscape: a pattern of fields, orchards, and houses, with the church in the center, all surrounded by the protective wall of forest and mountain. To the Calvinist theologian the village was little less than the symbol of piety, community, and mutual love, of "pure religion breathing household laws." The landscape, in short, possessed the quality of beauty insofar as it reflected the moral or ethical perfection to which all its inhabitants presumably aspired. Perfection or completeness resided not in the landscape itself, but in the spirit that had brought it into being and continued to animate it. This spirit was the Puritan spirit, that of a population devoted, in Dwight's words, "to the worship of Jehovah." Not every landscape possessed these qualities; Dwight was critical of other types of settlement. He condemned the backwoods communities of the New York or Vermont wilderness because these had no such religious origin. To Dwight and his contemporaries a landscape was beautiful only when it revealed or confirmed a moral or ethical truth.

This kind of appraisal is not one we in our generation are likely to find congenial, but it had merits. The man-made landscape that he found worthy of praise was certainly not lavish nor varied; it did not change or expand with grace; it was suited to a meager way of life. But his humanism never disdained the commonplace, never exalted the exotic and wonderful at the expense of everyday necessity. It never sought to wean men from society or to foster a fruitless nostalgia for the primitive. However devoid such humanism may have been of a feeling for the picturesque, it never created landscapes that were lonely; it endowed everyone who lived and worked in them with a kind of visibility, an identity tied to a fragment of the land itself. At all events, this landscape, nowhere more extensive than in the Connecticut Valley, was in those early days of the Republic the best we had. The Puritan village, stripped of its churchly characteristics, was the inspiration of the new rectangular landscape that came into existence west of the Alleghenies with the Land Ordinance of 1785. It was the eighteenth-century New England community, inhabited and self-governed by a small society of independent farmers, that Jefferson and others sought in fact to reproduce when they devised the range and township and section system, which still prevails over most of the United States.

As we all know, that particular agrarian dream failed to become a reality. But it took several decades to die, and I think we can say that it survived, although in an attenuated form, until after the Civil War. What eventually replaced the moral–ethical perception of the landscape was the vision of the engineer. We are only now beginning to study the origins and growth of the engineer's landscape, and the insidious manner in which the engineer's philosophy has affected our attitudes toward *every* landscape, even while we denounce it.

In his earliest guise, the engineer in America seemed to be exclusively devoted to the community — even the Puritan community. Toward the end of his life, Dwight noted with approval the construction of dams and canals throughout New England; at the same time Albert Gallatin, likewise a defender of the humanist tradition, launched a national program of internal improvements. Although many of these improvements were designed to serve the rising commercial and manufacturing interests, Dwight and his contemporaries managed to discover their moral justification; they not only created wealth, they discouraged idleness and taught skills. Forts, harbors, bridges, and roads, designed by engineers, were interpreted as signs of concern for the community and its welfare. It was not long after Dwight's death that the engineer further adorned the landscape by the building of railroads. But even this modification of the environment retained, visually at least, something of that civic quality suggested in the term civil engineer. For it was he who built the massive viaducts and bridges, who provided the rural as well as the urban landscape of America with a kind of granite infrastructure that still impresses us by its monumentality.

Only in the 1860s did the engineer begin to discard his civility, and that took place when he entered the employ of industry. His new clients, rich and ambitious, transformed him into the single most powerful environmental force in America, although a force entirely under their control. With the rise of the steam-powered factory, the multiplication of railroads, and the search for new natural resources, the concern of the engineer ceased to be civic or national and concentrated instead on the production, conservation, and use

of energy — energy from water, coal, gas, and wood, energy in the form of steam and electricity, and ultimately in the form of human labor. Inevitably, the American landscape reflected his efforts: not only in the rail lines, coal mines, hydroelectric dams, oil wells, and the multitude of factories and company towns; even the contemporary superhighway expresses the engineer's skill in conveying energy from one side of the nation to the other. And it cannot be forgotten that it was the engineer's obsession with plentiful and reliable energy that largely inspired the conservation movement of 70 years ago, as well as our own contemporary manner of interpreting economic difficulties.

Thus we are confronted with another implicit definition of environmental values: to the engineer (and to the engineer-minded society) a landscape is beautiful when the energy-flow system is functioning with unimpeded efficiency. Is it necessary to point out how similar this is to the concept of the average ecologist?

For it was not simply the environment that the engineer modified; the whole temper of American life and thought was changed, and permanently changed. By the end of the nineteenth century the majority of Americans were already living in towns and cities; the majority of Americans, that is, had pretty well broken their ties with the rural landscape and had begun to forget the role that the landscape had once played in the formation of their character and identity. I do not mean to imply that the new industrial order invariably meant a lowering of the quality of the environment of the average American. Quite the contrary; many small farmers and farm laborers were happy to exchange their exhausted acres and squalid houses for less strenuous work in a factory and a home in a company town. Nevertheless, the old covenant had been broken or annulled; there were no longer any agrarian routines and duties to teach citizenship and piety; without attachment to some piece of land, men lost their visibility. And how were the values of the landscape to be perceived when they no longer taught a lesson? Furthermore, the urban American found that all significant experiences, good or bad, now usually took place in the company of many other people, often strangers, and in environments owned or controlled either by the public authority or by a corporation: factory, office, or store; beach, park, or sports arena — environments for which the average citizen did not and could not feel any responsibility.

We are prone to exaggerate the consequences of this alienation and loss of visibility. It is hard for us to admit that most human qualities, like hydroponic vegetables, manage to flourish even when they have no roots in the soil. But there can be no doubt that an entirely new relationship to the environment has evolved over the past century of engineer control, or rather two distinct relationships.

One, with which literature has made us very familiar, is the indignant rejection of the engineer's world, with its dirt, confusion, and crowds, and flight to the wilderness. The other reaction, far more general and far less articulate, and on that account generally ignored by students of environmental perception, was *acceptance* of the situation, a readiness to take whatever pleasures were made available in an increasingly urbanized environment. A lingering romantic tradition, popular in the academic and upper-class world, finds little of value in that acceptance, and laments the crowded holiday highways, the crowded ball parks, the crowded beaches, the meretricious forms of recreation. But what some of us call crowds, others call people, and many enjoy these pastimes not as surrogates for the vanished agrarian experience, but as something entirely new and rewarding.

In any case, whether we abandon the en-

gineered landscape in favor of the wilderness or whether we embrace it, we are expressing an identical attitude toward the environment; and that attitude is essentially that of the engineer. The landscape is no longer the locus of character formation, for carrying out traditional obligations; it is now a place where certain resources can be bought or had for free. Our objective is that of the engineer: to accumulate energy, whether psychic or physical, and then to transfer it to the city.

Finally, one more characteristic of the contemporary evaluation of the natural environment, although obvious enough, should not be omitted, because it too is the product of the engineer way of life. Our contacts with that environment are not only brief and infrequent, but scheduled, taking place on holidays and weekends, determined not by seasons but by the routine of urban work. So these contacts are events to be looked forward to, planned, and long remembered. The natural environment thus becomes the *setting* of an experience, rather than the experience itself.

And what is the nature of that experience? How does it differ from the traditional experience of the wilderness explorer? In three specific ways: the contemporary experience is not solitary, it is not contemplative, and it is less concerned with awareness of the environment as a distinct phenomenon than it is with the cultivation of *self-awareness*.

This is not the place to expatiate on this new search for self-awareness by means of new sports and skills of mobility and intimate contact with the less familiar aspects of the environment: wind, slope, surface texture, depths of water, aerial heights; they represent, I think, a potentially valuable search for identity by means of a new kind of environmental experience, and quite clearly they call for new kinds of environment, part natural, part engineered. Such activities are distinctly urban insofar as they do not reject the presence of others. And insofar as this search for self-awareness has its religious or mystical quality, it is important to bear in mind that solitude is not a necessary or even a desirable ingredient. Here again we are often the victims of a romantic tradition which has insisted that religious insight comes only to the solitary seeker. But the thousands who gathered on the shores of the Sea of Galilee were not unique. We have only to recall the crowds who collected on the Boston Common to hear Whitefield preach, the thousands who gathered in the frontier forest clearings for revivals, or for that matter the tens of thousands who gathered at Woodstock or Watkins Glen, to recognize that the open-air environment can offer as genuine an experience to the crowd as to the individual.

It follows, I think, that we must learn to provide places for this kind of experience. It is almost as if we were reverting to the attitude of Timothy Dwight: discovering landscape beauty chiefly in those environments where men and women achieve a more complete sense of their own identity. But the identity we are after is, of course, far removed from that of Dwight's hardworking, pious farmer, and it calls for a very different setting; far more spacious, far less domestic, far less detailed. It is for the environmental planner and designer to formulate these settings and to discover how and where they can be artificially created. There is, even now, no lack of suggestive examples: the freeway, the ski slope, the wide expanse of public lawn, the wide expanse of water, landscapes of space and freedom and unpredictability. Environmental art can improve and perfect them, and devise new ones.

A third definition of landscape beauty therefore suggests itself: a landscape is beautiful when it has been or can be the scene of a significant experience in self-awareness and eventual self-knowledge.

Qualitative Landscape Values: The Historical Perspective

Roderick Nash

Roderick Nash is Professor of History and Environmental Studies and Chairman of Environmental Studies at the University of California, Santa Barbara.

Frederick Jackson Turner, the interpreter of the American frontier experience, has received more than his share of critical lumps at the hands of historians. Some are certainly deserved. But Turner's 1892 "frontier thesis" contains some indisputably brilliant insights into the task of determining qualitative landscape values. Turner's central point is that the character and culture of a people are shaped by their environment. Americans were different, Turner explained (1920),[1] because they had come into contact with wilderness. This pioneering experience fostered individualism, independence, and a confidence in the common man that encouraged democratic forms of social organization. The New World environment, according to Turner, was a clean slate on which hopeful people could write their dreams for a better life. A sense of messianic idealism — the American mission — understandably developed as a central part of the American national character. The frontier, as Turner saw it, was a giant crucible: Europeans entered and Americans emerged. The process required only a few generations.

The Turner thesis lends substance to the idea

that the place makes the man. Far more important than clothes in this regard is the landscape in which a person is born and raised. It is extremely meaningful to know that someone is a Westerner, a resident of New York City, a New Englander, a Texan, or from Dubuque. We instinctively sense that a people acquire certain mental and even physical characteristics from a particular locality. Exceptions exist, of course, and there are many other influences on character and personality. But as the common heritage that everyone in a locality shares, landscape is an undeniably important factor in the development of common traits. For the same reason the physical landscape is valuable as an historical document. Historians should recognize that men leave a record of their ideas and actions on the land just as they leave it on paper. The only difference is the writing implements — axes and bulldozers make as revealing a mark as pencils and pens. I have long urged my students to see the landscape as a giant blackboard on which they can read important parts of the story of the nation's past. The members of my environmental history classes are in the library everytime they walk outdoors.

Because landscape helps determine what we are, it follows that man as a normally egocentric creature takes pride in being from a particular place, a distinctive environment. He applauds the mention of his home town. Frederick Jackson Turner, for instance, made it clear that by virtue of his contact with the frontier the American was not only different from the European but *better*. Despotism and subservient attitudes dissolved on the outskirts of civilization. Democracy was a forest product. So was the aggregation of attitudes, values, and ambitions that collectively define Americanism. The making of Americans simply could not have occurred in the Old World. New environmental circumstances — a dis-

tinctive landscape — was essential in developing a distinctive nationality.

Turner, along with Theodore Roosevelt and many of their contemporaries, also believed that the frontier environment was essential in sustaining the American style. Such views gave rise to concern about the disappearance of frontier conditions. In 1903 Turner wondered if American ideals "have acquired sufficient momentum to sustain themselves under conditions so radically unlike those in the days of their origins" (Turner, 1920:260–61). Roosevelt continually harped on the theme of over-civilization and the concomitant phenomena of a vanishing frontier. "As our civilization grows older and more complex," the big-game-hunting President thundered (Roosevelt, 1924–1926, vol. 18:23), "we need a greater and not a less development of the fundamental frontier virtues." The growth of civilization was, obviously, the transforming influence, and by the time an iconoclastic employee of the U.S. Forest Service named Aldo Leopold was writing in the 1920s, the wide open spaces were closing in rapidly. It seemed to Leopold entirely possible that Americans might eradicate all significant physical vestiges of their pioneer past. In company with John Muir, Benton MacKaye, and other harbingers of the wilderness preservation movement, he was deeply troubled at the prospect of a frontierless America. It seemed to Leopold (1924) that "many of the attributes most distinctive of America and Americans are [due to] the impress of the wilderness and the life that accompanied it." Acting on this insight, he had already launched a crusade to preserve wilderness on National Forest land. He received support from articles like Emerson Hough's in the *Saturday Evening Post* (1922:63), which argued that a "typical portion of the American wilderness" should be maintained in its wild condition to show future citizens "what the old

America once was, how beautiful, how splendid."

Wilderness preservationists like Aldo Leopold and Emerson Hough knew that the wildland they sought to save was not just a place for outdoor recreation. They recognized that landscape form had a great deal to do with defining and perpetuating a society's character. Given the opportunity to experience wilderness, successive generations of urban-oriented Americans could acquaint themselves firsthand with the conditions that shaped their culture (Leopold, 1925a:21, 56). In the process they would have a chance to acquire some of the pioneer characteristics that, as Leopold (1925b:602) put it, "if anything are the indigenous part of our Americanism." When linked to history in this fashion, the value of a physical landscape was, essentially, beyond price. At stake was a people's very identity. Speaking for himself, Leopold confessed (1945:414) that he was "glad I shall never be young without wild country to be young in. Of what avail are forty freedoms without a blank spot on the map?"

The link Aldo Leopold established between wildland and free men became increasingly important as the twentieth century unrolled. Many began to accord wilderness value as an antipode to an ever-more-restricting civilization. The mere existence of wild country would be insurance against the submergence of individuality by cities and machines. With George Orwell's portrait of an omnipotent future society in mind, wilderness guide Sigurd Olson argued that the wilder parts of the physical landscape helped preserve human dignity. "It is far more," Olson declared[2] (1972:156), "than hunting, fishing, hiking, camping or canoeing; it has to do with the human spirit." For ecologist René Dubos (1968:4–5), the main value of the American wilderness was the fact that it constituted a bulwark against "dehumanization." Supreme Court Justice William

O. Douglas believed that roadless landscape was "one pledge to freedom." With access to wilderness where he could escape the driving pace of a mechanized civilization, "man need not become an automaton." In such places the individual could find relief from "mass compulsions" and totalitarian tendencies. Wilderness, Douglas continued, is the nearest approximation modern man could find of the presocial state of nature. Deviancy, idiosyncracy, eccentricity, and originality could thrive in the wilds beyond the reach of civilization's control. Their survival seemed to Douglas an important symbol of the possibility of individual variance and thus, in turn, of freedom. Thus, for Douglas, as for Frederick Jackson Turner, the American wilderness was the ultimate source of America's liberal and democratic tradition (Douglas, 1960:101, 1961:14–5, 1965:26–7).

It remained for novelist Wallace Stegner to give the most eloquent recent expression to the importance, for the individual and his cultural values, of the wild parts of the physical landscape. The American, Stegner began, is different among men insofar as he "has renewed himself in the wild." Because of the influence of the wilderness on three centuries of American history, ideals of human liberty and human dignity became "something more than an abstract dream." According to Stegner, "we were in subtle ways subdued by what we conquered." Reflecting on the future, he expressed his conviction that "without any . . . wilderness we are committed wholly . . . to a headlong drive into our technological termite-life, the Brave New World of a completely man-controlled environment." For Stegner it was not even necessary to visit wilderness with a pack and sleeping bag. Just *knowing* it existed, knowing that civilization was not all-embracing, fortified man's spirit. For Stegner wilderness held out the possibility of new beginnings; it replenished the American dream of a better life for man on earth. When Stegner (1969:145ff.) termed the uncivilized American landscape "part of the geography of hope," he had these things in mind.

Recognition of the relationship of physical landscape to the national culture and ego began with the beginnings of American nationhood. Indeed, this was a major concern of the young nation. The problem was that victory over the British at Yorktown in 1781 and the subsequent signing of the Treaty of Paris did not really establish American independence. Politically, the United States might be a nation, but most of its citizens realized that true nationhood entailed more than mere separation. The new republic had to demonstrate its capacity for defense, government, and economic self-sufficiency. In addition, there was a cultural or intellectual requirement for independence. Eighteenth-century philosophers of romantic nationalism made it clear that every bona fide nation had a unique *Geist,* or spirit, manifested in its art, literature, and the character of its people. This distinctiveness formed the basis of national pride. If the upstart United States could not demonstrate such cultural uniqueness, its claim to nationhood was open to question, as was the validity of the American Revolution.

Almost desperately, as a consequence, Americans sought sustenance for their national ego. They needed something valuable and distinctive that could transform embarrassed provincials into proud and confident citizens. But difficulties appeared at once. Our short history, shallow traditions, and minor cultural accomplishments seemed paltry, especially in comparison to Europe's. For decades after the revolution this realization frustrated American arts and letters, branding it with imitation and self-pity. But gradually cultural nationalists began to sense that in one respect their coun-

try *was* different: the New World had no counterpart in the Old. Specifically, it was *wilder.* Seizing on this distinction and adding to it newly minted assumptions about the aesthetic, religious, and romantic significance of wilderness, eager American patriots argued that, far from being a liability to culture as was traditionally assumed, wilderness was actually a cultural asset. To be sure, most Americans of the early national period continued to relish the destruction of wilderness, but recognition of the cultural significance of wilderness had a major role in changing their attitude to an appreciation of it (Nash, 1973:67–83).

As Americans explored the meaning of wilderness as a cultural resource, several reasons for pride came to light. Some argued that proximity to the wild sublimity of the American landscape would inspire artists and poets to great achievements. Wilderness, moreover, would furnish the subject matter for American arts and letters: European models could be thrust aside and native creativity released. Others contended that if pure nature were the medium through which God spoke most clearly, then America with its abundance of wilderness had a distinct moral advantage over the Old World, where centuries of civilization had deposited layers of artificiality on God's works. Another line of argument held that a wilderness environment produced a distinctive and desirable national character. The American, it was widely thought or, at least, hoped, combined the best of savagery and civilization into a kind of superman, superior to both the Indian and the European.

With these ideas providing the intellectual foundation, in the anxious early years of their republic Americans turned repeatedly to wilderness as a source of pride. As early as the 1780s, Philip Freneau, desperately searching for some way in which to praise his fledgling country, referred to the Mississippi (Marsh,

1955:228) as "this prince of rivers in comparison of whom the *Nile* is but a small rivulet, and the *Danube* a ditch." A number of illustrated "scenery" albums also made clear the link between nationalism and nature. As early as 1820, plans were made for a volume entitled *Picturesque Views of the American Scene* (Weitenkampf, 1945:61) that would show "our lofty mountains . . . the unexampled magnitude of our cataracts, the wild grandeur of our western forests . . . unsurpassed by any of the boasted scenery of other countries." As romantic interest in nature increased in the following decades, there were numerous similar ventures. Nathaniel P. Willis's text for *American Scenery* of 1840 was typical with its assertion that "Nature has wrought with a bolder hand in America." According to Willis, the native wilderness presented "a lavish and large-featured sublimity . . . quite dissimilar to the picturesque of all other countries" (vol. I, 1840:5). In 1852 came Elias L. Magoon's *The Home Book of the Picturesque*, with an expression of gratitude to God "that there are yet wild spots and wildernesses left . . . whence thought may take the wildest range." Such places, Magoon believed, "have ever developed the strongest patriotism, intensest energy, and most valuable letters of the world" (1852:37–8). In the absence of an environment consecrated by thousands of years of history, the natural landscape was the nationalists' trump.

Although actual cultural achievement fell short of what the nationalists hoped, it is still true that much of what was distinctively American in our early arts and letters utilized the wild landscape. James Kirke Paulding's 1818 novel, *The Backwoodsman*, alerted American writers to the literary potential of wild country. Looking west, rather than to Europe, Paulding declared, would be "the means of attaining to novelty of subject." It is well known how James

Fenimore Cooper at first disregarded this advice and failed miserably with his first novel, *Precaution,* an English imitation. But in 1823 he turned to the wilderness in *The Pioneers* and became a national literary hero. This and Cooper's subsequent Leatherstocking tales were preeminently American fiction because they bore the stamp of the unique in the American landscape.

The history of American painting provides an excellent example of the way the native landscape figured in the development of American cultural nationalism. Prior to the 1820s, our artists were virtually enslaved by European styles and subjects. When they did attempt a landscape, it was usually in the English pastoral tradition with purling brooks, placid cows, and, perhaps, a rustic swain or two. No one ever thought of painting a landscape divorced from human significance. There was always some sign of man or his works in evidence. Nature was background and setting, never important for its own sake. But in 1823 a young English immigrant, who had seen the beauty of the upper Ohio Valley, resolved to abandon portrait painting and devote his considerable talents to depicting, as he put it (Flexner, 1962:39), "the wild and great features of nature: mountainous forests that know not man." With this statement, Thomas Cole made a sort of declaration of independence for American painting. In the next few years he ranged, sketchbook in hand, through the wilder parts of northern New York and New England. The result was a series of wilderness landscapes, such as his study of the Catskill Mountains, that won Cole artistic fame and launched the Hudson River School of American painting. Excluding man and civilization from many of his canvases, Cole delighted in depicting the raw, unkempt power of wilderness with symbols such as the shattered tree trunks and surging storm clouds that appear in

Landscape with Tree Trunks. The contrast of such paintings with the ordered, pastoral landscapes inspired by Europe was sharp.

In 1829 Thomas Cole sailed to Europe for a period of study. His admirers feared that exposure to the Old World might lure him away from the American wilderness as a subject for art. And Cole was moved by what he saw in Europe. The way the face of the land, with its ruins and castles, reflected a long and rich history especially impressed him. Back in New York in 1835, Cole had an opportunity to summarize his reactions in an address before the National Academy of Design. Europe received its due: "Time and genius," Cole declared (1835:4–5), "have suspended an imperishable halo" over the Old World landscape that rendered it "glorious." But, he quickly added, Americans need not feel inferior. While lacking a storied past (1835:9), "American scenery . . . has features . . . unknown to Europe. The most distinctive, and perhaps the most impressive, characteristics of American scenery," he explained, "is its wildness." Americans should be grateful, Cole concluded (1835:12), that God, not man, had marked their landscape, making it ideal for "the contemplation of eternal things."

In 1836 Cole completed a series of five canvases entitled "The Course of Empire," in which the meaning of wilderness for American civilization received dramatic explication. In the first painting, *The Savage State,* Cole showed a wilderness inhabited by a hunter race. Time passed, and when Cole depicted the scene again it was the home of a people living in the arcadian or pastoral stage. Wilderness had partially given way to a rural landscape, but in the right corner the artist retained an untamed mountain peak. Man continued to alter the face of the earth, and in the third painting, *The Consummation of Empire,* we see a flourishing civilization. Wilderness had

been reduced to that single peak in the right corner, but in so doing Cole implied that the society had cut itself off from the source of its physical and spiritual vitality. Although outwardly luxurious, this civilization was actually moribund, and in the next scene we see the inevitable result: barbarians from wilder environments swept down and reduced the great city to ruin. In the final picture all is desolation. But the symbolic peak still looms in the corner, and its influence is beginning to spread as wild vines and grasses cover the scars of battle. We are left to believe that in time wilderness conditions will be restored and the cycle repeated. We can also conclude that the landscape at any stage of development is symbolic, evoking strong responses in minds tuned to the movement of history.

The relevance of "The Course of Empire" to the United States in the 1830s was clear: Europe, having lost its strength-giving wild roots, was declining. America, because of its proximity to wilderness, both chronologically and geographically, was on the rise — the new race of conquerors. Yet this very growth and prosperity were reason for concern. Might not the nation commit the error of Cole's civilization, or of Greece and Rome, and, by severing itself from the influence of wild nature, become prey for a wilder race? From Cole and Henry David Thoreau to Theodore Roosevelt, this question haunted many Americans. It also created a frame of mind favorable to the idea of preserving wilderness. Cole's empire had permitted its original wilderness to be reduced to a single peak, forgotten amid the pomp and splendor below. America's parks and reserves, it was hoped, would be reservoirs of wildness in the midst of civilization and halt Cole's cyclical progression at the midpoint of perpetual greatness. Wilderness, moreover, could serve the nation as a kind of historical document reminding Americans of the frontier heritage that many believed was responsible for giving the national character a unique and desirable shape.

Thomas Cole died prematurely in 1848, but his pupil, Frederick E. Church, carried on the tradition of American wilderness painting. The crucial experience in Church's development as an artist was an 1856 camping trip of eight days into the Mt. Katahdin region of northern Maine. Greatly inspired, the artist returned to his studio and painted a Maine lake and surrounding mountains at sunset. A crude road and a few sheep in the foreground are the only reminders of civilization. Four years later Church painted the little-known but magnificent *Twilight in the Wilderness*. Again the setting was northern Maine, but this time all traces of the pastoral had vanished. In the brilliant sunset and brooding Katahdin-like mountains there is a suggestion of the apocalyptic expectations of the virgin continent.

Cole and Church painted wildernesses of the East; subsequent American landscape artists took their palettes and their national pride across the Mississippi. In the American West they found ideal subjects for both. Within a few years of his first visit to the Rocky Mountains in 1858, Albert Bierstadt was busy depicting their peaks, canyons, and lakes on gigantic canvases measuring up to 84 square feet. Turning to the Sierras in the 1870s and 1880s, he painted Mt. Whitney and Mirror Lake in Yosemite Valley. He also was one of the first to paint the Hetch Hetchy Valley, later the object of a classic battle in the early history of wilderness preservation. Bierstadt's exaggerated, dramatic style provoked criticism, but represented a sincere attempt to express his awe and delight in the American wilderness.

Many early western landscapists were necessarily explorers as well. Thomas Moran participated in the famous 1871 Ferdinand V. Hayden expedition into the Yellowstone country, and his drawings of its wonders assisted in the successful campaign for the national park the following year. Subsequently, Moran painted throughout the West. He especially loved the Teton Range, one of whose peaks bears his name. Working in watercolor, Moran depicted California's Sierras. He also accepted the challenge of capturing the size and color of the Grand Canyon of the Colorado. When Congress in 1874 appropriated $10,000 for one of Moran's studies of the Canyon to hang in the Senate lobby, wilderness received official endorsement as a mainspring of American nationalism.

William H. Jackson, a pioneer landscape photographer, accompanied Moran and Hayden on the 1871 Yellowstone expedition. Jackson's artistic medium soon became a potent new force in directing American attention to wilderness as a source of pride. Following him have come Cedric Wright, Ansel Adams, Eliot Porter, and Philip Hyde, artists who have used cameras to expand the potential of landscape art. Certainly the prints in the Sierra Club's Exhibit Format Series have gone far in this direction, and to an historian of ideas these books stand squarely in the tradition of nineteenth-century scenery albums in their attempt to use wilderness as an ingredient of American culture. It is highly appropriate that the Exhibit Format Series should have received international publishing awards, since for over a century Americans have been calling the world's attention to their landscape as something unique and precious.

I want to emphasize that the physical landscape constitutes one of the best available links to the past. Indeed, we should think of landscape as a document, like a book or an oration or a code of laws. When properly "read," the landscape establishes a dramatic sense of continuity with the past. We have all had the experience of drawing closer to history by experiencing a place of historic importance. It follows that if we desire to preserve a sense of history (and the alternative is a frightening collective amnesia) then we would do well to preserve the environments in which it transpired and that retain the capacity to evoke understanding.

Few Americans, for instance, can pass through Cumberland Gap without drawing closer to Daniel Boone and the flood of pioneers who followed him through that famous pass to the West. And to stand on the high plains, looking west at the front range of the Rocky Mountains stretching like a barrier of snow across the horizon, is to appreciate the achievement of the men who matched these mountains on their way to Oregon and California. Lectures and books, no matter how good, are poor substitutes for confrontation with the land itself. Another place where history makes itself felt, to me at least, is in the canoe country of the Quetico–Superior in northern Minnesota. When you travel the fur traders' routes, feeling the bite of canoe thwarts on long portages and exulting at the glimmer of water through the trees, you draw as close as it is possible to the voyageurs. Consider finally the incredible landscape of the Grand Canyon. To pass through it on the Colorado River by boat is to relive several pasts. The most recent is that of John Wesley Powell, whose pioneering river run of 1869 filled in one

of the last vast blanks on the American map. But before Powell is the past of the native American inhabitants of the Grand Canyon, and preceding them is the prehuman history of the earth itself. If we had dammed the Grand Canyon as we came perilously close to doing in the 1960s, we would have been the poorer historically. And insofar as we are products of the past, some of our own identity would have vanished as well.

In concluding, we might think upon the implication of the story told about an established western rancher. His lush irrigated fields stretched away from his comfortable, modern home as far as the eye could see. But right in the middle of the green land was a one-acre patch of the original desert: cactus, mesquite, bone-dry soil. Surprised visitors invariably asked why that land had not also been irrigated. The rancher's reply underscores the central point of this chapter. "Well, once it was all like that," he said softly, "and I didn't want to forget."

NOTES

1. F. J. Turner (1920), *The Frontier in American History.* New York: Holt, Rinehart and Winston, Inc. Turner's 1892 talk entitled "The Significance of the Frontier in American History" is the initial chapter in this book, which collects his major analyses of frontier influence.
2. "The Spiritual Aspects of Wilderness," quoted in Ezra Bowen (1972), *The High Sierra.* New York: Time–Life Books.

This Fair Land

Calvin W. Stillman

Landscape is important because land is important to us; we hold strong feelings about it; landscape is what we see when we look upon this that we love.[1] Yet land itself is not the essential matter for concern. The essential is something closer to the concept "nature," a term that I wish to discuss. I hold that nature comprises a great submerged interest in our culture, of the order of a great batholith, out of sight but always there, made evident by scattered outcrops of concern.

One such concern is expressed by the conservation movement, now so well documented by historians (Hays, 1959). This I can summarize as concern over scarcities, fears that necessary supplies will diminish because of human lack of consideration for others in exploitation of natural resources. Conservation activists have appealed often to the symbol of unborn generations and to the dangers of power lodged in wrong hands. The successor environmentalist movement has refined concern to such immediate life-support systems as

Calvin W. Stillman is a Professor in the Department of Environmental Resources at Rutgers University.

This chapter is a product of Project 268 of the New Jersey Agricultural Experiment Station.

air, water, and space. These concerns have been examined in detail by the best of all the research groups in this area: Resources for the Future, Inc. (Brubaker, 1972).

A large part of interest in nature is what Albert Schweitzer called "reverence for life." This is sheer, positive pleasure in seeing things live. The scale can vary from window box and houseplant, devoted dog and housebound cat, through suburban plot and exurban "farm," to wilderness experience (Nash, 1973). This feeling relates to the peculiar prestige accorded agriculture and forestry in American culture (Griswold, 1948), and the trifurcation of feelings for wild animals: loving them, hunting them, and treating them as vermin (Graham, 1973).

A third great area of concern is simply conceptual: satisfaction drawn from ideas about nature. There is something akin to religion in an all-encompassing world view that places its adherent securely in a scheme of things (Redfield, 1962:231–53). On the other hand, use of nature as a religion has a vital lacuna: in nature there is no ethical system.

At several periods of stress in our culture, nature has become a recourse for many minds under pressure. Our own time is noted for the appeal of such related notions as "the balance of nature," cycles (for instance in climate), and that lovely Lorelei, "ecology." As an idea system, nature has great potential for individuals, but for a society the same ideas can be dysfunctional. This the founding fathers understood in adding the First Amendment to the Constitution of the United States.

Land as a concrete manifestation of nature is a romantic subject for many of us; landscape mediates between physiographic reality and our ideas of what it should look like (Fairbrother, 1970; Jackson, 1972). Romance, however, is a mercurial substance, founded as it is on love and ignorance.[2] We have a large seg-

ment of the national press devoted to nature in many of its aspects; this "nature press" is worthy of study as a phenomenon of our culture. We have, in fact, a "nature business," not yet, so far as I know, dignified by recognition by academics. Bird seed sales run to $25,000,000 a year in the United States.[3] Anyone can find his own instance.

Each September students enter my institution following the holy grail of the times. These students are concerned with environment, with ecology, and with their personal missions of saving from man what they see as great, delicate, and imperiled natural systems. They have studied catalogues and have read into course descriptions fulfillment of their dreams. In each dream the student has a status and a role in the world he perceives to exist. In their courses as they begin to grind along, in prerequisites for degrees, finally in possibilities for employment, things happen to these roles and to these worlds. Broken blossoms begin to drift into my office about October, each year. My mission is to salvage as much as I can of the student, and of the dream, for each is precious — and from the dream material to fashion learning experiences of permanent value (Stillman, 1972).

We know a lot about land as a physiographic entity. We know a lot about what others have said and done about land. We have excellent histories of gardening, landscape, and agriculture in all its forms. We know a great deal about positions people have taken on questions of the relative values to be placed on the preservation of nature, on natural beauty, on exploitation of economically significant natural resources, on restoration, and on the artifacts of landscape gardening. We know very little about the relevance of land, nature, and landscape to individual personality structures. We do not know the meanings to persons of the actual experience of natural settings, of being able to look at nature, or of the associated idea systems.

Of one thing I am sure: the great living values of "nature" transcend the potentials of university-based scholars to define, measure, or analyze. This is a life that is within all of us, gloriously so; all that scholars can do is peer, criticize, and now and then peck at a morsel of something quantitative.[4] First, I shall examine some individual feelings concerning nature, land, and landscape. Second, I shall consider the manner in which individual feelings are transmitted through the social system. Finally, I shall make a very few comments on contemporary American society.

NATURE AND THE INDIVIDUAL

At one point in the Watergate hearings of 1973 the senior senator from North Carolina referred to "all us fellow-travellers on the road to the tomb . . . ." The Select Committee was in no way concerned with the amenities of nature, but was very much concerned with the values and ethics that the members assumed were shared by all men; their concern was with a vital component of the human environment. The chairman's phrase emphasizes that each of us is much like every other, and that each of us is mortal. True as are Senator Ervin's propositions, each of us spends much of his imaginative life trying to escape them. On the one hand, we generally accept the fact that each of us is part of nature; on the other, we each seek to establish an identity distinct from our environment. And each of us grasps at immortality.

The world "nature" takes its root from the Latin "to be born." Its meaning is far more than landscape, land, living things, or natural environment. That which is natural for us expresses a very deep sense of propriety, and of relationships in which our personal status is central. Nature expresses the way things *ought*

to be. Fundamental in the concept of nature as it is used in our culture is hierarchy, an external system — basically supportive — in which each of us has a place. Here lie nuclear ideas of belonging, of rights, and of property. These deepest personal feelings, those least often examined in the light of logic and comparative human experience, are most readily projected upon the world outside.

Edward Stainbrook has written (1969:5) that

In a psychological sense time tends to get mixed up with space, and immortality and infinity are projected against the background of the permanent, relatively unchanging earth. As a support for his own immortality strivings, man needs the sense and the security of the timeless duration of nature. As contemporary society accelerates and multiplies the demands for constant change, both for individual persons and for the collectivity, the need for a relatively permanent frame of reference which can allow change to occur without the sense of being lost in the process becomes increasingly important. Just to be in frequent perceptual contact with the reassuring, enduring earth is a psychological security factor of considerable importance.

Help in dealing with concern over mortality is one of the services offered by organized religion. Each religion provides a world view, a status for the believer, an explanation of nature, an explanation of how the world began, and a sense of purpose. The monotheistic religions in general, and in particular those which have so importantly shaped our culture, utilize a father figure as vector for interpersonal ethics. An ethical system is vital for a society, but may be of little help to an individual trying to get it all together (La Barre, 1954, 1970).

Western religions have not been very interested in nature per se; they have emphasized rather the glories of the afterlife. The prophets of the Old Testament showed a coldly practical view of their environment (Genesis, Exodus, Isaiah 62:4, 5; Psalms 23, 104); its supportive potential was related always to the power of God. Animal stories in our religious tradition appear to be folk imports. The domesticated livestock that appear in every Christmas crèche escape mention in the New Testament. Tales told of St. Francis of Assisi that emphasize his feelings about animals fail to mention his sense of religious order and emphasis on poverty. We hear little about the contemporary followers of the Benedictine Rule, such as the Cistercian monks who pressed back eastward the agricultural frontier of Europe, using plants, animals, tools, and their own labor with about as much sentiment as a modern commercial farmer (Glacken, 1967:303,349).

"You will find far more in the forests than in the books; trees and stones will teach you what no teacher permits you to hear," wrote St. Bernard in the twelfth century, while abbot of the Cistercian monastery of Clairvaux.[5] His interest in this learning was pragmatic: to do a better job of farming. No preservationist, elsewhere he wrote, "The landscape is changed from a wilderness and given meaning because human beings impose an order upon it; when men change nature they make it more useful — perhaps, even, more charming and more beautiful" (Glacken, 1967:213).

The princes of the Church took their comforts where they found them; they embellished country seats with gardens and fountains, and their urban quarters with art and the services of musicians. The great patrons of the arts and of learning through the Middle Ages, noble and clerical alike, were keenly aware of the good things of life, but there was no confusion as to which were the proper objects for worship. The process of conversion of the heathen led without hesitation to the leveling of groves sacred to earlier gods of local inhabitants. An example is Monte Cassino.

Folk religions generally, polytheistic religions, Hinduism and Buddhism, Taoism, all are more hospitable to nuances of meaning in nonhuman living things (Northrup, 1947). Much of the contemporary appeal of American Indian culture is the apparent meaning of nature to these peoples who are said to live closer to it than do we. I doubt, however, that meanings of nonhuman living things in polytheistic cultures can be considered as parallel to those meanings in an essentially monotheistic, ethically oriented culture. Of this I cannot speak with certainty, for I do not have the tools to test my hypothesis. I can state, however, that in my judgment there is little interest in any concept of nature in tropical and subtropical societies. Interest in nature appears to be associated with the northern peoples of the world, peoples known also for achievement orientation, aptitudes for science, explicit systems of interpersonal ethics, and aggressiveness.[6]

Sir Kenneth Clark has written (1969:269) that

For almost a thousand years the chief creative force in western civilization was Christianity. Then, in about the year 1725, it suddenly declined and an intellectual society practically disappeared. Of course it left a vacuum. People couldn't get on without a belief in something outside themselves, and during the next hundred years they concocted a new belief which, however irrational it may seem to us, has added a good deal to our civilization: a belief in the divinity of nature. It's said that one can attach fifty-two different meanings to the word "nature." In the early eighteenth century it had come to mean little more than common sense, as when in conversation we say: "but naturally." But the evidences of divine power which took the place of Christianity were manifestations of what we still mean by nature, those parts of the visible world which were not created by man and can be perceived through the senses. The first stage in this new direction of the human mind was very largely achieved in England — and perhaps it was no accident that England was the first country in which the Christian faith had collapsed. In about 1730 the French philosopher Montesquieu noted: "There is no religion in England. If anyone mentions religion people begin to laugh."

Whatever the recession of religion in England at this time, it was the period of a rising merchant class forcing a new ethic on British society. Government dominated by rural aristocracy, rotten boroughs, and favoritism and sinecures in appointments, all this was coming to an end. The movement culminated in the Reform Bill of 1832 and repeal of the Corn Laws in 1846. Foundations were laid for objective standards in the civil service. British society was to become logical, efficient, commercial minded, and dominant in the world.

The flowering of nature as reaction to logic and asceticism can be read also into the greater East Asian experience. The harshness of strict Confucian ethics in China aroused interest first in Taoist and later in Buddhist resignation and contemplation. In Japan, instances of military centralization and strong government were tempered by succeeding years of dynastic decline, marked by flourishing of the arts. The great landscape paintings of the Chinese Tang and Sung periods were done in periods of Buddhist reaction to asceticism. Heian Japan was a long period of erosion of central authority marked, among other things, by the world's first novel; Lady Murasaki's *Tale of Genji* (Reischauer and Fairbank, 1960; Lee, 1964).

Each of us knows personally the deep appeal of certain places, of plants, trees, and pets. Many of us wave the flag of an idea system that we *know,* down deep, is true. But social scientists know a lot about each of us — about the emotional stresses we have been through and about the satisfactions persons have found to help them handle these strains. Basic problems are similar for all people: problems of growing up and of human relationships, particularly those situations in which what we are told is clearly at variance with what we sense to be true. Schizophrenia accordingly is a matter of degree.

We each need recourse from stress. Some of us use other people, and some want to get away from other people, at least from some other people, for some of the time. Every recourse situation involves set, setting, and structure. Our escape must be right in terms of who is there with us; right in terms of the periscape (what we see when we look around us), and right in terms of the structured understanding of the world in which we feel comfortable.

Typical American recourses are travel, visiting, sports, alcohol and other drugs, art, music, hobbies, and nature. Each recourse requires the presence or absence of specific people, the right environment, and the feeling that all is well with the world. A joke is a drag if there is nobody to tell it to; travelers take snapshots of scenes they remember from their predecessors' postcards. Recreation is a personal matter, each to his own; what is one man's scenery is another's obscenery.

Parallel with positive recourses in American life, there are of course equally institutionalized objects that provide for disposition of paranoid fears and hostilities. Among those in recent American history have been immigrants, Demon Rum, lumbermen, the Reds, drug pushers, polluters, snakes, and sometimes, even, wilderness.

Landscape involves the imprinting on settled land of our hopes and fears, our values and status systems, our economy and technology. Each of us wants assurance that his view of the world (and his place in it) is secure. We expect to find reassurance in looking about. Walt Whitman said in 1855 (Blodgett and Sculley, 1965):

> There was a child went forth every day,
> And the first object he look'd upon, that object he
>   became,
> And that object became part of him for the day or a
>   certain part of the day,
> Or for many years or stretching cycles of years . . . .

One might only add that the child's footprints are still there to see.

Special intensity of feelings for nature are reserved for animals and for landscapes that appear to offer them hospitality. Francis Klingender has left with us a great history of animals in European art (1971). Leo Marx (1964:8) has dealt extensively with feelings for nature in American literature, and offers us this morsel from Sigmund Freud:

The creation of the mental domain of phantasy has a complete counterpart in the establishment of "reservations" and "nature-parks" in places where the inroads of agriculture, traffic, or industry threaten to change . . . the earth rapidly into something unrecognizable. The "reservation" is to maintain the old condition of things which has been regretfully sacrificed to necessity everywhere else; there everything may grow and spread as it pleases, including what is useless and even what is harmful. The mental realm of phantasy is also such a reservation reclaimed from the encroaches of the reality-principle.

Civilized man, oppressed by the restrictions of a demanding culture, may well dream of freedom and happiness in nature. Clark (1969:272) tells us of Rousseau on his island in the Lake of Bienne: "in listening to the flux and reflux of the waves, he became completely at one with nature, lost all consciousness of an independent self, all painful memories of the past or anxieties about the future, everything except the sense of being. 'I realized,' he said, 'that our existence is nothing but a succession of moments perceived through the senses.'"

Just as there is a negative for every positive, nature can mean terror for those whose minds are suitably oriented. William James wrote (1902:160) that

To believe in the carnivorous reptiles of geologic times is hard for our imagination — they seem too much like mere museum specimens. Yet there is no tooth in any one of those museum-skulls that did not daily through long years of the foretime hold fast to the body struggling in despair of some fated living victim. Forms of horror just as dreadful to the victims, if on a smaller spatial scale, fill the world about us today. Here on our very hearths and in our gardens the infernal cat plays with the panting mouse, or holds the hot bird fluttering in her jaws. Crocodiles and rattlesnakes and pythons are at this moment vessels of life as real as we are; their loathsome existence fills every minute of every day that drags its length along; and whenever they or other wild beasts clutch their living prey, the deadly horror which an agitated melancholiac feels is the literally right reaction to the situation.

Alistair Graham loved animals, became a biologist, and secured a position in the game administration of Kenya. "It came as a revelation to me," he writes (1973:15), "that the love of wild animals was often a manifestation of intense hatred." Graham writes further (1973:26):

As I began to think about the meaning of what I saw conservationists doing, I saw many manifestations of childish behaviour. For instance, all conservation was characterized by contradiction and lack of rational purpose. Game wardens who pronounced themselves dedicated to preservation would casually poison a leopard because it was a nuisance. While poachers were denounced in the bitterest terms, sportsmen made merry among the same quarry. . . .

One could not escape the resemblance in all this to the irrational impulses of a child who sees no incongruities in random loves and hates, starts and stops, dos and don'ts. I noticed too how fierce the most ardent of preservationists were when their beliefs were challenged. The intensity of their aggression on such occasions was quite out of keeping with their meekness toward animals.

Nature loving has been a shy emotion in the United States, not quite manly (Theodore Roosevelt notwithstanding). Members of the conservation movement, and the successor environmental movement, have screened their feelings with arguments that hid private values in the guise of public interests. That their fundamental feelings for nature should have been so well buried is the factor relevant here; this is the opening that Graham exploits. But Graham, with his logic, rationality, and scorn, ignores the positive social values that can be served by providing members of the public with a safe place for disposal of their paranoid hostilities.

NATURE AND SOCIAL GROUPS

Concern for environment is normal and pandemic. But, effectively, anyone's environment is mostly other people — it is not just air, water, and landscape (to paraphrase Hippocrates). To the extent that there is an environment common to all persons, it has long since been taken in hand under the rubric of the common health, safety, and welfare. Our fundamental support services are watched over by public health personnel who monitor the quality of our air and water, watch communicable diseases, and tell us where accidents are likely to happen. Theirs is the objective environment.

Judging an environment only in terms of "quality" is a subjective matter; government concern is questionable, at least. To "save" such an environment raises just the question asked of those who would save "freedom": "Just whose?"

To get others to agree on a subjective matter requires either a substantial commonality in assumptions regarding the nature of the world or a very great deal of argument. The first is easier; hence we find that environmental campaigns tend to enlist individuals already similar in essential social characteristics. The task of the crusaders is to convince outsiders that what is good for me is good for thee (Paul Samuelson has denoted this as a fallacy of composition). The problem could be described as one of bridging a generalization gap.

A special field of environmental advocacy is the evaluation of landscape. The requirements for seizure of this concern seem to me to be three:

1. A positive feeling for nature as a recourse in the totality of life.
2. Identification with the social system that either produced, or values, the landscape in question (in short, to hold a reassuring status in the system, and to be basically satisfied with the performance of the local public health department).
3. Attachment to what Richard Hofstadter calls the paranoid style in American politics.

A landscape can be seen as an object of value, a matter of consensus within a group, or a symbol of life of a group. In any case, it is the evaluation that matters, the meaning of what is there as seen by its perceivers. There can be no objective, interpersonal, intergroup value in a landscape. Nor can there be any objective, interpersonal, intergroup determination of what is natural beauty. Achievement of a consensus on natural beauty is an indication of dominance within the community concerned. Examples are to be found in the standards of local zoning boards.

In our society, wealth and prestige are associated with ownership of land. This reflects partly the former economic importance of agriculture, partly feeling for nature, and partly cultural lag in assertion of status. There is a presumption in favor of landscapes of the most recent respectable aristocracy. Fashionable details of past landscapes — particularly those reproducible economically — become symbols for homes of families on the way up the social scale. Thus the trim shrubbery, the unused front lawn, and the panels of rail fence of American suburbia. [The notion of the single-family detached home, with its own grounds, has a venerable ancestry regardless of its present drift from respectability (Arensberg, 1955).] But love of nature as we understand it, love of wild areas, is culture-bound. Not all Americans share these values. For one example, Barzini tells us of the quite different Italian heritage (1965:79):

Life in the raw can be notoriously meaningless and frightening. Italians feel uncomfortable when surrounded by nature. They have for centuries cut down ancient woods where the pagan deities found their last refuge and solitary majestic trees. They long ago found ways to force vegetation to obey their will; they prune bushes into sculptured forms, they created gardens which were as similar to green cities as possible. Gabriele D'Annunzio, who was perhaps more Italian than any other Italian, spent the last years of his life passionately uprooting trees and bushes in his beautiful garden on Lake Garda (planted years before by a nature-loving German) to put in their place stone pillars, stone walls, marble arches, and allegorical statuary. He even transported and installed among the flower beds the iron prow of a first world war torpedo boat.

For me, beauty in landscape consists in leaving everything alone to grow in its own untrammeled way, unless there is a worthy reason for controlling something. I can identify with the freedom of untrammeled life, and I can identify with the objectives and the values of the persons who have exercised control. I find cultivated farms pleasanter to gaze upon than those abandoned to broom-sedge and brush. I doubt that my feeling has anything at all to do with shapes, or colors, or relative sizes of areas of shades of green. I enjoy the landscape of the New Jersey Turnpike north of the Raritan River and of the western reaches of the Indiana Turnpike through East Chicago and Gary. These industrial landscapes belong there, and I'm glad to see them, sweaty, rusty, smoking, and dirty as they are. I detest what I consider to be displaced symbols: fields without function, fences "for looks," lawns that cannot be played on, that are forbidden to dogs and children. I retch at the expanses of green that surround the more pretentious factories and research corporations, where the misplaced symbol evokes the college campus.

One's own sense of personal status requires confirmation from others. Symbols of status are studied by admirers, and if they fit, they are adopted. Feeling for nature is associated with high status in the United States; hence to express these feelings can be in part to define one's sense of personal status. Hofstadter wrote (1965:52–3) that

In a country where physical needs have been, by the scale of the world's living standards, on the whole well met, the luxury of questing after status has assumed an unusually prominent place in our civic consciousness. Political life is not simply an arena in which the conflicting interests of various social groups in concrete material gains are fought out; it is also an arena in which status aspirations and frustrations are, as the psychologists would say, projected. It is at this point that the issues of politics, or the pretended issues of politics, become interwoven with and dependent upon the personal problems of individuals. We have, at all times, two kinds of processes going on in inextricable connection with each other: interest politics, the clash of material aims and needs among various groups and blocs; and status politics, the clash of various projective rationalizations arising from status aspirations and other personal motives.

There is a dynamic dimension to status politics also: what happens as time brings social change. Established status in the United States, as in northern Europe, has been associated with land; as prestige slips from an established group, emphasis on the old symbols is exaggerated. The members of the rising class are charged with ungrammatical language, uncouth habits, unethical behavior, and disrespect for the land. At the turn of the century, Hofstadter wrote (1955:137) that

The newly rich, the grandiosely or corruptly rich, the masters of great corporations, were bypassing the men of the Mugwump type — the old gentry, the merchants of long standing, the small manufacturers, the established professional men, the civic leaders of an earlier era. In a score of cities and hundreds of towns, particularly in the East but also in the nation at large, the old-family, college-educated class that had deep ancestral roots in local communities and often owned family businesses, that had traditions of political leadership, belonged to the patriotic societies and the best clubs, staffed the governing boards of philanthropic and cultural institutions and led the movement for civic betterment, were being overshadowed and edged aside in the making of basic political and economic decisions.

It was in these years that John Muir organized the Sierra Club, and the American Forestry Association and the National Audubon Society were founded. Early symbols for embattled lovers of land and nature were the redwoods and Hetch Hetchy Valley.

Descendants of the proud pioneers who wrested a nation from the wilderness found themselves hard at work saving what they could of the wild from later comers. Arguments within committed groups centered on beauty, scarcity, and delicacy of natural phenomena. In reaching out to the larger public, arguments necessarily had to emphasize economics of tourism, intrinsic values — sometimes almost mystical, and the essential rightness of the views expressed. Through it all runs a flavor of embattled aristocracy. But to join the movement was to share in its cachet.

In the last decade there has been such a proliferation of local environmental issues as to permit statistical analysis of their characteristics. I should like to discuss a few of these, all recent and all located between the Hudson and the Delaware. In each, a preexisting symbiosis was disturbed when a local element was discovered by an outside group to have great significance, and the outside group possessed the skills and the capital to exploit the situation.

THE GREAT SWAMP JETPORT

Morris County, New Jersey, is one of the wealthiest counties in the nation. Few areas in the United States more nearly reproduce the flavor of upper-class Britain. The county seat lies in rolling country between the crystalline Reading Spur of the New England Upland and the tilted diabase of the Wachung Hills. Between these uplands the horsey set gambol on their estates, avoiding the wet and brushy lowlands cradled by the nearest Wachung ridge. The latter area is just 23 miles from Wall Street, where many of the estate owners maintain offices.

The Morris County symbiosis of man and environment was long-established. Social structure was imprinted clearly on the landscape. Fields and fences, houses and gateways, hedges and discreet screening trees spoke to the passerby as clearly as had St. Bernard's trees and stones. Disturbance occurred in 1959 when the Port of New York Authority picked the wet and brushy area as the site for its fourth jetport for New York City.

Outrage was instant and vocal. Estate owners and their allies organized the New Jersey Jetport Site Association in 1961. They raised among themselves several million dollars for political campaigns and for preclusive purchase of land. Much of this land was transferred to the federal government for a wildlife refuge, the public to be admitted only in small num-

bers and subject to observance of the proprieties. The manifest purpose was protection of the area's birds; the Port Authority's concern had been merely for men that fly. The latent aim of the defenders was much more complex: preservation of "home" as they knew it; creation of just the sort of preserve Freud noted as fantasy, keeping at arm's length not only jet noise, but also blue-collar and black workers and residents.

With victory apparent, the association was converted in 1965 into the North Jersey Conservation Foundation. Aims were broadened into education and then municipal conservation activities. Great Swamp slipped from the center of the stage. The Port Authority is biding its time.[7]

CONSOLIDATED EDISON AND STORM KING

Cornwall, New York, is a sleepy community on the Hudson just north of this river's intersection of the Reading Spur. The rugged mountain scenery is well known to travelers, prized by descendants of the very old summer colony (dating back to the 1820s, at least), and ignored by the majority of residents. The established gentry lived in rambling homes high above the river, prizing their isolation, their association with Storm King, the nearest and most famous of the Hudson highlands, and the lack of development on ridge-top lands to which they had easy access. This high-status group was small, its income and social ties firmly rooted in New York City. Nothing much had happened in town within memory of living man.

Disturbance occurred when New York's public utility, Consolidated Edison Company, found the highlands ideal for a large pumped-storage electrical facility. Relief difference was on the order of 1,000 feet, and water supply was infinite. Their plans were announced in

September 1962, 11 years before this page is written. Construction was finally scheduled to begin in November 1973.

Opposition began from organized hikers. The late Leo Rothchild, Conservation Chairman of the New York–New Jersey Trail Conference, expressed outrage at industrial invasion of this rough and wooded area, well known to members of his associated hiking clubs. Rothchild aroused the resentment of the local gentry in a meeting held in the offices of the National Audubon Society, The Jersey Jetport Site Association advised on strategy. The Scenic Hudson Preservation Conference thus was formed (Stillman, 1966).

Strategy took the form of public relations and recourse to the law. A public relations firm was retained. This in turn assigned an able if flamboyant account executive, who rolled out press releases and appeals for funds with the energy of a Niagara. Able use was made of the organization's masthead; the Storm King issue became the cynosure of New York City's upwardly mobile. The hikers were soon relegated to the background and forgotten. Directors of the organization themselves seem to have lost control of tactics and policy as the appeals rolled out and funds rolled in. By late 1970, $1,000,000 had been raised, it was said mostly in small amounts. Storm King ranked in national conservation esteem with the sanctity of the redwoods and Grand Canyon. The original aim had been "to save natural beauty"; later the arguments were couched in terms of technical considerations — structural and electrical — and a very dubious charge that Atlantic fishery resources were threatened.[8]

NEW JERSEY'S WETLANDS

Most of New Jersey's ocean shoreline is sandy coastal plain, often protected by barrier beaches. Lazy streams drain the low-lying uplands. Development through the 1950s was for recreation and retirement. Acres and acres of waving spartina grasses gave the shore an open and peaceful appearance. Boating, fishing, and shellfishing — vocational and avocational — characterized an easygoing symbiosis of man and environment.

Extension of highways and pressure of demand for housing brought the Jersey shore into the commutersheds of Philadelphia and New York by 1960. This was noticed not by residents, but by entrepreneurs seeking large tracts of land for rapid development into housing priced for quick sale. The spartina marshes thus came to have a wholly new meaning. The outsiders brought techniques of canalization and filling — developed earlier in Florida — which enabled them to build row on row of little houses on long "lagoons" leading in from seawater. The outsiders brought also techniques of attracting private capital in the necessary large amounts (Neutze, 1968; *New York Times*, 1972).

Construction became the major industry in many shore communities, particularly in Ocean County (Nieswand et al., 1972, 1973). Opposition to the inroads of developers was limited at first to small local groups, such as the Conservation Society of Long Beach Island.

Politics in New Jersey has its resemblances to those of Great Britain before 1832. Local conservation leaders were able to appeal to a statewide network of the likeminded, which included estate owners and other adherents to bucolic ideals. Political leaders in New Jersey defer to this group. The result was statewide wetlands legislation in 1970, which first froze all such development and then established strict controls. This was resented bitterly in shore communities, and was an issue in the 1973 gubernatorial campaign.

The motivation in this instance was the preservation of a landscape familiar to those who held significant power. Legal action was imposed on local communities by consensus of persons, few of whom made their homes or earned their livings in these communities. There was no significant local gentry to carry the ball; there was no need for a great fund-raising campaign.

TOCKS ISLAND DAM

Ever since disastrous floods in 1955, the U.S. Army Corps of Engineers has been perfecting a plan to control the waters of the upper Delaware River. This centers on a medium-sized dam 5 miles north of the Delaware Water Gap. The flood-control plan has broadened, adding to its initial provisions those of electric-power generation (now peaking only), water supply for North Jersey, low-flow maintenance for the lower Delaware (vital for flushing wastes from Philadelphia and Camden, and for the future of the Delaware Bay oyster fishery), and recreation. The U.S. National Park Service is in charge of a planned 60,000 acres of public open space on both sides of the 12,000-acre reservoir.

The area affected is the first valley within the Appalachian range, behind the Kittatinny Ridge, from the Water Gap 40 miles up to Port Jervis, New York. This valley is one of the longest-settled and most isolated parts of formerly colonial America. It has been used by the relatively few sportsmen and recreationists who have known of it. All this use now will be ended; the river will be changed into a lake; the fish themselves will change. Residents and recreationists have kept up a steady but seldom-heard opposition.

Quite late in the day statewide conservation groups have made an issue of this project. A leader has been the local chapter of the Sierra Club. As with the Storm King controversy, arguments have centered on technical considerations; effects on fishing, and the added general charge that "the ecology" will be affected.

Here again there is no identifiable local gentry and no great fund-raising plan. The innovation was the Corps of Engineers' response to the 1955 flood, using Congressional appropriations as their working capital. Statewide groups appear to be objecting directly to a change in an existing state of affairs.

I think that the following generalizations are valid for these issues:

1. A clear conflict has existed between the interests of at least two groups.
2. The interest of one group in each case is a general value accorded nature.
3. This interest in nature is never manifest; it is latent; it is overlain with arguments made to sound as technical and scientific as possible.[9]
4. The groups pressing their interest in nature freely identify their cause with the public interest, and seek victory without compromise.
5. In not one of these instances have conservationists recognized a role for mass public recreation or for public definition of the amenities of nature (with the modest exception of the hikers at the very start of the Storm King case). A proclivity of conservationists is to save nature by keeping the public out of it.
6. Since conservation activists are drawn from the more affluent and politically effective segments of society, their frequently significant impact on public policy has imposed real costs on other members of society (Economist, 1973). These costs have not been recognized nor charged back to their initiators.

I conclude that landscape values in my part of the country tend to be those of an effective minority that isolates itself from the public generally, using land as an insulator, other peoples' or public land if possible. Landscape values and landscape policy can be judged in terms of this self-isolating process.

WILLIAM WORDSWORTH, WHERE ARE YOU?

Landscape, land, and natural beauty involve values that are real to many persons. These values enter our national political process. All persons who hold these values should be free to urge them on the body politic. All such persons also are liable to the pressures of others, with their values. We end with the dilemma of justice: what is fair? How can we build into our system coordination, efficiency, and stability in decision making regarding land use (Rawls, 1971)?

Nature is a recourse of demonstrated meaning to many persons. This recourse should be available to all, included perhaps among the responsibilities of public-health personnel. The catholicity of this value has not been urged by the outspoken advocates of nature's virtues. Their light has been hidden under a bushel of rationalizations. One is their use of the term "environment."

"Environment" is a term so all-inclusive as to be operationally useless. Even the more limited term, "the public interest," has been shown to be without value in public policy determination (Schubert, 1960). There is not an environment; there are as many as there are living organisms in the world. Even if we confine our concern to human organisms, there still are many environments — several billions. Concern for what is common to all is already in hand. Concern for the total environment of humans is meaningless without identification of the individuals concerned. To act "for the environment" is to jump halfway across the stream. The official format for environmental impact statements in New Jersey is a good example. Information is demanded concerning effects upon each of a long list of physiographic segments and processes. Nowhere is there the further demand for effects of these segments, accordingly altered, upon humans.

Unless we can define the human meanings of segments of environment and consider these in terms of their meanings to real individuals, use of the term "environment" is likely to remain a code word for protection of special interests.

Certainly there are within the amenities of "nature" meanings of great value. But these inhere in the persons who hold them, not in the views, animals, and flowers so evocatively portrayed in Sierra Club posters and in the pages of such magnificent productions as *Audubon* magazine.[10] Many of these values have social merit in enabling members of society better to adjust to their situations in life. There is an immense area here for sensitive research and for imaginative public administration, as in the field of parks and recreation. Considerations of justice, however, must not be put in such crude terms as acres of open land per thousand population; rather we must seek justice in performance of the human *functions* of natural amenity.

For some of us nature is beautiful, its study a page from the humanities. For others of us, nature is a chapter from a volume on sports. And possibly for all of us, nature has functions that we do not usually discuss in polite society. Justice in access to nature, I repeat, must center first on the individual and on his particular need. Studying the meanings of nature in this manner, we find ourselves belatedly in debt to Wordsworth, who wrote (Clark, 1969:279)

> *One impulse from a vernal wood*
> *May teach you more of man*
> *Of moral evil and of good*
> *Than all the sages can.*

NOTES

1. My dictionary defines "landscape" as "a portion of land which the eye can comprehend in a single view, esp. in its pictorial aspect," and "love" as "a feeling of strong personal attachment induced by sympathetic understanding, or by ties of kinship; ardent affection" (Webster's, 1953:472, 498).

2. The reverse of the coin is, of course, disaffection combined with ignorance. This I submit results in suspicion, a product, like romance, that is subject to dissipation by further knowledge. Teachers are such spoilsports!

3. This nugget of information was supplied to me by George Lenz of Kenyon & Eckhardt Advertising, Inc. A glance at contemporary television commercials provides further evidence of the existence of the batholith — and of the alertness of the advertising fraternity in exploiting its possibilities.

4. For a magnificent presentation of human feelings for nature, see Susanne K. Langer's recent work (1967, 1973).

5. Early in 1967 I found the following in a fourth-floor walkup on the south side of Paris: "Aliquid amplius invenies in silvis quam in libris. Ligna et lapides docebunt te quod a magistris audire non possis." Not until I had Glacken's volume was I able to confirm the source. The translation is Glacken's (1967:213).

6. South of the tropics there exists very little temperate-zone land. All of it is dominated by immigrants from the Northern Temperate Zone: Africa south of the Zambesi, the Antipodes, Chile and Argentina. For a full discussion of the variables associated with achievement orientation, see McClelland (1961). For an understanding of the worldwide impact of developments in this characteristic, see McNeill (1963). ·

7. In 1968 a senior agricultural agent of Morris County pointed out to me in a volume of codified statutes the power of the federal Secretary of Transportation to take practically any federally owned land for a valid transportation purpose.

8. My colleague, Professor James W. Westman, informs me that 85 percent of all Atlantic striped bass are spawned in the Chesapeake, and that the small numbers spawned in the Hudson would be subjected to negligible effects from the Storm King plant.

9. Hofstadter has noted the predilection for academic-style documentation in the writings of the paranoid right (1965:36). Graham writes of the preservationists in Africa (1973:27).

10. A classic example of casting an argument as between an identifiable human group and "an environment," rather than another human group, is in Josephy (1973).

Qualitative Values in the Landscape

Garrett Eckbo

The landscape has many dimensions. The *physical* landscape surrounds us in space and time, a product of the interaction of people and nature. The *social* landscape expresses the local, regional, national, and worldwide relations among the people with whom we live. The *economic* landscape determines how well we live. The *cultural* landscape embodies the creative contribution of our times to world cultural history.

Here we shall deal with the physical landscape, a four-dimensional sequential pattern of earth, rock, water, plants, man-made structures, air, weather, light, and energy. This environment surrounds us continuously throughout our lives. We cannot be separated from it. It is a direct result of the impact of human social, economic, and cultural values upon nonhuman ecosystematic landscapes. Today it is almost impossible to find a landscape anywhere in the world that does not incorporate responses to such impact.

We, and everything that we need to sustain physical life, come out of the existing landscape and cannot be separated from it.

Garrett Eckbo is an independent landscape architect and consultant in urban and environmental planning and a Professor in the College of Environmental Design at the University of California, Berkeley.

31

Nevertheless, we do separate ourselves from it in our consciousness and day-to-day attitudes. We live as though we were separate, alien, and superior beings visiting a strange world, transients killing time between birth and death, immaterial spirits storing up points for Judgment Day, or cynics consuming all that we can of earth's material resources because we cannot take them with us.

This may be seen as a result of the Judeo-Christian tradition, in which man was in the beginning separated from this natural world and given dominion over it. However, the other major cultures of the world, even when they purport to preach the indivisible unity of man and nature in this everyday world, have done little better in preserving or conserving their landscapes and resources. Witness the long-time devastation of the most ancient sites of human cultural development — China, Central Asia, the Middle East, the Mediterranean. Only in Japan, where high sensitivity and a poverty of natural resources have eliminated the incentive for landscape exploitation, and in the tropical and subtropical areas, where the exuberance of natural growth has always been able to heal the scars of handicraft development, have people been able to continue to live in close and intimate relations with the scenes of nature. Now modern technology and economic motivation are providing the means to break down these last barriers to environmental degradation. Japan, the most heavily polluted urban culture, has the least control of destructive land use, uncontrolled high-density development, and rampant speculation in land values. The jungles of Africa, Indonesia, and the Amazon are being cleared by ruthlessly exploitive development.

At any given time and place the landscape expresses directly the values that have shaped human development, modification, change, or replacement of the original scenes of nature. These values begin with the fundamental needs for food, shelter, and clothing; they expand with the growth of technical and cultural concepts, which make possible the improvement, refinement, and enrichment of those commodities; they expand also with the development of surplus and mass production and the resultant opportunities for trade and the exploitation of labor and markets; and they expand still further with the growth of family, group, regional, national, and international community consciousness and cultural aspirations.

New environmental developments express directly the values and aspirations of those who produce them. As those developments age, they gradually become elements of local cultural history. Newer developments express newer values, which may be more or less different from those which preceded them, depending on the rate of cultural development. In the Old World cities of Europe and Asia, we find a conglomeration of value expressions, layer on layer of historical artifacts. In the New World cities of the Western Hemisphere, now 300 to 400 years old, yet in the North dominated largely by twentieth-century forms, cultural expression is much more clear and direct. New World citizens go by the thousands to the Old World to view cultural artifacts that they can no longer understand, replicate, or equal. Old World citizens, infected by New World values and aspirations, are less and less able to preserve or conserve their historical environmental artifacts.

Inasmuch as the environment expresses individual and group values and attitudes, how are they originally determined and developed? One might say through four avenues: heredity, education, communication, and experience.

Heredity provides basic capacities, tendencies, needs, and instinctive reflexes. Environment determines how these develop. Attitudes, values, and aspirations result from environmental conditioning.

Education by family, school, and employer is the process by which each new arrival on the scene is assimilated by society and indoctrinated with correct social values and attitudes. Education conveys to the student selected segments of current knowledge and value systems which are considered proper for that individual's likely social status. In our society, the range of educational opportunity is broad, from the narrow outlook of ghetto schools that force students into the streets early in their lives, to the multifaceted opportunities offered by our better universities. These extremes house only a minority of our total student body. Most move through a median range of studies, which are largely prosaic and uninspired.

Communication includes, but is much larger than, education. Beginning with direct verbal interchange, it expands to the speaker–audience relation, the circulation of the printed page, and the wireless distribution of the spoken word and the visual image over the air via radio and television. At each step the proportionate relations between source and audience expand geometrically, and the character of the message changes in accordance with the medium. The scope of communication processes has expanded from local through regional to national and international. Their importance, relative to education, has expanded concurrently. Formal education conditions people for nine to twenty years of their lives. Communication conditions them all their lives. The two together comprise a total social educational process. This process attempts to prepare and condition people for, and adjust them to, their societies and environments. The emphasis is on verbal interpretation, although the visual content has increased with photo magazines and television. Nevertheless, it is the printed caption or verbal commentary that guides our interpretation of the picture.

Experience is everything that happens to a given individual from birth, or before, to death (perhaps after). It includes education and communication in a larger whole. When experience confirms the messages of those two components, society and life remain tranquil. When it does not, credibility decreases and there is trouble. As we know today, experience may come through one segment of communication in such a way as to damage the credibility of other segments.

The accumulated total lifelong experience of each individual equips him or her with a set of interpretive–evaluative screens through which pass all the environmental experiences perceived through the sense organs. This is the way that values are applied to the landscape. In those who have decision-making power over changes in the landscape, accumulated experiential screens become sets of attitudes that determine the direction of their decision making. These attitudinal sets are basically four: subsistence, profit, conservation, and culture. All exist in North America, but profit is dominant. The general impact of the ecological–environmental movement is to reduce the role of profit and increase the roles of the other three.

Subsistence, the basic search for food, shelter, and clothing, is a dominant value for all societies which have not yet been able to raise a majority of their population above that bare level. One cannot think effectively about business deals, preserving ecology, or creating beautiful landscapes on an empty stomach. Such problems are minor in North America — although greater than we think.

Profit is still the dominant drive of our society. I need hardly elaborate on that statement. Profit-oriented valuation attitudes see the landscape through dollar signs. We have all experienced the fundamental communication problems generated by that peculiarly distorted abstraction of the real world.

Conservation, as a movement, developed in the late nineteenth century in response to the environmental destruction and waste of natural resources generated by uncontrolled profit seeking. It became a process for sound sustained-yield management of resources, amenities, and development activities. Although still minor in the total decision-making picture, conservation has made substantial gains in reducing exploitive waste and destruction. During the past decade, it has received substantial, expansive, even overwhelming support from the sudden growth of environmental movements and concerns. Ecology and environment are now definitely part of the national value system. But just how is not quite clear. In the most extreme form, they seem to demand rigid and precise preservation of every vestige of natural ecology that has survived the overwhelming 300-year continental development debauch. They do not seem to be particularly interested in such esoteric ideas as building new ecologies at the interfaces between man and nature. Yet, only through such ideas can a new and more beautiful landscape emerge.

Which brings us to culture. This I define as the creative social force responsible for maintaining movement, diversity, flexibility, amenity, and qualitative focus in civilizations. Culture embodies the inspirations and aspirations of local, regional, and national communities, and the direct, more or less refined and stylized expression of their philosophical attitudes toward landscape–environmental qualities. The physical landscape, wherever it has been so changed by people as to make that change visually apparent, is a direct cultural expression, even as are the various arts and sciences.

Culture accumulates, but cultural accumulations become collections of archaeological artifacts unless they are an integral part of daily community living. Culture regards history as relevant experience, but it begins a fresh review of the world and its future every day. Culture focuses, in many ways, on the qualitative aspects of the interaction between people and people, people and nature, and people and landscape — the latter a product of interaction between people and nature. Culture is the qualitative conscience of society in relations with its environmental production processes.

In summary, subsistence approaches the landscape in fundamentally utilitarian terms, which range from desperate to practical. Profit approaches it in terms of how much cash flow can be generated in the right directions by calculated manipulation. Conservation approaches it in terms of managing profit seeking in order to preserve or conserve natural–historical resources and amenities. Ecological environmentalism approaches the landscape in terms of precise natural science plus a romantic–poetic conviction about the preservation of nature. Culture approaches it in terms of the qualitative sequential experience that it provides for its inhabitants.

The environmental planner–designer may approach his work from any one of these viewpoints, or, more likely, from a combination in which one is weighted over the others. Theoretically, professionals emphasize cultural values. However, they do at times appear to be led astray by others.

The ultimate objective appears to be a steady state in which people, nature, and the four values achieve an equilibrium in which all work together to produce the best of all possible worlds. Radicals will say that the profit motive must be eliminated to achieve this. Conservatives will say that the profit motive is indispensable as a catalyst for all others.

Ultimately, we must confront the problem of verbalization versus visualization. We are verbalizing about direct, physical, visual experience. Words only intrude on a screen of interpretation and preconception between landscape and experience. They are irrelevant to the direct quality of the experience. Yet so conditioned are we to verbal interpretation of the world, we must even verbalize about it to ourselves before we feel secure in our experience.

Verbalization is, of course, viewed as that supreme cultural achievement which distinguishes us from other animals. Beginning with individual and group discourse and the impact of centrally placed speakers on audiences of expanding size, the continuing inventions of printing press, wireless, and television transmission have enormously increased the impact of verbalization by a minority on the majority. Beneficial though this may have been to international culture and commerce, it has created a major separation between people and environment. Most of us tend to live in a world of verbal abstractions, verbalized values that may have only a tenuous connection with the real world around us. It is becoming necessary to seek ways for returning to the direct naïveté of environmental relations that is experienced by children, primitives, animals, some old people, artists, designers, and scientists. Only when we are able constantly to see the world as it really is will we be able to sort out our values and determine which are relevant and which irrelevant.

In a recent book about teaching (Postman and Weingartner, 1969) the authors analyze relations between perception, language, meaning, and transaction somewhat as follows:

We do not get our perceptions from the things around us. We create them ourselves by filtering our encounters with what is out there through our nervous systems.

What we perceive is largely a function of our previous experiences, assumptions, and purposes.

We are unlikely to alter our perceptions until and unless we are frustrated in our attempts to do something based on them.

Each individual perceives what is out there in a unique way.

Perception is a function of the linguistic categories available to the perceiver. That is, perceptions are interpreted in terms which are shaped by the language in which the perceiver thinks. It is possible for direct visualization, whether through naïveté or training, to bypass this.

The meaning of a perception lies in how it causes us to act.

Perception conceived as the making of meanings becomes less static, and more oriented toward process, change, and unique individuality.

People relate to their environments through continuing reciprocal transactions, which can continue to produce new meanings.

This analysis leads me to conclude that we must distinguish between environmental design and ecological design. The former deals with what is out there in ways that may be proprietary, paternalistic, alienated, or personalized. Ecological design deals directly with relations and transactions between people and environment.

One way to think about ecological design is through consideration of relations between horticulture and nature. Good gardening follows precise rules, regulations, and schedules. The garden is kept neat, tidy, and trim at all times. Grass is mowed regularly, edges trimmed, weeds removed, leaves and litter transferred to the compost pile, shrubs and trees pruned, and the garden is sprayed on schedule for pests and diseases. Bear in mind the definition of a weed as a plant in the wrong place.

The wilderness lover, on the other hand, may decide to relax and let nature take its course. The results will depend upon the location and condition of the site, but they are bound to be interesting and not entirely predictable. Whether motivated by romanticism or indolence, life with nature can be at least as interesting as life with horticulture. The choice is a function of philosophy, temperament, and attitude.

However, this is not a simple black-and-white choice. There are not just two alternatives. Rather there are innumerable variations between the two extremes through mixtures of horticultural and natural processes. One may begin with nature and introduce exotic elements and cultural practices at special times in selected areas. Or one may begin with a well-planned and developed garden, and allow it to be selectively invaded by natural volunteers in order to enjoy their unpredictable relations with the original order.

Such choices in practice, and the attitudes toward nature, horticulture, and design that generate them, will vary with the natural landscape region in which the choice is made. All the romantic and poetic attitudes toward nature seem to have come out of the temperate regions of northwestern Europe, northeastern North America, and northeastern Asia. The arid and semiarid regions of the Mediterranean, Middle East, and Central Asia produced the controlled geometric gardens of Moorish, Mogul, Moslem, and Renaissance cultures. Tropical and subtropical regions produced no recognizable landscape cultures before the work of Roberto Burle Marx in Brazil.

Before the blossoming of pluralistic modern landscape design in the 1920s and 1930s, the relations between nature and horticulture were formalized in academic theory as formal and informal design — *le jardin francais et le jardin anglais*. Now this arbitrary dichotomy has been expanded to that between development and conservation.

The current confrontation, sharpened and refined by the ecological–environmental movement, is again not simply a choice between black and white. The interface between conservation and development, between people and nature, is where the action is. It is here that the most exciting potentials exist for new ecologies, new environmental cultures, new complexes of landscape art embodying enriched relations between construction and open space. Such concepts are also, of course, distrusted because they have been the breeding ground for environmental disaster, destruction, and devastation. Conservation–open space–recreation concepts are the soft and ultimately inexplicable alter ego to our hard-nosed world of development, progress, and hard work.

Relations between conservation and development, people and nature, positive and negative cultural potentials can only be resolved through the planning–design process. Through repeated cycles of survey, inventory analysis, hypothesis, and synthesis, the governing policies and final forms for all change in the environment are determined. Whether or not the process is carried out by professionals, it provides the basis for decisions that will determine the qualitative level of future relations between people and environment.

Environment–ecological planning–design processes are analogous to seduction relations between men and women. They may lead to beautiful continuing relations — or end as inconclusive one-night stands.

The resolution of relations between conservation and development cannot be determined through purely rational processes. As with successful life, which necessitates balanced interplay between reason and feeling, environmental problems can only be resolved through combinations of reason and intuition, systems analysis and inspired conceptualizing, science and art.

If professional planner–designers, artists,

and technicians are to be considered as environmental resources available for major service in solving our problems, changes in their structural relations with society will be needed. Professionals who spend half their time and energy in entrepreneurial promotion or bureaucratic administration are only contributing half their potential to developing that new environmental culture which we need so desperately.

John B. Jackson, in his outstanding chapter in this volume, describes the historical progression in North American landscape values from the moral values and transcendental truths sought in the early nineteenth century, through the materialist concentration on energy production of the late nineteenth and early twentieth centuries, to today's developing focus on significant experience. I wonder if this sequence is linear or circular. In the eyes of those whom we called the counterculture in the 1960s, significant experience and transcendental truth may merge in new concepts of environmental–ecological goals.

The Economics of a View

As our attitudes regarding the importance of various social issues change, so do our perceptions of what we observe around us and the language that we use to describe what we perceive. The very phrase "landscape assessment" has a meaning quite different today than it did even 10 years ago. It would be interesting to be able to step back a decade and poll a cross section of people interested in land use to ask them to define the term "landscape assessment." We might obtain answers such as, "It probably deals with problems of tax assessment," or "I guess it involves the procedure for determining market values of real property for setting sales prices," or "It probably deals with the difficulties of placing dollars on recreational lands for more accurately conducting cost–benefit analyses for river-basin projects." These answers all reflect a strong economic bias toward the word assessment. Yet today persons involved with landscape-assessment research include primarily landscape architects, psychologists, historians, and ecologists; economists are conspicuous mainly by their absence.

The number of disciplines with more than

Ross S. Whaley is Head of the Department of Landscape Architecture and Regional Planning at the University of Massachusetts.

casual interest in landscape values indicates that considerations of land value in our society have gone beyond simply the market price of real estate. We now recognize that the values inherent in land and the landscape include a vast array of both benefits and costs — some direct, some secondary; some tangible, some intangible; and some private, some social. One benefit of living in one of the wealthier nations of the world is that we can now afford the luxury of contemplating the secondary, the intangible, and the social impacts of our decisions. This is not to suggest that these are trivial concerns by any means. Rather, it is to point out that these concerns have arisen only in the past few decades among the wealthier nations of the world.

Prior to that time, land was valued primarily as a factor of production. Wild, undeveloped land had little or no value of itself. Land became useful as it became productive of food, fiber, and minerals, or as it was prepared to accommodate homes and the structures of industry and commerce. Consequently, the tools of economic analysis that were developed had two characteristics: first, they tended to be descriptive rather than predictive, and, second, they dealt solely with land as a private commodity and ignored the broader social consequences of land use.

The question facing the economist was, "What is the value of the contribution of land to the productivity of our economy?" Land took on value because it contributed to the production of consumable goods. The amount of this contribution was determined by two qualities of land: its fertility (or richness in the case of mineral-bearing land) and its location. The roots of the theory of land value based on its fertility are found in the works of Ricardo, who explained increasing increments of land value, which he called rent, on the basis of relating the fertility of various parcels of land.

The greater productivity of the more fertile land generated additional profits (rent), which were taken as the value of land.

In a similar manner, the location theorists attributed value to land on the basis of increased profits that resulted from locational advantages. Reduced transportation costs associated with land in a good location increased the profits to the owner. Thus, the measure of land value was the additional profit generated because of preferred locations. The early location theorists attempted to explain land use on the assumption that activities would take place so that the combination of uses would maximize the profits generated from the land. Attempts to generalize this theory started as early as 1826 with the pioneering efforts of Von Thünen. The computer has given rise to a cadre of location theorists, who have had some success in simulating locational patterns, particularly in urban areas.

Although these efforts have added richly to our basic understanding of why different parcels of land take on different values, the crudity of the models leaves economists as rather poor forecasters of land prices, or of the total value of land in various uses, or of the locational behavior of various land users.

Not only have these efforts been of little avail in the forecasting of land values or locations of particular land uses; they have the additional shortcoming of treating only the private costs and benefits associated with land use and ignoring the substantial social costs and benefits resulting from particular uses of the land. In the use of land probably more than any other part of our economic life, there are substantial social costs and benefits. Historically, this has been recognized even in our capitalistic society by the right of the people to collectively own land for parks, highways, watershed protection, or timber production. More recently we see wide acceptance of the imposition of public controls over the use of private land in such things as zoning, stiffer restrictions on building permits, and that rediscovered utopian process, land-use planning.

The economist has been involved in the public-land-use planning process in several ways. As economies of regions started making substantial shifts in response to the greater mobility of the population, regional analysis developed as a subdiscipline within economics, and gained its own legitimacy with the formation of its own association and journal. The major thrust of the regional analysts was the study of the interactions among economic sectors of a community or larger region so that predictions could be made regarding the impact of a change in one sector on the remainder of the economy. The goal of these predictions was to determine the prospective economic welfare of the region, generally expressed in terms of regional income or employment. From predicted employment simple multiplication would supposedly yield estimates of population, and thus the need for housing, schools, and an array of other public services. The final step in this process would be to estimate the tax receipts and public expenditures to determine the degree of economic self-sufficiency of the community. Although the techniques of the regional analyst have added measurably to the sophistication of land-use planning and have advanced our ability to deal with the secondary impacts of community development, they have still left a major gap in dealing with the intangible, nonpecuniary social impacts of land use.

A second major role of the economist in planning land use has been at the project level. The most notable examples have been river-basin analysis and the refinement of cost–benefit analysis as a decision-making tool for large investments in dams and other water-management projects. In these endeavors more than any other, the economist has had to face head on the dilemma of measuring intangible benefits and costs. There was no way to duck the inconvenient question of the value of expanded or diminished recreational opportunities resulting from a dam project. Although the problem could not be dodged, the popularly applied solutions to the problem were in many instances naïve at best and totally wrong at worst. It would be interesting to study the number of dam proposals for which the cost–benefit ratio was acceptable only because of the best-guess approach in evaluating the intangible benefits. This is mentioned not to suggest political shenanigans in the use of economic analysis to justify the goals of a particular agency, but to point out that some decisions were undoubtedly made on the weakest part of the analysis.

The criticisms leveled at the theory of rent, location analysis, regional analysis, and cost–benefit analysis are not made as a condemnation of the discipline of economics. To the contrary, economics has made valuable contributions to the development of analytic tools for land-use planning. However, the late 1960s saw changes in societal views that had social implications for the inadequacy of the traditional measures of societal welfare used by economists and acceptable to the public at large. A major segment of the population looked around and decided that they were not particularly pleased with the state of their environment. The richest people in the world started to question the necessity of the tremendous social costs which seemed to be inextricably linked to the financial wealth that had been generated. No social issue outside of war has had as much press devoted to it as concern over the quality of our environment. One lasting memento of this era was the passage of the National Environmental Policy Act (NEPA) of 1969, which institutionalized the need for analysis and prediction of environmental impacts of at least those of man's actions which involved expenditure of federal tax dollars. Equally as significant as the NEPA have been comparable changes in attitudes at state, county, and municipal levels. Sometimes these changes were articulated in laws and municipal ordinances. More often than not the changes were simply new people, expressing new concerns at every hearing, town meeting, or at any other occasion where they could express their outrage about environmental degradation.

The result of this awakening about the status of the quality of our environment has had mixed blessings. On the positive side is the significant progress in the reduction of water and air pollution. Lake Erie, for example, is now being restored. Land-use controls imposed at all governmental levels are resulting in a more compatible arrangement of land uses. The scientific community is seeking to better understand man's interference with the earth's natural processes. Others are attempting to study man's perception of the landscape so that these values can better be incorporated into the planning process. The net result of this tremendous range of efforts can only provide more information for the decisions governing land use.

The negative side of the environmental awakening is the rush for simplistic solutions. Just as the economist of the 1950s suggested decision-making schemes based on a singular criterion of maximizing profit, the ecologist–planner of the early 1970s seems all too comfortable with his singular criterion of minimizing impact to the physical environment. Just as the economist calculated total benefits and often ignored the distribution of those benefits, the ecologist–planner calculates the impact on the environment, but ignores the impacts of proposed land-use controls on land values and construction costs. Just as the

economist often ignored the intangible costs and benefits because his analytical tools were not that refined, the ecologist–planner assumes that society in general shares his value system because his analytical tools are also not sufficiently refined.

That we have not yet developed all the tools necessary for adequately incorporating environmental concerns into land-use decisions is not an insurmountable problem. They will be developed. The problem is that, in the absence of more comprehensive analytical tools, there is a tendency to sell unwarranted conclusions with emotionalism. This behavior is acceptable for the interest group or lobby, but is not appropriate for the professional involved in land-use planning and decision making.

What is the role of the planner? A definition of 1928 applies even today. MacKaye (1962:147) states,

the function of every sort of "planner" . . . is primarily to uncover, reveal, and visualize — not alone his own ideas but nature's; not merely to formulate the desire of man, but to reveal the limits thereto imposed by a greater power. Thus, in fine, planning is two things: (1) an accurate formulation of our own desires — the specific knowledge of what it is we want; and (2) an accurate revelation of the limits, and the opportunities, imposed and bequeathed to us by nature. Planning is a scientific charting and picturing of the thing (whether logging road or communal center) which man desires and which the eternal forces will permit.

This definition in its simplicity combines the attitudes of the economist and the ecologist. It also suggests that there are really not two solutions to optimum use of the land, but one, which can be achieved by balancing "what it is we want" and the "limits and opportunities imposed and bequeathed to us by nature." Balancing these apparently conflicting objectives poses an insolvable dilemma if we attempt to satisfy all man's wants while maintaining an unimpaired landscape. The dilemma has a hypothetical solution if we try to allocate land so as to maximize the differences between total costs and total benefits, including social and intangible values. We should recognize that man's demand upon the land is infinite, and that whatever use is made of the land extracts a cost in terms of changing it from its natural state.

The major dilemma in combining the talents of the various disciplines concerned with assessing changes in landscape values is that each specialty has developed its own measurement devices, and there may be little or no comparability between them. The economist most often uses dollars as his measure of change. The hydrologist uses cubic feet per second of water or some measure of sediment load. The ecologist may use kilograms of biomass or some measure of ecological diversity. The different units of measurement lead to inestimable difficulties in comparing gains in one sector with losses in another resulting from a change in land use. These drastically different measuring rods also are the major cause of the lack of interdisciplinary coordination in land-use planning. Simply, the professional participants in the planning process speak different languages. To suggest that communications between disciplinary groups can be likened to the tower of Babel is probably not too absurd an analogy.

Although the problem of finding comparable measures of all costs and benefits from changes in land use is a difficult one, it is not without solution if the problem can be reduced to one of indexes. That is, what is needed is an ordinal ranking of the effects of change. This is different from the traditional approach of the economist, who has attempted to find cardinal measures of costs and benefits. Much attention has been paid by the economics profession to imputing dollar values to nonmarket exchanged commodities or services such as water or recreation.

Reducing the measurement problem to an ordinal indexing one rather than attempting to find comparative cardinal measures raises optimism for future success in more thoroughly incorporating landscape values and other elements of environmental quality into land-use decisions. Although this approach to valuation does not allow a simple statement as to the worth of a particular view, quality of water, mix of vegetation covering a rolling countryside, or mix of social and cultural characteristics of a community, it should enable us to make comparative estimates as to whether changes in land use impose either gains or losses in these attributes and the relative magnitude of these gains and losses.

A hypothetical procedure for evaluating these gains and losses would involve six steps:

1. Identification of the important elements affecting evaluation of our living environment.
2. Identification of the significant attributes of those elements which enable us to make a qualitative statement about their condition.
3. Development of local, community, or regional standards for each of the elements.
4. Evaluation of current land use against the standards.
5. Evaluation of alternative future land uses against the standards.
6. Selection of that combination of future uses which appear to have maximum gains and minimum losses.

Identification of environmental elements The first step in this process of landscape assessment is the identification of the elements of our living environment to be included in our analysis of land-use change. Because of current usage we tend to think of natural characteristics of the landscape as the only ones appropriately included under the term "environment," and often forget the social, cultural, and economic components. This oversight, of course, brings us full circle to our starting proposition that what is needed for adequate land-use planning is a means of integrating the array of disciplinary concerns into the planning process.

The list of elements to be included in an adequate evaluation of proposed land-use changes is in itself a chore worthy of considerable research. What is it that people view as important in assessing the value of their surroundings? For implementation, the elements will have to be subdivided into specific components, but a rough first approximation might include the following:

1. Natural environment
   Watershed protection lands
   Agricultural lands
   Forest lands
   Wetlands
   Open spaces
   Floodplains
   Wildlife protection lands
2. Public service environment
   Transportation
   Communication
   Education
   Health services
   Police and fire
   Sewerage disposal
   Solid-waste disposal
   Electric supply
   Water supply
3. Private service environment
   Food sales
   Clothing sales
   Entertainment services
4. Housing environment
5. Cultural environment
6. Social and neighborhood environment
7. Economic environment
   Employment
   Income
   Taxes

This list is far from complete, but should serve as an indicator of the kinds of elements that comprise our living environment. The diversity of these elements forewarns us regarding the difficulty we shall have in the steps to follow.

Identification of attributes For each element it is necessary to determine what measures should be used to determine the contribution of that element to the well-being of individuals living in or dependent upon the land being analyzed. As an example, the appropriate measures of forest land might include acreage by species composition, by size of trees. For the cultural environment the number of museums, theaters, and significant historical preservations probably would be included in the measure. For housing the number of living units by size, age, density, and condition might be appropriate. This step is aimed at finding the proximate criteria that measure the contribution of each element to the well-being of individuals.

Development of community or regional standards The question of "standards" as a guide to land-use decisions has been and will continue to be a hotly debated subject. The opponents of "standards" object strongly to simple criteria as acres of park land per thousand population or number of hospital beds per thousand population as estimates of acceptable amounts of certain services or land uses. Their case is a good one when one observes the tendency for generalized "standards" to be applied arbitrarily over large geographic areas or possibly over the country as a whole. If the planning unit is a particular region of a state, municipality, or community, the concept of "standards" unique to that region should not be unacceptable. In this sense "standards" can be thought of as an approach to responding to Benton MacKaye's admonition to determine "an accurate formulation of our own desires —

the specific knowledge of what it is we want." Rather than a single point estimate of what it is we desire in each of the elements mentioned, I would suggest a range of "standards" including the following:

Minimum   Minimum desirable
Average   Optimum

For each environmental element there is a set of attributes which will describe the minimum acceptable level of that element, another set of attributes which describe the minimum desirable, and so on. The process whereby we establish these levels for many of the environmental elements is another needed area of research. Some levels are easier to determine than others. For example, the "average" attributes may be nothing more than statistical averages for all similar regions or communities. The "minimum" in many instances may be established by law such as air quality standards, water quality standards, and floodplains. By far the most difficult "standards" to establish are the "minimum desirable" and "optimum." In some instances these are matters of professional judgment; in others they can only be determined by social consensus. In spite of the difficulties, there is no reason to expect that, in any real-life planning situation, standards cannot be quite accurately approximated.

Evaluation of current and proposed conditions
To evaluate changes in land uses it is necessary to compare the impacts of alternative land uses against each other and against current land use. It is for purposes of these comparisons that some method of indexing becomes essential. What is proposed here is that for the region under study each environmental element be compared to the "standard." This could be done by converting the various levels within the "standard" to a numerical index ranging from 0 to 100. Thus, each environmen-

tal element would receive an index number. A rough guide to the assignment of index numbers could be

		0
Minimum		25
Minimum desirable		50
Average		75
Optimum		100

The summation of the index number for all elements would give a composite rating of the environmental quality of present land uses. It is important to note that this composite ranking has no meaning except as a comparison to alternative land uses in the same region or community under consideration. It cannot be used for valid comparisons between regions. However, for planning purposes comparisons between regions are rarely important.

The system described, from identification of environmental elements, through establishing standards, to comparing alternative land uses of a particular area, is not meant as a panacea to the problems of the land-use planner. Rather it is meant to suggest only three things. First, it hopefully serves as a reminder that we cannot afford to just look at the natural landscape in our zeal for environmental protection. As important as the natural landscape is, consideration of its use must be linked with other elements that comprise our individual living environments and influence our social welfare. Second, the system suggests that there may be ways to combine both direct and indirect and tangible and intangible benefits and costs into the land-use decision-making process. Third, it suggests that we are in the very beginning of the research needed to understand the influence of our environment on either individual or social well-being. The concept of a "standard" must start initially with psychology and sociology and an understanding of human perceptions of their surroundings. From there it is still a long way to determining the value of a particular view.

The role of the ecologist–environmentalist–planner is to identify and predict what changes will occur in the landscape as a result of a change in land use. The role of the economist is to develop a scale of measure that will serve as a common denominator to compare all the costs and all the benefits in a meaningful way. It is only through a merger of the contributions of the landscape architect, ecologist, psychologist, and economist that we can, as Benton MacKaye put it, "render actual and evident that which is potential and inevident" (1962:148).

Preservation Policy and Personal Perception: A 200-Million-Acre Misunderstanding

Charles E. Little

In the spring of 1972, a consultant in landscape preservation was invited to a New England town undergoing extraordinary growth. The consultant was taken on a tour of the town. He was shown the village green and the Revolutionary houses. He was asked to climb to the top of a drumlin to view a lush valley sprinkled with white farmhouses and laced with stone fences. He was driven to country-road vistas of apple trees in bloom and soft meadowlands. At the end of the day, the consultant sat on his host's deck overlooking a woodland and a dramatic ridgeline of greening hills and reflected on what a fine place this town would be to live in.

The following morning he had to get to work to earn his consulting fee. He met with conservation commissioners and with planners, and he discussed with them planned unit development, municipal costs and taxes, hydrological problems, recreational needs, and government grant programs. At length, a map was unfurled, a map being the sine qua non of discussions like these. It was an open-space preservation map said to represent one of the most ambitious plans in the whole state. The

Charles E. Little is a Washington, D.C.–based writer and consultant in land-use policy.

consultant took a long look at the massive areas colored in various shades of green, but he was at a loss to be very helpful. In spite of his lengthy tour the day before, only in one or two instances had he been shown the land that was proposed for preservation.

What this hardly unique experience suggested to the consultant was that there must be two sets of values: one, a mapped set of landscape-preservation values capable of being rationalized as public policy; the other, which he had been instructed in the day before, landscape-preservation values associated with actual personal perception. Only in a very minor way did they overlap. The *place* and the *plan* were essentially two different things.

Under ordinary circumstances, this gulf might not be very important, for the political processes characterized by town meetings, boards, and commissions made up of local residents, the effective political clout of civic and neighborhood organizations, might tend in time to coalesce the two sets of landscape values into one transcendent plan — a proper synthesis.

The trouble is, given the current disenchantment with local land-use control in favor of returning regulatory powers to the states, that these ordinary circumstances of local landscape dialectics may be on the way to oblivion. If, as is said, some 200 million acres of land will be urbanized in the period remaining to us in this century (Reilly, 1973), it is perhaps of more than routine importance to landscape planners and aestheticians to recognize how seriously we have been co-opted by "scientism" and the inhumane quantifications that can produce a landscape preservation plan so at variance with the realities of ordinary perception. For as the decision-making process is removed further and further from the people — as would be the case if municipal control is seriously weakened by state-level regulations

— then the landscape "expert" gains power. Given the current level of ignorance of those of us who pose as experts, the results could be disastrous.

Here is some of the background. Since the emergence of environmental quality as a national goal, air and water quality have been addressed by government, industry, and public-interest organizations with a relatively high level of conceptual consistency. New quantitative measurements of pollution, based principally on public health, have provided a foundation for methodologies that can be agreed upon sufficiently to sustain rational debate. Air and water quality can be measured on the basis of purity. Total purity is the ideal, unachievable, but nonetheless the ideal, meaning a 100 percent absence of measurable pollutants. Thus, air and water quality goals can be set and depolluting technologies applied. Given quantitative systems of measurement together with a clear national understanding of the common interest, legislation can be enacted — and enforced — to see that the common interest is served.

Thus, for two of the three primary components of the biophysical environment, the road to progress, if not solution, is well marked. But for the third primary component, the land, the story is quite different and of uncertain outcome. There is no direct quantitative method to measure the quality of the land nor can there be. A standard of purity, 100 percent absence of pollution, is perhaps possible to conceive of theoretically as primeval wilderness in which man functions as a biological, nonmanipulative organism. But such a standard is of no value to a species needing to live, work, and spend leisure time in community, and who can (and therefore must) alter the biophysical environment to maintain and improve its civilization and culture.

Because environmental quality standards as

they apply to the land, and would govern the use of land, cannot be achieved through quantitative measurements of pollution, the land-use decision-making process has traditionally been ad hoc, local, and without reference to secondary effects. The control mechanism was located, and has remained, at the lowest of government levels for good reason — so that decisions about the land could reflect, theoretically at least, the value judgments of those who have the most intense relationship (economic and otherwise) to the land, and have the most effective access to government processes for redress.

In an agrarian economy such a scheme had few serious drawbacks. But many believe, given the complexities of metropolitan settlement patterns in an industrial-cum-technological age, that Jeffersonian local control of land use has been found wanting. Metropolitan-scale infrastructure, inequalities of property-tax income, and the specialization and physical separation of differing land uses have so distorted local decision making that many have given up on local control as a way to express a coherent value system. Local interests, some say, cannot be responsive to the manifold needs of the larger, metropolitan community.

As a result, there is a strong effort to return the land-use apparatus to the states. But there is no corollary affirmation of landscape "values" in this changing of the guard. The principal purpose of the recent land-use policy bill introduced in Congress was to deal mainly with the question of who should make the decisions, rather than the development of a clear public policy informing the decisions to be made.

That the development of national policy is desirable is, at this point, beyond question. But given the nearly complete absence of national consensus on the matter of landscape quality goals, there is no identifiable reference point

for the beginnings of reform. This is, of course, the reason why proposed federal legislation has so far failed to come to grips with any component of qualitative policy save a need for more or better planning — an essentially circular approach.

However, we are not without constructs, most of which come from the processes of rationalizing governmental action in behalf of landscape preservation. Landscape preservation based on cultural values that stand in opposition to the materialistic utilitarian values promulgated by the industrialists of the nineteenth century is a relatively new phenomenon, although the impulse — the Edenic search — spans millenia (Marx, 1964). The city garden, the pastoral landscape, and the wilderness retreat are as old as literature itself, and are based firmly on landscape aesthetics and the "spiritual values" of nature (Shepard, 1967).

But as the agrarian economy was displaced and as the industrial revolution created its upheavals of both land ownership and society, the potential for imminent loss of many highly treasured landscapes became increasingly a cause for alarm. William Wordsworth, in perhaps some of the longest letters to the editor ever published (*Morning Post*, 1844), decried the proposed railway spur from Kendal to the edge of Lake Windermere. "Is then no nook of English ground secure/From rash assault?" he complained in a sonnet accompanying one of his letters. Wordsworth, who had spent a lifetime documenting the value of a dynamic man–land relationship that could lead one into a deeper sense of God, self, and human worth, feared in the 1830s that his beloved Lake District would be trampled to death by thousands of city folk induced thither not by the natural scene but by gaming houses, boat races, and other false lures.

Meanwhile, on the other side of the Atlantic,

Henry David Thoreau feared for the landscape of Concord, Massachusetts.

That devilish Iron Horse whose ear-rending neigh is heard throughout the town, has muddied the Boiling Spring with his foot, and he it is that has browsed off all the woods on Walden shore, that Trojan horse, with a thousand men in his belly, introduced by mercenary Greeks.

Both Wordsworth and Thoreau came to approximately the same conclusion — basically a preservationist position. Thoreau complained (1862) of the potential effect of private ownership of land.

At present, in this vicinity, the best part of the land is not private property; the landscape is not owned and the walker enjoys comparative freedom. But possibly the day will come . . . when fences shall be multiplied, and man-traps and other engines invented to confine men to the public road, and walking over the surface of God's earth shall be construed to mean trespassing on some gentle-man's grounds. . . . Let us improve our opportunities, then, before the evil days come.

A few years earlier, Wordsworth, who had the ocean at his back rather than a still unbroken wilderness, set forth a practical solution that has come to be accepted and acted upon in most nations of the world — a national park. In his geography, *A Guide to the Lakes* (fifth edition, 1835), he urged that the Lake District be preserved (finally accomplished in 1949) as a "sort of national property, in which every man has a right and interest who has an eye to perceive and a heart to enjoy."

But the Romantic consciousness of a landscape aesthetic that was more profound than mere "scenery" could not, in spite of its persuasive exponents, survive the philosophical onslaught of the utilitarians and the ineluctable economics of laissez-faire capitalism. Thus, constructs for landscape preservation were invented that assiduously avoided such nonstatistical phenomena as aesthetic perception. The language of the utilitarians was pressed into service, if not its values. Preserva-

tion became conservation, dating, for all intents and purposes, from 1864 when George Perkins Marsh published *Man and Nature.* "Conservation" is straight out of the utilitarian book and antithetical to the Romantic view. As Gifford Pinchot put it at the turn of the century, in connection with the conservation of forests, "the greatest good for the greatest number for the longest time." Cost–benefit became the rationale for landscape preservation, and still is in many respects even today.

It was Aldo Leopold in the 1930s who saw how utilitarian conservation — for recreation as well as resource husbandry — was essentially seductive of landscape aesthetics and a philosophical sham to boot. But at the same time that he proposed the validity of experiencing the natural landscape on its own terms, he was constrained to base his persuasion on a new justification, which in the hands of fools and Philistines was as separable from aesthetics as was economics. That justification was, of course, ecology. And as utilitarianism was twisted out of shape, so has been ecology as a rationale for land preservation. No fault of Leopold's, of course. The problem lies in the difficulty inherent in mistaking subsidiary rationales for the primary value. Aware that this might happen, Leopold warned (1949) about confusing the servant (ecology) with the master (perception). "Let no man jump to the conclusion," he wrote, "that Babbitt must take his Ph.D. in ecology before he can 'see' his country. On the contrary, the Ph.D. may become as callous as an undertaker to the mysteries at which he officiates."

Landscape planners and preservationists have not heeded his warning. Just as aesthetic perception was displaced by cost–benefit economics (and later by recreation-as-social-uplift) as the basis for public decision making, so ecological determinism tends to do the same thing. Professional environmentalists are now thoroughly hooked on ecology as a primary rationale for public action in respect to land preservation and control.

With this background in mind, let us now examine the public-policy justifications for landscape preservation.

Land is "saved" (from bulldozers, draglines, and other instruments of destruction) in one of three ways. It is bought or, preferably, bought back from private interests by the public; or private interests are required by the public not to destroy their land if there would be a dire secondary effect of such destruction. Hence, some wetlands are zoned against filling; shoreline industry and commerce are barred. Or, finally, private interests are paid not to destroy their land. This payment comes in a variety of ways, although most of it is in the form of negative income: allowing developers to build at higher densities, reducing taxes on farmland, and so forth.

Since the exercise of any of these public actions tends to remove land from the economic sector, the public decision to do so must be convincingly rationalized. Therefore, rationalizations, which are essentially post hoc, are commonly proposed as the *primary* motives for preservation. While the impulse to preservation is derived from a nonrational aesthetic sensibility, the justifications are invariably rationally nonaesthetic.

What follows is an irritatingly simplified and heavily biased analysis of the rationales commonly set forth in an effort to see where they have led. Ideally, the point will be made by this process that the confusion between the rationale and the primary impulse — aesthetics — holds great dangers.

Three rationales will be treated here: economic benefits of preservation, the social necessity for outdoor recreation, and ecological determinism in land-use planning.

Environmentalists discovered the value of cost–benefit analysis as a device to rationalize public decisions at the municipal level in 1958. This was the year that Roland Greeley published a famous letter in the Lexington, Massachusetts, *Minute Man* to the effect that if the town of Lexington would buy up 2,000 acres of vacant land it would *save* the taxpayers money. Greeley, a planner and professor, knew what he was talking about. He calculated that the cost of schools, fire and police protection, sewage, drainage, and welfare costs would add up to "far more" than the annual cost — some $75,000 per year — for retiring a $1,000,000 open-space-acquisition bond.

For landsavers all over the country this piece of news was roughly comparable to the invention of the wheel. In the suburbs of big cities, environmentalists made their own calculations to prove that the preservation of land, any land, was cheaper than the zoned alternative, which was usually single-family houses on half- or full-acre lots.

Developers, the traditional enemy of the landsaver, fought back. The Urban Land Institute, under a grant from the National Association of Home Builders, tried to prove (Mace and Wicker, 1969) that single-family homes *could* pay their way if the calculations were made differently. Moreover, the developers found a way to characterize themselves as social reformers, asking where all the poor people were going to live if the suburbs were to become one gigantic nature preserve. But it was too late. The Open Space Institute (Little, 1969), among others, took up the cry and publicized the new municipal math far and wide. In a valiant effort at compromise, Whyte (1964) and others had proposed cluster development as a way to save open space, maintain zoned densities, and reduce construction costs. But the compromise failed, by and large, since it served neither the landsavers, who were hardly interested in houses of any kind, nor the developers, who smelled a larger opportunity.

If, they reasoned, the primary rationale were economics, then they could fashion an effective petard for the landsavers. This they did and called it planned unit development. By agreeing that development should pay its own way, and by agreeing that a modicum of open space should be preserved, they backed their way into builder's heaven. They proposed uncommonly high densities, including garden apartments, some highrises, and townhouses along with a smattering of single-family homes — their old standby. Such a scheme, which could allot as much as a quarter of a large site to "open space" of one kind or another, would also pump fresh blood into the tax base, since not all tenants or owners would be of that uniform species that produce 2.4 school-aged children. Moreover, through economies of scale a planned unit development could provide many of its own municipal services.

If there have been any "Yeah, buts" recorded by landscape preservationists and putative aestheticians, they have been stomped to death in the stampede to the metropolitan countryside to build new communities that look like little chunks of city arbitrarily sprinkled about the rural scene. Possibly some would except from this negative assessment the Columbias and the Jonathans. The point is arguable. The fact remains that the countryside accessible to metropolitan centers is not the countryside the landsavers had in mind at all, in spite of the fact that cows sometimes cohabit with the condominiums. So much for the new municipal math. By capitulation to cost–benefit analysis, landscape preservationists not only failed to make a convincing case, but in fact probably encouraged land-development patterns wholly inconsistent with even the most rudimentary pastoral aesthetic.

The ecological justification does not have nearly so much direct danger attached, and, intellectually, the postulates of ecological determinism are attractive. Many have even tried to relate ecological balance with aesthetics. Fraser Darling has said (Fraser Darling and Eichhorn, 1967) that landscapes in balance are also beautiful to behold. One can believe this or not. To be sure, there is nothing wrong with ecology as a way to understand how the biosphere functions. Moreover, the ecological justification — as a rational system — is potentially helpful in the preservation of wetlands, alpine environments, deserts, and other such habitats that contain a delicate interlocking of creatures, plants, climate, and topography. Such insights are not endlessly projectable, however, to every copse or lea.

Ecology as an approach is, of course, neutral. It can be useful or not to the landscape preservationist, depending on the circumstances. But ecological *determinism* is not neutral. It tends to insist (McHarg, 1969) that all land-use policy questions can be answered by understanding the biological linkages. Moreover, in the hands of those who believe that the hydrological cycle is the prime indicator of ecological balance, the determinations made thereby are worse than incomplete. They are boring and irrelevant to real people who are trying to figure out how to maintain a humane environment.

Like the landsaver's cost–benefit analysis, ecology has been eagerly embraced by developers. In the old (pre-ecology) days, the best a developer could do was to leave as many trees standing as possible. Or, like the developer who was the president of a local Audubon Society in Westchester County, he could dig up and transplant all the wildflowers on his site on Sunday so that he wouldn't have to worry about what his bulldozers would do on Monday. These days land developers prepare maps showing unbuildable gorges, swamps, and outcrops splashed with green ink and labeled "conservation area." Nothing wrong with this, of course. Except that it may delude the landsavers into giving up a fine visual landscape, such as a meadow or even an old apple orchard, that may have absolutely no value under a system of ecological determinism.

The third justification for preservation that is often mistaken for a primary value is the need for outdoor recreation. We may define outdoor recreation as a set of leisure-time activities necessary to the underclasses and categorically different from the interests of those who plan recreational facilities for them. Where the intelligentsia of the out-of-doors treasure the slap and gurgle of a canoe moving across a wilderness lake, the masses are required to toss beer cans out of a hired aluminum outboard roaring across a reservoir. If the wilderness lake is too crowded, it is judged a failure. If the reservoir is not crowded enough, it is judged a failure.

On the banks of the Hudson River, landsavers had argued for years that a certain point of land jutting into the river, favored by many for bird watching, rock sitting, and similar activities, should be set aside. The county stepped in, set it aside, covered a meadow with a parking lot, blasted aside rocks for a boat launching ramp, installed swings, picnic tables, charcoal grills, grass, and signs that said "No —" and immediately complained that there wasn't enough money for maintenance. Some people liked that point of land once, for what it was. Now nobody does; it has been demoted to a "facility."

The story of the national parks is too dreary to dwell upon. The reader is directed to Edward Abbey's *Desert Solitaire* (1970) and the Conservation Foundation's *National Parks for the Future* (1972). The question is not *whether* many of the national parks have become tawdry, ridden with automobiles, and callously operated by that segment of the tourist industry with the largest share of market (larger even than that of Disney), which we call the National Park Service. Rather, the question is *why*.

The reason for this state of affairs is that the policy justification of national parks has been substituted for the primary values that led to their preservation in the first place. The justification was "outdoor recreation" — one of the least expensive ways a society based on the exploitation of resources and labor could pretend that it believed in the sanctity of nature and the dignity of man. Also, two weeks among the tall trees would make for a more efficient and less troublesome work force, not to mention the offsetting profits to be made by the "leisure-time" industry. Everybody could be happy, except, of course, those who were expected to find solace and renewal in natural surroundings.

The selling of outdoor recreation as a justification for landscape preservation simply had led to the destruction of landscapes rather than their salvation.

The problem is particularly acute in cities, where parks are thought to fail as landscapes unless they are so heavily used that they cannot be anything but failures as landscapes; and where recreation planners are unable to differentiate between social space — turf — and parks; and where the good social space — streets (Rudofsky, 1969) — functions as parking lots for those with money enough to own cars, but who refuse to bear the cost of parking, asking instead that poor people provide it for them on their streets and be taxed unjustly and disproportionately to pay for traffic cops, street maintenance crews, and the like.

Such is the tortured logic that derives from mistaking outdoor recreation for a landscape "value."

What we have been illustrating here, in these three examples, is philosophic deception — and it is mainly self-deception. In part, it may be because landscape preservationists and aestheticians have had no courage that the state of affairs vis-à-vis landscape quality has turned out so badly in the United States.

When one loses faith in the leadership, one must resort to the wisdom of the people: no small assignment. To that end, three experimental landscape "value sessions" were held recently in an inner-city area, a suburban area, and a rural area, all of them in or near Minneapolis, Minnesota. In all, about 36 people participated in this project, a pilot study that might lead to a full-blown program entitled, for lack of something better, "American Land Forums."

The Forums were introduced as follows:

The Conservation Foundation of Washington, D.C., in connection with its project "Expectations of the American Land," is initiating a series of citizen forums in cities, suburbs, and rural areas throughout the United States. The objective of these meetings is to get behind the rhetoric of land use planning to a basic understanding of how Americans really feel about their land and landscape.

The Foundation believes that the insights so gathered can have a significant impact on national, state, and local land use policy. And the insights will be timely, for today many basic assumptions about growth and development are being questioned. Major legislation such as the National Land Use Policy Act and state-level initiatives concerning land regulation suggest that during the next three to five years we will have to create fundamentally new policy directions concerning our use of land.

Each of the forums, made up of approximately twelve participants, will engage in an informal and candid discussion about personal values as they are associated with this emerging public consciousness that the American land has a "cultural" meaning as well as an economic one.

Cultural meanings are concerned with such expectations of the land as these:

— Ecological expectations: the degree to which land should perform ecological work, mitigate the extremes of environmental forces, provide a sense of natural "balance."

— Aesthetic expectations: the degree to which the land should provide scenic beauty.

— Social expectations: the degree to which the land should provide an optimum setting for community, social diversity, and amenity.

These expectations are the terms in which noneconomic values are generally expressed, rather than discussion top-ics in and of themselves. The discussion should instead focus on personal experiences and beliefs in connection with the land and the basic impulses, as well as they can be expressed, that have led to the growing demand that land use policies be developed that will make our communities worth looking at and living in. What is sought in each forum is passionate statement rather than a critical analysis of planning technique. Moreover, a spontaneous interaction between forum members is of greater value than are considered responses to questions posed by the moderator.

The responses were predictable, useless, but deeply affecting. The moderator posed no question, although he feared he might have to. The discussions took off spontaneously and ran on their own fuel. And although many of the participants were concerned with environmental affairs, their responses in this kind of setting may be significant and not necessarily at variance with those of any citizen who has thought for 15 or 20 minutes about landscape quality.

No one spoke of the need for outdoor recreation facilities, although they did speak of walking in the woods. No one spoke of ecology, although they did speak of environmental hazard. No one spoke of the cost–benefits of open-space preservation, although they did speak of the real estate profits earned by others.

But it is hard to write the truth about these meetings. The responses could be used to prove just about anything anyone wanted to prove. This much can be ventured: they indicated confusion, maybe even despair, on the part of virtually all participants.

So much confusion surfaced, in fact, that "values" of the kind an expert advisor of decision makers would dearly love to record, ascribe numbers to, and see decisions made by seemed almost moot. As one participant observed to the moderator at the end of a session, "What's the point of talking about 'values' when the processes of the political and economic systems are immune to such values?"

This view was unique only in its bluntness. The very first topic taken up in a meeting of farmers in a rural county on the far edge of the metropolitan area was a story that had the sense of legend about it, a circumstance that had taken place 30 years before but was felt to have a kind of universal applicability.

"Albert," began one of the farmers, "you might want to tell him about what happened when the federal government took over . . ."

"Well, I'll tell you. We seen men walking across our lands, and they must have been taking soil samples, that's all I can figure out. We were wondering what they were doing. And then, all at once, the last week in March, there comes a federal officer — big cap and stripes on his sleeves — and gives us a warrant to move in 30 days. How in the world can you move 35 sows and 25 cows and 300 chickens in 30 days? That's the kind of orders they gave us."

"When was this?" asked the moderator.

"This was on the tail end of World War II," said Albert.

"Why was the land taken?"

"Well," said Albert, "they just condemned it to put some kind of factory on it. I don't remember just quite right."

The mythic force of the legend dominated the session. Stories were told about developers that threatened to take this rural community to court unless they upzoned; there were stories about farmers who thought they had to sell out. One man recollected about his uncle who had done this. "He turned around and sold for about $1,200 and bought other land for $450, so he has a cash reserve in the bank for his old age. And he still has 160 acres. But it wasn't quite what he wanted. No, it never is."

"When we moved out of that area," said Albert, back at the myth again, "we were just like orphans. We couldn't adjust to no differ-

ent area. It takes a while, because every square foot of that land you've got to know."

"I can't move out," put in another. "I'll stay here — I'll fight. I'm going to stay on my land until . . . as long as I can."

"I'm going to live and die on my farm," said a third, "I'm attached to the community, churches, friends, neighbors — all that's worth something to me. You can't buy that with money. Isn't that right?"

"Right. That's right."

"Yes," said Albert.

Later, of course, they all agreed that a man'd be a fool not to sell for $1,500 or $2,000 an acre.

In a suburban session, the forum members spoke for a while about tearing up Montana to coal-stoke the industry of Minneapolis.

"I think it's immoral to go out there and do to Montana what they did in northern Minnesota to get the iron ore out," said a lady who wrote a column for a suburban newspaper.

"That's hardly a scratch on the surface compared to what strip mining's done to the South," observed an architect.

"I've been to Kentucky; I've been in Appalachia," said a schoolteacher, shaking his head.

Then someone asked, "Okay, well, that's the position you take. All right. We're not going to take the coal out of Montana then, so the industrial plant in this city is not going to keep growing anymore; then what's going to happen to this metropolitan area if you don't take the coal out of Montana?"

The wife of a physician complained that such a discussion was not really relevant. "A lot of us are involved on scales that are much smaller than that, in problems that are a lot easier to cope with and don't cause the situation where push comes to shove, where you have major forces clashing."

"Most of us here," she went on, "are involved in issues that have to do with relatively small acreages of land — a matter of 20 feet on one side or another of a stream, whether to build on these 5 acres here or whether to move over a few hundred yards. And we can't get anywhere even with *those* kinds of land use problems."

Later they talked about an ecologist who had been appointed to a governmental commission.

"He was on our team when we were trying to clean up the creek and save it," one lady said. "Now he's on the commission and I don't even go to their meetings any more, because I have never heard them turn down any developer when he asked for anything."

"But in that position he can't be arbitrary or capricious to anybody," put in a man who wanted to be fair.

"Oh, bullshit," said the lady who wrote the newspaper column.

In the inner city, a professor at the University of Minnesota said, "I get so damn depressed, you know. I've become a radical sort of environmentalist, mau-mauing state agency meetings and things like that. I am distrustful of planners, I'm distrustful of people that come to me and say they're going to help me with my urban landscape, particularly if they are officials, because I think that the urban landscape is up for sale to the highest bidder."

Tales of civic frustration ran around the table, of freeways and highrises that were constructed despite their efforts to prevent them.

"You know," said one woman, "I'm sick of going over to the legislature and lobbying and looking eye to eye with guys making 35 thou a year to do what I do on behalf of the environment for nothing."

"All we're doing," the moderator observed, "is talking about governmental processes, not perceptions of a more humane landscape."

"I'm sorry," said the woman.

"I'm not sorry," said the professor. "No, I wouldn't be sorry because I happen to feel very strongly that the process is impeding the vision, not the lack of vision impeding the process."

And so it went. But in spite of their confusion, their despair that anything could be done, and their panic over the loss of *place*, visions of landscape quality crept in.

"I need trees," said an employee of the 3M Company in the inner-city session. "Trees are now used as economic things — all the same type, all the same heights, all harvested when they're 25 years old for economic purposes. They're not grown for my needs. My needs are for a huge tree that's tangled, jumbled, not economically worthwhile at all."

"You know," said a woman. "I heard something that was *very* interesting. St. Catherine's College is right in the city, but close to the river, and they have a little woods in back, but it's very little. And they saw a *deer* in there."

"No kidding."

"I mean, that's amazing when you consider that the deer must have come through back yards."

"That's really an exciting thought, that a deer can actually get into the city. If the city could re-create itself so that this kind of thing could actually occur . . .''

Diversity was what the city residents recommended. "As soon as you simplify the environment, you lose the safety," one said. And they were concerned with small spaces, not large parks, which they thought could just as well be natural areas. They disliked both suburbs and automobiles! Suburbs because they destroyed the countryside, which they did not want to have destroyed; cars because they destroyed the city. They discussed gardens — for flowers and vegetables in small spaces. And they thought that the bulk of the streets could be done away with; used instead for gardens and trees, as well as for "genuine urban densities."

They spoke of funny, surprising little places in the city. And decided that you don't get that kind of thing with planning. In fact, the point was made that planning is probably antithetical to true urban diversity: the jumble city, productive of a good urban lifestyle.

Safety, urban surprise, and that recurring theme — trees — came together in the remarks of a young woman who was a Vista volunteer. "There's value in ugliness. I live above a warehouse, and I can leave my door unlocked. My windows are open. I frequently lock myself out, but I can crawl up into an open window in a matter of about 5 seconds. And because my place appears to be ugly it is very safe. Nobody suspects that anybody would want to live there."

And then she revealed her secret. "In the back I've got my roof garden and I look out my window and there's an old box elder tree which fills up my window. So what if a box elder is a weedy tree? It's nice and green. I lay in bed and see it against the sky. Of course, if I lay in bed the other way I see an office building."

If in the city the perceptions were related mainly to lifestyle, in the suburbs there was a more abstracted notion of natural beauty. "I have a real love for idle land," said a high school science teacher, "land that man can just keep his cotton-picking fingers off of and just let it go its way."

The talk was of childhood summers in the out-of-doors and of the effort to re-create that spacious sense for their own children in a metropolitan milieu.

There was one exchange that seemed to express not only the suburban view of the landscape, but also the most profound kind of value in terms of preservation. It took place near the end of the session.

One participant put the question this way to an avid preservation advocate, "But why? Why do you care?"

The woman answered, "It's sort of like a sense of security. We look at the natural order of things as ongoing. To see a river continue on is life."

And a man added, "A man's sanity depends on associating with and being able to know that the river is there, and that it's going to be there. Whereas everything else we're associating with is going to be here today and gone tomorrow. Yet, you know, that river . . ."

It may be, the moderator ventured later, that the suburbs are just as dangerous as the city but in a different way. Man is undependable in the city, and that is dangerous. But in the suburbs, nature itself seems undependable, since the landscapes are so massively transformed. "Getting back to nature" may involve something other than recreation. Perhaps it is a compulsive effort to reestablish the permanence of "the natural order," an escape from the placeless suburbs to natural dependability.

"You don't have to get too far away," said the science teacher, "to be a long ways away. And I think this is an important value."

The farmers were experts on real estate economics, sensitive to environmental hazard as might be expected, and grieving over the encroaching realization that they were anachronistic.

One farmer, a bit of a poet, put it this way: "Most of those new people like to have a farmer living near them, so they can sit and look out the window and watch everything he does. And they do that. The older people and the kids especially. A lot of people say, 'Oh, we watch you all the time. We listen to you sing!' "

The moderator of these three sessions despaired, and still does, of making some kind of useful analysis of all this. Perhaps it can be done after many more forums are held. Or perhaps not at all.

But everywhere he went he was struck by the

people's sense of loss of *place*, of personal "locatability." The changes are too many, too big, too fast even for the most exuberant and adaptable of citizens. And the people sense their lives are in disarray. They believe that they are being manipulated by government and business, but they seem reluctant to admit that a humane landscape and living environment is wholly out of reach, if only they could really *organize*. And when that thought is uttered, their hopelessness returns, sometimes with a shrug and silence, sometimes with a kind of protorevolutionary stridency.

At the forums there was excessive talking and unburdening, a reluctance to end the sessions. One of them ran to 4 hours and continued past midnight in a parking lot.

There is no instruction in this chapter for the planner or the preservationist, perhaps not even for the aesthetician. One hopes that it is enough to raise a few questions. Still, there would appear to be a difference between authentic landscape values deriving from ordinary perception rooted in the necessity for a dependable *place* and the dry intellectual constructs that preservationists have developed to justify their arguments and which they then confuse with reality.

If we continue to mistake the one for the other, we may well fail; for without humanizing our planning concepts, we may be unable to create humane or particularly meaningful metropolitan landscapes. We shall fail, not because we are wrong in the narrow intellectual sense, but because we shall move no one.

And that is the problem. There has been a good deal of puzzlement on the part of many planners and preservationists about how to justify aesthetic perception. We have invented such arguments as ecological balance, outdoor recreational opportunities, and economic benefits, sensing danger in proposing public action on the basis of personal perception.

Perhaps we cannot justify a humane landscape this way. Perhaps we can, but few have had the nerve to try. Most of us, excepting people like Lady Bird Johnson, have been embarrassed to voice a flat-footed celebration of *place*, without the diversionary tactic of ringing in a brass band of ecological, sociological, and economic scientism.

Landscape perception and the impulse to the preservation of place is, perhaps, no more or less than an authentic existential act, free of deterministic rationalism, undertaken as a way to dignify a man and to make his surroundings more humane.

Camus' classic existential metaphor is Sisyphus, who is condemned to push a stone up a hill only to have it tumble down again as he nears the crest. The hero of this legend is not the rational stone, which with a regularity characteristic of its essence, obeys Newton and rolls downhill. The hero here is the man, Sisyphus, who, Camus holds, not only endures but also finds joy in his task. Sisyphus was heard in the "value" forums reported here.

In these technologically parlous times, the impulse born of aesthetic perception and the fruitless search for Eden is, surely, absurd. But it is authentically affirmative of life. What further argument for landscape preservation is needed?

LANDSCAPE PERCEPTIONS

The concept of perception is complex. When related to the landscape, it involves the reception and processing of information gleaned from the landscape. The landscape is the source of both the stimulation and the information. It is important to recognize, however, that perception is conditioned by a range of factors in addition to landscape stimulus and the receptor organs. It is influenced by an individual's previous experiences; by his values, beliefs and attitudes; by his social and economic well-being; and by his expectations for the future.

Landscape perception as a subset of the broader concerns of environmental perception and as a subject for systematic research has been recognized only recently. The majority of the scholarly work in this area has been done within the past decade and is a reflection of the growing public interest in landscape problems during that period. It is also a reflection of the questioning of, or the searching for, the validation of assumed public landscape values. In a previous chapter Charles Little has, for example, raised the issue of the importance of knowing the values of the users of the environment if meaningful landscape design and management programs are to be achieved. Calvin Stillman, in a companion chapter, suggests that any consensual landscape values that predominate are those of an effective minority — a body elite. He suggests that there can be no objective, interpersonal, intergroup value in a landscape or in the determination of natural beauty. If such is true, Little's request becomes an impossible one to fulfill. John Jackson and Roderick Nash infer however that there have been and are generally held landscape values that have endured and that they encompass both the cultural (man-influenced) and the wilderness landscape.

Garrett Eckbo states that values are culturally derived; that is, they are learned and are a product of the milieu in which man is born and reared. He also infers that as the world moves toward an industrialized society, cultural differences decline.

The authors of the preceding chapters have posed an array of provocative and challenging interpretations of the concept of landscape values, interpretations that are very relevant to the concept of landscape perception. Landscape values influence landscape perception. The values we hold relevant to an object, issue, or environment influence our perception of reality — of the way in which we receive and process information about that object, issue, or landscape. We must also recognize that there are a number of value orientations toward the landscape, including aesthetic, economic, and ecological, and that these values may not necessarily be consonant. The cultural derivation of values may also strongly influence the relative importance or hierarchy of these various value orientations. Thus, agreement on the relative aesthetic values of a number of landscapes may be little indication as to the importance of aesthetic values to the individuals involved.

The student of landscape perception is presented with a number of theoretical and applied issues, many of which are exemplified by the previous discussions on landscape values. For example, what is the nature of inter-

personal and intergroup differences in landscape perception; what differences can be explained on the basis of cultural background, personality characteristics, and social and economic well-being? Another issue is that of the universality of certain values heretofore assumed to be exemplary of the general public. Does the nineteenth-century romantic naturalistic landscape prevail in the latter third of the twentieth century? Is it raw nature that is valued; is it the naturalistic landscape as altered and influenced by man; or is it the man-dominated, man-made, urbanized landscape that is most highly valued? By whom? And for what purposes? A third issue is that of the consonance of different landscape values — aesthetic, economic and ecological — or stated in other terms, value as scenery and value for other physical uses, such as housing, recreation, or conservation. Do aesthetic judgments of landscapes differ significantly from preferential assessments of the landscape for specific users, and do economic values relate to perceived aesthetic values? These issues relate to the substance of landscape perception studies. They suggest the why, they provide direction to the researcher, and they help to define the problem domain.

Another set of issues must be confronted in a state-of-the-art assessment, the set relating to methodology, to questions of techniques for presenting the landscape stimulus, recording perceptual responses, and validating or assessing the relevance of findings. The study of landscape perception presents major problems in the presentation of stimuli to subjects. If real-world landscapes are used, limitations of time and money can severely constrain both the sampling of subjects and landscapes. If simulations are used — drawings, photographs, or models, for example — how do responses to simulated landscapes differ from responses to real-world landscapes?

How does one measure perceptual responses to environmental stimuli such as landscapes? Techniques and instruments developed initially for use in the experimental laboratory for dealing with nonphysical phenomena or for assessing personalities pose questions of utility and efficacy when used for assessing landscapes. For example, how effectively can verbal responses and semantic scales represent the preception of visual–physical phenomena?

Concern with the validation of findings is an integral part of the preception research paradigm and leads to the search for a predictive function. A traditional criterion for assessing relevance is the comparison of a psychological response with a physical measure. If variations in response can be associated with variations in the physical measure, the latter may have utility as a predictor of the former. The search for reliable physical measures, for landscape dimensions, is therefore an issue of considerable importance that commands the attention of both researchers and practitioners. The researcher strives for explanation, for an understanding of the relationship between the stimulus and the subject. The practitioner is concerned that the dimensions used in the analysis of landscapes and in the development of landscape plans represent the values of a broad sector of the public and not just those of the professional conducting the analysis or preparing the plans.

The chapters that follow in this section touch on all these issues. They sometimes present conflicting viewpoints and frequently present alternative approaches to the same or similar issues. For example, three of the chapters (S. Kaplan; Zube et al.; Brush and Shafer) deal in part with efforts to define predictive models. The objectives are identical, but the points of origin of the three efforts vary considerably. Stephen Kaplan's work derives initially from the psychological theory of information processing and exhibits a strong intuitive bent in the interpretation of the findings. Brush and Shafer's work proceeds from a concern with developing tools and techniques for the landscape manager and relies on the use of a mathematical model. The work of Zube et al. had its origin in concern with the validity and utility of the assumptions commonly made by landscape planners in the conduct of their work. It has resulted in a mathematical modeling approach similar to that of Brush and Shafer.

The chapters are arranged in a sequence that proceeds from theoretical issues through questions of method to those which have a strong orientation to application. Barrie B. Greenbie addresses several salient issues, including that of objective "reality" versus subjective perception, in which he distinguishes between the individual's capability of seeing and the individual's interest in seeing. He also deals with the question of objectivity versus subjectivity in environmental response, and suggests that there may be basic perceptual elements such as shapes, relative scale, and spatial dimension which are stable across cultures in terms of the emotions that they elicit. He suggests that the stability of these emotions can be validated by plotting the strength and nature of emotional responses — what Manfred Clynes called the essentic form. Greenbie suggests that landscape assessment includes both objective values as indicated by essentic form and subjective values, which are a reflection of what one plans to do with the landscape. The latter point is illustrated with a study of neighborhood boundary perception in a New England city.

Stephen Kaplan reports on the evolution of a predictive model of preferences for outdoor spaces. He views the environment as a source of information and suggests that perception is a highly inferential process; thus, humans should prefer patterns of spatial information that aid them in making sense out of that environment. Two broad categories and six variables are discussed as having some role in the prediction of preference. The two categories are the promise of further information and legibility. The variables of mystery and complexity are contained under the promise of further information. The legibility category contains the variables of identifiability, coherence, spaciousness, and texture. These variables are essentially intuitively derived. It is of considerable interest to note, however, the strong parallel of these variables or dimensions to the traditional concerns of the designer with elements of spatial composition and structure. Kaplan also suggests that some variables may underlie all group landscape preferences, but that they may be weighted differently for different individuals or groups.

Ian C. Laurie, drawing upon his recent work for the Countryside Commission of England, presents a case for the use of the artists' or aestheticians' perception of values as a surrogate for those of the general public in landscape planning and management activities. He argues that there are stable landscape values that are not solely those of a professional elite, but rather that artists and designers are, by virtue of their training, perceptive of a wider range of values than the general public. He suggests the assessment of beauty in the landscape and not preference as a primary objective. Beauty is defined as a product of the formal qualities of the object being perceived and the characteristics and cultural values of the observer. He questions the adequacy of preference as a guide to aesthetic quality because of the implied utility element in preferential decisions. Laurie makes an important distinction between the comparative visual quality of

landscapes and the visual quality of a single landscape. He suggests a strategy for the comprehensive evaluation of the English landscape that draws upon the heightened perceptions and techniques of skilled artists and designers.

Rachel Kaplan addresses a number of important research caveats and methodological issues, and draws upon her collaborative research efforts with S. Kaplan for illustrative examples. Among the issues are the objectivity–subjectivity continuum, the identification of predictive variables or landscape dimensions, and the question of the experts' values versus "the people's" preferences. Her approach to the latter issue provides an interesting contrast and at the same time lends some support to Laurie's argument. It should be noted, however, that she uses the term preference in a manner that does not imply the utility element posed by Laurie. It is used here simply in reference to scenic preference. She questions the reliance on physical dimensions, such as land form, and land use as predictors of preference and suggests an alternative approach that defines more subjective variables based on dimensional analysis of preference ratings for landscapes. And, attention is focused on the very important issue of sampling the landscape. A warning is raised that, in exercising great care to define the sample of subjects from which preferential or evaulative responses are to be elicited, one does not overlook the problem of sampling the landscapes to be rated.

Kenneth H. Craik distinguishes among three kinds of landscape assessments: descriptive assessments, evaluative appraisals, and preferential judgments. The last two recognize the same distinction as made by Laurie, that of the potential utility element in preferential judgments. Craik focuses on the first kind of assessment, landscape description. He explores the relationships between observer characteristics and environmental perception as expressed in individual differences in landscape descriptions. His findings are based on "real-world" experiences and not on responses to simulated environments. They suggest significantly different subject typologies on the basis of landscape descriptions. That is, subjects with different personal characteristics perceive the landscape in such a way that the information gleaned and the manner in which it is processed cause them to describe the landscape in significantly different ways. These findings appear to support the categorization of kinds of landscape assessment and point up the need for further investigation of the nature of responses within categories and of the relationship of responses between categories.

Ervin H. Zube, David G. Pitt, and Thomas W. Anderson present findings from a number of studies related to frequently encountered assumptions of the landscape planner. The studies draw on techniques used in the experimental laboratory as well as those suitable for use in natural settings. All the studies are focused, however, on the art of application. The issues addressed include the use of physical dimensions for scenic-quality prediction, expert versus nonexpert values, and the use of simulation for landscape evaluation and description. Their findings on several of the issues, for example, on expert versus nonexpert values, tend to support the observations of R. Kaplan and Laurie, but also suggest a potentially significant cultural variation. Simulation is found to be more reliable for eliciting evaluative judgments than for descriptive assessments, confirming, at least partially, the explicit assumption of S. Kaplan as to the efficacy of using photography. Zube et al. are also concerned with the development of a predictive model with utility for landscape planning and management programs, and discuss the use of physical dimensions for such purposes.

Robert O. Brush and Elwood L. Shafer discuss a predictive model based on previous research on preferences for "natural" landscapes. The model employs a mathematical approach, using multiple regression analysis to predict preference.[1] Physical resources, such as vegetation, rock, grass, and water, and the compositional zones of foreground, middleground, and background are measured in black-and-white photographs for which preference ratings have been obtained. These data are entered into the predictive model and serve as the basis for testing the scenic impact of various landscape-management practices, such as clearing a stand of trees or creating an impoundment. In contrast to the variables used in the S. Kaplan model, which relate to landscape characteristics, this approach relies exclusively on physical resources in the landscape that can be measured and are the materials manipulated by resource managers and landscape architects. Challenging questions are posed by these two approaches as to efficacy: which provides greater prediction and utility, which is the most readily understood (by both public and professional), and which provides the greatest ease of application?

In summary, these chapters are illustrative of a range of approaches and of the diversity of questions related to landscape-perception studies. They do not provide ready solutions to the complex problems encountered by the practitioner. They do, however, provide insights that are of value in a general way, they identify some of the traditional assumptions and values that have been supported empirically, and they suggest where others should be approached with caution in the future. This section is a modest addition to the body of knowledge the practitioner has to draw upon when seeking solutions to land-management problems and participating in local and/or regional design and planning programs.

NOTE

1. The following are definitions of some of the terms used in this section and other chapters that employ mathematical approaches or statistical analyses.

   The *level of significance* of a statistical test indicates the probability that a hypothesis that is true will be rejected. A level of significance of $p = .001$ means that a true hypothesis will be rejected only 1 in 1,000 times.

   Correlation provides a measure of the degree of linear association between two variables. The correlation coefficient (R) varies from $+1$ to -1. A coefficient of zero indicates that there is no linear correlation. A positive correlation means that a large value of one variable is associated with a large value of the other variable. A negative coefficient means that a large value of one variable is associated with a small value of the other.

   Regression provides a measure of the degree to which a mathematical function explains the relation between a dependent variable (Y) and one or more independent variables (X). The coefficient of multiple determination of R^2, is a ratio that indicates how well a regression equation fits the sample data, that is, the percentage of the total variation in Y that is associated with the regression.

   A *t test* is used with two groups of paired data to decide whether they are from the same population. The *degrees of freedom* (df) indicate the size of the sample. The df is 1 less than the number of pairs of data. The t test assumes normal distribution. The significance level (e.g., $p < .001$) indicates the probability that the two groups are not from the same population.

   The *F test* is a ratio used to test whether two samples are from the same population. The degrees of freedom (df) indicates the size of each sample and is 1 less than the number of observations in each sample. The significance level ($p < .05$) indicates the probability that the two samples are not from the same population.

Problems of Scale and Context in Assessing a Generalized Landscape for Particular Persons

Barrie B. Greenbie

THE PARADOX OF SCALE

Landscape assessment as a specialized field of activity is primarily a function of planning. Although it may well extend our basic knowledge of ourselves and our environment, and is clearly of interest to theoreticians in the behavioral sciences, its primary excuse for existence is the solution of problems in the "real world." To use the new cliché of funding agencies, it is *mission oriented*. As such the results must be applicable to particular times and places. In short, the usefulness of landscape assessment as a tool depends on *what* is being assessed and for *whom*.

On the other hand, such a field of activity — perhaps we can now call it a discipline — relies on the presumption that it is possible to develop a standard set of criteria that will be more or less independent of the specific characteristics of particular environments and more or less generally applicable to a wide range of man–environment relationships. The establishment of such criteria, to the extent possible, is of course a primary objective of this volume and a major interest of all contributors. Some of the studies presented here indicate

Barrie B. Greenbie is an Associate Professor in the Department of Landscape Architecture and Regional Planning at the University of Massachusetts.

that such criteria can in fact be established. This in turn presupposes that there is some degree of commonality in the human perception of the environment, which, if we can identify and tune into it, will enable planners and designers to organize our surroundings in more generally satisfactory ways. The work of Zube, Craik, and Fabos, and the Kaplans, among others, certainly suggests that there is such commonality, and in fact it would be highly surprising if there were not, since we are after all one species with common sensory apparatus.

It seems to me that there are two aspects of human perception which relate to this problem. One has to do with what a particular individual is *capable* of seeing or otherwise perceiving, and the other has to do with what he or she is *interested* in seeing.

Klausner (1971:65) notes that the role of physical perception of the environment relative to a cultural one increases with what he calls the *extremity* of the external situation. Presumably, the closer we get to a purely physical response, the more similar will human perceptions become, since the cultural differences between individuals are much greater than differences in our physiology, even among highly contrasting races. Thus, on a normal day 100 radio listeners may be tuned into 75 different programs from rock to Beethoven to ballgames, but if a sudden catastrophe occurs, they may all tune into one, or at least one class of program, the news. There is good reason to believe that perception of the *danger* of environmental deterioration in recent years preceded aesthetic or moral interests in ecology on the part of the public. There seems to be an element of brinkmanship in perception, and this is no matter of comfort, as Aesop's pitcher found out.

It is useful to consider three determinants by which any one of us finds experiential satisfac- tion with a particular environment or object within it. One is what E. T. Hall (1966) calls "infraculture." It is phylogenetic and has to do with the basic structure of our nervous system and its propensities to respond to various stimuli. It will be common to all human beings except for relatively minor variations. The second and third are ontogenetic. Of these, one will be a function of our direct life experience with the nonhuman environment and the satisfaction gained individually from it. The other will be a reflection of the environment as it influences the other individuals in our group, especially those on whom we model our self- image, and its effect on our relations with them. This last determinant of perception includes style or fashion; in our time it is the least stable and the least capable of inducing lasting inner satisfaction; but it may well be the most crucial in governing our decisions, be- cause it is one of the powerful forces that bind us to a social group. Whether or not it is a reliable basis for assessment of anything as rel- atively durable and irreplaceable as the land- scape is one problem we have to cope with.

This points up the difficulties of determining such an elusive entity as, for example, "en- vironmental quality." The problems of assess- ing objectively the quality of anything are underscored by the meaning of the verb "to qualify." In other words, we must take note of the highly relative nature of the noun and make the best effort we can to be as specific as possible, that is, to acknowledge the *context*. If we are talking of water quality in terms of bio- logical oxygen demand or what is safe to drink or swim in, we are considering one thing. If we are trying to determine the water quality that makes for satisfactory vacation home sites, we are considering something else. Clearly, the former is simpler than the latter. For example, a friend of mine who has a camp on a lake has been attempting to get his neighbors to cooperate in a plan to open a dam, lower the water level, and allow the lake to be cleaned of pollution to reduce odors and algae, a familiar problem. So far he has been unsuccessful, because some of his neighbors are more concerned with keeping the water level high enough to be able to park their boats by their door. The "quality" of that lake thus varies considerably for these different people. However, most of them will probably agree, at least privately, that the lake stinks, and will support projects to clean up water in general. Their attitudes in this instance are a function of a particular set of details in the environment in combination with a set of interests peculiar to the circumstances surrounding that place.

Behind the problems of landscape assessment and most other planning activities, there is a paradox in the contemporary human condition that I call the *paradox of scale*. On the one hand, the sheer size of populations and the complexity of the relationships among them require that people be considered in large aggregations. Human needs must be defined in terms of abstractions and met in terms of generalities. On the other hand, everything that makes human life ultimately satisfying is specific to personality, culture, time, place, and circumstance.

The Evolutionary Generation Gap

Anthropologists tell us that the human animal developed its basic psychophysical characteristics back in the Stone Age (Dubos, 1968), and that our societies were apparently limited to very small, cooperative tribes with strong territorial and dominance structures (Morris, 1967, Ardrey, 1970; Calhoun, 1971) in which each individual knew his fellows and his environment personally and sensuously. Members of some village societies still retain this social pattern in urban and rural areas. However, the

technological systems that urbanizing peoples depend on call for vast impersonal relationships based on abstract conceptualizations, which human beings are obviously capable of inventing, but with which most of us do not seem to be able to live comfortably on a day-to-day basis.

MacLean (1970; 1973) has postulated three anatomical levels of the brain that correspond to the evolution from vertebrates, to mammals, to primates and man. The elaboration of the brain stem provides, in his words, "the raw stuff of awareness," which we share with all vertebrates. With mammals we share the "limbic system," or old cortex. To this MacLean ascribes the neural circuitry that makes emotion possible, which in his theory functions to enable an organism to respond selectively to its environment and to identify individuals in a social group. The neocortex, the new brain, which is increasingly elaborate in primates and fully developed only in man, apparently contains the circuits pertaining to anticipation and planning. Particularly in man, it seems to govern abstract thought and language. What is most significant about MacLean's theory is that these three functional levels are imperfectly integrated. He calls this uncertain organ the "triune brain" and refers to the problem as the "brain's generation gap."

I am not in the least qualified to comment further on this theory from a neurological point of view. The human brain is undoubtably the most complex thing in nature. The theory interests me as a useful heuristic description of the apparent dichotomy that does not seem to exist in practice between intellectual and emotional processes. Because of the nature of the problems to which land-use planning is addressed and the techniques it must employ, much of what is usually practiced calls on the kinds of abstract images that, in this theory, only the new cortex can manage. But if Mac-

Lean is right, most of what makes life worthwhile for most of us apparently exists in the mammalian old cortex, the limbic system. This system evolved when our ancestors got all their information sensually from the relatively near environment.

In our time, the size and complexity of environmental problems, the essential unity of the planet, the interconnected biological and geological systems, such as food chains and river valleys, and the vast interrelationships of industry require comprehension, classification, and organization on a large scale. The human senses are not adequate even to the task of monitoring the problems, which is now being assigned to remote sensors in outer space. Yet human senses, and for that matter animal ones, are what ultimately determine whether or not an environment is desirable or livable.

Regional land-use and resource planners use such aggregating devices as floodplains, river systems, slopes, heavily forested areas, coastlands, and so forth. Urbanization is measured in quantities like persons per square mile; maps are often at a scale no larger than 1 mile to the square inch. General categories of land are marked off for this or that purpose, for uses such as "industry" or "high-density residence," "conservation," and the like. But as we know, even the impersonal processes of natural ecology do not operate only on that level. The difference between the north and south slopes of even a very small hill may represent separate universes of life (Watts, 1957). A particular plant may grow only in a very special and complex combination of shade, sunlight, soil chemistry and mineral content, temperature, moisture, and so forth. Some types of agriculture require periodic flooding; others cannot stand it. A very small marsh may be the last remaining habitat of an endangered species in an entire region, for obscure reasons not replaceable somewhere else.

Good building sites vary considerably; a pine wood is not an oak forest; a meadow is one thing and a city park another. Steep slopes will erode badly under one type of soil condition and construction technique and may be very stable under others. Such sites cannot be adequately mapped, measured, evaluated, or planned entirely on a large scale. And yet some aspect of many environmental problems cannot be dealt with except on a large scale. The Skylab astronauts can spot the birth of a hurricane, while a sailor knows only that a storm is brewing. But for the crew of a small boat caught in the storm, there is little information Houston can give that will help. It is even unlikely that any data gained from space can help win the Bermuda race. Skylab is telling us things about the weather we have not been able to learn here on earth. But the subtleties that make for an April shower or an October morning require attention to particulars. Many city dwellers today have neither April nor October in their landscape, regardless of the time of the year.

Ultimately, all landscape assessment related to human satisfaction turns on the question of aesthetics, which is the most indeterminate problem of all. The nature of beauty has bedeviled philosophers from the dawn of language, and perhaps before. Nevertheless, we may safely conclude that no human society exists without the sense of it, whatever it is. But whatever else art may or may not be, it is *never* wholly abstract or generalized. Frank Lloyd Wright — I believe, or perhaps Louis Sullivan — summed it up: "Art can be no restatement."

It has often been noted that preindustrial cultures unconsciously produce aesthetic environments (Rudofsky, 1964). The peculiar ugliness of industrial cultures, which has yet to be remedied in postindustrial ones, seems to be a function of mindless repetition. Primitive handcraft cultures follow general rules and techniques, but the aesthetic component enters by virtue of the phenomenon that nature never repeats itself exactly, and neither does human thought and activity.

The landscape must be assessed not only in terms of man–environment relations, but also man–man relations. Klausner (1971) has described the relative nature of our satisfaction with environmental events in his chapter on "Social Implications of Filth and Noise." The reaction of a pilot to the noise of an airplane, he notes, will be quite different from that of the owner of a home over which the airplane flies. In fact, man–man relations become very critical among decision makers themselves, even when they have adequate and accurate information regarding the landscape, because questions of bureaucratic status or power enter the picture. McBride and Clawson (1970) observe that most land-use decisions in the United States are largely the result of incremental negotiations between small landholders and local officials. Regional planners, quite correctly noting that most problems of population and resources today transcend municipal boundaries, are constantly frustrated by the fact that it is next to impossible to overcome territorial possessiveness sufficiently to achieve effective joint action between local governing bodies. McBride and Clawson argue, however, that this is not due to the impotence of local officials, as is often claimed, but to their effectiveness in keeping a hand on their proprietary interests.

In a way I have chosen a role as devil's advocate, but the devil in this case has two faces and talks out of both sides of his mouth. I shall refer now to two studies that provide support on both sides of the question. One deals with

the most particular and subjective level of human feeling and objectifies *that*. The other points up the high degree of subjectivity that exists even on the most objective, generalized map-level view from which planners normally work.

SENTICS: OBJECTIFYING THE SUBJECTIVE

Manfred Clynes, former Director of the Biocybernetic Laboratories at Rockland State Hospital in Orangeburg, New York, appears to have quantified at least one aspect of the mental perceptual state we call quality. He has shown that those intense but hitherto elusive concomitants of experience which we call *emotion* can not only be identified and measured quite precisely, but *have a characteristic shape*.

The name that Clynes (1969) has given his discovery is *essentic form*. This is the space–time configuration of a specific neurological activity within the brain, which appears as a curve on an oscilloscope. It is a concomitant of a mental condition that he calls a *sentic state*. Elsewhere (Greenbie, 1971, 1972) I have presented in more detail some speculations regarding its potential for the subject we are concerned with. I will summarize only the main points here.

Clynes postulates that these neural patterns within the brain are genetically programmed into its cell structure along with other physical characteristics. They exist as interval circuits that are quite independent of actual events in the environment. He uses as an example the color "red" (Figure 1). "Redness" as a quality is represented in the brain by a precise set of neural processes that is absolute and unchanging, processes invoked in our brain when we

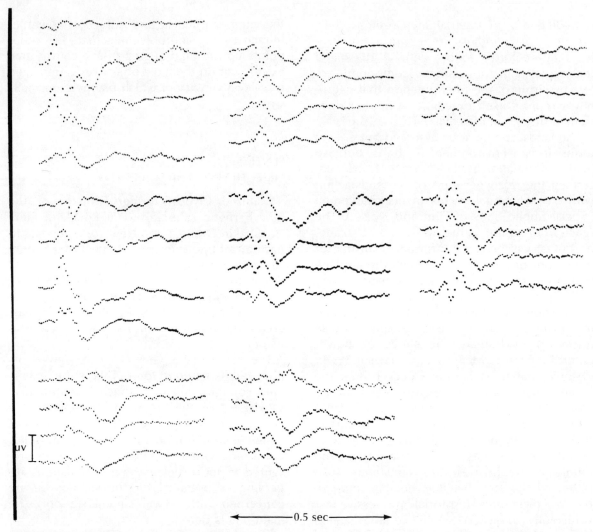

uv

←——0.5 sec——→

Figure 1
Comparison of responses of different individuals to red–black stimulus. Source: Clynes, 1969.

think "red." This is different from the perception of objects in the environment to which we will attach the word "red" as an adjective. A "real" object will be more or less red depending on adjacent colors, light intensity, our remembered experiences associated with the color, and so forth. But although a sentic state is internal and self-sufficient, it may be cued by the words in the natural language that a given culture has evolved to correspond to certain basic emotions, such as "love," "hate," or "grief."

The Measuring Instrument and What It Measures

The device by which Clynes measures the sentic state of an individual is a button attached to two transducers on which the subject, sitting in an upright but relaxed position, places a finger (Figure 2). The transducers measure very subtle changes in pressure in two separate directions, one line of movement away from or toward the body, the other up and down. Each transducer is connected to a computer via two separate channels. In the sentic state, there will be a characteristic pattern corresponding to the relative pressures along these two coordinates. Fifty responses to a particular word like "love" are averaged by a computer. The two separate curves representing these averages are read out on the screen on an oscilloscope and photographed by a Polaroid camera. The visual record of the two curves in parallel with each other is the essentic form for that particular sentic state (Figure 3).

To test the conclusion that essentic forms observed in this manner are biologically programmed and not the result of cultural influences, Clynes (1970) conducted experiments in different countries. Except for minor divergencies, the results were remarkably consistent throughout these cultures (Figure 4). But while Clynes has thus demonstrated basic similarities in emotional states among all human beings, he has also been concerned with the uniqueness of each person's emotional life.

He has paid particular attention to the way in which music conveys, on the one hand, the universal emotions, and, on the other, expresses the individual personality of both the composer and the performer. Each work of music has what he calls an inner pulse, which

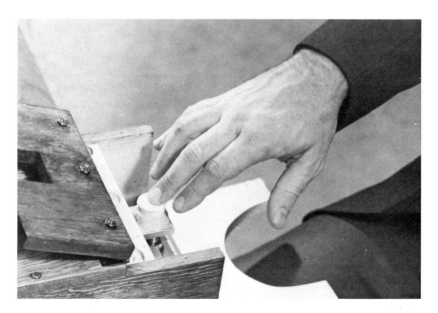

Figure 2

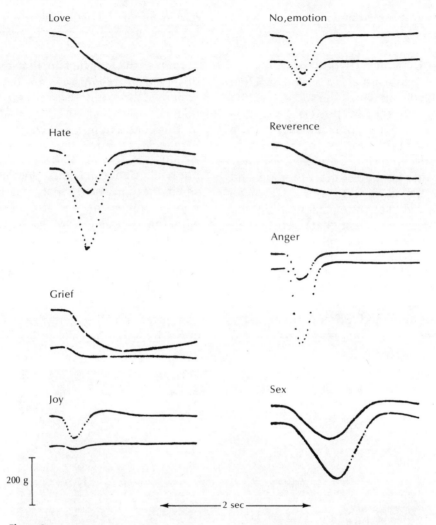

Figure 3
Essentic forms of emotions. Upper trace shows each emotion in the vertical component of transient pressure, lower trace the horizontal component (at twice the scale). Each form is measured as the average of 50 actons. Source: Clynes, 1970.

gives it its peculiar emotional quality (Figures 5, 6, and 7).

The way in which essentic form may correspond to artistic form in a visual art is vividly suggested by Clynes in Figure 8. His studies with sentics also suggest that there is a basic emotional need within us for natural forms that relate us in a fundamental way not only to each other but to the nonhuman environment as well. He reports that "the shapes of trees have an inherent affinity to the structure of our retinal data processing characteristics, the 'har-

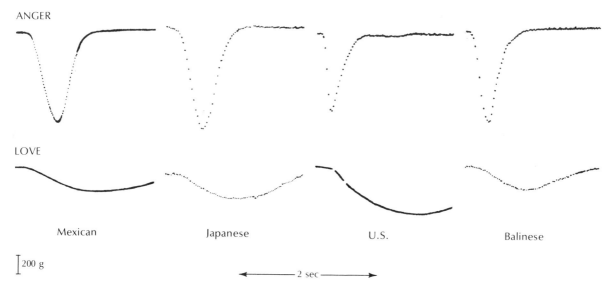

Figure 4
Essentic form of love and anger. Source: Clynes, 1970.

mony' of nature is also the harmony of our nervous system organization" (1970:23–4).

Eibl-Eibesfeldt (1971) has shown with motion pictures the similarities of the facial expression of emotion in such diverse peoples as the French, Samoans, Balinese, Papuans, and Waika Indians; to further emphasize their phylogenetic character, he has compared them with those of a 10-year-old deaf and blind girl. However, it is difficult to determine precisely to what extent these expressions represent identical *feelings* in different people. Clynes's work with physiological response to colors and his demonstration of the similarities of essentic form among diverse cultures go much further toward substantiating intuition and other evidence in this regard.

Essentic Form in the Landscape

The apparent fact that the basic units of emotional feeling are unvarying and have a precise spatio-temporal characteristic and that they may correspond to various stimuli in the environment gives us, it seems to me, a most important independent variable by which we can begin to examine responses to complexities in the environment, whereas before we had only a barrelful of dependent variables, none of which could be pinned down. The apparent fact that in diverse languages certain specific words can be located which will evoke the basic emotion and bring about a sentic state suggests that there are other basic perceptual elements, such as shapes, relative scale, and spatial dimensions, which can evoke very specific sentic forms and have characteristic essentic forms.

If we can find the key elements that consistently produce appropriate essentic forms from the environment, we shall have come close to identifying those aspects of aesthetics that are governed by phylogeny. By using these as references, we should also eventually be able to determine the most satisfactory forms based on more complex ontogenetic cultural

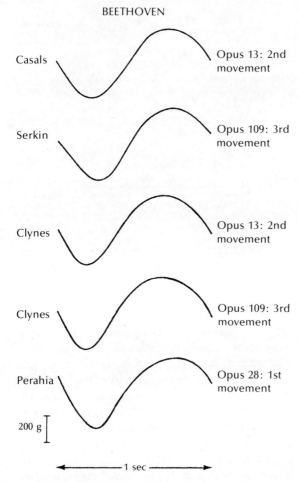

Figure 5
Essentic form of the inner pulse. Source: Clynes, 1970.

CONTRASTING COGNITIVE MAPS

I would now like to turn to a study that I participated in, which demonstrates the diversity of human responses to the same more or less objective phenomena. This was an experiment in cognitive mapping performed as part of a study of the relationship between neighborhood boundaries and community well-being in Springfield, Massachusetts (Greenbie et al., 1973). Our first problem was to get some sort

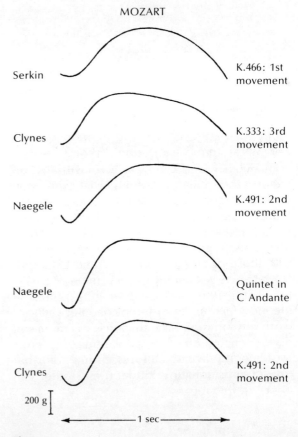

Figure 6
Essentic form of the inner pulse of Mozart. Source: Clynes, 1970.

responses to different environments, just as it was possible for Clynes to distinguish the essentic form of a performance by Casals in contrast to other performers, which also produced an immediate response from listeners. Figures 9–13 suggest some possible ways in which essentic forms might be found in a range of landscapes.

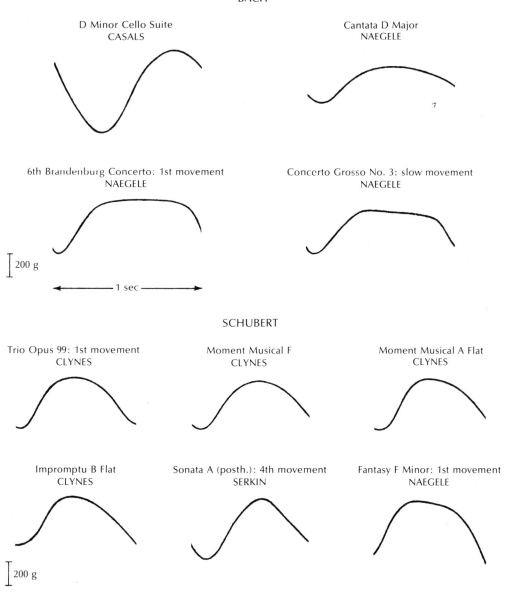

Figure 7
Baroque music. Source: Clynes, 1970.

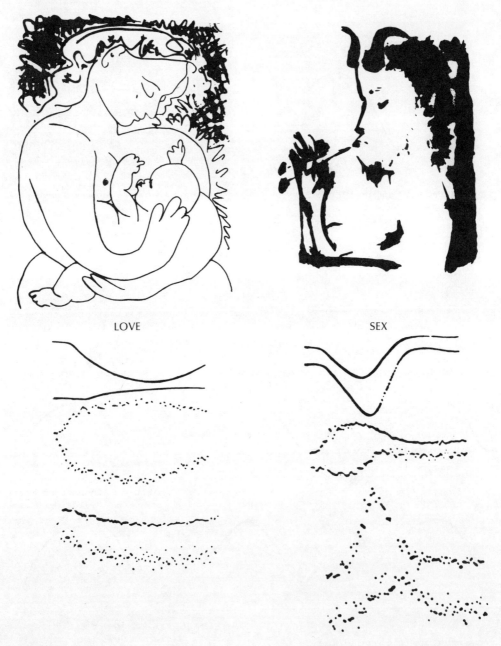

LOVE   SEX

Figure 8
Source: Clynes, 1970.

Figure 9
The shape of these Aztec pyramids suggests the spatio-temporal form that in Clynes' work corresponds to the word for "sex"; the mountains beyond suggest the essentic form for "reverence" (see Figure 3). Clearly, such correlation here and in the other photos cannot be literal, but the forms in this case may pertain to some underlying emotion that combines energy and affinity. Photo by Greenbie.

of handle on the concept of "boundaries." The strategy we devised was to compare the boundary perceptions of five different groups.

Researcher's Perceptions

The first group was the research team. Two of us who were unfamiliar with Springfield and who possessed no preconceptions about its neighborhood composition conducted a survey of the entire city by car using a large-scale street map as a guide. In addition, we made a low-level survey of the city by airplane and in the process obtained some interesting information from the pilot, who was a native of the city. We delineated everything that fell into one of the two categories: obvious physical edges or barriers that divide residential areas in some way, and abrupt changes in residential character that might comprise a symbolic boundary.

Figure 10
Here in this Amherst College war memorial the "reverence" of the mountains and rolling hills in the middle-ground contrasts with the circular shape in the near ground, which suggests the enfolding essentic form for "love." Photo by Greenbie.

Included in the first category of boundaries were large tracts of open space, industrial parks, steep inclines, ravines, rivers, lakes, railroad tracks, and superhighways. In the latter category were changes in housing type (from medium-rise apartment buildings to single-family housing, for instance) and overall changes in the residential environment. Our perception of boundaries is shown in Map 1. The heaviest outlines surround well-bounded areas; the fine lines delineate areas we considered to be moderately bounded.

Perceptions of Neighborhood Boundaries by Public-Health Nurses and Taxicab Drivers

The second study group consisted of eight taxicab drivers from a dispatcher's office in downtown Springfield and eleven public-health nurses. Both groups were interviewed by the same investigators. During the entire interview a set of prepared instructions was presented to both groups to assure as much consistency as possible.

Figure 11
Traditional Dutch rooftops here have a playful quality that suggests Clynes' essentic form for "joy." Photo by Greenbie.

Each respondent was given a large-scale street map of the city and was first asked to locate any neighborhoods he or she knew by name by writing the name near the center of each neighborhood. The respondents were then requested to locate the boundaries or edges of each neighborhood by drawing a solid line were the respondent felt fairly sure of them and a dotted line when uncertain. They were also asked to complete an answer sheet for each neighborhood that they had identified. On this they were requested to list the main streets of the neighborhood and to name the landmarks along these streets that mark the beginning and end of the neighborhood.

Map 2 is a composite of the neighborhood maps drawn by the eight taxicab drivers, with four boundary-line widths. The heaviest lines represent the opinion of four drivers, and the finest lines the opinion of only one. There is clear agreement only on two neighborhoods. Map 3 is a composite of the opinions of the eleven nurses. Here the heaviest lines follow a boundary drawn by eight or more, the next

Figure 12
The rooftop and conifer trees here suggest the essentic form for "sex." Photo by Greenbie.

heaviest the opinion of four, and, as in Map 2, the finest line is a boundary drawn by only one. The degree to which these perceptions correspond with those of the researchers can be seen by comparing these maps with Map 1. Only one area is consistently perceived as bounded in the same way.

Residents' Perceptions

The third study group was a sample of people who live in three of the areas that showed up most clearly in the delineations of the first two. Two of these were "most bounded" and one "moderately bounded." The residents were not asked to draw maps, but only to provide verbal descriptions, which we ourselves put on a map. One hundred questionnaires were distributed by the public-health nurses to the clients in these areas. In addition, 49 residents were interviewed on the streets, in bars, and in stores, using the same questionnaire as a guide.

Respondents were asked to give the name of

Figure 13
By contrast, this scene conveys the outward flowing quality so often evoked by mountains or the sea, suggesting the essentic form for "reverence." Photo by Greenbie.

their neighborhood, describe its center, to give street names, and to list any landmarks that distinguish the beginning, end, and center of the neighborhood. The results are shown on Map 4, and the differences in boundary perceptions when compared with the other groups is quite startling. Again the South End turns up as most sharply and consistently bounded. This is an area that has traditionally been an Italian, working-class, ethnic neighborhood, but in which recently the pro-

portion of Puerto Ricans and blacks has been steadily increasing. Eight of the ten residents interviewed there identified the neighborhood by name, the South End, without any hesitation, and seven agreed completely on the boundaries. These boundaries were also the same as those perceived by the researchers, drivers, and nurses.

The primary landmark in the area was the statue of Columbus (one woman said it was a statue of President Kennedy), which almost all

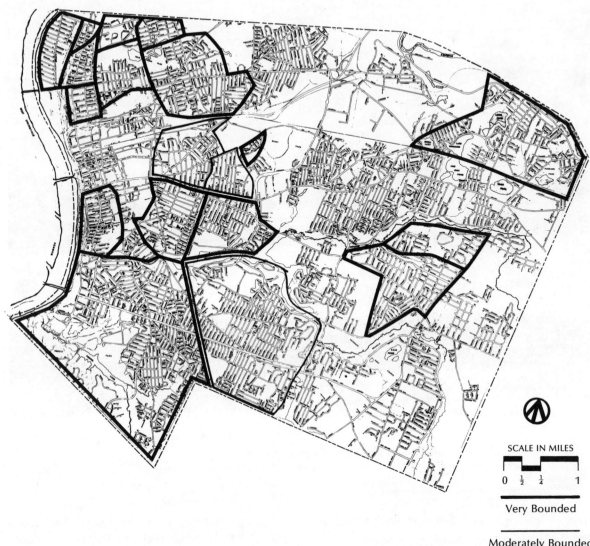

SCALE IN MILES

0   ½   ¼   1

Very Bounded

Moderately Bounded

Map 1
Researchers' perception of bounded areas.

gave as a distinguishing feature of the southern boundary. Of the northern edge, residents spoke vaguely of the business center, and only a few mentioned the Civic Center.

Somewhat less defined, but clearly perceived as a neighborhood, was an area generally known as the North End. Fifteen residents were interviewed of whom five were Puerto Rican and five French Canadian. Of the Puerto Ricans, two had no name for their neighbor-

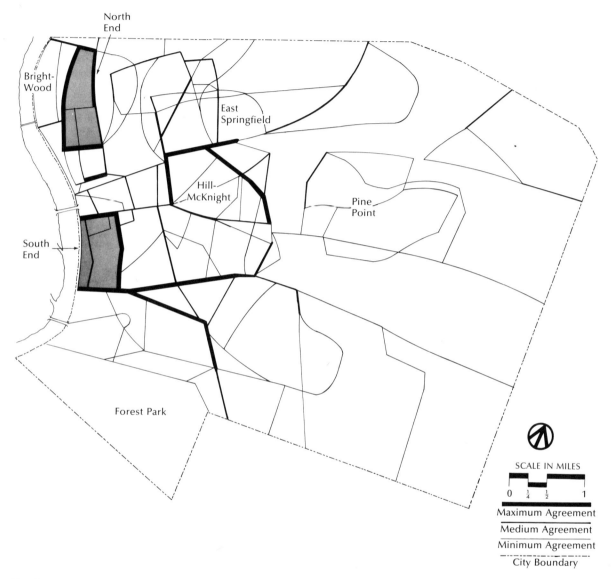

Map 2
Springfield's neighborhood boundaries as perceived by taxi drivers.

hood and were unable to describe it geographically. Only one Puerto Rican respondent
felt that his neighborhood bordered a distinct
French Canadian community to the north.

However, the French Canadians were more
specific and particular about their neighborhood. Four of them called it "Brightwood" and
adamantly declared that it extended no further

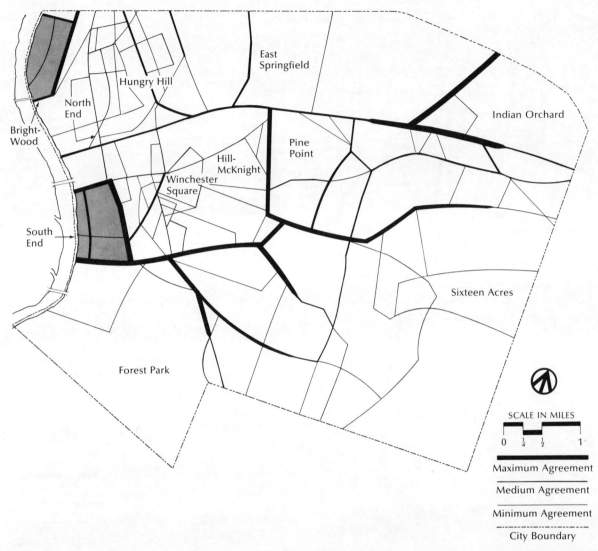

Map 3
Springfield's neighborhood boundaries as perceived by public-health nurses.

south than Jefferson Street, where the Puerto Rican North End, they felt, began. The fifth Canadian was a young woman who worked for the Memorial Square Neighborhood Development Program and described her neighborhood as the project area, a relatively artificial neighborhood drawn according to housing conditions.

There were no landmarks in the North End that were mentioned as consistently as the statue of Columbus in the South End, but several respondents referred to the Memorial

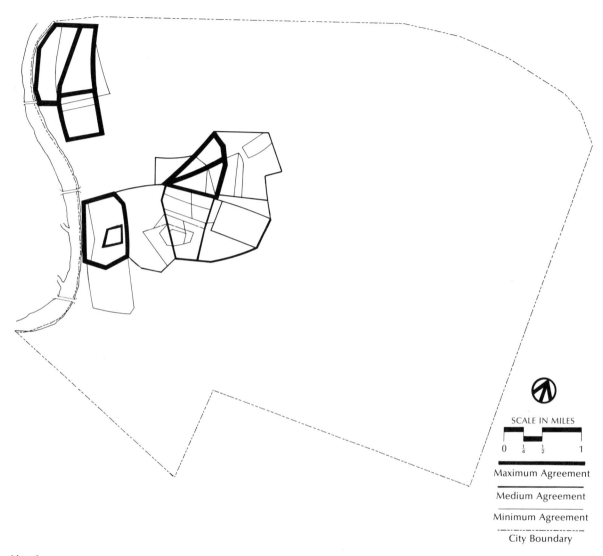

SCALE IN MILES

| 0 | ¼ | ½ | | 1 |

━━━━━━━━━━
Maximum Agreement

────────────
Medium Agreement

Minimum Agreement

-·-··-··-··-··-··-··-
City Boundary

Map 4
Neighborhood boundaries in three areas of Springfield as perceived by residents.

Church situated in a triangle formed by two major streets. Some emotional Canadians encountered in a bar spoke angrily of a former public library, just west of this triangle, which had been an important community symbol in their youth, now abandoned because, accord-ing to them, attacks on the librarians had made it unsafe. Without mentioning them by name, they made it clear that in their mind this was the result of the Puerto Rican influx into the southern portion of the area. By contrast, one of the Puerto Ricans interviewed expressed

Figure 14
The eastern boundary of the South End is clearly delineated by bluffs. Photo by Greenbie.

hostility toward the area because it was a run-down place to live, but no hostility as such to the older population.

In the third and less "bounded" area, according to the other groups, only five out of 24 residents perceived the area generally known as Winchester Square as one neighborhood with that name. As can be seen by Map 4, there is a very complex array of internal boundaries here. A third of the respondents described small individually defined neighborhoods,

usually only one or two blocks in area, whose center was frequently the respondent's own home. The nurses saw two separate neighborhoods separated by a weak boundary, the drivers heavily defined the northern part, and we ourselves saw the southern part as most bounded.

Our airplane pilot, by contrast, identified the entire area, as "Winchester Square" and said it was "all black." However, in his own area, generally known as one neighborhood called

Figure 15
The South End terminates less clearly on the north in the central business district.
Photo by Greenbie.

Forest Park in the southwest of the city, he was able to identify a complex array of Italian, Irish, and Jewish subneighborhoods.

City Planners' Perceptions

Our fourth study "group" was the official map of Springfield's Planning Districts, based on census tracts in combination, which we took to indicate planners' and census takers'

views of the city's boundaries. The degree to which this view corresponds with the others in our study can be seen from Map 5. Only the South End Planning District conforms closely to resident and other perceptions.

My purpose in introducing this small study, in association with a summary of Clynes's complex work, is to underscore the areas where commonality in human perception will give way to diversity. In his classic *Image of the*

Figure 16
All residents of the South End agreed that this statue of Columbus marked the boundary on the south (one woman said it was a statue of "Kennedy"). Photo by Greenbie.

Figure 17
No one in the North End mentioned this Spanish-American War statue, but several residents referred to the Memorial Church behind it. Photo by Greenbie.

Figure 18
Some Canadians in the North End seemed upset at the fate of this library, but the Puerto Ricans seemed unaware of it. Photo by Greenbie.

City, Kevin Lynch (1960) observed that there is a rather consistent tendency to perceive the landscape in terms of the very elements we look at, especially edges (or boundaries), nodes, (or intersections), and landmarks. As Lynch carefully pointed out, his respondents were relatively homogenous socially, and they appeared to have the same general motivational relationship to the landscapes considered. I see no contradiction at all in the fact that, although we found the same general consistency in response to certain *classes* of landscape features, for example, highways, railroads, factories, we discovered considerable discrepancy in which *particular* ones were singled out for attention.

In our study we deliberately selected groups who had different professional or daily activity attitudes toward the landscapes in question.

We may conclude, therefore, that the landscape is assessed not only in terms of whatever intrinsic responses its forms may evoke, as investigated by Clynes, but also in terms of what one plans to *do* with it, and what constraints or opportunities it offers in relation to individual goals or purposes. These phenomena have been investigated in detail by Suttles (1968, 1972). As shown for urban residence by Newman (1972), the landscape also will be judged in terms of its potential for danger or security and its relative capacity for reinforcing or disrupting personal social relationships. Our study proved to be quite inconclusive in respect to a number of things we were attempting to find out, but one relationship stood out quite clearly. When a strong and visible cultural, or ethnic, identity coincides with very obvious physical boundaries, as in Springfield's

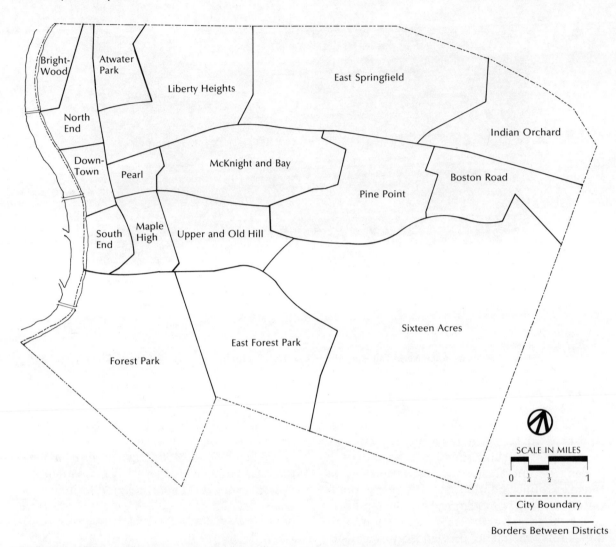

Map 5
Officially recognized Planning Districts of Springfield.

South End, the consistency of perception will be considerably heightened.

In the matter of landmarks, which, as Lynch suggests, can be quite significant in landscape assessment, the culturally determined symbolic content will be most important. Again, in the Italian South End we found the most persis-

tent references to a landmark, the statue of Columbus. Its emotional meaning was underscored by the elderly lady who first referred to it as simply the "statue of the President," and, when pressed to be more explicit, said it was "Kennedy." We may suppose that on the level of MacLean's paleomammalian brain a hero is a hero, whether he discovers the tribal environment in 1492 or rediscovers it in 1960. In the more culturally heterogenous North End, only one group, the French Canadians, placed emphasis on a landmark, the library, which had an obvious symbolic meaning for them that it lacked for the other group.

In conclusion, then, I think our greatest problem in developing a useful approach, or a body of technique, or a discipline — whatever we want to call it — in the *activity* of landscape assessment is not in locating and describing those variables which may produce an underlying common response in people, but in organizing whatever information of this kind we can obtain in a way that will allow it to be applied selectively, in context. This is not to suggest that the objective problems are easy or that we have begun to solve them, but simply that their solution is only the beginning of the job. Although landscape assessment must start as a science, it has no choice but to wind up as an art. Thus, we shall do well to remind ourselves and others that landscape *assessment* is a tool for use in landscape *architecture,* not a substitute for it. This will be obvious to many of us; I fear that for many decision makers, especially those in the bureaucracies of planning, it often is not.

An Informal Model for the Prediction of Preference

Stephen Kaplan

Landscape assessment can be viewed as a procedure for identifying landscapes likely to be preferred by humans. In this process the choice of variables is the central problem. Clearly, it is desirable to select variables that will predict preference. In addition to being effective predictors, such variables should make theoretical and intuitive sense as well. Theoretical sense makes one's efforts more coherent, better organized, and more widely generalizable. Intuitive sense is necessary if one wishes to share one's understanding with others. Variables that seem arbitrary or obscure are unlikely to be used by the experts whose effectiveness we hope to enhance.

It is difficult to specify how one goes about making intuitive sense. In part it is an attitude rather than a procedure, and in part it depends upon good fortune in uncovering variables that are both sensible and efficient. But in our work an important factor has been that of working with a broad theoretical framework which itself makes reasonably good intuitive sense.

This work was supported in part by the U.S. Department of Agriculture–Forest Service. Portions of this paper were presented as part of a Symposium on Environmental Aesthetics: Outdoor Environment as a Source of Affect, American Psychological Association meeting, Montreal, 1973.

Stephen Kaplan is a Professor in the Department of Psychology and the Department of Computer and Communication Sciences at the University of Michigan.

This basic theoretical framework has its background in perception and, more particularly, in a functional approach to perception. Two basic themes emerge from such an approach. First, it is assumed that perception is oriented to getting along in the world, to making sense out of the environment. Second, the process of perception is highly inferential. A great deal of knowledge, experience, and interpretation enters into what may seem to be the straightforward process of looking.

A number of implications of this approach have proved helpful in the search for suitable variables in landscape assessment. First, information is central to the organism's survival. Thus, considering the landscape in terms of the information it provides is likely to be helpful in discovering what underlies preference. Second, information that aids in making sense out of the environment is likely to be particularly salient. Information that allows an individual to make more accurate inferences about his whereabouts should be highly valued. Likewise, the individual should also value the possibility of gaining new information about his environment. Thus, the third point is that the acquisition of knowledge should also be related to environmental preference (S. Kaplan, 1973b).

One central concern of the perceptual process is the interpretation of space. For an understanding of why spatial information is so important, it is necessary to refer back to the conditions of human evolution. Comprehension of large areas was vital for early man to locate prey, to find desirable plant food in season, and to find his way home again (Flannery, 1965; Peters, 1973; Pfeiffer, 1969).

Like other perceptual processes, the perception of space is highly inferential. We construct our spatial world through the selection, analysis, and interpretation of spatial information.[1] This inferential process takes a two-dimensional pattern of light falling on the retina and interprets it in three dimensions. (Thus, the spatial interpretations that participants make of two-dimensional photographs in our research and in other studies is hardly surprising. The perceptual apparatus is highly biased toward spatial interpretations, and people in our society have extensive experience with photographs as representations of the three-dimensional world. To criticize photographs as artificial and inadequate in landscape research is to fail to appreciate the nature of human perceptual mechanisms.)

To date we have identified six variables that seem to have some role in the prediction of preference. We have tentatively grouped them into two categories in terms of the information that they seem to provide. One category, concerning the order or structure apparent in the scene, suggests factors that aid in making sense of or interpreting the environment. This is closely akin to the concept of legibility that Lynch (1960) has applied to the extended three-dimensional environment. The other category concerns the amount of information that appears to be available or is likely to become available as one advances into the scene. This category thus applies to settings where there is the possibility of acquiring further knowledge about the environment. The next portion of the paper deals with the evolution of the six concepts and of the organizational scheme that has been growing up around them.

IN PURSUIT OF PREFERENCE: A FRAMEWORK

The Promise of Further Information

The first study in the series was Wendt's honors thesis concerning the identification of the separate urban and nature domains (Kaplan et al., 1972). Complexity was the primary predictive variable in that study (besides, of course, the domain distinction itself). Since the chapter by R. Kaplan in this volume deals with several details of this study, I shall not repeat these, but focus instead on the role that study played in the emergence of preference predictors. By ordering the slides in terms of preference, it was clear that there were variables in addition to complexity that went into preference within the nature domain. Certain specific features, like the presence of water, were striking in their influence. Such primary landscape features, although not lending themselves to dimensionalization, are of undeniable importance. Another variable, however, seemed more continuous and less content specific, and appeared in a variety of different settings. There was high preference for a photograph of a path that went straight for a while and then turned and disappeared from view. Another highly preferred item was a brightly lit field partially obscured by nearby foliage. The two examples have little in common in terms of either the two-dimensional pattern of stimulation or the three-dimensional settings they depicted. But both of them communicated a feeling of mystery.

In thinking about the concept of mystery, and particularly in trying to describe it clearly to subjects or judges, the idea of being able to enter the scene to gain further information became increasingly compelling. In all cases that seemed appropriately characterized by "mystery," some information was suggested but hidden from view. The attraction to go deeper into the scene not surprisingly had its influence on the preference value of that scene.[2]

A number of comments are called for with respect to this concept. First, it clearly depends on the spatial interpretation of the visual array. One can hardly feel attracted to enter a visual array that lacks depth. Second, there does seem to be a functional interpretation for this concept. As I have suggested, an organism like man whose survival is based on knowledge would have to *like* acquiring new information. Thus, a scene that promises new information would be preferred precisely because of this promise. Let me hasten to add that this tendency is by no means uniquely human; it should be characteristic of any far-ranging animal whose resources and dangers are widely distributed in space. Thus, as we all know, the bear went over the mountain (to see what he could see).

Although one might be tempted to argue that curiosity by any other name is just as familiar, in fact certain subtle additions have crept in. First, mystery concerns the *promise* of new or additional information, rather than new information per se. Second, by casting the concept in these terms, its kinship with the complexity variable becomes evident. Both concepts address themselves to the issue of information that could differentially characterize different portions of the array. A complex scene promises more information just as a mysterious one does, except that in the case of complexity the additional information requires more time and inspection, rather than a change in vantage point. It is evident that a scene can be relatively high in both these qualities, or in either one without the other.

Legibility in Scenes of the Environment

The next step in the identification of possible predictors of preference came in the context of a different set of material. In addition to photographs of the outdoor environment, this set included graphics, that is, sketches by designers of the same sort of environments. Our intent was to find out if certain types of graphics were more effective than others; we ended up learning a good deal more than we intended.

We pretested this material by presenting it to a group of nondesigners, largely, as it turned out, psychologists and psychologists-to-be. We had expected them to be puzzled by some of the graphics — we were puzzled ourselves by some of them. But we had not anticipated the anger and hostility they provoked. Confrontation with something one could not make sense of turned out to be a distinctly unpleasant experience. Reflecting on this, we came to the realization that being able to identify or categorize a visual form tended to enhance its preference value. The identifiability variable is as yet not well defined. Clearly, in extreme cases its absence leads to considerable frustration. Proponents of ambiguity as a desirable feature of the designed environment take note! On the positive side, the variable is probably better understood in terms of familiarity, which in turn is not unrelated to a sense of place. Zajonc (1968) has shown that familiarity can have a powerful role in the prediction of preference in a laboratory setting. And Thomas Herzog, a colleague of ours at Grand Valley State College, has demonstrated that familiarity enhances preference for scenes of the outdoor environment as well. The concept also appears to be related to the Acking and Sorte concept of "affection", which they describe as "an age concept in the environment, but also a feeling for the old and genuine" (1973:472).

Another outcome of examining the graphics that had been ill-received was the discovery that some scenes failed to "hang together." They lacked organization; they were hard to grasp — quite apart from how readily one could tell what they depicted. Antidotes to this difficulty included textures that provided continuity among disparate elements, and elements that were identical or similar to each other. The grouping of elements together in space also helped with this property. Labeled "coherence," this concept has a kinship with gestalt principles of organization that cause elements to be perceived as groups. There is likewise a parallel with the information processing concept of "chunking." Although initially introduced in the context of memory Miller, 1956), this concept applies in the perceptual domain as well. The argument would be that anything that helps organize the many elements in a scene into a few major units (or "chunks") will aid in its perception, just as memory is aided by the formation of a few major units out of many different elements.

The concepts of identifiability and coherence arose out of experience with a particular set of stimuli. But they could hardly fail to have been influenced by Lynch's legibility concept. They clearly deal with order or structure and as such play an important functional role in orienting and in "knowing where one is." The differences between these two concepts are also instructive. The overall organization of the array, the order among the elements and the redundancy of the components, are readily apparent; in other words, coherence is perceived almost immediately. Identifiability, by contrast, depends upon inference. It is mediated rather than immediate; it requires a certain amount of classifying, of decision.

The same issue seems to apply to the complexity–mystery distinction. As we stopped to consider it, we realized that complexity, depending on the number of elements in the array, is immediately perceived. Mystery, like identifiability, requires an inferential process. At this point in our pursuit of the components of preference of physical environments we had four variables that fit into a two-by-two table. Two were aspects of legibility and two dealt with "information promised"; within each of these categories the two concepts differed in their immediacy.

Table 1

| | Degree of Inference Required | |
Source of Information	Little	More
Present Legibility	Coherence	Identifiability
Future Information promised	Complexity	Mystery

Of course such insights about possible predictors of preference lead one scurrying to the laboratory, the field, or anywhere that one can check them out. One of the most interesting possibilities for research of this kind arose in an applied context, the prediction of preference for the roadside environment. This study is at least as interesting for the ways in which it forced on us an extension of our conceptual scheme as it is for the test it provided for our previous concepts.

More on Legibility:
Gleanings from the Roadside

The project is a collaborative effort with Roger Ulrich, a behavioral geographer now at the University of Delaware. His interest in demonstrating the limits of the rational-man idea led him to study the choice between a fast expressway and an attractive parkway. This naturally led to a consideration of the factors underlying a choice clearly premised on aesthetic considerations. Although the data are not yet fully analyzed, certain preliminary findings are of sufficient interest to be worth describing briefly.

In the interest of sampling a wide range of roadside settings, this study began with a large number of photographs. Even a concerted effort at eliminating photographs with extrane-

ous elements and redundant themes only brought the total down to some 140 prints. To reduce that number to a manageable size for obtaining ratings, we asked several people to sort the photographs into categories of their own choosing. The groupings were remarkably reliable across participants. The controlling variable in these sorts, which some participants were able to articulate but which all appeared to be relying upon, was the notion of spaciousness.

Given the obvious salience of this new variable, judges were asked to rate each photograph for spaciousness as well as for coherence and complexity. Then 53 photographs were selected to include a representative range of each of these three variables. (Subsequently, a panel of judges also rated the scenes for mystery.) The subjects' task, then, was to indicate their degree of preference for each of the 53 roadside photographs.

In terms of their power in predicting preference, we found that a scene had to have a modicum of complexity, coherence, and spaciousness to be liked. Items rated low on these factors are not preferred. But it appears to make little difference whether there is a little or a lot of any of these. In other words, they form necessary conditions for preference. Mystery, by contrast, is effective throughout the entire range represented by these scenes. The more mystery the scene seemed to have, the better — following a typical regression pattern.

There is, however, another consistency lurking among these photographs. Following our usual approach (R. Kaplan, 1974), the results were subjected to dimensional analyses; these yielded eight content groupings. Inspection of the different groupings formed by these content domains points to the fineness of texture as a key distinguising factor. Within each content domain the scenes seemed to be fairly uniform in fineness or coarseness of texture — expanses of mowed grass versus scruffy underbrush, for example. The dimensions were also quite uniform with respect to the spaciousness ratings: at one extreme are embankments or other obstructions limiting the sense of space; at the other extreme are scenes of relatively open spaces. In terms of the other predictive variables, coherence, mystery, and complexity, the dimensions showed no such consistency.

By combining texture and spaciousness, one can categorize the majority of the dimensions unambiguously. The high spacious–smooth texture dimensions have by far the highest preference ratings, and the low spacious–coarse texture dimensions are clearly the lowest in preference.

Spaciousness is a welcome factor in this research; space is after all the hallmark of the outdoor environment, and it is rather ironic that it emerged as a predictive variable as late as it did. Texture too seems congenial, since it has a profound informational role as well as being so vital in defining space.[3] Note also that this study is based on black-and-white photographs of what are essentially natural settings. Color plays no role and contours range from soft to nonexistent. Thus, texture plays a critical role in defining the masses within the space, as well as the space itself.

These two factors were not discovered through use of the theoretical framework. They were discovered by getting a firm grasp of preference on the one hand and of dimensional structure on the other. But they are consistent with the proposed framework and extend it in an interesting way. Fineness of texture is a legibility component; the finer the texture, the more clearly the figures are distinguished from ground. It is also an immediately perceived factor. The combination of dealing with the order of the information and the low need for inference places texture in the same cell in the two-by-two table (Table 1) as coherence. Since coherence was intended to include redundancy factors, it may be that texture is a more explicit, more concrete component of coherence. Indeed, when more components of coherence are identified, the larger and vaguer concept might well be dropped.

Where does spaciousness fit in our previous table? I would argue that spaciousness is rather an inferred than an immediate factor, but it is also clearly a component of legibility. In fact, spaciousness might be defined as the visible availability of options for locomotion, of places to go. This factor would thus take its place in the same cell of the table as identifiability. Indeed, it could be considered as identifiability of a more specific kind, of running room, if you will. Although one of the most fascinating concepts in the prediction of preference that we have considered, spaciousness is also one of the least explored. At this point, both spaciousness and texture are included in the revised 2-by-2 table based on the tentative findings of a single study.[4]

Some Circumstantial Evidence

The empirical basis of this table is undeniably slim. At the same time, there is cir-

Table 2

Source of Information	Degree of Inference Required	
	Little	More
Present Legibility	Coherence Texture	Identifiability Spaciousness
Future Information promised	Complexity	Mystery

cumstantial support from other sources. One indication of the reasonableness of these proposed factors comes from viewing them in terms of the information-processing requirements that prevailed when our species evolved. Survival under those uncertain and dangerous conditions must have placed a high premium on the skills of recognition and prediction (S. Kaplan, 1972). Recognition, that is, comprehending where one is and what the objects are in one's immediate environment, although vital, is useless without prediction — the capacity for anticipating what might happen next.[5]

As indicated previously, an organism must not only be able to handle information; he must *like* to do so if he is to survive. Thus, humans would be expected to prefer an environment where both recognition and prediction can be achieved without undue effort. In other words, there must be sufficient structure to make sense, to comprehend, to recognize, and sufficient uncertainty to make prediction nontrivial. Prediction in an environment where nothing happens does not enhance one's predictive facility. Likewise, predicting in an environment without order is equally futile. But an environment that promises further information is a clear challenge to prediction.

One of the most striking parallels to the proposed set of factors involves what is perhaps the most concerted attempt in human history to comprehend the aesthetic visual experiences characteristic of nature. The Japanese garden is more an imitation of the visual experience of nature, and of the most aesthetic instances at that, than an imitation of nature per se. In the literature of the Japanese garden can be found explicit mention of mystery and of the means of enhancing spaciousness. The concern for careful control of texture, and particularly for the use of fine textures, is obvious. Coherence is dealt with in terms of grouping

elements, of unifying textures, of repeated elements, and in the total banishment of anything potentially distracting. Identifiability is achieved through the use of elements that capture the essence of the objects they stand for. In fact, through the use of highly standardized, highly familiar forms the elements achieve that ultimate identifiability required of the symbolic. Interestingly enough, of all the proposed variables, complexity plays the smallest role. The Japanese garden could in fact be viewed as a challenge to complexity theory; in its planned austerity it represents a vivid example of a low-complexity, high-preference environment.

ALTERNATIVE APPROACHES: SOME LIMITATIONS

It has been the concern of this chapter to provide a somewhat systematic framework in an area that has tended to go to extremes. By and large, the prediction of visual preference has been dominated by the unifactor theories on the one hand and by lengthy lists of factors on the other. Let me comment on each of these.

The unifactor theory in this area has been primarily the optimal complexity theory (see, for example, Berlyne and Madsen, 1973). It is somewhat of a squeeze to explain all human visual preference on the basis of a single variable, and one might wonder how it has been pulled off as successfully as it has. I think I am beginning to understand how this has been possible. The bulk of the laboratory work in this area has used nonsense forms of one kind or another. Nonsense forms are characteristically randomly generated. They thus contain no order — by definition. Given that people are concerned with order, with legibility, one would assume that people would prefer that level of complexity upon which they could most readily impose order. I believe the laboratory research has shown us that an intermediate level of complexity most readily permits the imposition of order. This is by no means a trivial finding. It is also not in any broad sense an adequate theory of preference.

In the real-world environment there is a great deal of order. Man builds in at least a somewhat orderly way, and nature is profound in its patterns of redundancies. A good designer does not merely attempt to control complexity; he creates order. He uses texture, repeated elements, sequential dependencies, and undoubtedly other vehicles of legibility yet to be discovered. In this context, it is particularly disheartening to see designers looking to psychology for guidance and taking back with them the unifactor approach better suited to computer-generated random forms. Worse yet, they have translated complexity to ambiguity (Rapoport and Kantor, 1967). Another weakness in the discussion of these issues has been the tendency to talk in terms of a bipolar dimension, of unity versus diversity. Given such a framework, one clearly has to search for an optimal level. And given the recent emphasis on complexity, it is clear that legibility must suffer. But we find no evidence that the legibility and "information promised" components are negatively correlated. Rather it is fruitful to search for the ways to enhance *each* of these domains.

The primary alternative to a unifactor approach, exemplified by numerous textbooks, has been the list. One can think of many terms referring to "good" aspects of design. Granted they may overlap or partially overlap. Granted some may be subcategories of others. If one is in a list-making mood, one can simply write them down. Lists, however, present problems, and not only because there is nothing to prevent them from growing indefinitely. They also foster arbitrariness or indecision, depending on one's temperament. The designer, who

tends to be relatively decisive, chooses from the list whatever he feels like taking. The longer the list, the more optional it all appears. The scientist working in this area, wishing to avoid arbitrariness, is readily paralyzed because it is by no means obvious where one should begin.

The proposed approach is intended to allow enough richness to characterize the man–environment interface without skimping. On the other hand, it itends to provide the analytic tools to keep the concepts organized, related to each other, and within a systematic framework. They are constrained from growing into optional status. There may be a variety of ways of achieving legibility and a variety of ways of promising added information, but neither can be considered unimportant in a setting where human preferences are at issue. The results obtained to date suggest that the proposed framework is a useful one in pointing to the importance of both aspects of information in comprehending environmental preference. It does not however answer the question of *which* factors within these categories are salient for a particular type of environment. At the same time, our data indicate that not even complexity reliably participates in the prediction of preference. Further research is clearly called for to find the relationship between the kind of environment and salient dimensions.

SOME IMPLICATIONS

The proposed framework has a number of implications for thinking about preference, both for design and assessment. Three are perhaps particularly salient.

First, there is something to be gained by thinking of humans as profoundly concerned with information, as being motivated both to make sense of their world and to learn more about it. Correspondingly, the environment can be viewed as a source of information, both in terms of the two-dimensional configurations that meet the eye and the three-dimensional world that is then inferred.

Second, the framework encourages the study of and concern with those factors that lead humans to infer the presence of depth or space. The designer in the Western tradition has tended to focus on the placing of objects in space as opposed to enhancing the experience of space per se. The ordinary (Western) human, however, seems to be quite sensitive to spaciousness in his judgment of preference (whether in spite of or in ignorance of his cultural heritage is not entirely clear). For the designer seriously in search of information on factors that enhance the sense of space, there are a variety of complementary sources. The literature on the Japanese garden is of great value, particularly if it is read in terms of salient cues rather than symbolism. The former appear to suffer far less in translation. The perception chapter of any introductory psychology textbook offers additional material, as do a number of books concerned with graphic art.

Third, there is in all landscape-assessment studies the persisting concern for individual differences. Even when high agreement is found among a particular group of participants, there is always the worry that some other group might feel differently. And although, in general, the level of agreement found has been impressive, there remains the concern that those groups who might not agree are the very groups that have all too often been ignored when planning decisions are made. But perhaps the problem is miscast. Groups with less experience with natural environments, for example, may indeed have different preferences.[6] This would suggest a two-pronged policy. On the one hand, it would be important to preserve landscapes

appreciated by the less experienced. On the other hand, with increasing experience, these same people might prefer environments very much like those preferred by other experienced individuals, thus underlining the importance of preserving those landscapes appreciated by the more experienced segment of the population.

But the most fruitful approach to this problem would seem to be not one of ascertaining how different such group preferences are, but of identifying what the pattern of variables is that underlies preference for these various groups. It may well be, for example, that the same variables are appropriate for different groups, but that their importance or weighting differs. An initial study of group differences using some of the variables discussed here suggests that this is indeed the case; the difference between groups can be explained in terms of differing emphasis among the same set of variables (R. Kaplan, 1973a).

The designer in search of a guiding framework may find some useful clues in the foregoing discussion. Some mention, however, should be made of the designer who secretly harbors hopes for a *formula*. Very briefly, he is unlikely to get it and would be unhappy with it if he did. Those who need to be convinced that science is unlikely to provide that ultimate formula are encouraged to read Weaver (1960) and Kuhn (1962). Those who think that they would like to have the ultimate formula that eliminates difficult and messy decisions are encouraged to think about what their role would be once such a formula were known.

Fortunately, for those who like a bit of uncertainty and challenge in their lives, *science* is likely to continue producing generalizations and frameworks while *reality* is likely to continue to be complicated and erratic. Thus, considerable skill will continue to be required in the application of scientific knowledge. The framework proposed here in no way threatens to replace the designer. It is intended to sharpen his eye, to enhance his intuition, and to provide a floor under his efforts. It is intended to multiply talent, not substitute for it.

NOTES

1. The idea that our perception of the environment is not given or immediate, but an achievement, has been stressed in the writing of such functionalists as Brunswick (1943) and Ittelson (1962). Hilgard (1950) has a thoughtful paper on this topic. Neisser (1967, 1968) added the notion of construction; that is, our experience of the environment is a synthesis rather than the picture it seems to be. That this approach entails internal structures corresponding to objects frequently experienced in the environment has been pointed out by S. Kaplan (1973a), who also argues for the central role of these structures in the organism's cognitive map.

2. R. Kaplan (1973a:272, 274) discusses the relationship of the "mystery" concept to Cullen's (1961) "here and there" and describes its use in other design contexts.

3. For an excellent discussion of the role of textural gradients in depth perception, see Gibson (1946).

4. It is not the case that these variables are unprecedented; parallels in the empirical literature exist, although they are hardly blatant. Thus, for example, spaciousness, texture, and order appear among the many variables considered in a stimulating study by Rabinowitz and Coughlin (1970). Wohlwill, too, has obtained independent evidence for one of these variables. In a recent symposium paper he described the predictive value of "depth," clearly a direct parallel to the spaciousness variable (1973a).

5. This predictive capacity had already been explicitly identified as an essential component of adaptive or intelligent behavior in 1943 by Kenneth J. W. Craik, a brilliant young British psychologist who met an untimely death 2 years later. Samuel (1959) depended on the same idea (which he called "look-ahead") in the construction of his famous computer checker player.

6. Such a difference in environmental preference arising out of differences in experience has been reported by R. Kaplan (1973b) in the context of gardening activities.

Aesthetic Factors in Visual Evaluation

Ian C. Laurie

The need for visual quality landscape evaluation in the planning profession is commonly accepted as a product of the increased pressure for change in the landscape and of a growing need to protect the scenic qualities of the landscape as a resource in limited supply. Evaluations have therefore arisen in the last 10 years from the needs of planners to solve new and more urgent problems affecting the landscape. Evaluations of landscape may be either purely philosophic and aesthetic; *or* they may be quantitative and use applied measurement techniques in the fields of geography, planning, environmental psychology, economics, and landscape design. A need or an interest in

In preparing this chapter I am grateful to several colleagues who have offered valuable comments and criticisms. I should like to thank Sylvia Crowe, David Baldwin, John Jones, David Robinson, Jonathan Wager, Larry Wakefield, and Don Wilson for their willingness in giving this assistance. The work was originally prepared as an occasional paper for the Landscape Evaluation Research Project being carried out between 1970 and 1974 for the Countryside Commission for England and Wales at the Centre for Urban and Regional Research at the University of Manchester. The opinions expressed in this chapter do not necessarily represent the views of other members of the project or of the Countryside Commission.

Ian C. Laurie is a Senior Lecturer in Landscape Design in the Department of Town and Country Planning at the University of Manchester, England.

the evaluation of the visual quality of landscape has developed within all these disciplines, and it is vital to ensure that the subject is studied comprehensively.

Evaluation of visual quality in landscape is, however, mainly derived from longstanding appraisals of the relationships of man and nature, with a developing aesthetic awareness of landscape (particularly since the eighteenth century) in the form of philosophic, literary, and graphic preoccupation with the aesthetic qualities in scenery. We need, therefore, to examine the problems of landscape evaluation in a wider historical perspective, and to consider the problems of technique in terms of aesthetic philosophy and the viewpoint of the aesthetic designer.

Landscape evaluation may be defined as "the comparative relationships between two or more landscapes in terms of assessments of visual quality"; in this context, assessments are the "process of recording visual quality through an observer's aesthetic appreciation of intrinsic visual qualities or characteristics within the landscape." Many factors affect the way we assess landscape as a basis for evaluation. This chapter endeavors to close a gap in the present approach to visual evaluation of landscape by considering the techniques of the aesthetic designer who assesses and evaluates the visual qualities of landscape on the basis of an aesthetic philosophy and an aesthetic terminology.

In giving emphasis to visual evaluation in this chapter it is nevertheless recognized that landscape can be perceived through the other basic senses, and the important evaluations of ecological and land-use functions should also not be overlooked. Essentially, visual quality evaluation is but one form of sensory perception of landscape and only one aspect of comprehensive landscape evaluation for regional planning purposes. For the purpose of helping to make realistic policies for the future of the landscape, only an attempt at a broad and comprehensive study of all aspects of landscape is likely to be acceptable to all those in any society who use the landscape and respond to it.

Existing Methodologies

Recent techniques of visual quality evaluation have concentrated on the following:

1. Measured techniques based on the observer's or the survey designer's reaction to the visual qualities of the *physical content* of landscapes in the field, that is, observations based on the quality of individual components.
2. Assessments of landscape preferences based on photographs or slides used as surrogates.
3. Descriptive classifications of tastes and preferences for scenery as displayed in literary sources or by behavior patterns.
4. Subjective evaluations in the field of the landscape seen as a whole.

There are three characteristics of these studies that appear to be significant:

1. With only one or two exceptions, they have not been compiled by, or involved, creative designers or individuals with special competence in aesthetics.
2. The terminology of art and design has not been used and little attempt has been made to isolate and evaluate purely aesthetic qualities.
3. Aesthetic emotions[1] and other associational reactions[2] to the visual appearance of landscape, including "utility preferences,"[3] have not been specifically separated from each other (by accident or design) in the tech-

niques used. These omissions are briefly discussed in turn.

Originators of methods It is doubtful whether aesthetic philosophers, artists, and designers believe that aesthetic qualities (feelings and emotions) can be *measured* or whether they accept a need for such evaluations. Perhaps, simply, they have not been consulted or are unaware of the need, and this may explain why they have not been involved. Artists and designers would generally accept, however, that aesthetic qualities can be described and interpreted, and that aesthetic values can be held and are reasonably consistent within different cultural groups, but subject to gradual modification and change of taste and fashion over long periods.

The evidence for consistency in the assessment of aesthetic qualities lies in the general measure of agreement about the value of works of art selected for art gallery collections and for reproduction in art books, works selected for use in art education, and the consensus found among art critics as well as in the work of creative artists themselves. Inconsistency is more evident among assessments of new works of art (as it appears to be also with aesthetic qualities for new landscapes), because society has not yet established its value judgments for what is beautiful in what is new.

The need for evaluation (that is, the motivation behind previous and current approaches) is based on the assumption that aesthetic standards are held and sought after, and that they are an important cultural facet of our society. Whether held by a minority or a majority, and whether articulated or not, is of lesser importance to us than the knowledge that aesthetic standards exist and are beneficial to the individual and through him to society at large.

We may then ask, are aesthetic standards for landscape important and are people aware of them as being significant and ultimately important to them?

The evidence for the existence of purely aesthetic satisfaction from the sight of landscape seems to derive from two main factors: behavioral patterns and aesthetic education.

Behavioral patterns Large numbers of people go to see beautiful scenery seemingly on their own initiative and exclusive of any associated recreational or social benefit other than an aesthetic experience. For example, they go

1. To isolated viewpoints for the enjoyment of panoramic views.
2. To look at beautiful natural phenomena: sunsets, waterfalls, rough seas, calm lakes, wild flowers, animals, trees in autumn color, gardens in bloom.
3. To look at the beauty of man-made activity in landscape: boats on water, gliders in the sky.
4. To drive in the country to enjoy looking at the scenery.

Aesthetic education The demand for aesthetic education about landscape in education courses, books, films, television programs, and pictures is considerable, as can be seen by the supply of goods and services that has been developed to meet this demand.

It seems, therefore, that purely aesthetic values, preferences, and standards exist and are widely sought. They have, however, been largely ignored in existing techniques of assessment of visual quality in landscape, and we must assume that this is because artists have not been involved, or because it is believed that they would not accept any form of measured values being given. If evaluations of landscape are made without recognition of these purely aesthetic values, it would seem that the policies based on such evaluations might have limited acceptance by society. A community may feel unwilling to accept the evaluation of the landscape that their predecessors have helped to create, and which has been acknowledged as possessing visual quality by artists and writers, when the landscape has been given, say, a less than adequate visual quality score by less sensitive observers. If landscape policies that may result in a fundamental change in the landscape are to be based on such scores, there would seem to be a risk of even less acceptability. We need therefore to determine what purely aesthetic qualities exist in landscape, and to consider the involvement of artists, designers, and writers in landscape evaluation to describe and interpret these qualities.

Aesthetic qualities The aesthetic terminology of artists and designers is widely used and is accepted in some measure in all art forms as a working analytical means of giving verbal description to aesthetic qualities, but its use is not much in evidence in existing methodologies. The terms derive generally from the concept of order in nature and from man's ability to create visual order so as to stimulate and satisfy pleasurable feelings and emotions that he calls aesthetic. The assumption is that man can have an intuitive understanding of the mathematical laws of nature, that the eye and brain are infinitely subtle instruments for assessment, and that the voice, hand, and brain are infinitely subtle means for communicating such an intuitive response.

Common terms used in art and design to describe the concept of an ordered relationship from the interaction of aesthetic factors are unity and composition. Additional descriptive terms include variety, contrast and balance, form, mass, shape and outline, space, spatial relationships and enclosure, proportion and scale, texture and pattern, rhythm, light, and color and color relationships. It seems relevant to determine the application and meaning of this terminology in assessing the visual qualities of landscape — if it is conceded that landscape produces the same aesthetic response as a work of art.

It is generally recognized that landscape, even though it may not be composed by man, does provoke an aesthetic reaction, although it has not received, particularly in this century, the same critical attention as works of art. The aesthetic response to landscape is a stimulus to artist and writer. It can be argued that the observer of landscape is more involved and less detached than the observer of a work of art because landscape envelopes him spatially, and that his aesthetic experience is extended by often having the sensory awareness of sound and smell to add to that of sight when appreciating landscape. The response to landscape can also be extended by the variety of emotions obtained by the participation of the observer, who is able to create new compositions for himself by continuously varying his viewpoint in the exercise of landscape appreciation.

Associational reactions The lack of any separation of associational reactions from purely aesthetic reactions is the third significant point that can be seen in an examination of existing methodologies. Associational reactions are intimately bound up with the aesthetic emotion engendered by all objects. It is arguable that they cannot be separated, although both the techniques of assessing purely aesthetic factors using descriptive design terminology and of analyzing the visual impact produced by the components of landscape attempt to reduce or eliminate these associational reactions. On the other hand, evaluations of general preference ("Do you like" surveys) of landscape tastes, perception studies based on imagery (for example, mental maps), and "where would you like to be/go/live" surveys attempt to measure mainly associational reaction. Clearly, such measures of *general* preference for different types of landscape are an inadequate guide to inherent aesthetic quality, and could be grossly deceptive and unacceptable, because they contain a variable "utility preference element" (that is, a response based on associating the landscape with some forms of use or activity).

The principal factors that have been omitted from many recent visual quality evaluations have now been mentioned, and the problems of making purely aesthetic evaluations can now be examined. The main difficulties seem to arise from two factors:

1. The vocabulary of assessment (or description).
2. The selection of assessors.

It seems likely that the vocabulary of art and design suggested previously might (in the absence of any other) be generally acceptable. If this is the case, it would be necessary to select those who are experienced and trained to make purely aesthetic judgments (as far as possible free from associative reactions and use-preference factors) and are familiar with aesthetic analysis. (It is doubtful if such disassociation can be made by persons untrained in this skill.) This means in practice, therefore, primarily landscape artists and landscape designers. This selection in no way implies an elitist view that only trained designers appreciate beauty, but simply that training develops skills of rationalizing judgment and a vocabulary of description and methodology of assessment, and it is therefore realistic to make use of this. Trained assessors do, of course, only act as the representatives of the society in which they work and which trains and establishes the judgments that (if the necessary democratic controls exist and are used), are

subject to confirmation, modification, or rejection by society in making its decisions. Feeling and response to beauty itself is not, of course, necessarily the product of training or education, and its manifestation is seen in all sections of society.

As purely aesthetic preferences are more abstract than individual subjective associations or collective tastes in any group, the premise is advanced that an attempt should be made to develop, at a regional scale (as this is a planning requirement), ways of comprehensively assessing the aesthetic qualities of landscape, using persons of high visual sensitivity who are capable of interpreting its visual qualities. This premise is examined later in this chapter, but to see the problem effectively we must first examine the nature of beauty in landscape so that we can more closely determine the qualities that are assessed in any overall measurement of visual quality for the purposes of landscape evaluation.

Beauty in Landscape

The nature of beauty It is perhaps significant that the recent literature on landscape visual quality evaluation rarely uses the word "beauty," preferring the euphemisms "visual quality" or "aesthetic value." Beauty is, however, the word that has particular meaning to the painter, the designer, and to those who specialize in interpreting our aesthetic feelings. It is the nature of beauty that has been given the most penetrating thought and study by philosophers, artists, and writers when considering how visual objects are appraised. The word has meaning and obvious relevance in the visual evaluation of landscape.

It has long been generally accepted that there is beauty in nature and that man derives his concepts of beauty from nature. Nature is not in itself a work of art, but it has the similar underlying facets of order and unity. (These are now being more widely understood through an understanding of the principles of ecological science.) Nature can, however, become part of a work of art by being ordered and manipulated with underlying aesthetic appreciation (for example, the park landscape).

Eric Newton, the English art critic, writes in his book, *The Meaning of Beauty,* that beauty is a recognizable quality — a quality that arouses pleasure to the senses.

Beauty is a desirable commodity. But not all men are equally susceptible to it. Nor are all men agreed about its abode. Moreover it varies with period. It is subject to the laws that govern fashion. . . . It also varies with its geographical position. . . . Variation in national or racial standards of beauty are as noticeable as in period standards (1950:18).

The less sensitive the spectator to formal beauty the more association will weigh with him in his final assessment. (1950:69)

Beauty is that aspect of phenomena which when perceived by the senses and thence referred to the contemplative faculty of the perceiver, has the power to evoke responses drawn from his accumulated experience.

The test in any given case, of its presence and intensity is a sensation of pleasure in the perceiver caused by the gratification of his desire to repeat his experience on a contemplative level, such desire is itself generated by experience on any level.

Therefore the richer the experience of the beholder and the greater his capacity for contemplation the more complete his equipment for perceiving beauty — the "better," as the phrase goes, his "taste." (1950:212)

It would seem from these observations alone (and other aesthetic writers have broadly similar views on these aspects) that beauty is a subject of study related to our intuitive and emotional enjoyment of landscape and, therefore, the value we give to it. As a cultural phenomenon, it may be that beauty (and ugliness) in landscape creates a higher emotive response than associational reactions. Or that the combination of an aesthetic response with associative reactions and use preference when

all are positive feelings of pleasure is the highest total response possible. We have not established means of measuring all these reactions, but it would seem wrong not to recognize their existence fully and to examine how society as a whole assesses these purely aesthetic qualities in landscape. It would appear to be an essential aspect of any study of landscape evaluation. We need next to examine, therefore, the concept of beauty in relation to landscape.

The form and content of beauty in landscape Beauty in landscape derives from two main sources which cannot be separated in assessments because they interact:

From the object The intrinsic formal qualities of individual object(s) whether natural or man-made (that is, shape, proportion, color, and the like); the aesthetic relationship between these individual objects (that is, their spacing, scale, composition, and so on); the relationship of an object or group of objects to a setting.

From the observer The inherent physiological, emotional, and psychological makeup of the observer; the relationship between the observer and society; the relationship between the observer and the object(s).

These are now considered separately, solely for the purposes of analysis.

Beauty derived from the object(s) The formal qualities of the objects and the formal qualities of relationships between them and their setting, as perceived by an observer, can be described in analytical design terms. Aesthetic thought suggests that there must be a degree of order and unity in the formal relationships to produce pleasurable aesthetic feeling.

Conversely, complete disorder, uncontrolled randomness, the chaos of destruction, and unrelieved incongruities in most cases produce ugliness in landscape. Examples are seen in derelict industrial landscapes, parts of the urban fringe, and "spoiled" recreational coastlines. The ultimate is possibly the devastated landscapes caused by war.

A landscape may appear to have beauty if

1. A single object is beautiful in itself but is in an uninteresting setting. For example, a tree in a demolished slum area, or wild flowers on a waste heap, or an old barn in a flat prairie landscape. The eye is stimulated by the quality of contrast between the object and its setting, as well as by the intrinsic quality of the object itself.
2. If the relationship between objects ugly in themselves is beautiful, for example, the distant view of mill chimneys grouped in a mill-town landscape, or a cluster of conical waste heaps grouped on a flat landscape. The spatial relationships become more important than the objects themselves.
3. If ugly objects are in an *ordered relationship* to a beautiful setting, for example, a power station with its large masses of buildings on an open coastline or in a mountain setting, producing a sympathetic scale relationship between the object and its setting.

Unfortunately, it is more common to find beautiful landscapes damaged by ugly objects, providing a detrimental contrast, or ugly or unsympathetic visual relationships between objects and their setting.

The perception of beauty from the qualities of objects that make a landscape is therefore highly "volatile" and easily enhanced or impaired. Further, because aesthetic qualities depend on visual relationships that change with the position of the observer in the landscape, beauty in the landscape must also be dependent on the position or positions from which the landscape is perceived. It must also be dependent on the net balance in the ob-

server's mind of the overall response to the beauty and ugliness of the objects that make up a landscape and their visual relationships within a given area.

Appreciation of beauty through the observer The inherent qualities of the observer condition the strength and quality of his response. Visual beauty is felt and recognized more by some people than by others. Adequate vision, imagination, knowledge of the way the object functions, a contemplative turn of mind, and an emotional temperament may be desirable characteristics that are inherited, but upbringing and education can induce and develop the responses as in other human faculties.

The response to beauty may also derive from the standards of beauty and the overall cultural values and heritage of the observer's society. It is an inevitable part of the educational processes for some indoctrination to exist, and even the most unreceptive person will be affected by it.

The third source of response to beauty felt by an observer comes from his relationship with the object seen. A receptive attitude, a suitable climate, atmosphere and lighting for the object, a comfortable or pleasant viewpoint, freedom from distraction, opportunity to examine in detail as well as "in the round," familiarity with the type of landscape concerned and knowledge of its many parts, or emotional attachment to it because of personal associations, all affect the response he feels.

Conclusions The capacity of observers to appreciate landscape beauty with a high degree of discernment is important: it requires visual sensitivity and trained perception, emotional response (pleasure and feelings), the ability to comprehend order in nature, a rich experience of different landscapes, historical insight, intuition, and the ability to contemplate on things seen.

The observers must have a relevant common

fund of experience because of differences that occur nationally, and possibly regionally, in any society in its standards of beauty.

The observer is likely to appreciate natural beauty better if he has an understanding of the functions of nature and landscape, that is, ecology and landscape design.

Associative responses are more likely to assume a greater importance in observers who have less capacity, opportunity, or education for appraising beauty, and whose perception and awareness of visual qualities, therefore, are possibly less objective.

The beauty of a landscape as perceived by an observer must depend on a combination of the inherent qualities of the objects in it seen individually, in relation to each other, and seen in relation to their setting. These relationships will vary depending on the position(s) of the observer, his receptiveness, and the physical conditions existing in the environment when he makes his assessment.

The beauty of a landscape must be the result of an overall positive response to the accumulation of a set of positive and negative aesthetic responses from a wide assimilation of landscape experience in any given area.

If these conclusions are related to methods that have been adopted in landscape evaluation for obtaining responses to landscape content from observers in the field or by the use of photographs, it may be judged that many existing "visual quality" assessments may not, paradoxically, appear to measure adequately visual quality or beauty. Observers have usually not specifically been required to concentrate on purely formal aesthetic qualities, they may not have been specially selected for their capacities to perceive beauty, and they may not have been given the opportunities needed to make adequate perceptive judgments. In particular, they may not have been specifically required or encouraged to take adequate time to

see and experience the landscape from movement within it and so develop the intuitive feeling on which to base their responses. Finally, the landscapes they have been asked to assess may not have had sufficient underlying unity, so the aesthetic qualities that derive from unity in nature cannot be fully appreciated.

There are difficulties in defining any underlying visual unities in landscapes that have not been designed as compositions or do not have strongly dominant natural factors giving consequent visually dominant characteristics. Where these unities exist they heighten the aesthetic response, but a high response may also occur from landscape because of its continuous nature and from the sharp contrast sometimes found between two visual units (the "edge effect"). Furthermore, preoccupation with numerical ranking limits the recording of the intrinsic visual qualities with which policies are concerned. "Broad-grain" assessments of visual quality may, however, be a useful basis for evaluation (that is, comparisons) of scenic beauty in a limited form and in a specific content. They are primarily a nondescriptive measure of those limited aesthetic qualities that can be derived from viewing a landscape as a whole from a distance. Judgments are made and a degree of consistency among observers can be obtained in these judgments. What, therefore (in existing methods), is the nature of these judgments?

It is suggested that such judgments are *spontaneous aesthetic reactions for comparative purposes with a high associative content;* that is, they are largely associational responses concerned more with utility preferences, rather than detached abstract aesthetic judgments of visual quality or beauty in landscape, and they are not a measure of the intrinsic visual *qualities* of landscape.

If this is so, it would seem that the aesthetic objectives of broad-scale landscape evaluation of visual quality must be more modest and generalized and that visual quality in the context of regional planning can be best interpreted as "visual amenity" or "general pleasantness of appearance."

This concept has overtones of use value as well as aesthetic meaning, and it is considered important that this distinction should be made. Assessment of visual quality is an aesthetic exercise that requires an aesthetic response; therefore, the awareness of ugliness and beauty are the upper and lower levels of judgment values. It is a phenomenon of the human race that we all develop and hold such values or believe we do. But we look to the creative artist, writer, and designer in our society to have a greater percipience of such values and to have a heightened response to ugliness and beauty. This awareness and skill produces a finer scale of values, and may also produce a wider range of values so that the top and bottom of their scales should be farther apart than for others in society. The implication of this analysis seems to be that recent landscape-evaluation techniques are based on limited assessments of natural beauty. The scales they represent are likely to be more modest than those produced by the artists whose values society recognizes, upholds, and generally follows.

Furthermore, the requirement in existing techniques for an *areal* definition of visual quality in landscape is an important limitation on the techniques as measures of natural beauty. Aesthetic value in nature may extend from the smallest flower, a tiny stream, or a single tree to the broad panoramas from the top of a mountain or across a fen, a moor, or a river estuary. In addition, the beauty or ugliness of an object may be modified or even reversed by its setting or the distance from which it is viewed.

It follows, therefore, that within an area of defined visual quality there may well exist infinite variations of natural beauty in different-sized individual objects (or landscape components), in their settings and groupings, and in the distance at which they are seen.

It may be argued that, if instant associative reaction governs the nature of the evaluation, it is relevant information for the formulation of landscape policies, and it is irrelevant to consider whether these evaluations give any assessment of beauty in landscape. It can be said that decisions regarding the recreational use of landscape are associative with previous or potential recreation experience, or that decisions regarding protection are mainly related to general landscape character rather than aesthetic value, or that decisions regarding siting of buildings, structures, or routeways are based more on associations of the development with the visual character of towns in which they are usually seen; that is, they are questions of congruity rather than disruption of aesthetic unity in the landscape.

It can also be argued that the exercise of making comparative judgments rather than judgments on the inherent absolute qualities of landscape in isolation demands a more rapid response, so that the comparison is assisted by a concentration on the simplicity of superficialities rather than on the confusion of complexities. We can also recognize that the time given to make judgments in the field is controllable within reasonably practical limits.

On the other hand, it may well be that the purely aesthetic landscape assessment is nearer to the responses of those who know a landscape best and whose responses are strongest where change of any sort is contemplated. In a democratic society, awareness of such responses may be of considerable importance to the policy maker.

It seems reasonable to surmise also that the judgments made in existing techniques might be less consistent if the landscapes assessed were preselected on two bases: first, on the basis of previously assessed aesthetic unities of some form such as those that tend to arise from areas of recognizable specific ecological character. This would then produce heightened response from those among the observers who recognize the aesthetic unity qualities and would alter therefore the range and possibly the distribution of assessments. The second basis would be the inclusion of landscapes subject to recent change for which observers had not yet acquired associative familiarity. There might also be less consistency if some of the observers were more specialized in aesthetic judgment. This would then presumably produce a wider and more discriminating distribution of value judgments.

To overcome these difficulties in the practice of landscape evaluation, it is suggested that the attempt should be made to devise evaluations which are more comprehensive to supplement any assessments of general visual quality. They might be based on the following:

1. The assessment of formal aesthetic qualities in landscape.
2. The use of observers of high perceptual capacities and a high degree of acquired skill in landscape appreciation.
3. The selection of landscapes having an underlying visual unity as a "survey unit."

The implications of these suggestions are now considered.

Evaluation of Aesthetic Qualities

If perception of beauty is based on "an intuitive response to complex interrelationships in phenomena," the relationships need to be fully classified and understood. Examples of visual qualities that can be sought and observed systematically are given in Table 1.

Table 1
Landscape Visual Qualities Assessments

General Qualities To Be Sought and Observed

1. Uniformity of character from homogeneity of vegetation and building materials.
2. Evidence of design and composition in the landscape.
3. Richness (that is, quantity and quality) of natural features and incident.
4. Absence of incongruities and conflicts of materials, scale, and color.
5. Lack of visually disturbing detractors.
6. The condition and character of buildings, bridges, fences, walls, gates, and the like.
7. Absorption of buildings into the landscape.
8. Relationship of linear elements to landscape.
9. Dominance and quality of undisturbed natural landform.
10. Presence of trees where landform is not dominant.
11. Sharp contrast of landforms and vegetation types.
12. Relationships of woodland plantation to landform.
13. Good outline of water areas.
14. Edge quality to water areas and watercourses.
15. Regularity of field and woodland patterns.
16. Spatial interest and spatial diversity.
17. Incidence and quality of panoramic views.
18. Vegetation health.
19. Cleanness of air and water.
20. Presence of wild flowers.

1. Not all the qualities would appear together in any landscape and their importance would vary.
2. The many interrelationships possible between the qualities indicated would be as important to record as the individual qualities themselves.
3. Absence of individual qualities would not necessarily be detrimental to overall quality.

Measurement of these visual qualities may be of assistance, but essentially the intuitive response for which descriptions and interpretation can be attempted for the purpose of formulating policies obviates the need for measurement. The extreme subtlety of the relationships that exist can only be determined by the eye and mind subconsciously. Table 2

Table 2
Visual Qualities Assessment Checklist

A. Characteristics and Components from Which Visual Qualities Are Derived	B. Quality Impact on the Landscape			C. Inherent Qualities of Characteristics and Components																	
				Proportion			Scale			Outline in Plan			Profile in Elevation			Shape/Form			Color			Texture/Pattern
	+	0	−	+	0	−	+	0	−	+	0	−	+	0	−	+	0	−	+	0	−	+	0	−
1. Overall identity/imageability (sense of unity and diversity of interest, balance of contrast and uniformity)																								
2. Spatial interest and continuity																								
3. Views and landmarks																								
4. Viewpoints																								
5. Landform																								
6. Natural herbaceous vegetation																								
7. Cultivated vegetation																								
8. Trees and shrubs																								
Hedgerows																								
Small woods																								
Plantation																								
9. Parklands and gardens																								
10. Water areas																								
11. Watercourses																								
12. Main routes																								
13. Walks																								
14. Major features and structures																								
15. Minor features																								
Small buildings																								
Gates																								
Bridges																								
Fences																								
16. Atmospheric qualities																								
17. Wildlife and domestic animals																								

Note: Shaded area indicates where an assessment can appropriately be recorded.

1. The checklist indicates in summary form a range of aesthetic qualities that may be recorded in landscape. The objective is simply to indicate those qualities which give a landscape its perceptional character, as an aid to the making of policies for the conservation of that landscape.

2. The checklist recognizes that qualities are derived from the landscape seen as a whole, from the relationships among the objects seen in the landscape, and from the objects in relation to their landscape setting (columns B and C).

3. The checklist acknowledges that visual qualities may derive from the aggregate effect of small qualities as well as the single effect of a large quality.

4. Those qualities derived from movement through landscape as well as those obtained from viewing the landscape at selected viewpoints are included.

5. The checklist does *not* indicate specifically those additional qualities that derive from the visual relationships among the characteristics and components of landscape, except in as far as they affect the overall identity.

6. The checklist is *not* a score sheet, but could be a useful *aide memoire* to assessors and could be used to produce summary indications of the range of visual qualities in any landscape.

7. If the qualities are recorded as positive (+), neutral (0), or negative (−), indication is recorded of the visual impact. Such assessments have no significance if expressed in more specific measured terms, however, or if aggregated in any way.

presents a checklist for assisting in the assessment of visual qualities. The assistance that such checklists offer is in reminding observers of the more *general* visual qualities which may be present in a landscape (Table 1) and in providing a means of recording the overall and the specific inherent qualities created by the characteristics and components of a landscape (Table 2). The checklists incorporate the terminology of landscape aesthetics as described earlier in this chapter.

In themselves the terms are only a descriptive analytical means of communicating formal visual qualities by the use of words that have generally agreed definitions and meanings. They are the words used by the critic, teacher, and aesthetician. The creative writer who describes and interprets landscape values may also use them, but he and the creative landscape artist will not usually be concerned simply with descriptive communication of what is seen. In addition, they will seek to interpret the values in what is seen and to develop or heighten our awareness of them. In doing so they will create new aesthetic values inherent in their own work, and we must be aware of the possibilities of confusion. (The landscape artist, of course, does not use words but communicates the qualities which the words endeavor to express in other media.)

The terms used to define formal aesthetic qualities show that there is a large range of aesthetic factors which affects the visual appearance of landscape. It should also be apparent that the relationships among the factors are complex and considerable in their effects. The ability of the eye and mind to assess these rapidly over a considerable spatial area is believed to be great, but a full comprehension inevitably requires considerable time and repeated visits (as anyone preparing evidence on the visual qualities of landscape for a public inquiry well knows!). We need to recognize that on occasion "familiarity breeds contempt," and the value accorded at a first response may decline on repeated observation. It is, however, a test of true aesthetic quality if the response given initially is maintained or even increases over a period of time; therefore, the value of lengthy and repeated observation is in measuring the degree of permanence in the value judgment. It seems likely also that observers may vary considerably in their capacity to process so many variables; among different observers some may subconsciously omit assessment of, or underemphasize, certain factors, and conversely others may give them greater emphasis. A system of evaluation of aesthetic factors based *only* on numbers and not on description and interpretation therefore seems inappropriate in attempting to measure purely aesthetic qualities, and the use of the checklists ensures that a more descriptive evaluation is made on a standard basis. Even broader forms of assessment are needed, however, and it is suggested that these are provided by "evaluation panels."

Use of skilled observers and evaluation panels More comprehensive sets of aesthetic value judgments prepared by skilled observers forming evaluation panels would accomplish the following:

1. Describe a greater range of visual qualities with a higher degree of discernment.
2. Develop a greater range and sensitivity of landscape policies.
3. Enable the resources needed to implement policies to be more fully determined (because the effects of change could be more clearly assessed).
4. Achieve a wider measure of interest and therefore support (because of the greater interest and concern in aesthetic qualities than in using numerical scales of visual quality).

Purely aesthetic values derived from land-scapes can best be recorded and communicated in words, diagrams, photographs, drawings, and paintings to provide a comprehensive "aesthetic guidebook" by writers, artists, and designers. This approach is well known in tourist trade, but objectivity is often lacking there. In a narrower but more specialized form, it is the approach of the landscape designer, although he may attempt the broader approach.

At present no succinct but comprehensive record of the visual and associational qualities of landscape on a regional basis usually exists in a single form, and no evaluation technique has attempted to produce one, or to produce a series of such assessments for different land-scapes within a region on a comparative basis.

The basis of such regional evaluations of visual qualities would be a compendium by an evaluation panel of writings, pictures, photographs, maps, and diagrams, which would record and communicate in as much detail as possible, reflecting as many aesthetic creative skills as possible, the aesthetic and other associational values of easily recognized and comprehended landscapes. It would include existing records as well as new specially commissioned work. Essentially, the richness, variety, and individuality of the compilations would be their strength as an aid to policy making. Their other great strength would be in the integrity and artistic quality of the writers, artists, and designers who compiled them and the degree of support they received from those who lived in and used the landscapes concerned.

The basis for the concept is not new. It exists already in the amassing of local history records in schools and libraries, in the surveys and evaluation of buildings and historic towns and villages by planning authorities and civic and amenity societies, and to some extent in the

haphazard and sporadically distributed evaluations of landscapes by artists, writers, or landscape designers who happen to have been born in or worked in specific landscapes in different parts of the country.

In England, the landscape policies now applied to the Lake District, the Yorkshire Moors, or Wessex may owe more to the values created by the artists and writers who found themselves living and working there in the past than perhaps we fully recognize today.

The essence of the method is to amass evidence of those immeasurable and unique qualities in landscape at least comparable in significance and substance to that achieved from the compilation of measured data. This would be for the benefit of all who make decisions and policies concerning the future planning and management of landscape.

As in the establishment of all values in society, the works amassed and produced would be appraised by the communities living in the landscapes as well as by the planning agencies, and some general understanding of the values established should result, thus ensuring that they are fully reflected in the policy- and decision-making processes.

Evaluation of landscape areas regionally on, say, a four- or five-point scale might well be added, based on the team's consensus opinion, but this would not form the main objective of the evaluation because (as has been argued earlier) rankings are inadequate as a complete basis for making landscape policies.

Selection of evaluation panels To prepare a descriptive evaluation based on aesthetic and associational factors would require the services of teams of artists, landscape and art historians, writers, and designers such as have been engaged for the preparation of tourist guides, garden guides, and guides to buildings of interest. It is suggested that such teams or panels should be especially constituted under

the direction of the planning agencies, and should include local as well as nationally experienced persons. Their composition would embrace skills outside those normally held by the local authority. Regional teams might well be formed and a national landscape inventory and evaluation compiled within a period of, say, 5 years. As in the precedents mentioned, careful preplanning of the form and content is required, so that comparative evaluation of the material obtained and produced is possible.

Selection of landscapes To produce a descriptive aesthetic evaluation of any region would require agreement on the size of the landscapes to be evaluated; determination of some appropriate measure of overall visual homogeneity would form the basis of the subdivision of the survey for classification purposes. Many of the difficulties arising from the choice of survey unit for measured evaluation techniques would not occur, and lack of uniformity in the means of classification would not appear to matter greatly. With nationally orientated guidelines, and using map and air photo coverage and local knowledge of the area, the assembled team could no doubt agree fairly easily and quickly on the basis of a subjective consensus response to the divisions of landscape within a region. A regional survey of main ecological divisions may well assist, of course.

Conclusions The object of a visual qualities assessment would be essentially to ensure that we are, as a society, responding creatively to our environment and that values are being identified not only for more traditional landscapes, but for the new landscapes that are continuously being created. A panel would not primarily be making comparative assessments, but rather recording and interpreting intrinsic qualities in landscape and so providing the essential data that would guide and influence meaningful policy making. They would keep the society in which they work more aware of the more obvious qualities in landscape. They would also emphasize the less obvious, the rare and the unique, the unusual and the hidden, the qualities that are seen and felt when our sensory perception is heightened by the interpretative artist. In some areas much of this has already been achieved by environmental agencies and planning authorities in the last decade, but their actions have not extended far into the environment of the country landscape and its aesthetic qualities; it remains largely unrecorded in any permanent form. It is envisaged that the assessments would record landscapes as scenery in all its many aspects and evocatively in all its moods.

Although all landscapes would be recorded in positive and sympathetic terms, it seems unlikely that those landscapes which have few positive qualities would evoke as much response as those that have many. There is much that is of little visual stimulus in man-made landscape. The recording would not therefore lead to a more protectionist attitude toward the countryside as a whole, but would ensure that the changes proposed in those areas that had aesthetic qualities, both great and small, would be known and appreciated by the developer, public, and planning authority before the development took place.

Summary

A technique for the aesthetic evaluation of the landscape should embrace purely aesthetic assessments made by persons who have acquired the necessary skills and value judgments. The visual evaluation of landscape has a long history; therefore, any technique of evaluation and appreciation of landscape is likely to be based on the accumulated and

often superimposed concepts of the past. History also shows that visual assessment is an aesthetic study, and that the concepts of beauty and of beauty in relation to landscape have to be examined. Appreciation of beauty in landscape depends on the emotive and observational capacity of the observer, his knowledge of the landscape, the position from which it is experienced, and the total accumulation of numerous aesthetic experiences derived from it. It will also depend on the content and formal qualities of the landscape, their relationships, and the general setting and visual relationships of the objects within it. Existing evaluation techniques appear to measure immediate associative reactions and numerical ranking rather than recording purely visual qualities (beauty and ugliness). It is argued that although this may be useful it may not be sufficiently adequate for detailed policy making, and that therefore a more comprehensive system of evaluation is needed with greater emphasis on determining and recording purely visual aesthetic qualities. Accepted design terminology applied to the landscape assessment of visual quality is seen as a basis for a broader visual evaluation, but the interrelationships among aesthetic factors are subtle and complex and can best be recorded in a combination of media. Such an evaluation technique would need to be prepared by a team of observers of high perceptual capacities and a high degree of acquired skill in landscape appreciation, drawn from varied disciplines concerned with art, literature, history, philosophy, and design. An evaluation panel could determine the division of landscape based on visual unity and prepare an inventory and comprehensive descriptive record and assessment of landscape values for each region based on national guidelines and within prescribed time limits.

NOTES

1. Aesthetic emotions are defined as the response to what is seen through recognition of the abstract qualities in objects. They may be pleasant from the beauty in the object(s), or unpleasant from the ugliness in an object(s); "I don't know why I like it but I do."
2. Associational reactions are defined as the response to what is seen through recognition of events that have occurred in the environment of an object(s) or of similar object(s). These events may have been personal to the observer or to his knowledge have been experienced by others. They may be pleasant or unpleasant reactions; "I like it or it interests me because it reminds me of . . . ."
3. Utility preferences are defined as the response to what is seen through recognition of existing or potential use of an object(s) for a functional purpose or activity; "I like it because I will be able to do something there or do something with it."

Some Methods and Strategies in the Prediction of Preference

Rachel Kaplan

There seems to be a pervasive split in many human endeavors between those who are concerned with what "really matters" and those who are more concerned that "whatever one does be done right." Many years ago, William James identified the dichotomy between the "tender-minded" and the "empty-headed." As I read the work in landscape assessment, I worry that here too the distinction applies. There seems to be the one extreme — call it the scientific, perhaps — where the concern for objectivity and quantification is so pervasive that the results seem irrefutable, but hardly pertinent to the questions that need answering. At the other extreme — dare I call it the designer as artist? — the prose is guided by deep faith in insight and expertise, and while the pertinent questions are certainly being faced, the objectivity is questionable. I do not mean to imply that none of the work in this

Rachel Kaplan is an Associate Professor in the School of Natural Resources and the Urban and Regional Planning Program and Lecturer in Psychology at the University of Michigan.

Portions of this chapter were presented at the Symposium on Affective Response to the Outdoor Environment at the meeting of the American Psychological Association in Montreal, 1973. The work discussed here was supported in part by the U.S. Department of Agriculture — Forest Service.

area has ventured into the more dangerous, vulnerable openland between the less ambiguous extremes. The attraction of multidisciplinary efforts, and of genuine problems that require practical and prompt solutions, is that they allow a certain amount of trespassing, permitting an interaction of rigorous standards and qualitative concerns. This is not an easy task, but an exciting one.

It is striking how mild the literature in this area has been; harsh and critical words are rarely spoken. A rather limited set of papers is cited and re-cited; one man's conclusions are unquestionedly repeated by his colleagues. Criticizing one's fellows is not a gentlemanly pursuit; on the other hand, perpetuating ineffectual approaches to important problems is a luxury we can ill afford. I claim no inside track on the truth. On the contrary, my firm conviction is that there is no one truth to guide these efforts. I would, however, like to raise some methodological problems that I feel have hampered work in this area; within that context I shall also discuss some of our research in the area of environmental preference.

THE VISUAL WORLD

The landscape is basically a visual experience. People in fact experience much of the physical environment visually. The pervasiveness of our visual and spatial modes of operation is too easily forgotten as we wend our way through verbal morasses and convince ourselves that language is uniquely our form of cognition. We are probably at least as visual as we are verbal (S. Kaplan, 1972), and, furthermore, it turns out that a great deal about our everyday environmental experience is difficult to react to in a verbal way. Yet an unfortunate amount of the research that deals with man's experience of the environment is basically verbal. It is

verbal in two ways: the form of the stimulus material and the form of the subject's task. Two studies dealing with residential environments (Lansing and Marans, 1969; Menchik, 1971) provide good examples of studies for which visual forms of presentation would have greatly enhanced the kinds of conclusions that could be drawn. As far as the task is concerned, there are numerous studies entailing open-ended questions requiring descriptions of the environment. The problem with these is not merely that content analyses are laborious, but that the verbal approach limits the insights to be extracted from the data. We have found, for example, that if you ask people why they say they prefer the parkway to the expressway they will tell you "because it is green." But actually, the expressway is "green," too. It has mowed grass and trees as does the parkway. And lots of other roads that are "green" are not preferred. The respondents are not trying to be dishonest, nor to be glib, nor are they stupid. Rather we may be asking the question in the wrong way.

In a similar fashion many questions that pertain to people's experience, awareness, concern, or pleasure with respect to the environment require visual information. Words are not in danger of being eliminated; the hope is that a more easily imaged form of input will not be neglected. Thus, visual displays are called for when studying such questions as: What it is about a little old village that its inhabitants would like to maintain as the road of progress, inevitably, comes through town? What about the rural countryside is important to the people choosing to live there, and what are the defining characteristics of such environments for its people? What things are considered scenic and should be included in deciding scenic highway routes? What consequences of carrying capacity limitations are people aware of?

ASSESSMENT OF WHAT?

When we undertake the task of landscape assessment, we are confronted with many possibilities and few landmarks. What shall we assess? What are the salient aspects of the environment? For whom are they relevant? To some extent the answers to these questions are based on how cautious a strategy one wishes to adopt. Much research in this area reflects a preference for a safer, more objective approach. In this section I shall contrast these approaches with an alternative, which may at first glance seem to be going about the problems entirely backward. The choice of variables of course reflects considerably more than riskiness of strategy; there are necessarily complexities and ramifications not touched upon in the brief discussion that follows.

In the Name of Objectivity

There have been several thorough reviews recently of the various approaches proposed and used in landscape-appraisal studies (Craik, 1972b; Fabos, 1971; Zube, 1973a). From these it is evident that a variety of basic strategies has been employed to find generic schemes that are strong in objectivity. Landscape architects and planners have found landform and land-use concepts to be of central importance in environmental assessment. Their decision is aided and abetted by the information readily obtained from geological survey maps and aerial photographs. The resulting categories are attractive for a variety of reasons (Fabos, 1971), not the least of which is their apparent objectivity. The same concern also underlies the distinction between "esthetic evaluation of landscapes and preference for landscape," which has become part of the lore of this field (Zube, 1973a, citing Craik, 1972b, who cites Fines and many others). There is no need here to list the kinds of variables that such studies have utilized; I shall, however, return to what seem to me to be some shortcomings of these strategies in a later section.

Objectivity is the hallmark of science and reliability might be considered a corollary. Given categories that are readily defined, one would expect high agreement among people classifying scenes into these categories. With proven reliability one can rest assured that one is not studying idiosyncratic reactions, that the empirical process is shared and shareable. In fact, however, the agreement among raters of these relatively objective variables is not as colossal as one would like to think. Impressive significance levels sometimes obscure another side of the same truth. Thus, for example, Coughlin and Goldstein (1970) report a correlation of .55 between their two judges. Given the large number of settings, 92, this is a significant correlation. But the degree of overlap in the ratings (only 30 percent common variance) is less impressive. Comparably, Craik (1972a) presents lists of hundreds of highly significant results. But here too particular characteristics of statistical tests obscure some surprisingly low agreement among raters. Thus, it was possible and not unusual that less than half the people agreed on a particular category, where three options were available, but the significance level was a confidence-inspiring $p <$ .001.

The fact that reliability is not foolproof even with relatively objective judgments does not mean that objectivity should be ignored; on the contrary, the fact of the disagreement is important to acknowledge. Some distinctions are clearly more amenable to consistent ratings than are others. We do not have any a priori basis for knowing what variables are more likely to enjoy reliable ratings, nor whether the "objectivity–subjectivity" continuum plays an important role in this. In any event, low reliabilities provide a vivid demonstration of the fickle nature of the animal for whom we assess the environment! They also clearly show the problems of assuming that we, as experts, can simply make universally acceptable or agreed-upon decisions.

Role of the expert It is exciting, instructive, efficient, and sometimes even necessary, to examine a large collection of pictures and make decisions about the relative importance of different principles they may portray or to decide what the basic, underlying components are in landscape evaluation, or to assign differential weightings to various properties of the environment. In these senses, the expert necessarily affects the course of the decision-making process. And the effect is strong and pervasive. The very choice of variables for evaluating the environment has ramifying implications and a direct line to impact. A more subtle but no less powerful tool that the expert uses in the privacy of his study involves the assignment of numeric values to different levels or categories of variables and the subsequent playful manipulations of the different quantities that evolve. These weightings are quickly translated into new variables and qualitative differences.

This procedure is not uncommon and obviously tempting. Let me here cite a single example, a document on highway landscapes by Edwards and Kelcey, Inc. (1972:34–5). They use five components to compute the "total scenic value," and the combinatorial rule is multiplication. Three components have an upper limit of 2 ("angle of view," "viewing time," and "travel directions observable"). The last of these is the only component that cannot assume a value of zero. The "quality of scene" component can be designated "eyesore" (value = 0), "substandard" ($\frac{1}{2}$), "average" (1), "above average" (2–5), or "unique or extremely high quality" (10). The fifth component, "number of

viewable objects," has no upper limit. There are thus many potential ways to obtain a "total scenic value" of zero, and as long as many objects are viewable, the total score can be extremely high.

Often such metric decisions are not exposed to any empirical evaluation. But their subtle effect can easily go unnoticed even in sophisticated research. Thus, Wohlwill (1968:308), for example, utilized a "complexity" measure to predict preference that involved five attributes (amount of variation in "color, shape, direction of dominant lines, textures, and natural versus artificial"). The combinatorial rule involved "summing across the five attributes." Thus, two scenes may have the same total "complexity" score and yet share no similarity in the sources of variation (for example, a scene with many shapes and few textures as opposed to a diversely textured scene with few shapes).

Categorizations define equivalence classes. The designations of numeric weightings assume metric properties that generally go unstated. There are important consequences to the decision of adding or multiplying, to permitting variables to assume values of different orders of magnitude, to combining values that may be highly correlated versus those that are independent of each other. The decision as to which categories are salient and the additional decision as to their alchemy are powerful "voice of the expert" stipulations with ramifying consequences. There is no question that such decisions must be made, and often there is no "right" way to approach these problems. On the other hand, it is vital that the decisions be justified whenever possible and that the underlying assumptions be recognized.

Starting from Preference

Objectivity is clearly a virtue; it is comforting and important. It belongs in the list of things not to be questioned. But it is not a substitute for understanding. An understanding of the factors involved in preference is likely to lead to an objective means of assessment, but it seems less likely that the opposite is the case. That is, the study of preference based on variables chosen for their objectivity seems unlikely to lead to any broader understanding. Indeed, an overconcern with objectivity has tended to produce myopia; theoretical sense and even common sense are abandoned in an effort to squeeze prediction from unlikely but reliable variables.

Craik has said that "the comprehensive assessment of places is clearly a complex, expensive, and in some respects curiously nonpsychological endeavor" (1971:60). While it is indeed complex, it need not be "curiously nonpsychological." Perhaps the great emphasis on the objective and efficient has fostered this condition.

In the course of research we have pursued on the rural countryside we have had firsthand experience with the limitations of some physically oriented variables in terms of their lack of psychological impact. We have found the landform/land-use approach to landscape assessment to be efficient and convenient, but the equivalence classes formed by this procedure often seem tangential to the salient variables. If one arrays a dozen scenes representative of a single landform/land-use combination, even if they are taken along the same short segment of the road and each is taken at the same roadside angle, one might readily find the scenes falling in a great diversity of categories based on more "subjective" visual distinctions. Undoubtedly, elevation differences matter, especially if extreme or few and far between, as does the presence of water, billowing factory smoke, or barns and farmhouses. There are certainly many instances when manifestations of landform and/or land-use involve features of the environment that are salient for many people viewing them. But the landform/land-use distinction does not reliably provide a handle for environmental qualities that are of focal significance for the human observer of the passing scene.

The study Craik has undertaken in conjunction with Litton's theorizing in this area provides a further example of primarily physically oriented variables. Craik found relatively high agreement among his raters on issues such as "the distance to the most remote elements in the scene," panoramic view, focal view, appearance of clouds, and many others. But these failed miserably in the prediction of aesthetic judgment (Craik, 1972a). At the same time, the kinds of issues Litton raises in his section labeled "aesthetic criteria" are in no way assessed by these ratings. The latter include the qualities that landscape architects have long been interested in and have used as guiding principles in their work: Litton (1972) discusses "unity," "vividness," and "variety," in particular. These partially overlap the qualities of coherence, complexity, diversity, mystery, and legibility — to name a few — that are frequently found in the nonempirical, nonpsychological literature on design (Cullen, 1961), the art of the Japanese garden (Eliovson, 1971), and the deficiencies of our built environment (Parr, 1965, 1967).

An alternative approach Our research program in landscape assessment has been a search for predictors of environmental preference. Preference in its blatant, personal, subjective form has served as the anchor. We have used it as a global concept, not with respect to any particular use or function. The preference studied has been not that of the taste setters but of the "people" (or "subjects" as we tastelessly call them). To some this is quite a backward approach. However, in the process — through pretesting insights, research results, and no lack of hindsight — we have "discovered" many things that seem to matter to people viewing their environment. We have also "discovered" that, although preference is undeniably subjective, the subjectivity is often shared to a remarkable degree. And when the agreement is low, that too is important. After all, in many cases it is the same environment that must be shared by these rival factions.

I do not wish to imply that these discoveries are ours alone. Quite the contrary, I am delighted that they are not. Coughlin and his colleagues (Coughlin and Goldstein, 1970; Rabinowitz and Coughlin, 1970) have reported many findings similar to what we have found. Zube (1973b) has shown substantial agreement across varying groups with respect to scenic preference. He too has found that urban–rural background and sex do not play an important role in accounting for preference. And he has shown in a variety of contexts that the natural/man-made distinction is pervasive in preference prediction.

SAMPLING AND SANITY

To make sense out of people's preferences for diverse environments, one must sample the environments broadly. At the same time, the threat of being overwhelmed by the resulting mountains of data calls for particular analytic strategies. Before turning to some examples from our own research in environmental preference, I would like to discuss briefly both some problems of situation sampling and some ways to keep the overall task manageable and meaningful.

The Need for Many Scenes

The sampling of people is often recognized as an important issue in research. One worries about their background, experience, age, sex, education, skills, and what not. But the sampling of situations (Brunswik, 1956) or views of the environment is too readily ignored and is at least as vital to adequate research in environmental assessment. When constructing something like a personality inventory, for example, it is well known that the instrument needs to be long, that validity requires the redundancy of items — even if the person who must complete the "test" is long since fatigued and perhaps even provoked. But when assessing the relationship of stimulus variables and aesthetic judgments, it is quite characteristic to base the results on an amazingly small and not necessarily homogeneous set of "items" (for instance, Calvin et al., 1972, Peterson and Neumann, 1969, and Wohlwill, 1968, each based their studies on 14 or 15 scenes in all). In his otherwise extensive review of research on the "assessment of places," Craik (1971) fails to comment on this issue. As a matter of fact, several of the favored tasks in this area of research, such as adjective checklists, are likely to reduce the chances of adequate attention to situation sampling because the repetition of such an arduous task with respect to each picture is indeed inordinately expensive and unduly demanding of the person making the ratings.

There is no simple solution to the sampling problem. The crucial issue in selecting appropriate material is adequate sampling of the domain of interest. Only by providing a range of material having essentially the same content can the reaction of the raters be interpreted. At the same time, the instances must not be virtually identical. This leads to a difficult problem of selection criteria and decision rules. A panel of judges is useful in obtaining agreement, but the investigator must still decide on the categories to be judged by the panel. It is necessarily a bootstrap process; entirely adequate sampling would require knowledge of the very dimensions the investigator is attempting to discover.

Out of Many, Few

If one takes the situation sampling approach seriously, one very quickly has a seemingly unmanageable amount of data. One can pursue several strategies in this situation. Coughlin and his colleagues seemed to approach their data from an informal, intuitive approach that led to a set of interesting results. This approach does suffer, however, in leading to findings that are difficult to remember or to use effectively. It also does not facilitate the task of understanding one's data the next time around.

Shafer and his colleagues, by contrast, have opted for a regression-equation approach. Thus, they have found that certain qualities that have a positive effect on landscape "aesthetic appeal" include, for example, "area of intermediate vegetation multiplied by area of distant nonvegetation," "area of intermediate vegetation multiplied by area of water," as well as several other components. The formula further states that some other aspects have a negative effect, including "area of water squared" and "perimeter of intermediate vegetation multiplied by area of distant nonvegetation," among others (Shafer et al., 1969:14–5). As Jacobs (1973:27) rightly asks, do such variables entail "appropriate aspects of the prediction of visual preference"? In other words, does the seeming rigor of such an approach compensate for the total lack of theoretical or even intuitive justification for the variables?

A third strategy for maintaining a manageable number of variables is exemplified by Wohlwill's (1973a) approach, which is based on a priori decisions of "nature," "man-made," and "mixed." Thus, a picture of a canal might be "mixed" while a visually similar river view would be in the "nature" category. Cabins in a park, bridges over streams, even farmland and urban parks would be in an amorphous "mixed" category. Although these designations are definitionally correct, they do not necessarily reflect the way people react to such scenes, and they may obscure certain other distinctions necessary to a more complete understanding of preference patterns (for example, there may be distinct residential categories within the "mixed" grouping).

We have approached the problem of reducing the data from a large number of individual scenes to a manageable number of meaningful domains in a still different manner. In all our studies, the definition of content domain is made on the basis of dimensional analyses of the preference ratings. As I am not aware of any other work dealing with visual displays that has used this approach, it may be worth discussing this strategy in more detail.

First, it should be made clear that the dimensionalization is based on the preference ratings, where the "items" are the photographs or slides themselves. Several studies in this area (Little, 1969; Sanoff, 1969; Calvin et al., 1972; and many others) have indeed used a series of visual displays and a factor analytic approach. But the factor analysis in these studies was of semantic differential responses — the "items," in other words, are polar adjective pairs. The results of such analyses are dimensions of response items; characteristically, they yield an evaluative scale (that is, preference) and some other scales that are akin to some of the attributes we have asked subjects to rate (for example, complexity, coherence, and mystery). They do not directly deal with content domains; they group adjectives, not pictures. By contrast, the dimensional analyses we do are based on a single rating, that of preference; the resulting collections of photographs define the content domains upon which subsequent analyses are made.

The dimensional approach I am advocating is not intended to replace the role a panel of judges serves in meaningfully selecting pictures to include. That step must be taken before one can be ready to obtain any preference information. The decision as to how to group the photographs in the final analysis, however, is based on this additional step. Elsewhere (R. Kaplan, 1972) I have described the rationale for this strategy and provided some background for the two forms of dimensional analysis we use: Guttman–Lingoes Smallest Space Analysis III, a nonmetric factor analysis (Lingoes, 1972), and the ICLUST "hierarchical cluster analysis" (Kulik et al., 1970). The use of two very different forms of dimensional analysis relates to the conviction I stated earlier that there is no one truth to guide these efforts. Each statistical procedure is influenced by its own assumptions and achieves its simplification on the basis of throwing away somewhat different information. Coming to terms with the different results of these procedures keeps one from adopting their "magic" with closed eyes. Such tools must not be permitted to replace intuition and interpretation.

The dimensional approach serves to identify interpretable groupings of items that will extend our understanding of meaningful content domains. It also serves as an indication of areas that are insufficiently sampled, despite the well-articulated set of criteria, the careful instruction to the panel of judges, and the wise selection decisions that led to the choice of visual displays. But all this is more easily appreciated in the context of concrete examples.

FOR INSTANCE

For purposes of illustration, I will describe a series of studies we have done that all use the same set of slides. [Examples using different stimulus material can be found in R. Kaplan (1973a) and in S. Kaplan's chapter in this vol-

ume.] Our interest in this research program is in the prediction of preference and particularly the role of content in preference. We were especially concerned with the argument that preference for the outdoor environment is explicable on the basis of the rated complexity of the scene (Wohlwill, 1968). Implicit in this argument is the implication that this effect transcends content. In other words, how complex a scene is, not what it is, will determine preference. Carried to its logical extreme, such a position would imply that humans would be happy with an environment devoid of nature as long as the complexity of what remained was properly manipulated. It is not, however, our intent to substitute content for scales that influence preference. Rather we are concerned with content *and* with such scales, as well as their interaction.

The 56 color slides used in these studies were selected to include four categories ranging from entirely natural scenes to predominance of nature, to predominance of man-made aspects, to scenes with virtually no natural features. The environments depicted in these slides were intentionally unspectacular, relatively local places. The nature scenes consisted of open, grassy stretches, meadow scenes, dense foliage, and stretches with more or less woodland. We also took pictures in the same park-like setting that included unpaved roads and some showing an occasional parked car. The urban scenes were various views of street intersections, stores, traffic situations, and tall buildings in downtown side streets. The scenes of predominantly man-made aspects were mostly residential areas with trees, lawns, and such.

Insight from Dimensional Analyses

In the first study in the series, the basis of Wendt's honors thesis some years ago (Kaplan et al., 1972), 88 subjects rated these scenes both for complexity and preference. What we found in that study was a dramatic preference for nature scenes to urban scenes with virtually no overlap in preference distributions. In fact, the urban scene with the highest preference rating by far was the one with the plaza containing a few small trees against a backdrop of skyscrapers! The urban slides were rated as significantly more complex than the nature slides, but complexity did not account for the preference across content domains. Within each of the domains, however, higher complexity scenes received higher preference ratings.

In analyzing the results of this study, the categories of "nature" and "urban" were the outcomes of dimensional analyses. We found that the careful categorization of slides made by the judges, in terms of the nature to man-dominated continuum, did not lead to a domain structure maintaining these decisions. Thus, the nature domain that emerged through dimensional analyses did in fact contain all the purely "nature" items, but also included ones with some clear man-influence. Although judges can easily agree on man-influence in the form of telephone poles, fences, unpaved roads, and such, these judgments do not necessarily reflect the structure of the content domain as viewed by a person whose attention is not drawn to these issues per se. Given our set of slides, the nature domain, as defined in terms of underlying patterns of ratings, consisted of all the nature scenes, whether or not these scenes also contained "intrusions." Comparably, the urban domain included all the items the judges categorized as containing virtually no natural features; but it also contained the item I have mentioned as the most preferred urban item — the downtown plaza — which the judges had categorized as "predominantly man-influence" because of the trees in the planters. In other words, the presence of

planters did not prevent this item from being seen as basically urban.

The dimensional analyses of these preference ratings also revealed the areas that were insufficiently sampled. The various "predominantly man-made" scenes, for example, did not form a single meaningful residential cluster, but rather helped us see that the underlying dimensionality of residential areas requires further effort.

These data provide one source of examples of the insights to be gained from the dimensional approach. Using a variety of visual displays in different studies, we have never failed to profit from this procedure. Whereas judges can make reliable, discrete judgments, usually with respect to a single issue, the very basis of multidimensional scaling procedures entails the interactive qualities of the ratings. This procedure can both reveal that some criteria included in the selection decisions were not in fact of importance in the subjects' ratings, and that the sampling procedure was inadequate with respect to some other criteria for enough items to form a meaningful dimension — or equivalence class. Such "discoveries" can be used to adjust the set of visual arrays to be included in a revision of a study; further, the insight obtained from the dimensional analysis can enhance our understanding of the underlying meaningful domains to be studied.

The Biased Rater

In further studies using these same slides, we viewed them as consisting of a set of nature scenes (22 in all), an urban set (12 scenes), and 22 other items. The slides are always shown in a number of random orders when ratings are being obtained.

We had two purposes in mind for the next set of studies: first, we were concerned to check the methodological issue of the independence of ratings, and thus had separate groups of subjects (each consisting of about 18 people) rate the slides in terms of *complexity* (how intricate the scene is, whether it contains many different elements) and in terms of *preference* (how pleasing do you find the scene, how much do you like it).

Second, the results of the first study led us to consider other variables that might be important in the prediction of environmental preference. These I shall return to in the next section.

Once again there seems to be more than one version of "truth" in examining the issue of independence of ratings, and the findings lead to rather different conclusions, depending on which of two approaches one takes. If one correlates the two sets of complexity ratings, those made by the subjects who also rated preference and those for which complexity was the only rating made, one can get a notion of the reliability of the ratings when the number of ratings being made is the only difference. Taking the nature and urban scenes together, we found a respectable correlation of .79 for complexity. Comparably, the correlation for the two sets of preference ratings was .69, supporting one's notion that the more subjective preference judgment requires a relatively large sample for a stable result. The .79 complexity correlation, however, suggests a fairly high agreement despite the preference ratings made by one group.

Another approach to examining the effect of possible bias in ratings is to relate the preference ratings to the independently obtained complexity ratings. Using either set of preference ratings, those originally made or those made as the sole judgment, we found a relatively strong negative correlation (−.52 and −.58 for the two sets of preferences) between preference and the independently obtained complexity ratings for the nature and urban

scenes combined, and no meaningful correlation between these variables within either the nature or the urban set. This is in marked contrast to the results originally obtained, in which we found a positive correlation within each domain. Since the initial finding was based on nonindependent ratings, this raises the possibility that preference ratings biased the judgment of complexity.

Clearly, this issue will demand further attention, both with respect to the role of complexity in the prediction of preference and with respect to the issue of independence of ratings. Wohlwill (1973a), for instance, presented results strongly supporting our original ones, using very different material, but based on independent ratings of "complexity" and preference. Thomas Herzog, our colleague at Grand Valley State College, has found no biasing effect when people are asked to rate different pairs of variables — although preference was never one of the pair. Typically, one asks a panel of judges to rate scenes on any number of qualities — but again, preference is excluded from the set. (In light of these results, the findings on the role of coherence and mystery reported by R. Kaplan, 1973a, will need to be reexamined.)

It must be emphasized that the underlying issue here is by no means a clear one. The very difference in the patterns of results when subjects are or are not asked to consider a scene in terms of preference and something else can help show what "matters" to them in terms of preference. It can be argued that this is precisely the approach taken by the semantic-differential procedure in which a mixture of blatantly evaluative, clearly subjective, qualities is juxtaposed with a variety of relatively objective ratings. Likewise, in adjective checklists, both evaluative and relatively objective ratings are scrambled in the same list. In other words, one might suggest that the rater's personal bias is an inherent feature of such procedures.

Additional Predictors

To return to the issue of the prediction of preference, let me first mention some other variables that were included in the study involving independent ratings of complexity and preference. In analyzing the results of the first study, the notion of mystery emerged as a compelling force in preference, and especially in preference for nature scenes. So we had a group of subjects rate these slides only in terms of *mystery,* which we explained to them as "the promise of further information based on a change in the vantage point of the observer. Consider whether you would learn more if you could walk deeper into the scene." Based on other insights (Kaplan and Wendt, 1972), we also had a group of subjects rate the scenes in terms of *coherence* (the extent to which the scene "hangs together;" repeated elements, textures, and structural factors within a scene may help it hang together). A five-point scale was used for each rating; the slides were viewed for 15 seconds each.

The overall negative correlation between preference and complexity obtained using either set of preference ratings (mentioned in the previous section) is attributable to the consistently strong, highly significant ($t = 4.92$, and $t = 6.76$, df = 34, $p < .001$) preference for nature scenes over urban scenes, and the consistently higher complexity ratings of urban scenes over nature scenes ($t = 7.08$ and $t = 3.80$, df = 34, $p < .001$). Turning to the two new predictor variables, we found that coherence did not play an important role in the prediction of preference, nor was coherence on the whole different for the nature and urban domains. Mystery, on the other hand, was a strong positive predictor and was rated as sig-

nificantly higher in the nature than in the urban items ($t = 4.09$, df = 34, $p < .001$). The correlation of mystery and preference, partialing out the effects of the two other predictors, was .64 for the nature and urban sets combined (.55 and .53 within each domain).

The prediction of preference based on the three predictors led to $R = .79$ for the nature and urban domains together (.64 and .55 within each domain) when using only independent ratings for each variable. These findings suggest that the three predictor variables (whose intercorrelations are always low, incidentally) offer an interesting beginning in the search for understanding of environmental preference. A much fuller exposition of their role in this work can be found in S. Kaplan's chapter in this volume.

Just a Glimpse

The last study in the series explored the effects of viewing duration. Preference was the only rating made, and the slides were presented for either 10, 40, or 200 milliseconds with different subject groups for each duration. Such brief exposures were used because they better reflect the amount of time often afforded for a glimpse of the environment in one's daily experience. Other research we have carried out using comparable scenes of the outdoor environment assured us that these durations are long enough for considerable extraction of information. The results of the short-duration study are most interesting. We found no difference among these brief durations in preference, within or across content domains. In fact, the correlation of preference ratings for the nature and urban scenes combined was an unbelievable .97. At least when viewed for a brief instant only, there does seem to be remarkable agreement on such a subjective variable.

The prediction of the preference ratings from the independently rated complexity, coherence, and mystery predictors (obtained in the previous study) was very similar to the results obtained with long exposure: coherence was ineffective, complexity was negatively related to preference for the two content domains combined and zero within each domain, and mystery once again was a powerful predictor. The only difference, however, was that mystery was positively related to preference for nature scenes (.41) and negatively related to preference for urban scenes ($-.52$). The latter was not the case in the long-exposure study. These results suggest that with brief exposure there is a heightening of an overall affective reaction: nature was positively viewed — to an even greater extent than in the previous studies — and the urban scenes were downrated — to an even greater extent than before. In fact, the separation between nature and urban ratings for brief durations is quite astounding; the nature preference was significantly greater ($F = 6.03$, df $= 2,53$, $p < .005$) and the urban preference significantly lower ($F = 4.86$, df $= 2.53$, $p < .05$) for the short durations as compared with the 15-second exposure.

IN SUM

A compact, reliable means of characterizing the visual environment would be of considerable interest. It represents a challenge that is both tantalizing and of practical importance. Focusing not only on the salient features of the physical world, but also on the qualities that are salient for the humans who live in it, makes the task still more valuable, but also more difficult. It demands that we explore variables that are difficult to assess, to define operationally, to assign numbers to, and to get respectable interobserver reliabilities for. But I would argue that our understanding of landscape assessment in general, and of environmental preference in particular, cannot proceed without attacking these thorny issues. And our understanding will not come from complicated regression equations that linearly combine factors that have no underlying reason to be combined. It takes more than meticulous research procedures to make sense of the universe; effective research strategy requires that one's goals be kept firmly in mind.

We are visual creatures in a visual world surrounded by perplexing rich stimulus arrays that we cannot afford to take for granted. We must apply sophisticated methodologies and analytic tools to the well-honed intuitions that have already surfaced in this exciting area. Far-reaching decisions that have direct impact on all of us are constantly being made, whether we generate effective research in this area or not. We need be neither tender-minded nor empty-headed. The ground between is fertile and the tools are not lacking.

Individual Variations in Landscape Description

Kenneth H. Craik

Among the many forms of human response to landscape it may be useful to define three kinds: *descriptive assessments,* which simply seek to depict, rate, or measure the attributes of specific landscapes; *evaluative appraisals,* which judge the relative quality of specific landscapes against some implicit or explicit standard of comparison; and *preferential judgments,* which express a wholly personal, subjective appreciation of (or repugnance for) specific landscapes (Craik, 1972a).

In previous research, I have attempted to develop landscape rating scales and a graphic landscape typology, partly based on the work of Litton (1972), as techniques for the descriptive assessment of landscapes (Craik, 1969, 1972a). Although a large array of landscape photoslides (ranging from 50 to 100) was used in the initial, and encouraging, appraisal of observer agreement, the assessment instruments

Kenneth H. Craik is an Associate Professor and Vice-Chairman in the Department of Psychology and Associate Research Psychologist in the Institute of Personality Assessment and Research at the University of California, Berkeley.

The research program is supported by National Science Foundation Grants GS 30984-X and GS 40097: Environmental Dispositions and the Simulation of Environments. Donald Appleyard and the author are the principal investigators. I am grateful to Susan Hopkin, Linda Sikorowski, and other project staff who assisted in these analyses.

have not yet been subjected to the challenge of field application. And except for a minor pilot study (Craik, 1972a), they have not been put to the test of substantive scientific utility. Nevertheless, they do hold promise for facilitating thorough, systematic investigation of the relationship of human response to objective features of landscape scenes (for example, observer position, sense of enclosure). Elsewhere, I have also attempted to delineate a psychosociological differentiation between evaluative appraisals, which have reference to a standard of comparison, and preferential judgments, which are wholly personal and subjective, and to suggest the policy implications of this distinction (Craik, 1972b).

In the present research, the focus shifts to individual variations among observers in their descriptions of landscapes. Observer descriptions of landscape can be considered from two points of view (Craik, 1971). In *environmental-assessment studies*, the intent is to establish characteristics of places. Consensual observer descriptions are treated as *trait designations* and thus as properties of the landscapes. In *environmental-perception studies*, the intent is to understand processes and factors influencing the responses of persons. Their descriptions are treated as *trait attributions* and thus as properties of the observers. For example, I might describe a landscape scene as "barren." If I were serving as a member of a landscape-assessment team and the majority joined me in making that response, *the scene* could be designated as "barren." Ultimately, a sample of barren scenes and lush scenes might be established and used in research on the effects of barren and lush landscapes upon human response and behavior. If, however, a colleague were to honor me by conducting a case analysis of my personal response to landscape, the question would be, "What is there *about*

Craik that led him to attribute barrenness to that landscape scene?"

In their well-known work on personality in nature, culture, and society, Kluckhohn and Murray (1950:35) noted that

Every man is in certain respects
a. like all other men,
b. like some other men,
c. like no other man.

My aim in this study has been to analyze the ways in which each of our research participants is like *some* other persons in their landscape descriptions. The strategy employed in the investigation identified basic dimensions of landscape description, established an empirical typology based upon these dimensions, and explored personality characteristics associated with each landscape description type. Thus, the study is an exploration in taxonomy (Sneath and Sokal, 1973).

The findings I am going to present are drawn from a current interdisciplinary research program under way at Berkeley which has two major purposes: to appraise the psychological effectiveness of a system of dynamic environmental simulation (Appleyard et al., 1973), and to explore the relationships between observer characteristics and environmental perception, broadly defined.

The research procedure can be described quite simply. Individuals are presented with a tour through an everyday physical environment located in Marin County, California. Following the tour, they are asked to describe the place they have toured. Subsequently, they are asked to describe themselves on a number of standard personality and attitude measures. Some research participants are taken on an auto tour through the place; some observe a color film of the auto tour; some watch a color film of a simulated eye-level tour through a scale model of the place; and some view a black-white videotape of the simulated scale model tour. Participation entails a day-long session (Table 1); we are becoming indebted to hundreds of environmental professionals and Marin County residents who have assisted us in this way (Table 2). The research program is still underway and reports of final results, particularly the appraisal of simulation, must be deferred.

Table 1
Environmental Research Program: Daily Schedule

8:45	Continental breakfast — welcome
9:00	Environmental tour (direct-film-video; site-model)
9:30	Mood checklist
9:35	Free description of tour List of noteworthy features List of regions
9:45	Map sketch
10:00	Route configuration (string)
10:15	Regional Q-sort deck
10:45	Information quizzes A and B
11:00	Coffee break
11:30	Recognition test
11:40	Environmental inference and description
11:50	Environmental evaluation
11:55	Environmental adjective checklist Landscape adjective checklist
12:15	Lunch and discussion (participants and staff) Film and description of the environmental simulation project
1:15	Personal and environmental background form (including living room checklist)
1:30	Familiarity with tour area
1:35	Marin County consequences
1:50	Environmental attitudes survey
2:05	Gottschaldt figures test
2:15	Social attitude scale
2:30	Barron–Welsh art scale
2:40	Leisure activities blank
2:50	Environmental response inventory
3:15	Adjective checklist Visual acuity test (individually administered)
3:30	Discussion and farewell

In this chapter, I would like to put the issue of environmental simulation aside altogether and consider a limited but important aspect of the research on environmental perception. Specifically, I shall describe our attempts to understand and account for the individual differences in landscape descriptions rendered by participants who took the *auto tour through the actual site* (Table 3).

METHOD

Selection of Participants

The strategy for selecting observers for the research project has been guided by an effort to maximize the external validity and representativeness of the research findings. Three major samples can be distinguished (see Table 2):

Countywide sample A subject pool has been established from the Marin County population that is equally divided in sex and reasonably representative in social class and geographical location of residence. The names are drawn from a telephone directory that lists subscribers alphabetically by street addresses. Individuals in the subject pool are randomly assigned to one of the four experimental conditions and invited by letter and telephone follow-up to participate in the program. In the auto-tour condition, one subsample completed only the posttour response formats ($N = 109$); two subsamples also provided evaluations and made inferences about points along the route ($N = 40$) or provided ongoing descriptive commentaries, which were tape-recorded during the tour ($N = 38$).

Research site sample A random sample of residents of the actual research site were also invited to participate and were assigned to the auto-tour condition ($N = 50$).

Professional sample A combined directory of San Francisco Bay Area environmental planners, architects, landscape architects, trans-

Table 2
Research Activity Schedule: Subsamples
I. Auto Tour and Color Film of Auto Tour (Summer 1972)

	Posttest Only	Prefer-ence and Inference A	Prefer-ence and Inference B	Free Descrip-tion	Total
County: auto tour	109	20	20	38	187
Site residents: auto tour	50				50
Professionals: auto tour	58			4	62
County: film of auto tour	113	21	22	36	192
Professionals: film of auto tour	57			4	61
	387	41	42	82	552

II. Color Film and Videotape of Model Tour (1973–1974) (projected)

	Posttest Only	Prefer-ence and Inference A	Prefer-ence and Inference B	Free Descrip-tion	Total
County: film of scale model	100	20	20	40	180
Professionals: film of scale model	60				60
County: videotape of scale model	100	20	20	40	180
Professionals: videotape of scale model	60				60
County: auto tour[a]	40				40
County: film of auto tour[a]	40				40
	400	40	40	80	560

[a] Samples added to check on history effects.

portation engineers, and real estate brokers and appraisers was compiled. Randomly selected professionals were invited to partici-pate and randomly assigned to the four treat-ment conditions, including the auto tour ($N = 62$).

The present results will be based upon the countrywide auto-tour sample only.

Auto Tour of the Research Site

The research site in Marin County embodies a broad array of land uses, including several types of residential areas, a shopping center, an older commercial highway strip, a light in-dustrial park, an office complex and some graz-ing land. The topography features low rolling hills with extensive grasses and occasional oak

Table 3
Research Paradigm: Environmental Perception and Assessment Studies[a]

Observers	Response Formats	Media of Presentation	Environmental Displays and Places
Samples:			
Countrywide	Mood checklist	Auto Tour	Marin site
Site	Free description: cards		
Professional	lists	Color film	Marin site model
	Map sketch		
Observer characteristics	Route configuration (string map)	Black–white videotape	
Personal and environmental	Regional Q-sort deck		
background form	Information quizzes A and B		
Living room checklist	Recognition test		
Familiarity with tour area	Environmental inference and		
Marin County consequences	description		
Gottschaldt figures test	Environmental evaluation		
Social attitude scale (LOC)	Environmental adjective checklist		
Barron–Welsh art scale	Landscape adjective checklist		
Leisure activities blank			
Environmental response			
inventory			
Adjective checklist (Gough)			
Visual acuity test			

[a] Based on Craik (1968, 1970a, 1971).

and bay trees. The small hills throughout the site create a system of differentiated places. The residential areas, mostly along the valley floors, are cultivated with vegetation that is not native to the area, including Eucalyptus trees, liquidambars, and oleanders.

A 25-minute, 9-mile standard auto tour was delineated to sample the residential, shopping, commercial, pastoral, and freeway segments of the area. The auto tour was made in contemporary U.S.-built sedans with research staff drivers. When more than one driver was required on a given day, assignment of participants to drivers was made randomly (cards with the names of drivers were shuffled and drawn by participants). When more than one participant was assigned to an auto, assignment to seating position was made randomly (cards listing seating positions were shuffled and drawn by participants). Quotas of 40 participants, balanced by sex, were set for the free description and the preference and inference response modes. On testing days when facilities and preparations for these conditions were adequate, the assignments to them of participants from the countyside sample were made randomly, within the constraints of efforts to meet the established quotas. The auto tours that formed the object of this report were conducted in July and August 1972.

Figure 1
View of the research site. Auto tour begins and ends in shopping-center parking lot,
left center of photo. (Looking north.)

Landscape Adjective Checklist

The landscape adjective checklist (LACL) consists of 240 adjectives frequently used in everyday life to describe landscape scenes. The LACL fills a significant need for brief, comprehensive descriptive techniques in environmental assessment (Craik, 1971, 1973); its development has been described elsewhere (Craik, 1971, 1972a).

Participants were asked to employ the LACL in recording their impressions of the landscape, terrain, and nonbuilt features of the tour area. The instructions for the LACL are as follows:

Directions: This booklet contains a list of adjectives. Please read them quickly and put an X on the line beside each one you would consider descriptive of the designated landscape. Do not worry about duplications, contradictions, and so forth. Work quickly and do not spend too much time on any one adjective.

The items of the LACL are presented in Table 4.

Figure 2
Aerial photograph of research site. Auto tour begins and ends in shopping-center
parking lot, lower right of photo.

The other response formats employed in the study are listed in Tables 1 and 3, but will not be discussed here.

Measures of Observer Characteristics

In addition to completing the response formats that recorded their impressions of the research site, participants completed a series of background, personality, and ability measures that assess a broad range of observer characteristics.

Personal and environmental background form (PEBF) This form was developed to record pertinent information concerning the participant's personal background, environmental background, and present life situation. Participants drawn from the environmental professions also provided information on their professional training and current practice.

Figure 3
Route of the auto tour through research site. Tour begins and ends in shopping-center parking lot, X. Major areas include the residential areas, A; shopping center and professional offices, B; light industrial park, C; and older commercial area, D.

Familiarity with tour area The purpose of this procedure is to attain a comprehensive assessment of the participant's prior familiarity with the research site. It yields two factor scores: one deals with acquaintance *via* auto travel through the area; the other with acquaintance *via* use of its facilities and establishments.

Environmental attitude survey (EAS) The EAS was developed in consultation with the advance planning staff of the Marin County Planning Department to assess attitudes toward important environmental issues facing the county, including conservation of open space, alternative transportation systems, and future development patterns.

Gottschaldt figures test (GFT) The GFT measures the ability of an individual to locate simple geometrical figures that are embedded and camouflaged in more complex figures. The test is presumed to relate to spatial ability, and since there is a stringent time limit, scores may

Table 4
Landscape Adjective Checklist: Endorsement Rates Greater than 10% Noted (countywide auto sample, *N* = 187)

1. active (26%)	48. dense	95. <u>hilly</u> (69%)	142. <u>pleasant</u> (55%)
2. alive (42%)	49. depressing	96. hot (36%)	143. pointed
3. Alpine	50. deserted	97. humid	144. polluted
4. angry	51. desolate	98. icy	145. powerful
5. arid (26%)	52. destroyed (11%)	99. imposing	146. pretty (38%)
6. artificial (18%)	53. dirty	100. impressive (26%)	147. pure
7. autumnal (16%)	54. distant	101. inhabited (48%)	148. purple
8. awesome	55. drab	102. inspiring (14%)	149. quiet (35%)
9. bare (19%)	56. dry (37%)	103. intimate	150. rainy
10. barren (12%)	57. dull	104. invigorating	151. rapid
11. <u>beautiful</u> (55%)	58. eerie	105. inviting (43%)	152. reaching
12. black	59. empty	106. isolated	153. red
13. bleak	60. enclosed	107. jagged	154. reflecting
14. blooming (42%)	61. eroded (20%)	108. lazy	155. refreshing (27%)
15. blue	62. eternal	109. leafy (35%)	156. relaxing (42%)
16. boggy	63. exciting (16%)	110. lifeless	157. remote
17. boring	64. expansive (25%)	111. light (27%)	158. restful (40%)
18. bright (39%)	65. extensive (29%)	112. living (39%)	159. rich (12%)
19. brisk (12%)	66. falling	113. lonely	160. rippled
20. broad (17%)	67. farmed	114. lovely (31%)	161. rocky (11%)
21. brown (45%)	68. flat	115. low	162. rolling (49%)
22. burned (37%)	69. flowery (33%)	116. lumpy	163. romantic
23. bushy (35%)	70. flowing (16%)	117. lush (13%)	164. rough
24. calm (30%)	71. foamy	118. majestic	165. round (14%)
25. challenging	72. foggy	119. marshy	166. rugged
26. changing (29%)	73. forbidding	120. massive	167. running
27. <u>clean</u> (71%)	74. forceful	121. meadowy (29%)	168. rushing
28. clear (26%)	75. forested (18%)	122. misty	169. rustic (11%)
29. close	76. free (23%)	123. moist	170. rusty
30. cloudy	77. fresh (39%)	124. monotonous (16%)	171. sad
31. cold	78. friendly (41%)	125. mossy	172. sandy
32. colorful (47%)	79. frightening	126. motionless	173. scraggly
33. colorless	80. gentle (32%)	127. mountainous (18%)	174. secluded
34. comfortable (44%)	81. glacial	128. muddy	175. secure (24%)
35. complex	82. gloomy	129. mysterious	176. serene (25%)
36. contrasting (46%)	83. golden (27%)	130. narrow	177. shadowy
37. cool	84. <u>grassy</u> (61%)	131. <u>natural</u> (52%)	178. shady (18%)
38. craggy	85. gravelly (12%)	132. nocturnal	179. shallow
39. crashing	86. gray	133. noisy	180. sharp
40. creviced	87. <u>green</u> (52%)	134. open (44%)	181. simple (17%)
41. crisp (13%)	88. happy (25%)	135. orange	182. sliding
42. cultivated (44%)	89. hard	136. overpowering	183. slippery
43. damp	90. harsh	137. pastoral (29%)	184. sloping (33%)
44. dangerous	91. hazardous	138. <u>peaceful</u> (51%)	185. slow
45. dank	92. hazy	139. picturesque (41%)	186. smoggy
46. dark	93. hidden	140. placid (23%)	187. smooth (12%)
47. deep	94. high (13%)	141. plain (11%)	188. snow-covered

Table 4 *(cont.)*

189. soft (12%)	202. swampy	215. undulating (14%)	228. watery
190. spacious (30%)	203. swift	216. unfriendly	229. weedy (18%)
191. sparse	204. tall	217. uniform (14%)	230. wet
192. spring-like	205. terraced (36%)	218. uninspiring	231. white
193. stark	206. terrifying	219. uninteresting	232. wide (13%)
194. steep (14%)	207. thicketed	220. uninviting	233. wild
195. still	208. threatening	221. unspoiled (11%)	234. winding (24%)
196. stony	209. timbered	222. unusual	235. windswept
197. stormy	210. towering	223. varied (32%)	236. wintry
198. straight	211. tranquil (29%)	224. vast	237. withered
199. strange	212. tree-studded (61%)	225. vegetated (40%)	238. wooded (24%)
200. summery (35%)	213. tropical	226. violent	239. worn
201. sunny (50%)	214. ugly	227. warm (33%)	240. yellow (17%)

reflect the manner in which the individual's cognitive processes are impaired by stress (Crutchfield et al., 1958).

Social attitude scale This questionnaire seeks to measure the tendency of persons to perceive the things that happen to them as being either beyond their control and outside their personal influence ("external locus of control") or a consequence of their own actions and within the sphere of their personal influence ("internal locus of control") (Rotter, 1966).

Barron–Welsh art scale (BWAS) The BWAS measures the similarity of an individual's preference for abstract line drawings to that of artists and appears to tap an aesthetic disposition (Barron and Welsh, 1952).

Leisure activities blank (LAB) In the LAB, respondents indicate the extent of their past involvement in each of a comprehensive array of 121 leisure activities. The LAB yields scores on seven factor scales (McKechnie, 1972).

Environmental response inventory (ERI) The ERI is a recently developed multiscale assessment instrument designed to measure an array of environmental dispositions — individual differences in the ways people think about and relate to the everyday physical environment (McKechnie, 1972).

Adjective checklist (ACL) The ACL is a 300-item list of adjectives commonly used to describe persons. The respondent checks those adjectives which he believes to be self-descriptive. The standard 24 personality scales have been scored (Gough and Heilbrun, 1965).

Visual acuity test The functional visual acuity of participants was assessed by use of the standard Snelling wall chart. Participants were tested individually; those who wore eyeglasses during the auto tour were tested with eyeglasses.

RESULTS

Landscape Attributions

Table 4 presents the items of the landscape adjective checklist, with endorsement rates greater than 10 percent noted. The majority of the countywide auto sample attributed the following characteristics to the landscape, terrain, and nonbuilt segments of the research site: clean, hilly, tree-studded, grassy, pleasant, beautiful, natural, green, peaceful, and sunny.

The array of additional noteworthy attributions is considerable. A total of 104 of the 240 adjectives were endorsed by at least 10 percent of the auto-tour observers.

Descriptive Landscape Factors for the Marin Site

The subset of 104 adjectives with endorsement rates greater than 10 percent was selected for principal-axis factor analysis, employing the "highest *r*" method of estimating communality. Varimax rotation of a four-factor solution accounts for 65.2 percent of the communality and yields the descriptive landscape factors presented in Table 5. The first factor, termed "serene–gentle" for convenient reference, conveys a sense of tranquility and low-keyed positive affect. The second factor, "dry–barren," seems to focus upon the tawny midsummer grass cover of the open hills that form a backdrop above and beyond the developed areas of the site. The third factor, "beautiful–picturesque," emphasizes a positive evaluation of the spaciousness of the area and also suggests an aesthetic-pictoral framework for appraisal. The fourth factor, "blooming–cultivated," appears to highlight the oasis-like character of the introduced plantings in the residential and other developed areas along the valley floors. Varimax factor-weight scores were computed on the four descriptive landscape dimensions for each participant, with the sample mean set at 50.0 and standard deviation of 10.0.

Typological Analysis of Landscape Descriptions

The four descriptive landscape dimensions formed the basis for a typological analysis, employing the BC TRY 0TYPE program (Tryon and Bailey, 1970). In the first stage of the program, individuals are assigned to core 0-types on the basis of an arbitrary sectioning of the factor score space. In this case, categories of high and low scores on each of the four factor scores were used, yielding 16 core 0-types. Table 6 presents the initial incidence of each core 0-type. By a process of iterative condensation, the program computes the coordinates of the centroids of each core 0-type and reassigns each individual to the centroid of that core 0-type to which he or she has the smallest Euclidean distance. After the first reassignment, each 0-type has changed. The process is then repeated on the basis of the new 0-types, and iterations continue until all individuals remain unchanged in their reassignments to 0-types. In the present analysis, 14 0-types emerge. Table 6 presents the incidence of each 0-type and the mean scores of its members on the four descriptive landscape factors. The overall homogeneity of each type is also presented in Table 6. This index measures the "tightness" of the profiles of individuals that compose a given type by comparing the variance of factor scores for individuals within the type to the variance for the entire sample. Complete identity of profiles for type members would yield an index of 1.00; no shared similarity of type members over that found in the sample as a whole would yield an index of .00.

Figure 4 displays the overall structure of the relationships among the 14 types of landscape descriptions. In this figure, the vertical scale is the Euclidean distance between the mean profiles of the various 0-types. The chart progressively combines 0-types with small Euclidean distances between them, two at a time, into higher-order clusters. The progressive condensation of 0-types is shown as one reads down the chart; reading up the chart reveals the breakdown of taxonomic structure, akin to the movement from genus to species to varieties.

Table 5
Descriptive Landscape Factors: Marin Site[a] (countywide auto sample, $N = 187$)

Factor I: Serene–gentle (19.6% of total communality)		Factor II: Dry–barren (15.8% of total communality)		Factor III: Beautiful–picturesque (15.2% of total communality)		Factor IV: Blooming–cultivated (14.6% of total communality)	
Adjective	*Loading*	*Adjective*	*Loading*	*Adjective*	*Loading*	*Adjective*	*Loading*
serene	.583	brown	.585	beautiful	.594	flowery	.585
quiet	.559	burned	.564	lovely	.554	blooming	.577
light	.544	dry	.563	impressive	.526	leafy	.547
soft	.541	bare	.538	inspiring	.497	green	.543
tranquil	.498	eroded	.518	invigorating	.495	cultivated	.512
restful	.494	steep	.483	picturesque	.486	lush	.507
friendly	.493	yellow	.477	forested	.480	pretty	.425
relaxing	.472	barren	.465	wooded	.445	vegetated	.418
placid	.472	arid	.437	exciting	.430	alive	.416
free	.452	plain	.432	spacious	.382	shady	.407
smooth	.439	hilly	.428	high	.378	colorful	.390
gentle	.438	monotonous	.426	refreshing	.374	varied	.386
still	.410	weedy	.420	rustic	.359	gravelly	.372
inviting	.398	round	.420	expansive	.358	tree-studded	.369
happy	.397	hot	.411	fresh	.351	grassy	.369
warm	.385	bushy	.403	mountainous	.348	pleasant	.337
comfortable	.376	destroyed	.400	natural	.340	extensive	.332
bright	.371	sloping	.387	meadowy	.338	winding	.270
secure	.361	distant	.383	contrasting	.312	flat	.255
brisk	.361	rocky	.351	calm	.304		
sunny	.359	artificial	.338	unspoiled	.285		
living	.354	rolling	.336	flowing	.284		
broad	.353	undulating	.311	uniform	−.312		
summery	.337	terraced	.293	inhabited	−.225		
simple	.331	golden	.271				
clean	.330	rich	.165				
crisp	.320						
peaceful	.319						
open	.313						
autumnal	.309						
wide	.308						
clear	.292						
pastoral	.280						
changing	.230						
active	.212						

[a] Each of the 104 adjectives is assigned to the factor on which it has the highest loading.

Table 6
Typological Analysis of Landscape Descriptions: Marin Site (Profile Levels, X̄; homogeneities, H)

Type	Incidence		Serene–gentle X̄	Dry–barren X̄	Beautiful–picturesque X̄	Blooming–cultivated X̄	Overall H
	Initial	Final					
T01	18	24	48.2	45.0	44.2	43.9	.92
T02	15	26	43.7	42.1	48.4	56.1	.90
T03	12	17	44.2	44.0	55.9	42.0	.86
T04	9						
T05	17	17	43.0	55.8	42.5	41.7	.88
T06	15	19	47.2	55.2	41.9	56.4	.86
T07	11	12	43.5	56.3	61.6	41.8	.84
T08	10	10	39.6	57.3	63.1	59.4	.81
T09	12						
T10	12	14	58.4	39.9	45.1	51.7	.90
T11	10	9	67.2	42.9	56.6	40.2	.81
T12	12	9	57.6	41.7	62.3	61.6	.85
T13	6	8	57.0	68.1	41.8	41.9	.78
T14	11	9	62.2	55.9	40.9	64.2	.71
T15	8	4	69.5	58.3	60.4	39.1	.76
T16	9	6	59.6	56.8	63.6	65.1	.67

Observer Characteristics Associated with Types of Landscape Descriptions

The typology reported in Table 6 and Figure 4 represents a taxonomy of landscape descriptions. Do individuals who rendered the same type of landscape description display other distinctive characteristics? To address this question, individuals sharing membership in a landscape description type were compared to the complement of that type (that is, all other participants in the countywide auto sample). Comparisons of each type with its complement were conducted across all measures of observer characteristics, which, of course, constitute independent sources of information that did not play a part in the derivation of the typology.

Reporting the associated characteristics of 14 types is an inescapably cumbersome task. The strategy adopted here is to report the findings for each type in a textual format, providing a composite sketch based upon attributes that differentiate the type from the complement to a statistically significant degree (beyond the .10 level).

Type 01   Low: serene–gentle (48.2)
           Low: dry–barren (45.0)
           Low: beautiful–picturesque (44.2)
           Low: blooming–cultivated (43.9)

Type 01 members have spent a greater length of time residing in a central city and the direction of their moves over their life course has been from farms toward central cities. They have fewer children than the complement sample and are more likely to consider them-

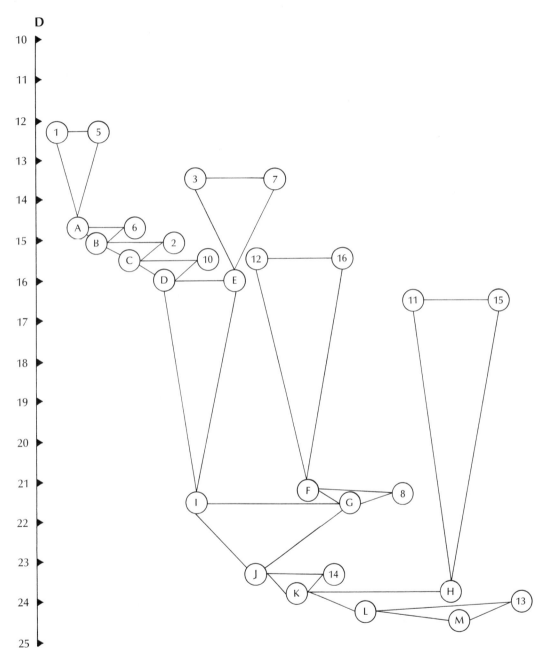

Figure 4
Hierarchical structure of landscape description types.

selves Republicans than Democrats. They are more favorably disposed to creating new, modern, efficient environments rather than preserving older environments. They assign higher priority to freeway construction and to planned "new towns," and would prefer to have a new freeway to San Francisco located close to rather than far from their home. They have also lived longer in Marin County than the complement sample. They belong to fewer social service, community, and religious organizations and read fewer magazines regularly. They assign higher priority to crime as an issue in the county. They tend not to spend their leisure time in home crafts or glamour sports, and they grant lower priority to using present agricultural land for recreational facilities (for example, state parks). However, they express a willingness to pay more (for example, through taxes) than the complement sample on alleviating traffic congestion, conserving open space, and developing recreational facilities.

Type 01 did not provide a positive characterization of the research site's landscape, but did give relatively greater emphasis to the serene–gentle dimension. A response style of checking fewer adjectives may be implicated in the specification of this type. However, the correlations of total number of adjectives checked on the LACL with comparable indexes for the Gough adjective checklist (self-description) and a mood checklist are only +.44 and +.30, respectively.

Type 02   Low: serene–gentle (43.7)
            Low: dry–barren (42.1)
            Low: beautiful–picturesque (48.4)
            High: blooming–cultivated (56.1)

Type 02 members are more often women who had active mothers, have moved more often from one section of the country to another, and have spent more years residing in small, isolated towns. The population of their present community in Marin County is smaller than that of the complement sample. The home range of their leisure activities is also smaller; they tend to be stay-at-homes rather than gadabouts. They are less likely to belong to conservation or ecology organizations and are unlikely to have mechanical pastimes. Their ideal county does not entail greater separation between communities or more open space. They give lower priority to express buses as a transportation goal and also grant lower priority to recreation as a countywide issue. They are more likely to favor the present level of local governmental control over private land (for example, via zoning) rather than greater controls. In the same vein, they tend to grant somewhat greater endorsement to present zoning regulations on agricultural lands. They are willing to spend more money (for example, through taxes) to control air pollution.

In their landscape description, this type has emphasized the blooming–cultivated dimension and presumably the compact, oasis-like residential developments in the research site.

Type 03   Low: serene–gentle (44.2)
            Low: dry–barren (44.0)
            High: beautiful–picturesque (55.9)
            Low: blooming–cultivated (42.0)

Type 03 members tend to be Protestant, to be older than the complement sample, and to have spent more years residing both in a central city and on a farm. Their educational attainment is lower. They rank crime higher as a countywide issue, give improved ferry service to San Francisco lower priority as a transportation goal, and are willing to spend less money on the development of recreational facilities. They tend to be positively disposed to the world of objects and technological processes, but less strongly so than the complement sample. They are unlikely to be found engaged in glamour sports, such as archery, horseback riding, and water-skiing. Type 03 members tend to be less familiar with the research site from the vantage point of roadway views, but equally familiar in terms of the use of facilities in the area. They attain lower scores on a measure of aesthetic sensitivity and also on a measure of spatial ability.

In their landscape descriptions, Type 03 members emphasize the beautiful–picturesque dimension. The adjectives loading on this factor dimension conveys the spaciousness of the area and suggests an aesthetic-pictoral framework of appraisal (for example, spacious, expansive, flowing, beautiful, lovely, inspiring, picturesque). The low scores on the Barron–Welsh art scale might appear to contradict this interpretation. But on the contrary, previous studies indicate that high scorers on the scale tend to prefer modern, abstract paintings, and low scorers prefer representational paintings, such as traditional landscape paintings (Barron, 1952, 1953).

Type 05   Low: serene–gentle (43.0)
           High: dry–barren (55.8)
           Low: beautiful–picturesque (42.5)
           Low: blooming–cultivated (41.7)

The fathers of Type 05 members had a higher educational attainment and higher occupational status than those of the complement sample. Type 05 members are more likely to engage in glamour sports and to be gadabouts, with leisure activities scattered widely throughout the county and beyond its boundaries. They are more familiar with the research site from the vantage point of roadway views and less familiar with it in terms of use of the area's facilities. They place higher priority on scenic highway improvement as a transportation goal, and rank recreation higher as a countywide issue while ranking public education and air and water pollution lower. They are less inclined to prohibit by law resort development along the Marin coastline. In personality, Type 05 members are below average on "abasement" and "succorance," and lower than the

complement sample. That is, they tend not to feel inferior nor to seek emotional support from others; instead, they are alert, poised, and decisive, with a quiet confidence in their own worth.

The wide discretionary home range, concern about scenic travel, and selective recreational pursuits of this type suggest the operation of unusually high standards of landscape appraisal, leading to broad-based comparative judgments that highlight the area's dry, barren features and play down the more appealing attributes conveyed by the other three factor dimensions.

Type 06   Low: serene–gentle (47.2)
           High: dry–barren (55.2)
           Low: beautiful–picturesque (41.9)
           High: blooming–cultivated (56.4)

Type 06 members had relatively better educated mothers and are less likely to be Protestant. Compared to the complement, they report a larger number of residential moves within one locality or city within their lifetimes. They grant higher priority to recreation facilities as a future use of present agricultural lands, rank public utilities higher as a countywide issue, and consider new towns as a more attractive form of future development than does the complement sample. They also give more support to local governmental control (for example, via zoning) over private land.

This type appears to focus upon the contrast between distinctive forms of land use in the research site — the dry, barren hillsides and the blooming, cultivated residential valley floors.

Type 07   Low: serene–gentle (43.5)
           High: dry–barren (56.3)
           High: beautiful–picturesque (61.6)
           Low: blooming–cultivated (41.8)

Type 07 members spent a larger number of their early years, as well as a larger portion of their entire lives, in a suburban setting, and have spent less years residing in a central city. They are more likely to have had Protestant mothers and to be Protestant themselves, and less likely to have no religious affiliation. They have more children than the complement sample and are more apt to be stay-at-homes, spending their leisure time close to their home. They also spend a larger percentage of their time indoors. They are more favorably disposed to new, modern, efficient environments than to preserving older environments, and they display a greater need for privacy. They travel a greater distance to work than the complement sample and grant higher priority to express buses as a transportation goal. They also assign higher priority to new-town developments as a future use of present agricultural land.

Type 07 members appear to be commuting suburbanites. Their emphasis upon the dry hillsides and spaciousness of the research site's landscape may represent a stress upon its distinctiveness and contrast to the urban environment.

Type 08   Low: serene–gentle (39.6)
           High: dry–barren (57.3)
           High: beautiful–picturesque (63.1)
           High: blooming–cultivated (59.4)

Type 08 members are more likely to have had an active father. They have spent more years residing in a small town and less years in a central city. However, the population of their present Marin community is larger than that of the complement sample. They are more likely to attain higher scores on a measure of spatial ability. Although their household has access to a greater number of cars, they also assign a higher priority to rapid transit as a transportation goal, and they more often employ travel modes other than car, bus, and ferry. They belong to a larger number of conservation and

ecology organizations than the complement sample and more often endorse the complete prohibition of resort development on the coast. To a greater extent than the complement sample, their ideal conception of the county entails fewer homes, less people, greater separation between communities, and more open space. They also more strongly endorse newtown development as a means of accommodating population increases. On the Gough adjective checklist, they show above-average scores on "number of unfavorable adjectives checked" and "succorance," which are also higher than those of the complement sample; they are below average and lower than the complement sample on "achievement" and "endurance." This pattern of mean differences suggests a somewhat rebellious and dissatisfied individual, unwilling to engage in prolonged effort but trusting in the benevolence and supportive intentions of others.

Type 10   High: serene–gentle (58.4)
           Low: dry–barren (39.9)
           Low: beautiful–picturesque (45.1)
           High: blooming–cultivated (51.7)

Type 10 members tend to be younger than the complement sample and are more likely to be unmarried. Their family income is lower than that of the complement sample and, if married, their spouse's educational and occupational status tends to be lower, as well. They are more likely to consider themselves Democrats. Their household has access to fewer cars and they express a greater willingness to use rapid transit. They are more likely to read a national newspaper and belong to a larger number of agricultural organizations. They are somewhat less inclined than the complement sample to modify the environment to satisfy human needs and to assert "man over nature." They are also less strongly inclined to set a population limit on the county, but are willing to pay more (for example, in taxes) for the development of recreational facilities. Overall, their appraisal of Marin County is less positive than the complement sample's rating, but still favorable. In personality, they are above average and higher than the complement sample on the "number of unfavorable adjectives checked" and on "autonomy," while below average and lower on "personal adjustment." Thus, this type tends to be individualistic, hard-headed, and self-willed, and perhaps also somewhat skeptical, dissatisfied, and aloof. They also possess greater visual acuity than the complement sample.

Type 11   High: serene–gentle (67.2)
           Low: dry–barren (42.9)
           High: beautiful–picturesque (56.6)
           Low: blooming–cultivated (40.2)

Type 11 members are more likely to have had Roman Catholic parents whose educational and occupational status were lower than in the case of the complement sample. They show a greater willingness than the complement sample to have low-income housing located close to their residence. They are more likely than the complement sample to be passengers instead of drivers when traveling by car, are willing to spend more (for example, via taxes) to relieve traffic congestion, and assign higher priority to rapid transit as a transportation goal. However, they also grant express buses a lower priority than the complement sample. Their ideal conception of Marin County is less likely to include greater separation between communities and more open space.

Type 12   High: serene–gentle (57.6)
           Low: dry–barren (41.7)
           High: beautiful–picturesque (62.3)
           High: blooming–cultivated (61.6)

Type 12 members had fathers with lower educational and occupational status. They have

a greater appreciation and understanding of the world of mechanical objects and technological processes than the complement sample, but they are also more disposed to preserving traditional environments than welcoming modern, efficient environments. They are willing to spend more money on the conservation of open space, recreational facilities, and air pollution control. They are less in favor of continuing the present zoning regulations on agricultural lands. They are less willing to use rapid transit facilities than the complement sample, and they assign rapid transit a lower priority as a transportation goal and as a countywide issue, and are less willing to have such facilities located close to their residence. They devote a greater percentage of their discretionary time to outdoor activities. In personality, they score above average and higher than the complement sample on "achievement," "endurance," "intraception," "number of favorable adjectives checked," "defensiveness," and "personal adjustment," while scoring below average and lower on "lability," "succorance," and "number of unfavorable adjectives checked." They tend to be able, hard-working, goal-directed persons, serious, self-controlled, and resolute in style, with an ability to work well with others despite a lack of spontaneity and verve.

Type 13   High: serene–gentle (57.0)
           High: dry–barren (68.1)
           Low: beautiful–picturesque (41.8)
           Low: blooming–cultivated (41.9)

Type 13 members had mothers with lower educational attainments and few community activities. They report more moves from one section of the country to another and from one country to another than the complement sample. They are more disposed to modify the environment in accord with human needs (the "man-over-nature" orientation). They are somewhat less enthusiastic in their appraisal of Marin County as a place to live, but favorable nevertheless. They are also somewhat more ready than the complement sample to leave the county if environmental problems increase in the next 5 years. They are more in favor of prohibiting, rather than limiting, coastal resort development. Compared to the complement sample, they are more in favor of low-density development than new towns to handle increased population. They are less willing to use rapid transit, less willing to spend money on traffic-congestion remedies, and assign a lower priority to rapid transit as a transportation goal.

Type 14   High: serene–gentle (62.2)
           High: dry–barren (55.9)
           Low: beautiful–picturesque (40.9)
           High: blooming–cultivated (64.2)

Type 14 members have spent a greater number of years of their life, including their early years, in a small isolated city. They are more likely to have had a Roman Catholic father and are more likely to consider themselves Democrats. They have a shorter commute to work than the complement sample. They belong to a larger number of organizations, including a larger number of urban-improvement, agricultural, and environmental organizations. Their ideal conception of Marin County would entail better-quality housing, and they are more willing to have low-income housing located in their own community. They are somewhat more inclined to have municipal and county governments encourage coastal resort development, and they show more support than the complement sample for public access to beaches through private property. Regarding present agricultural land, they assign higher priority to continuation of present zoning regulations and lower priority to its use for improved recreation facilities.

Type 15   High: serene–gentle (69.5)
           High: dry–barren (58.3)
           High: beautiful–picturesque (60.4)
           Low: blooming–cultivated (39.1)

Type 15 members and their spouses have a higher educational attainment than the complement sample and a higher yearly family income. Their leisure time is more frequently devoted to intellectual–cultural pursuits (going to plays, concerts, museums). They are more likely to read a national newspaper regularly and read a larger number of magazines and newspapers regularly. They score higher on a measure of need for privacy. They are more likely not to be affiliated with a major religion or any religion. They express greater willingness than the complement sample to use rapid transit regularly. Compared to the complement sample, they are less familiar with the research site from the vantage point of roadway views.

Type 16   High: serene–gentle (59.6)
           High: dry–barren (56.8)
           High: beautiful–picturesque (63.6)
           High: blooming–cultivated (65.1)

Type 16 members belong to a relatively larger number of organizations than the complement sample, including conservation and ecology groups and environmental organizations. They have a higher educational attainment and also read a larger number of magazines regularly. They tend to devote more of their leisure time to neighborhood sports and mechanical pursuits than does the complement sample. In contrast to the complement sample, they would prefer that coastal resort development be prohibited rather than simply limited and controlled, and they advocate greater local governmental control over land use. Their ideal conception of Marin County entails fewer homes, fewer people, greater separation between communities, and

more open space. They indicate a stronger desire that new shopping centers, freeways, and
community colleges be located far from rather
than close to their residence. They are less
strongly disposed to modifying the environment in accord with human needs (the "man-
over-nature" orientation) and are more likely
to perceive their personal lives as influenced
by external rather than internal forces. In personality, they score above average and higher
than the complement sample on "deference"
and "abasement," while scoring below average
and lower on "self-confidence," "autonomy,"
and "lability." This pattern of scores suggests a
reluctance to take the initiative and a tendency
toward enacting subordinate roles with others
in a dependable, steady, unassuming, and
subdued manner, which may reflect a lack of
self-acceptance and self-worth.

DISCUSSION

The general method employed in the present study yields a considerable amount of
practical information. If the research site fell
within the jurisdiction of a regional planning
agency interested in the environmental perceptions of its constituency, what use might
these findings be to it? First, the results answer
the question: How do the constituents describe the landscape of the site (Table 4)? Second, what summary dimensions underlie their
descriptions (Table 5)? Third, what kinds of descriptions emerge, taken over the configuration of landscape dimensions (Table 6)? And,
finally, what sorts of people render the various
types of landscape descriptions (textual summaries of associated characteristics)? Furthermore, these answers are based upon a reasonably representative sample of the regional
constituency, who actually toured the area
under analysis.

In particular, perusal of the landscape-
description types and their associated characteristics reveals practical as well as scientific implications. First, the various types of landscape
descriptions do indeed appear to be rendered
by persons who also differ in many other ways.
This observation is affirmed by a comparison of
Types 12 and 16, who agree in describing
the landscape as serene–gentle, beautiful–
picturesque, and blooming–cultivated, but
only Type 16 describes it as dry–barren; or by a
comparison of Types 05 and 16, who agree in
describing it as dry–barren but disagree on the
other dimensions. In each comparison, the
thumbnail sketches delineate a wide array of
personal differences between type members.

Second, there is the implication that holding
public meetings and consulting with environmental organizations do not provide a comprehensive basis for the agency to gain an
understanding of their constituents' environmental perceptions. Type 02 members, for
example, tend to be stay-at-homes, uninvolved
in environmental organizations; Type 16 members tend to belong to such groups. Thus,
the environmental perceptions of Type 16
members might be communicated to agency
staff at public meetings, whereas the views of
Type 02 members might be overlooked. Yet
Type 16 has one of the lowest incidences of
membership in our sample, and Type 02 has
the highest incidence (Table 6).

Our results might also serve as a check on
the assumptions held by the agency staff regarding the environmental perceptions of their
constituents. Type 07 members, for example,
appear to be prototypical suburbanites. Would
the agency staff have accurately predicted that
these commuting suburbanites tend to see
the landscape of the site as dry–barren
and beautiful–picturesque? Parenthetically, it
might be noted that priorities in taxonomic

exercises depend upon their purposes. It would have been possible to establish observer types on the basis of demographic–personal attributes and then examine the landscape attributions associated with each observer type. In the present analysis, we have elected to grant primary importance to the descriptive responses to landscape and secondary importance to other observer characteristics.

The present findings offer several directions for further psychological research. The associated characteristics of some landscape-description types display evident psychological coherence. In Type 05, for example, the pursuit of glamour sports, the extensive home range, the high priorities assigned to scenic highways and recreation, the high familiarity with the research site from the roadway, but low use familiarity, all appear to fit with the touch of landscape snobbery entailed in their unflattering description of the site. In the case of some types, the linkages between landscape descriptions and personality characteristics are less clear and warrant further investigation. Indeed, the exploration of the nature of types is an open-ended endeavor. Certainly, extensive case studies of members of each type would reward the effort they would entail. The generality of landscape descriptive styles to other sites could also be studied. Findings regarding other types point the way to more specific research. For example, the negative association of aesthetic sensitivity (as assessed by the Barron–Welsh art scale) to membership in Type 03 (who viewed the landscape as primarily beautiful–picturesque) raises the broader possibility that aesthetic sensitivity in the context of landscape may implicate quite different psychological factors than in the fine arts context.

Thus, this exploratory taxonomic analysis of landscape description illustrates the practical and scientific usefulness of a general methodological approach. Through objective modes of classification, empirically derived typologies have the capacity to integrate data bearing upon a wide variety of observer characteristics, at the same time opening up new directions of inquiry. Ultimately, of course, we must aspire to achieve a full understanding of the origin and functional relationships among the characteristics of each type.

Perception and Prediction of Scenic Resource Values of the Northeast

Ervin H. Zube, David G. Pitt, and
Thomas W. Anderson

*Ervin H. Zube is the Director of the Institute for Man and
Environment and a Professor in the Department of Landscape Architecture and Regional Planning at the University of Massachusetts.*

*David G. Pitt is an Assistant Professor and Extension
Specialist in Landscape Architecture at the University of
Maryland.*

*Thomas W. Anderson is a graduate student in landscape
architecture at the University of Massachusetts.*

THE LANDSCAPE PLANNERS' DILEMMA

The nature of many multidisciplinary planning and design activities is such that the practitioner is called upon early in the study process
to make basic conceptual and methodological
assumptions that will determine the course of
his activities for the duration of the study. Time
is provided for only minimal background research. The inevitable constraints of time and
money are a concomitant of most such endeavors. Interlocking deadlines are established
for different components of the planning program such that the meeting of these deadlines is essential if the contributions of other
planning-team members are not to be hin-
dered. Team member D is dependent upon the
contributions of team members A, B, and C
before he can start his work. Questions may be
raised as to the efficacy of the initial assumptions, but time and money constraints will tend
to reinforce the continued use of those assumptions. Given that there is also no practice
or tradition of postplanning or postconstruc-
tion evaluation, or of the professional assump-

tions relevant thereto, those initial untested assumptions become part of the "folklore" of the professions. As such they are likely to reappear with increasing frequency in future plans and designs.

The objective of this paper is to review and discuss a number of landscape perception studies that had their genesis in such a multidisciplinary planning activity and to assess the utility of those assumptions for future use. The several approaches followed in the conduct of these studies are also discussed. The planning activity that served as the research stimulus was the North Atlantic Regional Water Resources Study (NAR).[1]

The following discussion is organized in three sections: first, a brief review of the NAR and the assumptions posited in the development of the approach to landscape assessment; second, a review of a number of relatively discrete studies relating to the testing of some of the assumptions, which used a range of landscape simulation techniques; third, a discussion of a multivariant study employing both simulation and field experience.

THE NORTH ATLANTIC REGIONAL WATER RESOURCES STUDY

The NAR was a broad-brush, multidisciplinary study of the major drainage basins that empty into the North Atlantic Ocean between Canada and North Carolina, an area of 167,000 square miles (Zube, 1970; Riotte et al., this volume). The multiple objectives of the planning process were the enhancement of environmental quality, national efficiency, and regional development. The study was intended to review regional and subregional resource needs, to assess supply and demand, and to guide future development. An important component of the environmental-quality planning objective was the incorporation of planning and management recommendations specifically related to scenic resources.

Basic assumptions Basic assumptions relative to the scenic resources component — to the inventorying, classification, and evaluation of the NAR landscape — were made within the first 4 months of the 3-year work period. Questions as to the reasonableness and efficacy of these assumptions were the basis for the initial interest in a post hoc assessment and for the formulation of subsequent research questions. The assumptions were the following:

1. Scenic value is a function of relative landform elevation and diversity of land-use pattern. As relative elevation decreases in magnitude, diversity of land-use pattern increases in importance for the maintenance of high scenic value.
2. Water is a dominant visual landscape resource and almost always enhances scenic quality (an exception being pollution levels at which floating objects, discoloration, and/or odors become offensive).
3. All landscape settings (wilderness to urban or natural to man-made) have equal potential for high scenic quality as a product of landform and land-use pattern. (The NAR study did not include an analysis and evaluation of urban landscapes; however, this assumption was implicit in the study.)
4. The landscape perceptions and aesthetic values of the professional designer–planner are consonant with those of the majority of the inhabitants of the planning region and thus can serve as surrogate values.

TESTING THE ASSUMPTIONS

Over a 4-year period six studies have been conducted, addressed, all or in part, to the assumptions on landform, land-use pattern, water, naturalism, and expert versus nonexpert responses. A number of landscape-simulation techniques were employed, including line drawings, photomontages, black-and-white photographs, three-dimensional models and 35mm color transparencies. Modes of presentation for eliciting responses from these environmental displays included tachistoscopic projection, paired-comparison formats, and rank ordering.

Landform and land-use pattern The initial study (Albert, 1969) questioned the identification of landscape elements that had been used for differentiating or classifying landscapes.[2] Using a study population of 245 students, designers, engineers, and Grange members from southern New England, responses to 40 tachistoscopically projected 35mm color slides of New England suggested that the element of topography tended to be visually more dominant at a brief glance than any pattern element and that the three pattern elements most consistently recognized were forest, fields, and water.

A following study (Burns and Rundell, 1969) tested the assumption of landform and land-use diversity as critical dimensions of scenic quality. Photomontages were used in which, with the foreground held constant, five variations of middleground were created, consisting of from 65 percent open land and 35 percent forest to total forest. Each of the five variations was presented with and without a mountainous background in a paired-comparison format. The results of a random survey of the adult population of the town of Amherst ($N = 34$) tended to support the first NAR assumption. Differences in topography and in middleground pattern were related to preference. Landscapes with the mountainous background were preferred over their corollaries without the background, and landscapes with more open land, but still with a mix of open and forest, were preferred over landscapes with an all forest middleground.

The land-use diversity assumption was also tested in reference to the economic value of undeveloped residentially zoned land (Strom, 1973). It was hypothesized that land with diverse patterns of fields and trees (assumed to be more scenic) would carry a higher economic value than land with uniform or rectilinear patterns of either element.[3] A $\frac{1}{16}$ scale model was constructed to match an existing 11.9-acre parcel of land in Amherst, Massachusetts. Vegetative cover was systematically varied so as to provide six displays of varying percentages of cover and degrees of diversity in distribution pattern. Background information in the form of a written scenario, eye-level photographs (taken from the same positions for each of the variations), and a site plan were shown to each of 16 real estate appraisers in the northeast. The hypothesis was confirmed. Significantly higher appraisals were obtained for parcels with two thirds forest cover and with more diverse or complex spatial arrangements of forested and open lands.

These studies support the use of landform and land use as assessment variables and the assumption as to the qualitative influence on scenic quality. It must be noted, however, that in each case they represent contrived landscape simulations in which one or two dimensions were systematically varied. Unfortunately, the real landscape does not vary in uni- and bivariant ways but rather in multivariant ways. To identify other relevant variables or landscape dimensions, develop measurement scales, and gain an understanding of the nature of the multivariant interactions are obviously essential for explanation of responses to "real-world" scenic resources and for development of predictive capabilities.

Role of water The NAR assumption echoes a long-held belief in the significance of water as a component of scenic quality. The assumption was tested in three studies. The first used a set of line drawings in which the variables of water and topography were systematically varied (Halvorson, 1970.) Three drawings were prepared wherein the only variation was the steepness of slopes on background landforms. Each landform drawing was then duplicated with a water feature inserted in the foreground. Using a paired-comparison format, the displays were reproduced and distributed by mail to a random selection of 500 members of the American Society of Landscape Architects. The results based on a 39.2 percent ($N = 196$) return indicated consistent preference for water over nonwater scenes. Even the low topographic water scene was preferred over the moderate and high topographic nonwater scenes. In both the water and nonwater scenes, however, the moderate topographic configuration was preferred to the high.

Results obtained in a parallel study (Melillo, 1970) using black-and-white photographic prints suggest, however, a more complex landform—water relationship.[4] Landscape architects (60 professionals and students) from the northeastern United States consistently preferred landscapes with steeper topographic elements to those with more moderate topography. The kind (stream, river, or lake) or magnitude (minor or dominant) of water body present in the landscape did not appear to modify the influence of "rugged" mountainous topography on preferential ratings.

In a study of the scenic quality of the everyday rural landscape of the Northeast, using 35 mm color slides (Zube, 1973b), it was found that the presence of water was consistently related to those landscapes perceived to be of the highest scenic quality. The more rugged topographic sections of the study region were not included, however, in the landscape sample.

The results of these studies support in general the long-held assumption about the visual significance of water in the landscape. They suggest, however, that there may be some point on the landscape continuum where topography may be an overriding variable. Both elements are undoubtedly important, but their weighting may vary as the landscape context changes.

Natural/man-made dimension The implicit NAR assumption as to equal scenic values in all landscape settings suggested the addition of a natural/man-made dimension in the study of the scenic quality of the everyday rural landscape of the Northeast (Zube, 1973b). Predicted rank orders were generated for each of six sets of 35mm color slides on the basis of the combined scale values for landform, pattern, and complexity. The latter were included on the basis of the work of Wohlwill (1968) and Kaplan et al. (1972). When the landscapes were predominantly natural or consisted of natural materials such as in argicultural areas (as exemplified by three of the six sets of displays), the predicted rank-order evaluations using the NAR dimensions correlated moderately to highly with the rank orders of the seven participant subgroups. Correlation of predicted and obtained values ranged from .53 to .71, with a mean of .65. However, no significant correlation was found between the obtained rank orders and the predicted rank orders when complexity scale values were used. For the three sets of landscapes that contained one or more displays scaled as predominantly man-made, neither the NAR nor the complexity dimension was a meaningful predictor of rank-order evaluations.

These findings support those of Kaplan et al. (1972) of preferences for natural over man-made landscapes, but they do not lend support to the utility of complexity as a predictor within the natural or man-made domain. Nor do they support the implicit NAR assumption that all landscape settings (natural to man-made) have equal potential for high scenic value. A number of interpretations of these findings relating to the natural/man-made dimension are suggested, each of which merits further investigation.

1. That there is a cultural bias for natural landscapes over man-made landscapes.
2. That the man-made landscapes used in research studies to date have not included the most scenic of man's building accomplishments — that the sample of environments tested has been limited.
3. That the potential for equal scenic quality exists but has not yet been realized — that man has yet to build a landscape equal in quality to the best of nature.

Physical dimensions The importance of physical dimensions such as landform, land use, water, and naturalism to planning–design practitioners is that they can be assessed directly with the traditional tools and techniques of the profession (for example, topographic maps, aerial photographs, windshield surveys). Of greater importance to the practitioner is the use of dimensions that are understood by his constituency, be they fellow professionals on a multidisciplinary planning team, real estate appraisers, or a concerned citizen group. The striving for objectivity (R. Kaplan, this volume) on the part of planners and designers is in large part an effort to be responsive to their constituents by not hiding behind pseudoprofessional jargon and by explicating not only conclusions, but more importantly assumptions and process. In so doing it is not surprising that an approach is adopted which uses landscape dimensions that are a part of the existing professional domain.

A number of questions remain to be answered, however, in reference to the identification and utility of landscape variables or dimensions. Among them is the relative operational efficacy of these physical dimensions versus those such as complexity, mystery, coherence, and identifiability, which Wohlwill categorizes as relating to "information content" (1973b). If either are demonstrated to be more effective predictors of landscape preferences or values, it is important that they be defined precisely and that a means be found to make them operational for practitioners. Questions of scale and context also remain to be answered. Which dimensions are most useful at which scales (for example, site, neighborhood, or region)? And do the same dimensions have equal utility in all landscape settings from the Arctic to the desert?

Expert and nonexpert values The study of the everyday rural landscape of the Northeast (Zube, 1973b) also provided a comparison of landscape descriptions and evaluations by expert and nonexpert participants. Seven subgroups participated. The expert subgroup consisted of professional environmental designers ($N = 50$). The six other subgroups were natural resources students ($N = 24$), environmental design students ($N = 20$), professional resource managers ($N = 19$), technicians ($N = 19$), elementary and secondary school teachers and housewives ($N = 23$), and secretaries ($N = 30$). Twenty-seven 35mm color slides divided into six sets (four or five slides each) were used in paired comparison. Eighteen of the slides were of "real-world" landscapes and nine were of colored landscape drawings — all representative of the northeastern landscape.

The correlation between the seven subgroups on scenic evaluation of all 27 landscapes ranged from .43 (environmental design students and secretaries) to .91 (resource managers and teachers). The mean correlation for the 21 between-group associations was .77.

Even higher degrees of association were found in describing two of the "real-world" landscapes and two of the drawings with the use of 14 bipolar semantic scales (for example, urban–rural, beautiful–ugly, obvious–mysterious). Between-group correlations ranged from .58 (environmental design students and secretaries) to .96 (professional environmental designers and teachers), with a mean correlation for the 21 between-group associations of .85. Overall there was generally high agreement between the seven subgroups on both landscape evaluation and description. Similar indications of agreement between experts and nonexperts have been found in a number of other studies (Zube, Pitt, and Anderson, 1974; Craik, 1972a; Coughlin and Goldstein, 1970; Fines, 1968).

A MULTIVARIANT APPROACH

Several very broad issues can be distilled from the work reported on thus far. Among them are the efficacy of the use of simulation for landscape assessment, the extent of intergroup agreement on a range of landscape-assessment questions, and the adequacy of physical dimensions as predictors of scenic quality. A multivariant study was designed with the following objectives to address these issues (Zube, Pitt, and Anderson, 1974)[5]:

1. To investigate the extent of agreement between subjects on the evaluation and description of different landscapes when using both field experience and photographic representations for eliciting evaluative and descriptive responses to specific landscape settings.
2. To identify landscape dimensions hypothesized to be determinants of scenic resource values and which can be measured

by using aerial photography and topographic maps.
3. To analyze, for a given set of rural landscapes, the relationships between subjects' evaluative responses and the quantified dimensions.

The study involved two modes of landscape experience and two categories of landscapes. The two modes were the in-field experiencing of landscape and the use of color photography as a surrogate for in-field experience. The two landscape categories were landscape views (small sample) to be used for in-field experience and to be depicted in color panoramic photographic simulations, and landscape views (large sample) to be used for studying the relationship of values to dimensions and to be depicted in color, wide-angle photographic simulation.

The study landscape was the nonurban sections of the southern half of the Connecticut River Valley within Connecticut and Massachusetts. Colored photographic coverage was systematically obtained so as to document the range of nonurban landscape settings found within the entire two-state study area. Fifty-six views (large sample) were selected as representative of the range of identified landscape settings (Figure 1). Eight (small sample) of the 56 views in Suffield, Connecticut (Figure 2), representing a landscape diversity ranging from a New England village center through suburban and strip development to working farms and forest areas, were selected for detailed study and as the location for the field study.

Participants Thirteen subgroups totaling 307 subjects participated in the study. Five subgroups participated in the field portion of the study and eight in the nonfield portion as follows:

Field Study Subgroups		*Nonfield Study Subgroups*	
Pretest, residents of Amherst, Mass.	26	Professional engineers	30
Adult residents of Suffield, Conn.	22	Hartford center-city residents	11
Professional environmental designers	21	Professional environmental designers	24
Professional environmentalists	27	Professional environmentalists	33
Secretarial and clerical office workers	27	Professional and clerical office workers	28
		Undergraduate design students	23
		Undergraduate psychology students	18
		High school students	17
	123		184

Modes of response The subjects were asked to describe and evaluate each of the eight small-sample views using semantic scales and a landscape feature checklist, to rank order the panoramic photographs, and to Q-sort the 56 photographs on the basis of scenic quality. Field subjects had one additional evaluative–preferential assessment task. The tasks performed by the field and nonfield subgroups are summarized in Table 1. The discussion that follows will draw upon data from tasks 1, 3, 4, and 5 only.

Agreement on landscape description and evaluation The responses of each subgroup were correlated with those of every other subgroup for each response mode (for example, semantic scales, rank order, and Q-sort). Table 3 illustrates the consistently high and generally impressive degrees of association on all modes; 82 percent of all correlations are at the .80 level or higher. The two groups of designers, field and nonfield, correlated at the .84 level or higher on the use of the semantic scales with every group except Hartford center-city residents. Similar patterns of association are found for the designers or experts on the panoramic and Q-sort modes.

The most striking pattern, however, is that the black Hartford center-city subgroup, for each set of values, consistently exhibits the lowest degree of association with all other subgroups. Another much less striking but nevertheless obvious pattern is apparent on the Q-sort values. Excluding the Hartford center-city subgroup, 8 of the remaining 66 correlations are below .80. All these involve the field secretarial group.

These findings parallel those cited previously on the congruence of expert and nonexpert or users' values. They also suggest similar congruence between field and simulation evaluations. The findings on the Hartford center-city group suggest a note of caution, however. The data reported indicate a potentially important difference in landscape evaluation. The nature of the difference is not affective but one of magnitude on the semantic scales. The Hartford subgroup did not disagree with the other subgroups in terms of whether a landscape registered to the right or left of the midpoint on different scales, but they did vary considerably in terms of magnitude. Evaluative scales were less positively endorsed. And it appears that man-made structures, regardless of landscape context, were viewed more favorably. Although there were only 11 subjects in this group, the differences in response patterns points up the need for additional study.

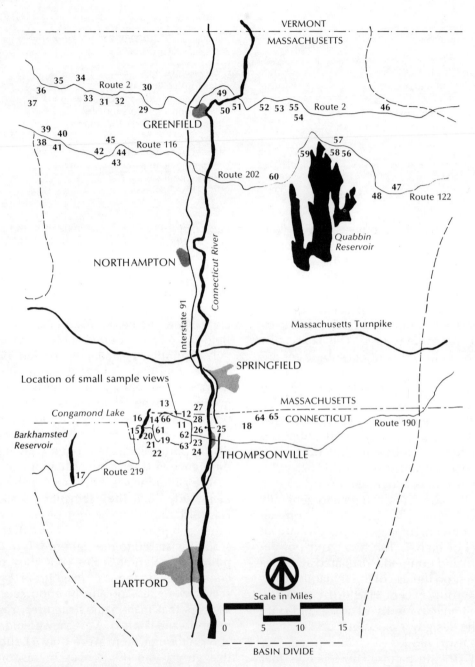

Figure 1
Landscape settings.

Table 1
Field and Nonfield Responses

Field	Nonfield
1. Visit eight view stations in Suffield and rate on 18 seven-point semantic scales (Table 2).	1. Study panoramic photographs of eight view stations in Suffield and rate on 18 seven-point semantic scales (Table 2).
2. Complete a landscape-feature checklist at each of the eight view stations.	2. Complete a landscape-feature checklist for each of the eight panoramic photographs.
3. Evaluate scenic quality and assess preference for recreational, residential, and travel use for each of nine landscape sections between the eight view stations.	3. Rank order eight panoramic photographs of Suffield view stations according to scenic quality.
4. Rank order eight panoramic photographs of Suffield view stations according to scenic quality.	4. Sort 56 views into seven scenic quality categories distributed 3–7–11–14–11–7–3.
5. Sort 56 views into seven scenic-quality categories distributed 3–7–11–14–11–7–3.	

These findings, inconclusive as they are, suggest the possibility of cultural and/or socioeconomic factors influencing landscape perception. They also suggest, rather convincingly, that profession — be it engineer, designer, environmentalist, resource manager, or teacher — does not seem to be strongly related to landscape perception.

One more issue must be raised in reference to the discussion of expert and nonexpert values: the distinction between existing and proposed landscapes. All the studies cited previously demonstrated agreement only on the evaluation of existing landscapes. As such they do not necessarily provide a basis for assuming similar levels of congruence on proposed changes in the landscape. Whether or not nonexperts would agree with the experts on

the aesthetic values of a proposed change in the landscape is yet to be tested. For example, the adult citizens of Suffied, Connecticut, agreed with experts and nonresidents of their town on the scenic evaluation of the eight view stations. Whether such apparent objectivity would be maintained by residents and nonresidents or experts and nonexperts on proposed changes that could impinge directly on the residents and indirectly or not at all on others is an interesting question. Equally challenging is the related question of the influence of the natural/man-made dichotomy: is it the same for all subgroups and are all man-induced changes in the landscape perceived as yielding more man-made and/or less scenic landscapes?

Evaluation or preference The field portion of this study provided an opportunity to address, in a modest way, the issue of a potential distinction between preference and evaluation. The practical and theoretical distinctions between landscape evaluation and landscape preference have been raised in a number of

Figure 2
Eight view stations in Suffield, Connecticut, that were used for field study. The mean values were obtained from the rank orderings of all subjects (*N* = 123) who participated in the field study.

recent publications (Craik, 1972b; Zube, 1973b). Are there differences among an individual or a group appraisal of the scenic quality of a landscape (an evaluative decision), the appraisal of that same landscape as one which is liked or disliked as scenery, and the appraisal of it as a place in which to recreate, travel, or live (a preferential decision)? If there is a distinction, it could have considerable practical value in explaining landscape planning and

View Station No. 1, Mean 4.81

View Station No. 2, Mean 6.21

View Station No. 3, Mean 6.62

View Station No. 4, Mean 4.97

management decisions to the lay public (Craik, 1972b:258). Such a distinction could also be of importance in dealing with environmental-impact assessment for which preferential appraisals could be a major factor in one's perceptions of proposed changes. The planner might find considerable agreement on the evaluation of the existing site and possibly of the potential aesthetic impact of a proposed project, but considerable disagreement on the appraisal of preferences for the use of that same landscape.

In attempting to probe this question, each subject in the field portion of the study was asked to indicate his or her preference and evaluation for each of nine sections of the landscape as they traveled between view stations. Using a five-point scale (very low–low–moderate–high–very high), subjects responsed to four questions at each section:

View Station No. 5, Mean 5.96

View Station No. 6, Mean 3.86

View Station No. 7, Mean 1.51

View Station No. 8, Mean 2.07

Table 2
Landscape Description and Evaluation Scales

Common	1 : 2 : 3 : 4 : 5 : 6 : 7 Unusual
Angular	1 : 2 : 3 : 4 : 5 : 6 : 7 Rounded
Like	1 : 2 : 3 : 4 : 5 : 6 : 7 Dislike
High scenic value	1 : 2 : 3 : 4 : 5 : 6 : 7 Low scenic value
Inviting	1 : 2 : 3 : 4 : 5 : 6 : 7 Uninviting
Bright	1 : 2 : 3 : 4 : 5 : 6 : 7 Dull
Smooth	1 : 2 : 3 : 4 : 5 : 6 : 7 Rough
Closed	1 : 2 : 3 : 4 : 5 : 6 : 7 Open
Varied	1 : 2 : 3 : 4 : 5 : 6 : 7 Monotonous
Pleasant	1 : 2 : 3 : 4 : 5 : 6 : 7 Unpleasant
Colorless	1 : 2 : 3 : 4 : 5 : 6 : 7 Colorful
Tidy	1 : 2 : 3 : 4 : 5 : 6 : 7 Untidy
Boring	1 : 2 : 3 : 4 : 5 : 6 : 7 Interesting
Obvious	1 : 2 : 3 : 4 : 5 : 6 : 7 Mysterious
Beautiful	1 : 2 : 3 : 4 : 5 : 6 : 7 Ugly
Hard	1 : 2 : 3 : 4 : 5 : 6 : 7 Soft
Light	1 : 2 : 3 : 4 : 5 : 6 : 7 Dark
Natural	1 : 2 : 3 : 4 : 5 : 6 : 7 Man-made

1. How strongly would you like to have a permanent residence in the landscape you just traveled through?
2. How strongly would you like to participate in outdoor recreation activities in the landscape you just traveled through?
3. How strongly would you like to pass through the landscape and enjoy the scenery?
4. How would you rate the scenic quality of the landscape you just traveled through?

Two of the eighteen semantic scales used at each of the eight small-sample views were also intended to tap the potential distinction between preference and evaluation. Whereas three of the between-view questions were related to the expression of preference for use, the semantic scale, like–dislike, was intended to tap preference as an appreciative or agreeableness response. The evaluative scale used was high scenic value–low scenic value.

Responses to the two semantic scales suggest that they are highly associated with a between-scale correlation of .80 for all subjects. The between-group variance ratios for the high scenic value–low scenic value scale were statistically significant ($p < .05$) at only five of the eight small-sample views. For like–dislike, the between-group variance ratios were statistically significant at seven of the eight views.

Two-way analysis of variance of the responses of the five field subgroups to the four questions indicated significant differences between both the groups and the questions. The subgroups did not agree on their responses to the questions, and there were significant differences between preferences for use and scenic evaluation. Or put another way, the four questions were not dealing with the same issue.

The variance between responses to the four questions at each sequence was analyzed using Duncan's multiple range test for the entire

Table 3

Correlation Coefficient (Pearson r)	Frequency of Between-Group Correlations (N = 78) for Three Response Modes		
	Semantic Scales	Panoramic	Q-Sort
.90–1.00	44	66	41
.80– .89	24	—	17
.70– .79	3[a]	1[a]	8[b]
.60– .69	8[a]	6[a]	—
.50– .59	1[a]	4[a]	1[a]
.40– .49	—	1[a]	—
.30– .39	—	—	5[a]
.20– .29	—	—	5[a]
.10– .19	—	—	1[a]

$r = .21, p = .01.$
[a] Hartford center-city subgroups.
[b] Field secretarial subgroup.

field population. Table 4 illustrates that the evaluation question, number 4, had the highest frequency of agreement with all other questions. Had there been agreement on the questions at every sequence, the cell values in Table 4 would equal nine. Questions 1 (preference for residential use) and 4 agreed at six sequences, and questions 2 (preference for outdoor recreation) and 4 agreed at seven sequences. It is interesting that the three preferential questions (1, 2, and 3 — preference for traveling through) agreed at only three sequences. Apparently, the preference questions, by themselves, are more closely related to the evaluation question than they are to themselves.

Table 5 is a further indication of only modest relationships among the four questions. Averaging the correlations across all nine between-view sequences yielded values ranging from .56 to .62.

There are a number of possible factors that enter into the preference–evaluation question: preference for a favored use or uses of a landscape; preference as an indication of the agreeableness or of one's appreciativeness of a landscape; and evaluation of a landscape as an aesthetic judgment. These findings suggest that there is considerable agreement between the assessment of the agreeableness or appreciation for a landscape and an evaluative judgment. They also indicate that the agree-

Table 4
Frequency of Interquestion Agreement

Question	1	2	3	4
1 (reside)	—	3	1	6
2 (recreate)		—	3	7
3 (travel)			—	1
4 (scenic value)				—

Table 5
Between-Question Correlations

Question	1	2	3	4
1 (reside)	—	.56	.57	.62
2 (recreate)		—	.60	.58
3 (travel)			—	.61
4 (scenic value)				—

ment between preferences for specific uses and between those uses and evaluative judgments is considerably less. A possible explanation for these differences is that of the personal context within which the decision for preference for use must be made. Whereas the evaluative and like–dislike decision may be made within the broader context of a cultural norm for scenic value, the preference for use decision may be more closely related to and influenced by the individual's personal attitudes toward life style and his or her actual recreational and residential behavioral patterns.

Stimulation versus field experience How do responses obtained as a result of experiencing landscapes directly compare with those obtained using simulations (colored photographs) in lieu of experience?

Evaluative responses were compared for the total field population (N = 123, five subgroups) and the total nonfield population (N = 184, eight subgroups) by using mean scores for the high scenic value–low scenic value semantic scale, mean scores for the rank ordering of the small-sample panoramics, and mean scores obtained for the eight Suffield views contained in the Q-sort of the total field of 56 views.

Mean values for each of the eight Suffield views were obtained for each of the three tasks and served as the basis for three sets of scenic-value rank orders. Table 6 indicates the

Table 6
Rank-Order Correlation[a] of Eight Views by Mode of Analysis and Group

	Field			Nonfield		
	SS	PA	QS	SS	PA	QS
Field:						
Semantic scale (SS)	—	.88	.76	.95	.92	.89
Panoramics (PA)		—	.93	.92	.92	.97
Q-sort (QS)			—	.92	.92	.97
Nonfield:						
Semantic scale (SS)				—	.99	.97
Panoramics (PA)					—	.97
Q-sort (QS)						—

[a] Spearman *r*.

rank-order correlation of the eight small-sample views by mode and by group. The results are generally impressive and suggest considerable consistency across modes and groups using field and simulation stimuli.

Table 7 indicates the generally high correlation between field and nonfield groups on the use of all 18 semantic scales at each of the eight

Table 7
Field–Nonfield Correlation on Semantic Scale Means at Each View

View	*r*[a]
1	.98
2	.98
3	.99
4	.95
5	.81
6	.68
7	.99
8	.97

[a] Pearson *r*.

view stations. Two-way analysis of variance of semantic-scale responses by field and nonfield groups at each of the stations indicates a significant difference (.05 level) between the groups at only one of the eight.

Utility of simulation Each study reported on thus far employed some technique of environmental simulation as a surrogate for field experiences. Each technique carries with it certain inherent advantages and disadvantages. For example, drawings, photomontages, and models provide the ability to control variance on specific dimensions in the landscape display. They are expensive to produce, but still considerably less expensive than transporting subjects to viewing stations in the landscape. However, one must question whether these techniques, frequently used to explain the essence of landscape designs and plans, are effective agents of communication in that the responses they elicit can be assumed to be reflective of the real world. For example, when descriptive responses to slides of real-world landscapes and to drawings that were intended to be mirror images of the real-world landscapes were analyzed, only one group (environmental design students) out of seven perceived the drawings as even modestly approximating their counterparts (Zube, 1973b).

There are indications, however, that for nondesigners, for those individuals who are not graphically oriented in their educational or occupational pursuits, the best mode is the one most closely approximating reality. The benefits gained by the ability to control variance in drawings may only be imagined if subjects are not able to relate those drawings to the real landscape. The more promising path to pursue in the future appears to be that of using photography as the closest approximation of reality (Shafer and Richards, 1971) and, where possible, validating those findings by field studies. Certainly, the findings from the latest study provide considerable encouragement as to the efficacy of using colored photographic prints for eliciting evaluative responses to the Connecticut River Valley landscape.

Landscape dimensions A number of landscape characteristics were investigated that have been hypothesized in the research literature and in previous planning studies to be highly correlated with scenic quality (Fabos, 1973; Zube, 1973a; Litton, 1968, Linton, 1968; Greene, 1972; Kiemstedt, 1971; Smardon, this volume). Twenty-three dimensions were developed from these characteristics. The dimensions can be measured using existing map and aerial-photographic sources. They are quantifiable and can be depicted in map format. The measurement techniques for the dimensions have been based, whenever possible, on the mensuration techniques of the planning, hydrology, geomorphology, and forestry professions. Several of the dimensions also required psychometric scaling techniques. The major categories and related dimensions are the following:

Landform
  Relative relief ratio: the range of vertical elevations (based on sample points) per unit area.
  Absolute relative relief: the range of vertical elevations (based on sample points) within the view area.
  Mean slope distribution: the mean of a random sample of slopes, the steepness of landform.
  Topographic texture: the degree of dissection of the land surface, the drainage density.
  Ruggedness number: the roughness of landform based on absolute relative relief, mean slope, and topographic texture.
  Spatial definition index: the amount of enclosure created by landform.
Land use
  Land-use diversity: the relative areal distribution of land uses within the view.
  Naturalism index: the degree of naturalism as indicated by land use.
  Percentage tree cover: the amount of land covered by trees per unit area.
Edges
  Land-use edge density: the amount of edge created by adjacent land uses per unit area.

  Land-use edge variety: the variety of land uses as indicated by the number of edge types per view.
  Land-use compatibility: an indication of the visual congruence of adjacent land uses.
Contrast
  Height contrast: the difference in height of the dominant elements of adjacent land uses.
  Grain contrast: the difference in the size of the individual elements of adjacent land uses.
  Spacing contrast: the difference in the spatial distribution of the elements of adjacent land uses.
  Evenness contrast: the difference in size, distribution, and height of elements of adjacent land uses.
  Naturalism contrast: the difference in naturalism of adjacent land uses.
Water
  Water-edge density: the amount of land/water edge per unit area.
  Percentage water area: the amount of surface water per unit area.
View
  Area of view: the size of the view area.
  Length of view: the maximum length of view.
  Viewer position: the relative vertical position of the viewer to the view.

Quantitative values were obtained for each of these dimensions for each of the 56 view stations using topographic maps and land-use data from current (1971) aerial photography. The intercorrelation of the 23 dimensions was analyzed and the affective value of each of the dimensions was ascertained — whether it was negatively or positively related to scenic resource values. The findings are as follows:

1. Essentially all of the landform dimensions are positively related to the scenic resource values, which suggests that, generally, as landform becomes more rugged and more pronounced scenic resource value increases.
2. Land-use diversity and land-use edge variety are both negatively related to scenic resource value, which suggests that as these dimensions increase scenic resource value decreases.
3. Naturalism index and percentage of tree cover are both positively related to scenic

resource value, which suggests that as an area becomes more natural or more tree covered its scenic resource value increases.

4. Land-use compatibility is negatively related to scenic resource value, which suggests that as adjacent land uses become more compatible scenic resource value increases.

5. Land-use edge density varies in relationship, but is generally positively related when cubed. This suggests that at the extremes of the dimensions as edge density increases scenic resource value increases, but in the midrange the effect is indeterminate.

6. Height contrast is positively related to scenic resource value, which suggests that as height contrast increases scenic resource values increase. Grain, spacing, evenness, and naturalism contrast are negatively related, which suggests that as these dimensions increase scenic resource value decreases.

7. The two water dimensions are positively related to scenic resource value. As water area or water edge increases, scenic resource value increases.

8. The two size-of-view dimensions are positively related to scenic resource value, which suggests that as area or length of view increases scenic resource value increases.

9. Viewer position was negatively related to scenic resource value, which suggests that the viewer inferior position enhances scenic quality more than the viewer superior position.

In most cases these findings support our intuitive feelings about the dimensions. The land-use diversity and land-use edge variety findings tend, however, to run counter to intuition. A possible explanation of this seemingly anomalous pattern may be that the diversity dimensions are related to landscape context and might be positively related if the diversity were measured, for example, within a forest landscape or a farm landscape. The interjection of a small subdivision into the context of a forest or agricultural landscape may add to diversity and detract from scenic value. It must also be pointed out that these findings are based on a limited sample (56) of the landscape of the Northeast.

Toward a predictive model Analysis of the distribution of values for each of the 23 dimensions indicated that the 56 view stations were not a representative sample of all possible values for the 23 dimensions. After stratifying the sites on the basis of the area of view, including only those 46 views where the view area was smaller than 65 acres (.10 square mile), and using only 14 dimensions, the results of regression analysis explained 65.6 percent of the variance. The top six dimensions accounted for 61.4 percent of the variance. Each dimension accounted for approximately 3 percent or more of the variance.

Land-use compatibility	27.5
Absolute relative relief	13.8
Height contrast	8.9
Water-edge density	5.5
Naturalism contrast	2.9
Land-use edge variety	2.8
	61.4

The level of explanation was further increased to 80.2 percent by using the reduced number of dimensions (14) and stratifying the views such that only the 29 most natural were included. The top six dimensions, each of which accounted for 5 percent or more of the variance, accounted for 69.0 percent.

Grain contrast	23.7
Mean slope	16.9
Length of view	9.7
Spatial definition	7.4
Area of view	6.5
Absolute relative relief	4.8
	69.0

SUMMARY

The seven studies that have been presented and discussed tend to support the majority of the initial NAR assumptions; more importantly, they also illustrate the complexity of the problem under consideration. In three cases the findings are congruent with the general thrust of the assumptions, but also indicate that there are confounding factors.

The landform/land use and water assumptions were demonstrated in a number of ways to be related to scenic quality. But it has also been demonstrated that the issue of context is very important. The context issue was addressed in reference to the man-made/naturalism question and in reference to scale. The findings from the regression analyses of the last study suggest that better prediction may be possible if attention is given to stratifying the landscape on the basis of the scale of the view area and/or on the extent of naturalism or of the impact of man.

All the studies reported on were confined to the Northeast and involved subjects from the same region. The question of context can also be extended to encompass geographic considerations. Are the assumptions and dimensions valid across geographic landscapes and populations?

The use of physical dimensions in scenic resource assessment has been supported, but the importance of better measurement techniques has also been demonstrated. There is some evidence that the relative importance of dimensions is also influenced by landscape context. That is, the predictive value of the dimension may change as the context changes. Some of the same categories of dimensions were involved in both of the regression analyses in the last study, but the specific dimensions were different.

The assumption of the congruence of the experts' values with the nonexperts' values was addressed in a number of ways. In general, the assumption was supported, with two potentially important exceptions. One is in the findings on the black center-city residents, which suggests a potential cultural and/or socioeconomic difference in landscape perception. The second is that, although the experts' assessment of the aesthetic value of a landscape may be congruent with other sectors of society, this is not necessarily true for the experts' preferential assessment of the use of the landscape.

A number of simulation techniques were employed in the studies. However, only the last study attempted to assess the efficacy of replacing the real-world experience with a surrogate experience. The findings are generally impressive, at least in reference to the use of color, wide-angle photography for assessing scenic resource values.

In summary, three of the assumptions were supported and the fourth, that all landscape settings have equal potential for high scenic quality, was not. In each case, however, qualifications on the assumptions were identified and a set of questions posed to guide the next iteration of research and practice.

NOTES

1. The North Atlantic Regional Water Resources Study of Visual and Cultural Environment was conducted by Research Planning and Design Associates, Inc., of Amherst, Massachusetts, under contract with the National Park Service with Ervin H. Zube as study manager.
2. Study conducted by John Albert while serving on a U.S. Army Corps of Engineers graduate internship.
3. Study supported by the U.S. Forest Service, Northeastern Forest Experiment Station, Amherst, Massachusetts.
4. Both the Halvorson and Mellilo studies were supported by a grant from Warner Burns Toan and Lunde, Architects of New York, New York.
5. Study supported by a grant from the Northeast Utilities Service Company of Hartford, Connecticut.

Application of a Landscape-Preference Model to Land Management

Robert O. Brush and Elwood L. Shafer

The regional planner's ability to recommend the right decisions about developing and utilizing, or retaining and protecting, natural landscapes depends a great deal on the public's reaction to natural scenic beauty. Predicting people's preferences for scenic landscapes is not a simple matter, but the landscape-preference model described in this chapter provides a straightforward procedure for estimating public reaction. By adding the perimeter and area measurements of certain landscape features, a landscape-preference score can be computed. Landscape-preference scores change as features in the landscape change, and decision makers can use this information to plan and manage natural landscapes for optimum scenic quality.

DEVELOPMENT OF THE MODEL

The following is a brief explanation of how the model was developed, what it involves, and how it was tested in previous research.

Robert O. Brush is a Research Landscape Architect with the Pinchot Institute of Environmental Forestry Research, U.S. Department of Agriculture–Forest Service in the Amherst, Massachusetts, field unit.

Elwood L. Shafer is Principal Recreation Scientist, U.S. Department of Agriculture–Forest Service, Washington, D.C. He was formerly Director of the Pinchot Institute of Environmental Forestry, U.S. Department of Agriculture–Forest Service, Northeastern Forest Experiment Station, Upper Darby, Pennsylvania.

Initial Experiment

Using the methodology and experimental material described by Shafer et al. (1969), interviewers measured the scenic perceptions of Adirondack campers. In the interview, a random sample of 250 campers was asked to rank preferences for one hundred 8- by 10-inch black-and-white photographs of landscapes. The survey provided a landscape-preference index number (or score) for each photograph. Theoretically, preference scores could range from 50 for the *most* preferred to 250 for the *least* preferred scene. Regression analysis indicated that a scene's preference score was related to the areas or perimeter measurements of six landscape features in the photograph.

Landscape Zones

Before the six landscape features used in the model can be measured, a photograph of a scene must be separated into three zones: an immediate zone in which the individual leaves of trees and shrubs are discernible; an intermediate zone in which only the forms of trees and shrubs are discernible; and a *distant* zone in which the forms of individual trees cannot be distinguished (Figures 1A and B). The model uses measurements of the area or perimeter of *major vegetation*, such as trees and shrubs; *nonvegetation*, such as exposed ground, snowfields, and grasses, and *water*, including streams, lakes, and waterfalls.

Field Tests

Subsequent testing demonstrated that the regression model's predicted landscape-preference scores were highly correlated with observed preference scores for landscape photographs — not only in other parts of the United States (other than the Adirondacks), but also in Scotland (Shafer and Mietz, 1970; Shafer and Tooby, 1973).

THE MODEL

Regression Equation

The landscape-preference model, with an R^2 of .66, is

$$Y = 184.8 - 0.5436X_1 - 0.09298X_2 \\ + 0.002069\,(X_1 \cdot X_3) + 0.0005538\,(X_1 \cdot X_4) \\ - 0.002596\,(X_3 \cdot X_5) + 0.001634\,(X_2 \cdot X_6) \\ - 0.0008441\,(X_4 \cdot X_6) - 0.0004131(X_4 \cdot X_5) \\ + 0.0006666X_1^2 + 0.0001327X_5^2$$

where Y = preference score (the lower the score, the more preferred the scene)

X_1 = perimeter of immediate vegetation — section of the photo where characteristics of individual leaves and bark of trees and shrubs (not grass) are easily distinguishable

X_2 = perimeter of intermediate nonvegetation — section of the photo where prominent features of nonvegetation (including grass) are visible, but not in the fine detail found in immediate zone

X_3 = perimeter of distant vegetation — section of the photo where only the broad outlines of vegetation shapes are distinguishable, but no details are visible

X_4 = area of intermediate vegetation — section of the photo where vegetation is visible but not in fine detail found in the immediate vegetation zone

X_5 = area of any kind of water — section of photo that includes water

X_6 = area of distant nonvegetation — section of the photo where shapes of nonvegetation cannot be distinguished

Measurement of Variables

The model's six predictor variables are measured on a photograph by laying over the photo a transparent $\frac{1}{4}$-inch grid. Perimeter measurements are obtained by counting the number of sides of grid squares that enclose each particular landscape element. Area measurements are obtained by counting the number of grid squares that cover the landscape feature in a particular zone (Figure 1B). A more detailed stepwise procedure for using the grid system to measure each variable used in the equation is described elsewhere (Shafer and Mietz, 1970).

Restrictions

When using the model, at least three points should be kept in mind. First, the value of any variable must not exceed the maximum value that occurred in the 100 original photographs. Violating this rule could force the model to produce spurious results.

Second, the model should not be applied to scenes that include prominent buildings, roadways, or other man-made structures, because these features were deliberately excluded from the original photographs on which the model is based.

Third, the model should not be used to evaluate the effect of any landscape element that does not occupy more than half the area of one $\frac{1}{4}$-inch grid square.

APPLICATION OF THE MODEL TO INDIVIDUAL LANDSCAPES

To illustrate how the model can be used in land management and planning decisions, we selected three very different scenes from the original 100 photographs used to develop the model (Figures 1A, 2A, and 3A). For each of the three scenes we gradually changed the amount and composition of the various landscape features, and determined, by use of the model, the corresponding landscape-preference scores. On the basis of the resulting scores, the most appropriate landscape-management procedures are recommended for each scene.

The types and degrees of modifications introduced in the three scenes represent only a few of the many possible changes, and do not include related economic and social considerations. Our principal aim in presenting the three examples is simply to show how to apply the model, and how the results can be used to make decisions over a wide range of resource-management conditions.

Throughout these three examples, remember that the higher the preference score, the lower the scenic quality. Thus, when a change is made in the landscape features that increases the model's predicted score, the scenic quality is reduced. Conversely, the lower the preference score, the higher the scenic quality.

Farmland Scene

The first scene of Iowa farmland contains low, rolling hills, with rows of trees separating a patchwork of fields and pastures, with the preference score $Y = 155$ (Figure 1A).

Perimeter of immediate vegetation If the perimeter of immediate vegetation (X_1) that exists in the scene is decreased gradually from 200 to 0 grid-square sides, scenic quality decreases by 14 percent to a preference score of

177. If the perimeter of immediate vegetation is increased somewhat in the original scene, the preference score does not change noticeably (Figure 1C).

Therefore, our first management recommendation for this scene is to maintain or increase the present perimeter of 200 grid-square edges of immediate vegetation.

Area of intermediate vegetation If a reforestation program, for example, were implemented in the intermediate zone, causing the area of intermediate vegetation (X_4) to increase, scenic quality would steadily decrease. On the other hand, if the present 188 grid squares of intermediate vegetation were reduced to 0, the scenic quality would increase (by 8 percent) to a score of 143 (Figure 1D).

The second management recommendation for this scene is to eliminate tree cover in the intermediate zone and replace with fields or pasture.

Area of Water There is no water in the present scene. Suppose, however, that regional planners were considering creating a lake (X_5) on this site. A lake that occupied 108 grid squares in this scene would create a dramatic positive shift of 23 percent in scenic quality; the preference score would shift from 155 to 119 (Figure 1E).

The management recommendation is thus to establish the proposed lake in the valley.

Area of distant nonvegetation The fields and woodland extend into the distant zone, where about two thirds of the area is vegetation. If fields in the distant zone of the original scene were permitted to revert to woodlands, thus causing a decrease in the area of distant nonvegetation (X_6), the scenic quality would remain essentially unchanged. However, if additional clearings were made in the distant zone of the original scene, abrupt decreases would occur in the predicted scenic quality (Figure 1F).

The recommendation is to permit vegetation to encroach in the distant zone or retain vegetation in its present condition in the zone.

Other variables also affected In each change described thus far in the farmland scene (and in scenes to follow), remember that the values of all other variables in the model (besides those variables shown in Figures 1C through 1F) may also change. For example, each time the perimeter of immediate vegetation (X_1) is changed, the values of many of the other variables need to be changed before the model is used to compute the resulting landscape-preference score.

Summary of recommendations Based on the predicted preference scores resulting from the changes discussed for the farmland scene (Figures 1C through 1F), management decision priorities and optimum $\frac{1}{4}$-inch grid measurement limits can be assigned to the landscape features involved:

Decision Priority	Landscape Features	Optimum Grid Squares	Predicted Scenic Preference Score
1	Area of water	108	119
2	Area of intermediate vegetation	0	143
3	No change	—	155

These summary recommendations assume that in the final decision only one of the four landscape conditions will be changed. If more than one kind of landscape change is anticipated, new preference scores need to be computed from the model. The same constraint holds for the next two scenes.

Recall also that any one predicted preference score is in relation to a wide range of possible scores for many types of landscapes throughout the United States. Therefore, if landscape changes improve a scene's score by 10 percent, for example, the improvement may be even more relevant when considered in terms of the amount of change possible within the affected landscape region. In such cases you should *not* evaluate the landscape score change in relation to the total range of possible landscape scores throughout the country.

In this context, *regional* landscape-preference models may be more useful than the general model presented in this paper. Regional models could be developed by the method described by Shafer et al. (1969).

Ridge and Valley Scene

The second scene, from northern Georgia, comprises a broad, open valley abutting a steep, wooded ridge with the preference score of $Y = 178$ (Figure 2A).

Perimeter of immediate vegetation If the perimeter of immediate vegetation (X_1) is increased from 0 to 202 grid-square sides, the preference score changes to 159, an 11 percent increase in scenic quality. When the value of X_1 is increased further, the scene loses some of its aesthetic appeal (Figure 2B).

Therefore, frame the scene by encouraging the growth of trees and shrubs in the foreground up to a maximum measurement of 202 grid-square sides for the perimeter of immediate vegetation.

Area of intermediate vegetation When the area of trees in the intermediate zone (X_4) is reduced from 390 to 191 grid squares, the predicted preference score changes to 161, an improvement in scenic quality of 10 percent (Figure 2B). Any further reduction in intermediate vegetation diminishes scenic quality.

The recommendation then is to reduce the area of intermediate-zone tree cover to 191 grid squares.

Area of water If a lake were created that oc-

cupied 183 grid squares in the intermediate zone, the predicted scenic preference score would change to 117, a 34 percent improvement over the initial preference score.

Therefore, create a lake in the intermediate zone with a measurement of at least 183 grid squares.

Area of distant nonvegetation If openings were made in the distant-zone forest cover that amounted to 44 grid squares, the preference score would improve by 5 percent (Figure 2B).

The recommendation then is to remove at least 44 grid squares of tree cover in the distant zone.

Summary of recommendations When the results of all proposed landscape changes are plotted on one graph, management decision priorities and associated ¼-inch grid measurement limits can be summarized fairly easily. Decision information for the ridge and valley scene are summarized from Figure 2B as follows:

Decision Priority	Landscape Features	Optimum Grid Squares	Predicted Scenic Preference Score
1	Area of water	183	117
2	Perimeter of immediate vegetation	202	159
3	Area of intermediate vegetation	191	161
4	Area of distant nonvegetation	44	169
5	No change	—	178

Figure 1
(A) Farmland scene; (B) separated into landscape zones by use of a grid. (C) Changes in the scene's preference score are shown for corresponding changes in perimeter of immediate vegetation; (D) area of intermediate vegetation; (E) area of water; and (F) area of distant nonvegetation. Asterisk in each graph marks the value of the measurement in the present scene.

A

B

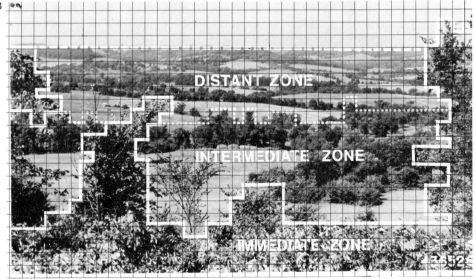

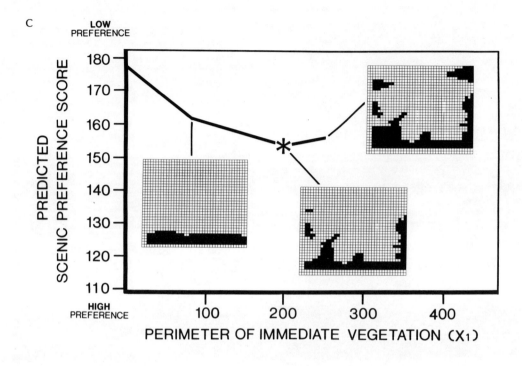

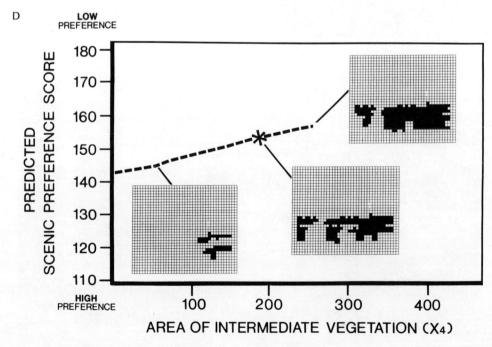

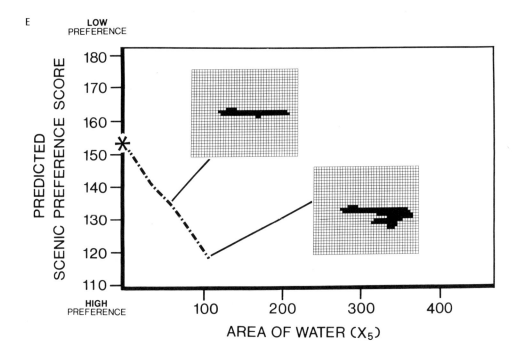

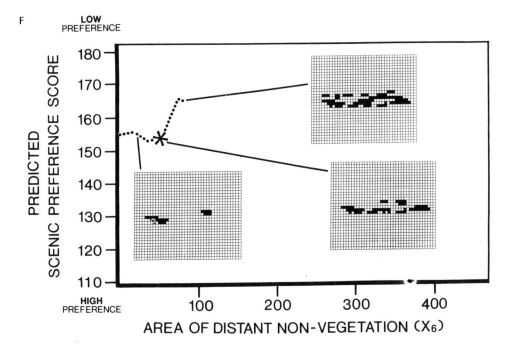

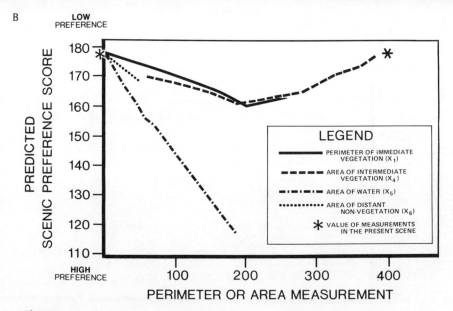

Figure 2
(A) Ridge and valley scene. (B) Changes in the scene's preference score are shown for corresponding changes in certain landscape features.

A

B

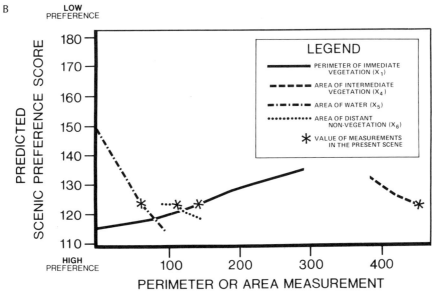

Figure 3
(A) Wildland scene. (B) Changes in the scene's preference score are shown for corresponding changes in certain landscape features.

Wildland Scene

The third scene includes a snowcapped peak, a lake, an alpine meadow, and a coniferous forest in Washington with the preference score of $Y = 124$ (Figure 3A).

Perimeter of immediate vegetation If more immediate foliage is allowed to frame the view, the appeal of the scene decreases considerably. However, if the immediate vegetation perimeter is decreased to zero, scenic quality increases slightly, about 6 percent (Figure 3B).

The recommendation is not to increase the perimeter of immediate vegetation in the scene; if anything, reduce it slightly.

Area of intermediate vegetation If the area of intermediate vegetation (X_4) is reduced from 451 to 383 grid squares, the scenic quality is decreased by 7 percent (Figure 3B).

In this scene, if other variables remain constant, the recommendation is not to reduce the present forest cover in the intermediate zone.

Area of water If the water area (X_5) in this scene is reduced, the scenic quality decreases. However, if the area of the lake is increased from 61 to 93 grid squares, the scenic quality increases considerably (Figure 3b).

Therefore, increase the area of the lake to at least 93 grid squares, perhaps even more.

Area of distant nonvegetation Creating additional openings in the distant forest zone, from 119 to 141 grid squares, improves the quality of the scene by 4 percent (Figure 3B). This landscape alteration is particularly relevant to forest management practices in wildland areas. Although the landscape-preference model is not too sensitive to the shape of clearings in the distant zone (because the measurements are made by $\frac{1}{4}$-inch squares), forest managers should ensure that the shapes of any such cuttings in that zone blend harmoniously with landforms and natural vegetation patterns. This recommendation also applies, of course, to cuttings made in the intermediate zone of this and other scenes.

The recommendation for the distant zone in this example is to create openings in the continuous forest cover of the distant zone to at least 141 grid squares, possibly more.

Summary of recommendations As in the previous two scenes, the summary of management recommendations is based on a graphic representation of all relevant changes in the landscape (Figure 3B):

Decision Priority	Landscape Features	Optimum Grid Squares	Predicted Scenic Preference Score
1	Area of water	93	115
2	Perimeter of immediate vegetation	0	116
3	Area of distant nonvegetation	141	119
4	No change	—	124

OTHER APPLICATIONS OF THE MODEL

Adapting the Model to a Computer-Based Resource Inventory System

Forest managers inventory timber by means of standard sampling procedures to obtain data related to the volume, basal area, number of trees, and other characteristics of a forest. The basic sampling units of the inventory are called plots or cruise lines.

A timber inventory or "cruise" can be made largely from aerial photographs. Cruise results are usually plotted on a map and show "compartments" of the forest with their various timber types, their age, their extent and the stage (if any) at which each should be cut.

Through available computer technology, the landscape-preference model could be incorporated in forest inventories so that landscape-preference compartments would be plotted on timber-management compartment maps. Such a dual map could be used to evaluate the impact on forest scenery of various timber-management options.

The procedure for mapping landscape-preference compartments on aerial photographs would work somewhat like this: At each sample plot, or at randomly selected points along timber cruise lines, the computer would conduct a 360-degree scan of an orthographic projection of the terrain as seen from that point — somewhat like a radar sweep. Except in this scanning procedure, the computer would analyze information in the three zones (immediate, intermediate, and distant) as specified in the landscape-preference model and predict the landscape-preference score for the first, second, third, and so on, best scene available.

The final result would be two overlays for the map of the forest that would show not only timber-management possibilities, but also scenic qualities (Figure 4). If timber production is the primary management objective, the harvesting operations could still be controlled so as to have the least detrimental impact on scenic quality. On the other hand, if enhancement of scenic recreational values is the major management objective, alternative forestry practices could be used to maximize scenic quality (as explained in the previous examples for Figures 1, 2, and 3).

Relating Landscape Preference
Values to Economic Land Values

How do the preference values determined from the model relate to economic values of the same landscapes? Some of our present research is attempting to answer this question. Results of an exploratory study suggest that a consumer's evaluation of real estate that overlooks a given natural scene correlates highly ($R^2 = .65$) with the scene's predicted preference scores. With additional research it should be possible to develop an equation that ties scenic preference values to economic land values. The results of such research should be useful in benefit–cost and environmental-impact analyses of the effects of proposed man-made changes in natural environments.

Pictures Versus Actual Scenes

Photographs are useful in landscape-management decisions only if respondents rank pictures in approximately the same order as they rank the actual scenes. A recent experiment on people's reactions to actual scenes and to either 8- by 10-inch color photographs or projected color slides of those same scenes strongly suggests that, if the photograph or slide includes most of the variation in the scene, respondents react essentially the same way to both the scene and the photograph. The semantic differential measurements used in this experiment included 26 adjective pairs to measure reaction to each of eight different environments, ranging from a junkyard to a woodland waterfall (Shafer and Richards, 1974).

Preference Models for
Metropolitan Environments

By expanding the method used to develop the initial landscape-preference model, the Forest Service research program intends to construct a landscape-preference model for metropolitan environments. We anticipate that the final model will contain more variables than the initial landscape-preference model

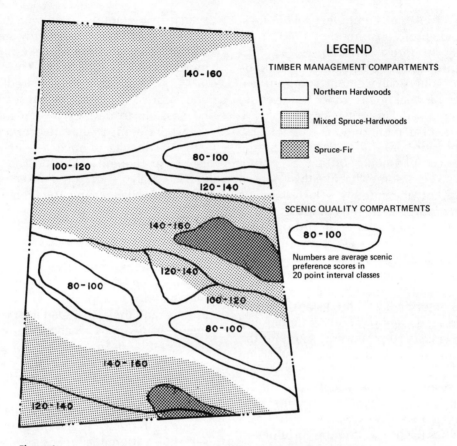

Figure 4
Map showing hypothetical timber management and aesthetic quality values for use in multiple-use management decisions.

discussed in this chapter. The metropolitan landscape model will probably involve area and perimeter measurements of vegetation, open space, and water, and additional measurements of city structures and people.

Only by examining an environment in terms of all its components simultaneously can we expect to evaluate the importance of the scenic contribution of any one component, such as vegetation, water, wildlife, or people, in a metropolitan scene.

Rationale of the Model

The model predicts quite accurately how people will rank (or score) natural landscapes. Apparently, the model's terms include those features that are important in a landscape's aesthetic appeal. The three landscape elements measured in the photographs — vegetation, nonvegetation, and water — are also the gross features in natural landscapes that man is capable of altering to an appreciable degree.

Edges of abrupt change Perimeter measurements stress the prominent *edges* between the forest canopy and open ground or water, edges that separate masses of contrasting texture and tone. Several recent studies of human eye movement in viewing photographs and paintings have shown that the viewer's attention focuses at points along such edges (Mackworth and Morandi, 1967; Gratzer and McDowell, 1971).

Amount of the features present The model's area measurements, and to some extent the perimeter measurements, reflect the relative *proportions* of landscape features in the landscape.

Textural gradients and overlapping landforms The use of three zones in the model takes into consideration the textural variation of vegetation and nonvegetation. The sense of depth in a view, as established by textural gradients and overlapping landforms, is generally recognized as a major factor in scenic preference.

Interactions among features A principal advantage of the regression model is the use of second-order terms (squared terms and cross-product terms) that describe interrelated or interlocking elements of the landscape. In the model, only the first two terms are first-order terms; the remaining eight terms are second-order. The presence of higher-order terms shows that a simple additive model is not adequate.

Importance of framing Terms in the model that are preceded by a plus sign generally cause a reduction in scenic quality and those terms with a minus sign enhance the scene. Therefore, the perimeter of immediate vegetation $(-X_1)$ seems to enhance scenic quality. However, in scenes where the intermediate zone is largely forested, the presence of foreground vegetation detracts from scenic quality

$(+X_1X_4)$. Likewise, in scenes where the perimeter measurement of distant trees is large, foreground vegetation detracts from scenic quality $(+X_1X_3)$. Furthermore, the ninth term $(+X_1^2)$ penalizes a scene's preference score if excessive amounts of immediate vegetation are present.

Importance of water Water, in combination with forest vegetation in either the intermediate or the distant zone, strongly enhances scenic quality, as indicated by the terms $-X_3X_5$ and $-X_4X_5$. Yet if water occupies a proportionately large section of the scene, it detracts from the quality of that scene $(+X_5^2)$. Such relationships in the model suggest that without the contrast of dark vertical masses of trees in the distance the presence of water could actually diminish scenic quality.

Intermediate and distant zone interrelationships At times, large values for the perimeter of intermediate nonvegetation $(-X_2)$ enhance scenic quality. However, the opposite effect occurs if large amounts of open ground are present in the distant zone. In such instances, the model penalizes scenic quality when trees are lacking in the intermediate zone $(+X_2X_6)$. In other cases, the model gives higher scenic quality ratings when the intermediate vegetation increases $(-X_4X_6)$. An example of this exception is an alpine scene where mountain peaks jut above the timberline. The distant-zone variables occur only in combination with other variables.

Why a Mathematical Approach?

Several leading researchers in the field of environmental perception have commented that regression analysis is too complicated for the average planner to use or understand. However complicated the technique may be, public preference for natural environments is itself a complex phenomenon. Not to use mathematics to examine this phenomenon would be like trying to fell a tree with a chain saw without turning on the power switch — one could hack away at the problem for a long time and not solve it because of failure to use the best tool available for the job. Multiple regression is particularly appropriate to the analysis of landscape preference because it takes into account not only the changes in a given landscape variable, but also the many subtle and unsuspected interreactions with other variables in the model.

The landscape-preference model provides a reliable and predictive tool for anticipating the public's reaction to changes in the scenic composition of natural environments. For decisions regarding the location of vantage points for viewing, or the removal or addition of forest cover or bodies of water, this model can be particularly helpful.

LANDSCAPE RESOURCES
AND MODELS

An essential feature of most large-scale planning programs is the assessment of the landscape resource. Assessment has focused primarily on problems related to water resource, recreation, or transportation planning during the past decade and has produced a considerable number of assessment techniques of varying degrees of sophistication. Visual and cultural landscape values are receiving increased attention as techniques develop and are being included in the planning program, along with other more widely recognized renewable resources, such as timber or water, and the nonrenewable, such as iron or oil. The following chapters describe some of the recent visual–cultural landscape-resource-assessment techniques, most of which have been designed for integration into more comprehensive resource-assessment processes. This section presents a sampling of the state of the art.

The term "assessment" as used here refers to the evaluation or judgment of the overall visual–cultural value of a total landscape or a part of a landscape. Until recently the identification and weighting of these values was based almost solely on the professional judgment of designers and planners. However, a more sophisticated and rigorous justification of these values is now being demanded by decision makers. In responding to this demand, researchers and practitioners have begun to document their evaluations with references to the literature on qualitative values and to the published findings from landscape perception research.

The writings of John B. Jackson, Roderick Nash, Garrett Eckbo, and others are familiar to most students of planning and design. Recently, however, the writings of these articulators of landscape values have been augmented by the efforts of behavioral scientists. The assumed traditional values are being probed, questioned, and tested. The implicit assumption of the authors of the following chapters is that the social norms, derived both from the literature on landscape values and from behavioral science research, provide a more accountable basis for planning than a designer's intuition and unsubstantiated professional judgment. The most common references to traditional values relate to design principles and to values of an historic or cultural origin. References to economic values are almost entirely absent. Ross Whaley, in a previous chapter, urges the inclusion of economic values in the assessment process. One author in this section, Richard Smardon, attempts to substantiate the visual value of a landscape, a wetland, with an economic rationale. Robert Brush and Elwood Shafer also touch on the relationship of economic value to landscape-preference value.

In contrasting the influence of economists with that of behavioral scientists, the question arises as to why behavioral science has had a greater influence on the development of landscape-assessment models. Perhaps perceptual psychology is more amenable to the "designer mentality" than is the rigor of economic accounting. Undoubtedly Kevin Lynch's seminal work, *The Image of the City* (1960), provided an important stimulus to behavioral scientists to begin studying people's perception of environment in nonlaboratory settings. Not only did he identify significant visual variables, such as legibility, but he also provided the impetus for subsequent studies, such as that reported by Stephen Kaplan in an earlier chapter in this volume.

The chapters in the previous section on human response to the landscape indicate that a common interest is developing between environmental psychologists and designers. The preceding section also indicates that the intuitive judgment of landscape planners is being reinforced by a more quantifiable value system. Visual–cultural landscape values are more frequently evidenced in the results of landscape-perception studies.

The objective of this section is to present a selection of some recent applications of landscape-assessment techniques. Five of the chapters are based on work done in the departments of landscape architecture at the Universities of Michigan, Massachusetts, and Wisconsin. These include the chapters by Bruce Murray and Bernard Niemann, Kenneth Polakowski, R. Jeffrey Riotte et al., Richard Smardon, and Julius Fabos et al. The chapters by Wayne Iverson and Rolf Plattner represent the work of public agencies, respectively, the U.S. Department of Agriculture Forest Service and the Basel (Switzerland) Regional Planning Office.

Interest in landscape assessment in the United States dates back to the nineteenth century (Fabos, 1971). The national park movement influenced by Frederick Law Olmsted and his contemporaries was an early example of the concept of placing high value on spectacular or unique landscape quality. During the 1930s the National Park Service classified the entire country into landscape regions with varied quality for recreation use. Similarly, in the 1960s, the Outdoor Recreation Research Review Commission incorporated visual–cultural attributes into their proposed recreation land classification system. In the mid 1960s, three studies that incorporated innovative techniques and were comprehensive in scope received considerable attention (McHarg, 1963; Lewis, 1964; Zube and Carlozzi, 1967). By the end of the decade there were dozens of studies contributing to the art and science of landscape assessment.

The majority of the techniques developed to date are designed to classify and evaluate large landscapes to support land-allocation decisions such as highway or recreational development. All the chapters included in this section deal with the application of assessment technique to large land areas. They are arranged generally in order of their dependence upon perception studies for the substantiation of the underlying landscape values.

Rolf M. Plattner relies very little on behavioral research. Rather, his model is based primarily on social norms expressed in Swiss law, and secondarily upon the designer's value judgments. Swiss law determines the general configuration of forest and agricultural lands that are to be protected from major alteration. Laws also influence the degree and types of recreational use of these forest–agricultural areas. Finally, a new Swiss law also supports the planners' evaluation to determine which portion of the land presently zoned for urban use (roughly 20 percent of the landscape in the Basel region) should be removed and designated for other land uses.

Within the broad categories of land use prescribed by law, Plattner places values on landscape elements such as unique areas and historical sites. This analysis is applied to each parcel of about 17 acres within the unurbanized sector of the Basel metropolitan region. The value of each element and feature of each cell are combined in a matrix. In addition, a concept of use compatibility of the landscape

elements and features with potential rural land uses is also developed. This process is designed to determine land allocations for uses such as electric power lines and ski lifts in the farm and forest landscape without too much impairment of the intrinsic values identified in the cells.

The national norms of Switzerland as reflected in Swiss law have provided the planner with an unequivocal basis for allocating land. The farms in the valley and the forests on the steep hills are all protected. The extent and configuration of urban development is controlled. The planner is left with the preparation of proposals that may only slightly modify or adjust the functional use of the landscape for limited recreation or power-line routing. Finally, the public has supported the planners' assessed landscape values via the public hearings.

The chapter by Kenneth J. Polakowski deals with scenic highway route selection for the Upper Great Lakes Region. The technique operates on two levels. The first level deals with the macro landscape assessment. Polakowski classified the region into what he calls evaluative districts. Each subregion has similar landform and vegetative characteristics. The overall visual quality is assessed quantitatively for each "district." At this first level one can make decisions that place highways in the most scenic districts or subregions. Polakowski draws upon several well-known regional classification and evaluation systems to support his value-assessment procedure (Fines, 1968; Zube, 1970; Hills, 1966; Linton, 1968).

On the second, or micro level, Polakowski places a subjective value on each potential view area. He calls it the "landscape scene composition value." In supporting this value, he traces the evolution of design norms and reviews the principles of visual organization from the Egyptians to Kevin Lynch (1960). He then translates these principles into quantifiable values to rank various scene compositions. According to Polakowski, this second system would place the road in the most scenic area within the district, selected at the macro level. Although this study is still undergoing development, its two-stage evaluation scheme seems to be very useful for scenic highway planning.

The landscape-assessment technique for selecting electric-power-line corridors developed by Bruce H. Murray and Bernard J. Niemann was designed on four levels. On the first two levels it analyzes the degree of potential disruption and the compatibility of power lines with various existing uses. On the third and fourth level it analyzes potential exposure and other detailed site characteristics. Summary computer printouts show areas where power-line location would be most appropriate on all four levels. The visual–cultural values are obtained from surveys of landscape designers, representative groups of the general public, and decision makers. An advantage of this technique is its ability to assess the preferred corridor locations from the points of view of the various interest groups. For instance, it would indicate where power lines should be placed if the naturalists' values were accepted. Thus, it provides an excellent tool for negotiation among public decision makers, corporations, and the affected interest groups.

The chapter on visual–cultural resources of the southeastern New England region by R. Jeffrey Riotte, Julius Gy. Fabos, and Ervin H. Zube provides a classification system for large-scale landscapes, a quantitative and qualitative evaluation system on various geographic scales, and a method of identifying the land-management devices that would protect existing qualities or enhance others. This technique uses findings from landscape-perception research to support visual–cultural values.

Wayne D. Iverson and his colleagues have developed a computerized assessment technique at the U.S. Department of Agriculture Forest Service's California Region. Their computer-aided delineation of landscape view areas has received considerable attention (Amidon and Elsner, 1968). This technique and those developed in other Forest Service regions provide a basis for evaluating the landscapes in public forest lands, which range up to many hundreds of square miles in area. This particular technique has applicability for forest management, for designating recreation areas, and for scenic road alignment. The significant contribution of Iverson's technique is that it can be used for assessing either large landscapes or small portions of landscapes. Even more important, it has predictive utility, as it can be used to evaluate the "visual sensitivity" of future changes in the landscape. Iverson's technique reflects both normative values developed within the Forest Service, and draws heavily upon perception studies.

The model by Richard C. Smardon presents a technique for assessing values of wetlands. This three-level eliminative model was designed to group the wetlands of Massachusetts according to their assessed values. On the first level the most outstanding wetlands are identified. On the second level the visual quality of all nonoutstanding wetlands is ranked qualitatively from best to worst. Decisions can be made at this level regarding the possible protection of those wetlands having the highest quality. The quality value ratings used in this model are derived from the research findings of behavioral scientists. The remaining wetlands are then assessed in terms of cultural variables, such as accessibility, which may increase the importance of a wetland of lesser visual quality. The final phase of the study considered economic values, and derived a maximum purchase price of wetlands for conservation purposes. This economic model produced a maximum possible dollar value for the wetlands from a point of view of visual–cultural quality, wildlife habitat, water supply, and flood storage capacity. This ranking by dollar value provides a scale against which other wetlands may be compared.

The assessment technique developed by Julius Gy. Fabos, William G. Hendrix, and Christopher M. Greene is a parametric correlation model. It is designed to assess human impact on landscape resources and includes visual–cultural values. The model was initially applied in the assessment of the resource value change of three towns within the Boston metropolitan region between 1952 and 1971. The quantitative values used in the rating techniques are based on interpretations of the research of behavioral scientists. The technique also incorporates the results of a preliminary study of the perception of land-use compatibility.

In summary, all these chapters reflect to some degree the influence of the research of behavioral scientists and/or economists. Whaley's suggestions in the first section for more collaboration with economists may provide further impetus in this area.

Even if we incorporate the economic rationale and improve our knowledge in the area of perception, we are a long way from identifying commonly held social values pertaining to land use. It appears, however, that we are learning and adapting the techniques of quantification already used extensively in resource planning by engineers and economists, and we are beginning to substantiate the intuitively held values of designers with the results of research in the social sciences. This approach provides us with a much broader base on which to evaluate numerous landscapes or sites according to their scenic values and to begin to develop quantitative simulation models to predict the potential impacts of alternative uses.

Is landscape assessment representative of a temporary fascination or does it have long-term validity? It not only seems valid to an increasing number of landscape architects but it also has much utility in decision making within a complex and pluralistic society such as ours. Subjective feelings about beauty are not adequate as the sole basis for the protection and management of scenic resources. Quantitative analysis and assessment, the "facts" and "figures," and the need for "objectivity" will continue to be demanded by decision makers. Indeed, not only do we have to advise decision makers that one tract of land is twice as suitable as another for a given use, we also have to be able to prove it! Quantitative assessment models of the type evidenced in this section will ultimately provide the necessary scientific rigor.

The Regional Landscape Concept for the Basel Region

Rolf M. Plattner

This chapter describes the landscape-assessment and design process, including the origin, public hearings, and revision of the Regional Landscape Concept (RELAC), for the Basel region of Switzerland. This process is an attempt to organize the utilization and protection of the landscape in a fast-growing urban area, and thus is an attempt also to increase the quality of life.

The physiographic region of Basel falls within the borders of three countries: northwest Switzerland and parts of Germany and France. Switzerland's portion is divided into three areas. In the north, the flat plains of the Rhine valley where it forms the boundary with Germany dominate the residential and industrial areas. The middle sector is formed by a plateau dissected by relatively narrow valleys. The southern portion of the region is formed by the Jura, a mountain range similar to the Appalachians, with altitudes of up to 3,000 feet. The Jura can best be described as a partly rocky landscape, well known for its scenic beauty. Timber production and dairy farming form the area's economic base.

The RELAC has been developed for the area

Rolf M. Plattner is a member of the Basel Regional Planning Authority in Switzerland.

188

of Basel-Stadt and Basel-Land, constituting 465 square kilometers, or 181.6 square miles. The three characteristic land-use types are zoned land, including residential areas, industrial areas, public facilities, and institutional uses, constituting 20 percent; forest covering 33 percent; and open farmland taking up 47 percent. Nonproductive areas, such as snow-covered alps, glaciers, and lakes, do not exist in the Basel region.

The Basel region proper covers about 2.5 percent of Switzerland's total surface, but its 521,000 inhabitants form 8.3 percent of the entire Swiss population. Switzerland's average population density is 60 inhabitants per square kilometer, or 153 per square mile. In contrast to this, the study area has 2,422 inhabitants per square mile. Basel and its suburbs form the second largest metropolitan area in Switzerland. Its population has increased substantially: 1850, 146,000; 1910, 264,000; 1950, 435,000; 1970, 521,000; 1990, 600,000 (projection).

Growth is generated primarily by the economic development of Basel's chemical industry. The per capita income in the region in 1971 was 17,500 Swiss francs (approximately $5,700), the second highest in Switzerland after Zurich.

The Swiss portion of the Basel region is governed by five cantons. The political structure of the cantons resembles that of the states in America. Each canton is responsible for its own planning activities, and regional planning concepts become law by cantonal approbation. To increase efficiency in all fields of intercantonal planning, Basel-Stadt and Basel-Land have decided to establish the Basel Regional Planning Authority, although each canton is governed by a different set of laws.

The RELAC is a landscape concept that has attempted to conform to the laws of each of its two autonomous cantons. In addition to the cantonal and city laws, Swiss landscape planning is greatly influenced by federal law. The following discussion and Figure 1 reveal this influence.

Federal laws regulating land use At the federal level, the Swiss constitution mandates planning activities by the federal and cantonal governments. Based on this article, the Federal Planning Bill has been proposed and is at present under discussion in the two political assemblies. The Federal Planning Bill promoting regional planning requires that cantons and municipalities coordinate their designation of all land uses to ensure the optimization of landscape resource values.

The federal government does not prepare a federal master plan, but only acts as a coordinator and publishes guidelines and objectives. The federal laws, however, have great influence on land utilization, especially the Forest Law.[1] Since 1902 all forests have been completely protected by law, which requires that wooded areas may not be reduced in size. The regulation stems from the need to cultivate forests as precautionary measures against avalanches and erosion. Today it is becoming useful as a means of restricting urban sprawl. Unless permission is given by the authorities involved, clear cutting is prohibited, and any cleared area has to be reforested as close as possible to the site and extent of the original forest area.

The Federal Act of Urgent Measures for Planning[2] is another important legal device that helps to preserve the landscape. It has required the cantons to establish "protection areas," resulting in a comprehensive restriction on any construction activity except for agriculture and forestry.

The Federal Bill for Water Protection[3] was designed to decrease water pollution and control urban sprawl. It requires the establishment of zones within which sewerage has to be treated. Outside those zones, permission for construction cannot be granted.

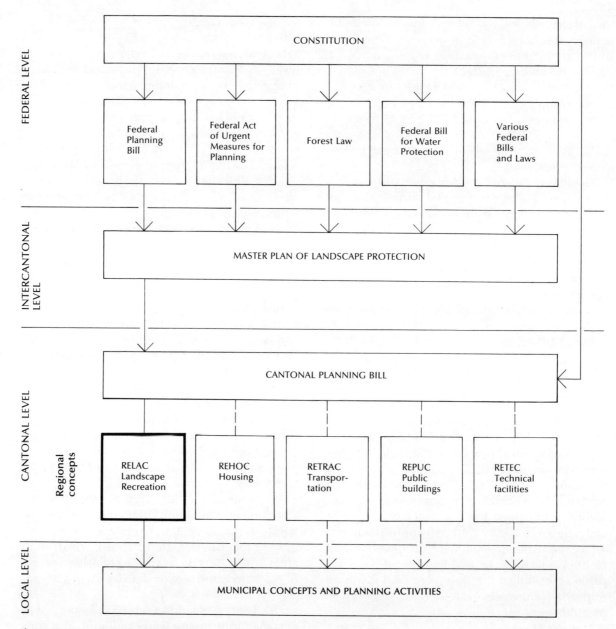

Figure 1
Hierarchy of planning activities in Switzerland.

Planning at the cantonal level At the cantonal level, the Regional Development Concept (REDEC)[4] encompasses the entire region of the two cantons Basel-Stadt and Basel-Land and portions of the cantons of Aargau, Bern, and Solothurn. REDEC includes planning proposals for the allocation of the main land-use functions and activities, in the form of a master plan as required by Federal law. Each canton may have an individual concept, but each has to designate areas for agriculture, recreation, and protection uses.[5] The federal law also defines the procedure for public participation, which has an impact on the revision process.

The cantonal planning laws are even more specific. For instance, most cantonal planning laws, including those of Basel-Land,[6] require that the configuration of four land uses be specified: urban (residential and industrial), landscape protection and recreation, transportation, and public buildings. The application of this law has resulted in printed maps and written reports containing measures for implementation. All regional concepts, including this one, are submitted to the parliament by the cantonal government. By approbation the concepts become law and mandatory for further planning activities on the local level.

Detailed planning at the local level Detailed planning occurs at the municipal level. It conforms to the constitution in that, on each level, the participation of the authorities involved has to be guaranteed.

Regional Landscape Concept (RELAC)

The Basel Regional Planning Authority first published the RELAC for public hearings and scheduled the final debate leading to approbation during the spring of 1974. It may be asked why all concepts (REHOC, RETRAC, and so on, as shown in Figure 1) were not published

simultaneously, and why priority was given to landscape planning. This procedure was adopted because no planning activity starts from scratch, but has to take into consideration innumerable earlier decisions. This attitude is by no means fatalistic or resigned, but rather appreciative of earlier political decisions. In looking back, the landscape concern has proved the weakest element in decision making. The landscape has had defenders who were ineffectual against the construction lobby and the highway administration. For too long the open countryside was considered a "white area," rather like the "terra incognita" of ancient maps. At this time, large portions of the population recognize the limited extent of green areas and understand the concept of "green–red balance" in which the more urbanized an area becomes, the less open land remains for recreation.

The lack of sufficient data concerning the landscape's value has been an additional reason for giving RELAC higher priority. Whyte's (1970) suggestion is true for Switzerland: "The land that is still to be saved will have to be saved in the next few years. We have no luxury of choice. We must make our commitments now and look to this landscape as the last one."

Areas that cannot be saved today will be lost tomorrow. It is especially important that recreation areas near urban developments be safeguarded. This policy is a social requirement in the way that social security insurance or hospital systems were in the past. In addition, the RELAC provides a catalogue and assessment of landscape values. Only by analyzing the value of the landscape for agriculture, recreation, and conservation can the required priorities be realized. In the past, the value of landscape has been neglected.

Each planning concept shown in Figure 1 has its objectives, which exert mutual influences. A short summary of the interaction of the various regional planning concepts is therefore in order.

Residential planning The Basel region consists of 76 municipalities, each with its own legal zoning ordinance. This instrument leads to a clear distinction between zoned land, where private and public construction activities are permitted, and nonzoned land, such as agricultural areas reserved for farming and forestry. The curbing of urban sprawl has been achieved by this regulation.

The theoretical capacity of the actual zoned land in Basel-Stadt and Basel-Land could accommodate 750,000 to 850,000 inhabitants, depending on the density assumed. By comparing the present population (440,000) with the projected figure for 1990 (490,000), it may be seen that any conversion of agricultural land into zoned land is completely unnecessary for the next two decades. The RELAC concluded that presently zoned land can be reduced, especially in areas where inappropriate zoning has been permitted in the past.

Transportation planning The transportation system includes the region's public and private transport. Planning and construction of highways have been completed, and recent emphasis has focused on the improvement of public transportation facilities. It is the formulated goal not only to connect residential and employment areas, but also recreation centers with nearby urban development to help especially children and the elderly.

Landscape planning Landscape planning comprises the allocation of rural and urban uses in such a way that they complement each other. When planning started, few Swiss studies existed in the area of landscape planning. In 1960 an inventory on the subject of landscape protection was drawn up. Because all the municipalities worked independently, the lack of coordination reduced the possibility

of implementation. The Swiss Confederation published additional material in 1968, including a report, "Landscapes of National Value,"[7] for areas requiring special protection.

THE ASSESSMENT PROCESS

The first version of the assessment process of RELAC included five steps after the general objectives had been formulated (see Figure 2). *Step 1* included the elaboration of different basic reports. *Step 2* comprised the listing of all conflicts that occurred in the comparison and analysis of the basic reports. *Step 3* was the application of the general objectives in spatial terms and relevant form, which showed how and to what degree the main objectives were realized by means of the different goals defined by the basic reports or by other regional concepts. The result of this step was the formulation of guidelines for the assessment process for different elements. *Step 4* determined the elements of land-use and landscape protection, including criteria for restrictions. All restrictions had to be defined in advance because their effects influenced the assessment process. Both the single element and its related restrictions were part of the written comment and of the maps. The matrix of compatibility (see Figure 3) explains this step. *Step 5* was the final assembly process, using the criteria, objectives, and guidelines in drawing up the two maps.

Step 0: General Objectives

Without objectives, no planning activity can be successfully realized. For the RELAC the following clear, programmatic objectives set the frame and content for the later work: protection from urbanization of the areas that were presently nonzoned; maintenance of agricultural areas; development at the most suitable

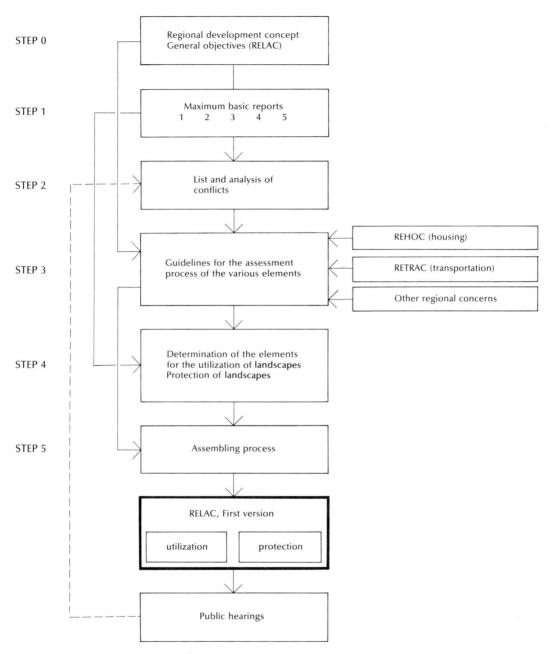

Figure 2
Assessment process for the Basel region.

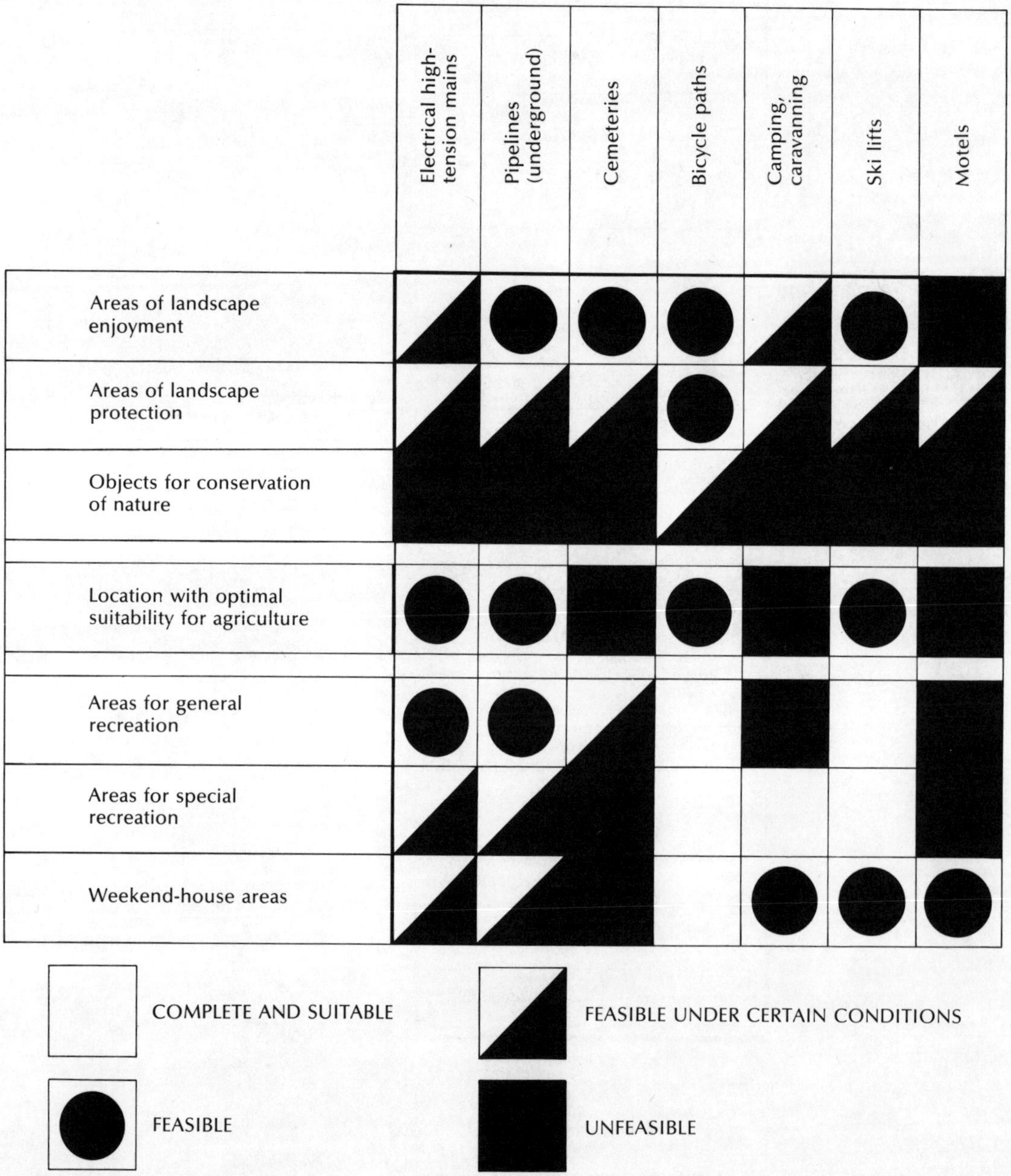

Figure 3
Matrix of compatibility (section).

locations under favorable socioeconomic conditions; protection of outstanding landscape areas; creation and implementation of new recreation areas with the concentrations of buildings and sports facilities located near present and future population centers.

Step 1: Basic Reports

The starting point consisted of the collection of existing data. Furthermore, leading experts were invited to write "maximum basic reports" on the values of various landscape resources. The Basel Regional Planning Authority ordered such reports for the landscape resources of agriculture,[8] nature conservancy areas,[9] valuable landscape areas for protection,[10] geology,[11] recreation and forest areas.[12] The authors were free to choose their own working methods, the only stipulation being that they had to use all existing data and documents. Each report included a summary of the maximum realistic goals and the means of achieving them, a summary of existing conflicts in regard to each landscape resource studied, and a cartographic analysis and display of suitable and unsuitable areas on the scale of 1:25,000.

Step 2: List and Analysis of Conflicts

The analysis of the maximum basic reports resulted in the discovery of a great number of conflicts. Many occurred in areas that were proposed for landscape protection, recreation in the open countryside, and agriculture. For instance, intensive and efficient agricultural areas produce smaller quantities of agricultural products if combined with recreational activities. Intensive and efficient agricultural productivity cannot be realized if landscape protection imposes restrictions influencing management and cultivation. Therefore, legitimate requirements in the fields of recrea-

tion, agriculture, and preservation demand the setting of priorities to reduce the conflict and the impact of regulations.

Step 3: Guidelines for the Assessment Process

The third step led to the development of guidelines for balancing and weighting the values of landscape resource elements. Spatial objectives, for example, must take into consideration topographic features.

In the *lower-lying part* of the region is the central city of Basel with its fringe of fast-growing suburbs situated in the valleys and forming urban linear development patterns all connected by private and public transportation. These linear development areas are separated by plateaux and mountain ranges. Recreational activities dominate the areas between townships and on the top of the plateaux. These open spaces are valuable for several types of recreation uses and are situated very close to urban development. In addition, they help to maintain reasonable environmental conditions in the nearby urban areas in terms of meteorology, water balance, and other factors. The recreational needs of the urban population are the most important consideration for these landscapes. However, high-quality farming areas should be maintained primarily for food production, and recreational activities should be permitted as a secondary land use.

In the region's *central area* the topographic features encourage intensive agriculture. Sufficient agriculture should be maintained to meet possible wartime needs, and, for obvious reasons, it is therefore imperative to reserve for farming those areas most suitable for agriculture. These optimal agricultural land reservations can also provide recreation sites as a secondary use. Recreation is more important than agriculture on the plateaux only when the land is less suitable for farming.

The *Jura* mountain range dominates the southern part of the region, creating a countryside of outstanding beauty and scenic values. The protection of the existing natural and cultural landscape requires the imposition of restrictions, especially for sites of national importance. This objective does not mean that a national park should necessarily be created but that agriculture and forest uses must be subordinated to the goals of landscape protection. The high scenic values suggest that this landscape is also attractive for general recreation. However, to maintain these recreational values, a comprehensive protection program is required.

Based on the spatial objectives, the system for analysis of the interaction of all elements has been worked out. A clear system is a prerequisite for a successful landscape concept. The system of superimposing various land uses has to guarantee the main land use and permit secondary uses also. In addition, the determination of the temporal sequence of different utilizations should be possible.

In summary, two factors determine the landscape resource use in the regional landscape concept. First is the setting of the highest priorities for agriculture or intensive recreation or conservation of nature. Second is the allocation of secondary land uses such as for various types of recreation, water resources, and so on. The first planning decision was to maintain agricultural activities as the main land use wherever possible. The recreation and landscape protection uses should be subordinate to the agricultural requirement.

Step 4: Determination of the Elements

Because the RELAC's goal is the determination of conservation, protection areas, and different land uses in the countryside, it includes two groups of elements: first, the elements that are essential attributes of landscape protection and, second, the elements that constitute essential attributes concerning utilization of landscape. I shall discuss the particular elements of landscape protection first.

Areas for conservation of nature The basic report includes 250 areas, measuring from 1 acre to 450 acres, that represent the highest level of concern and should be conserved as completely as possible for zoological, botanical, or geological reasons. For each area there exists a complete report describing conservation aims. Because the areas are relatively small, complete and comprehensive restrictions are legitimate. It is not a question of "beautiful places," but of unique and interesting areas. The main objective is to achieve as comprehensive a landscape-protection policy as possible without changing the main land use, such as agriculture, forestry, or recreation. In these protected areas, new roads and streets, new buildings of any size, fences, camping, caravans, changes in the soil composition, drainage, clear cutting, intensive farming, the use of pesticides, and mining are forbidden. Each restriction and each measure for protection is a function of the conservation objective.

Areas for landscape protection At the second highest level, the goal is to define areas of outstanding beauty and visual quality, in a countryside containing a great variety of unique and interesting natural objects and features. In maintaining protected areas, some buildings and facilities cannot be prohibited completely. The selection of areas for protection was based on high visual quality, forest–open land diversity, and views. They have been defined without consideration of their situation in relation to residential areas and urban development.

Areas for the enjoyment of landscapes Landscape areas for enjoyment are defined here as partially protected areas. They form the third level of protected areas. The main objective is to maintain and buffer these areas, but to permit effective agriculture at the same time. Therefore, buildings and facilities for farming, recreation, and public use are tolerated, but all development and use must be realized with additional caution. Activities that would result in permanent damage to the landscape, such as pits, mines, and dumps, are restricted. In summary, the main land use remains agriculture or forestry, with recreation as a secondary use in those areas.

Areas without restrictions for protection An area of low or nonexistent visual quality is defined as an area requiring no protection. It is not available for private development but is used rather for agriculture and recreation. The building regulations are compulsory for these areas also.

Additional regulations for protection Additional regulations cover historic buildings, natural and archaeological sites, and monuments. The main objective of preservation is a gradual restoration in the future; therefore, any changes that would reduce the quality of the objects are restricted. Villages, groups of old buildings, churches, town halls, fountains, and the like form an integral part of the countryside and need comprehensive protection.

The second group of elements in step 4 was defined as those elements which constitute essential attributes concerning utilization of the landscape by allocating the various types of land uses that are in evidence in any countryside.

Agriculture and Forestry All nonzoned areas are reserved fundamentally either for agriculture or forestry. Any private development that is not related to one of these uses is not permitted in these areas.

Recreation areas To determine the size of recreation areas is a difficult problem. Suggested standards are very broad and vague. For instance, the Swiss Institute of Technology sets the figure of 10 to 14 square meters per inhabitant for intensive recreation; German area needs range from 20 to 44 square meters; Chapin (1965) recommends about 14 square meters per person.

The adaptation of these general standards becomes impossible when the following limitations are considered: modes of recreation and their development are difficult to predict; new preferences and trends alter the demand in size and location; it can be assumed that increasing urbanization, growing leisure time, and the absolute and relative increase in the numbers of people demanding recreation will force planning authorities to reserve more sites suitable for recreational uses.

Since there is no consensus on standards, all areas suitable for recreation have to be reserved in the RELAC. It is not the planners' function to prescribe types of recreation, but it is their task to reserve in advance the most valuable and suitable areas. In the future, the percentage of car owners in the population will probably not be an indicator of the standard of living. More likely, the number of greenbelts and the size of playgrounds in the vicinity of residential areas will help to determine the quality of life.

The RELAC should meet the growing demand in recreational areas and at the same time it should be used to control "recreational sprawl" by allocating two types of area for recreation.

In the *areas of general recreation,* where the main land use remains agriculture and forestry, general recreation is a nonconflicting or contained land use. The only facilities permitted in those areas are subordinated to agriculture and forestry, such as family playgrounds, picnic areas, hiking trails, bicycle paths, barbecue sites, and small shelters. Subordination of these facilities to agriculture favors therefore a linear-type development of recreation. Parking facilities should be provided at the edge of general recreation areas so that visitors have to enter on foot.

The evaluation process for designating areas for general recreation took into consideration the following features. The suitability of sites for recreation has been defined as the distance between sites and residential centers, which should not exceed 20 miles or one half-hour's drive. The visual aspect of the landscape should be characterized by forest–open land diversity. The sites have to be accessible at all seasons. Finally, general recreation sites should not be designated in areas most suited to agriculture because of their agricultural productivity value.

The *areas for special recreation* constitute sites reserved for sports facilities, where buildings, stadiums, fields for large-scale ball games, and parking facilities are needed. The main purpose is to concentrate sports facilities to reduce investment costs. Since they are frequently used, special recreation sites should be located as close as possible to residential areas. Location within walking distance of nearby municipalities increases the accessibility of the site to the regular visitor, and especially to elderly people and schoolchildren.

Matrix of compatibility The application of the elements concerning landscape protection is fundamental to the realization of any planning concept. The matrix of compatibility was designed to guide the practical application of RELAC. It shows the compatibility of each element with all major probable rural land uses, such as electric high-tension lines and ski lifts. The range of compatibility is ranked in four possible categories: complete and suitable; feasible; conditionally feasible; unfeasible (see Figure 3).

Step 5: Assembly Process

Five fundamental steps have been completed before the start of the assembly phase: definition of general objectives; preparation of basic reports; listing and analysis of conflicts; the drawing up of guidelines for the assessment process to determine the mutual feasibility and influence of each element concerning protection and land use; and the determination of the element that is to receive priority over others.

The basic reports contained written summaries and maps on the scale of 1:25,000 of the sites involved. The maps were transferred to transparent folios and the whole planning region was divided up into rectangular cells, each representing 6.25 hectares, or 17 acres. (On the scale of 1:25,000, 6.25 hectares equals 1 square centimeter.) The corresponding areas of the basic reports were outlined on the transparent folios with self-adhesive dots. Each folio contained one specific feature and was compared with all other existing folios, each representing the existence of a given landscape element. Opportunities and conflicts became evident among the landscape elements when one folio was laid on top of another. Finally, an evaluation diagram was prepared to aid in the determination of the priorities among the elements in each cell.

Evaluation diagram In Figure 4, only the 11 most important and decisive steps out of the total of 35 on the complete list are described. The evaluation diagram was the basis of all decisions made during the process of assembly and the preparation of maps. For each decision, it included the geographic area (region) concerned; the initial ideas considered in the maximum basic reports (basic reports); the assessment, weighting, and the reasons (comment); and, finally, the dominating element (elements).

The entire process resulted in two sets of

proposals, each proposal being mapped separately. The first map shows the areas for protection. It specifies not only the areas but also the degree of protection. The second map shows the various proposed specific uses and the intensity of uses. The two proposals collectively can also be used for the determination of utility lines, such as electrical high-tension lines.

HEARINGS AND REVISIONS

Public Hearings

Necessity The value of hearings in the planning process is underestimated. Hearings involve not so much discussion as the guarantee of public participation, which is becoming increasingly necessary and an integral part of the elaboration process. At least 30 percent of the time devoted to the study was reserved for hearings, which involved the administration, representatives of the municipalities, and private citizens.

Objectives The objective of planning is to win the approbation of political bodies. The objective of public hearings is to prepare for approbation by reducing errors, obtaining cooperation and information for the revision process, and creating confidence. Finally, everyone is influenced by planning concepts and the resistance likely to occur should be minimized as soon as possible; at the same time, cooperation for later realization is fostered.

System of public hearings The hearings were conducted on the broadest possible basis and covered all relevant branches of federal, cantonal, and local government. In addition, representative private organizations were invited. The Basel Regional Planning Authority was eager to give oral explanations if required. By the end of 1973, over 50 meetings had been held. The statements by the institutions in-

volved were considered official only if a written report was submitted.

Results of public hearings The result of public hearings was, in general, positive. In most cases, the planning authorities were encouraged to formulate even more severe restrictions. For the revision of the RELAC, critics presented useful suggestions. The bipartite elaboration for land use and protection was accepted, but the bipartite publication on two separate printed maps was rejected. Complaints were made that the concept had become too complicated. The authorities involved did not comprehend the need for two maps to illustrate one concept; they also wished to be better informed of its consequences. It was also seen that suspicion must be allayed by a policy of complete openness in the planning process; otherwise unfavorable political consequences may ensue. In addition, the great majority of more than 1,500 proposals submitted suggested real improvements and helped in the revision of the concept.

Revision of RELAC

The first phase of the concept was the design process followed by public hearings. Together they led to the revision of the concept. The assessment system was maintained because the public hearings have approved the process.

Inquiry on Recreation

The areas of general recreation are based on a specific basic report in which the number of pedestrians, the number and location of barbecue sites, and the complaints of farmers about damage have been registered. Nevertheless, the planning authorities wanted to verify the assumptions by asking the public's opinion through the medium of the region's leading newspaper. In the inquiry, held during the

REGION
- Total Basel region
- Lower Basel region
- Middle Basel region
- Upper Basel region

ELEMENTS
- Enjoyment of landscape
- Landscape protection
- Landscapes of national value
- Conservation of nature
- General recreation
- Special recreation
- Tourist centers
- Zones for weekend houses
- Agriculture

comment (see legend)   1 2 3 4 5 6 7

BASIC REPORTS
- Conservation of nature
- Forestry
- Landscape protection
- Agriculture
- Existing residential areas and transportation
- Recreation
- Inquiry with municipalities
- Other basic reports

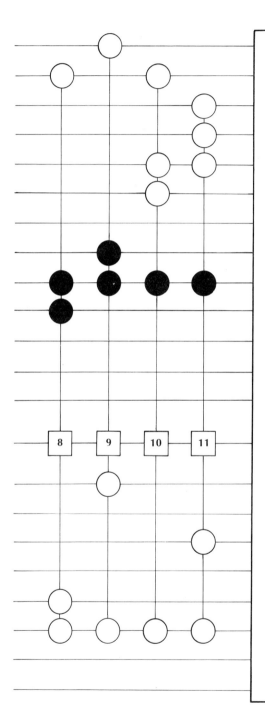

Figure 4
Evaluation diagram.
1. In areas of mountain-type farming, landscape protection and landscape enjoyment have priority over agriculture.
2. Areas of landscape protection, defined according to basic report; in "Pleated Jura" mountain range extended with "Landscapes of National Value."
3. Areas for conservation of nature have priority over agriculture in the entire planning region.
4. Areas of landscape protection according to basic report only that are not situated in areas suited for optimal agriculture remain protection areas.
5. Agricultural land use has priority over recreation in areas suited for optimal agriculture.
6. "Landscapes of National Value" have priority over agriculture, even in optimally suited areas.
7. Plateau Jura: overlapping of areas suited for optimal agriculture with areas for enjoyment of landscape at delicate locations.
8. Allocation of areas for general and special recreation at locations on the top of the plateaux, near and between urban developments.
9. Areas for general recreation and areas for protection of nature: no conflict; overposition is possible.
10. Entire lower part of the Basel region has high suitability for general recreation because of location near urban development. Superposition with areas for the enjoyment of landscape or areas of landscape protection.
11. All areas for general recreation are overlapped with areas for enjoyment of landscape, if they are not defined yet as areas of landscape protection.

winter of 1973–1974, readers were asked to list their favorite recreation areas. This information resulted in more comprehensive knowledge of general recreation, and the mode of inquiry may be defended in that this type of recreation is highly user oriented.

Present Situation and Summary

At the time of writing, the revision of the RELAC was scheduled for completion in the spring of 1974. The new version was to be presented at a public hearing and then discussed in the parliaments. Little resistance was anticipated because of permanent contact with politicians and because a comprehensive presentation of the first version removed misunderstandings.

In summary, it may be concluded that the results of the landscape-assessment process represented the values of the public at large, although the public was not involved in the establishment of those values. Prior to the public hearings, the landscape values were determined through the assessment process presented here purely by professionals, yet the public favored the maintenance of farms and forests and the protection of valuable landscape elements.

NOTES

1. *Eidgenössische Oberaufsicht über die Forstpolizei.* Bern: EDMZ, 1902/1971.
2. *Bundesbeschluss über Dringliche Massnahmen auf dem Gebiete der Raumplanung,* March 17, 1972. Bern: EDMZ, 1972.
3. *Bundesgesetz uber den Schutz der Gewässer gegen Verunreinigung,* October 8, 1971. Bern: EDMZ, 1971.
4. "Regionales Entwicklungskonzept (REK)." Liestal: Basel Planning Authority, 1971/73.
5. Butler, M., and R. M. Plattner (1973). "Bericht über den Stand der Landschaftsplanung in der Nordwest-Schweiz." Liestal: Basel Regional Planning Authority.
6. "Baugesetz des Kantons Basel-Landschaft," June 15, 1967. Liestal: Basel-Land Department of Construction, 1972.
7. "Katalog der Landschaften von Nationaler Bedeutung (KLN)." Basel: Swiss Association for the Conservation of Nature, 1972.
8. "Landwirtschaftsgutachten." Liestal: Basel Regional Planning Authority, 1970. Out of print.
9. Ewald, K. (1970). "Naturschutzgutachten." Liestal: Basel Regional Planning Authority.
10. Stern, M. (1971). "Gutachten über Landschaftsschutz." Liestal: Basel Regional Planning Authority. Not available.
11. Weiner, G. (1971). "Geologie — Gutachten." Liestal: Basel Regional Planning Authority. Not available.
12. "Erholung und Forstwirtschaft." Liestal: Basel Regional Planning Authority, 1971. Not available.

Landscape Assessment of the Upper Great Lakes Basin Resources: A Macro-Geomorphic and Micro-Composition Analysis

Kenneth J. Polakowski

Kenneth J. Polakowski is a Professor in the Department of Landscape Architecture at the University of Michigan.

The purpose of this chapter is to present the research methods and results of a resource-assessment study concerned with scenic values along the existing highway system in the Upper Great Lakes Basin. The project is a part of a five-phase regional recreation planning study that is coordinated by the Institute of Environmental Studies at the University of Wisconsin and is funded by the Upper Great Lakes Regional Planning Commission. The five phases of the project are environmental considerations, recreation user demand, transportation network, scenic highway study, and land-use controls.

Objective The purpose of the Scenic Highway Study is to define and locate highway corridors that would connect the National Recreation Areas in a 50-mile-wide zone, starting at the boundary of Minnesota and Ontario, along Lake Superior, south and then east across Wisconsin and Michigan's Upper Peninsula; then across the Mackinac Straits and following along the Lake Michigan shoreline to Sleeping Bear Dunes National Recreation Area. The Scenic Highway System would connect eight national recreation areas and cover a total distance of 600 miles.

Procedure This procedure for determining the corridors with the highest scenic value was established by recognizing the vastness of the study area, the limited opportunities for detailed data collection, and a dependency on the research conclusions of investigators concerned with landscape assessment. Also, the research was applied only to the existing highway system and was not to be used for determining the location of new highway corridors.

The research methodology that evolved was the result of recognizing those project conditions and formulating a procedure on two major levels.

Macro assessment
Phase 1: Analyze the scenic quality of the entire Upper Great Lakes Basin from a macro geomorphological/land-use pattern framework.
Phase 2: Determine and locate the most significant recreation and historic destination points of the traveler and establish two alternative highway corridors from a macro framework that will link the destination points.

Micro assessment
Phase 3: Establish a theoretical basis for a landscape-assessment system that is capable of selecting the best of the alternative routes from an aesthetic basis that evaluates the composition of the landscape type.
Phase 4: Determine the highest-quality landscape scenes within a landscape type by analyzing the micro-composition of the photo scene and its relationship to the actual, physical characteristics within the scene–site.

Phase 5: Determine the significance of employing this assessment technique by conducting user-preference studies to substantiate the research-project conclusions that determine the landscape scenes within the various landscape types which contain the highest visual interest.
Phase 6: Select the existing highway corridor that contains the highest scenic value in accordance with the preceding procedure.

The focus of this chapter is to present a landscape-assessment approach that can evaluate an extensive landscape from a broad reference and is capable of integrating those findings into a scene–site analysis technique that recognizes the significance of the arrangement or composition of the landscape scene. The actual application of the micro technique to the Upper Great Lakes Basin and the user testing of the macro–micro techniques cannot be fully described because the research is still in progress.

MACRO ASSESSMENT

Phase 1: Scenic Resources of the Upper Great Lakes Basin

Influential regional assessment methods The method for landscape assessment evolved from an analysis of various research techniques concerned with very large regions that were of the consensus that regional scenery is the result of the composite image that the type of landform and the land-use pattern projects on the mind of the observer. A detailed review of the research literature and an applied description of this assessment method is found in Thornbrough (1973). A brief description of the work of the following investigators will clarify the concept and variants of this landscape-assessment approach.

Zube et al. (1970) categorize the region into three types of landscape divisions: series, systems, and units. The landscape series, either natural or man-made, is the visual impression of a dominant form over a large area. The landscape system and units are segments of the series and are determined by the degree of contrast, spatial variety, and presence of water features.

The classification system used by Hills et al. (1970) bases the land unit upon the degree of relief that the landform contains within an area of 1 square mile. This seems to be a logical system to measure the degree of contrast within the region's landform.

The landform categories as described by a geomorphologist are suggested by Linton (1968) as a reliable method of classifying a region's ground form because of data reliability and ease of inventory for large regions. Linton also evaluates the landforms according to relief, water features, and contrast. The region's scenery is dependent on the use pattern, natural or man-made, that occupies the various landforms.

Consequently, the research methodology that was applied to the Upper Great Lakes Basin is a composite of research methods that are compatible with the project's scope and scale. The primary purpose of this first phase was to analyze the entire region in a manner that was efficient, reliable, and capable of evaluating the resources from a macro framework, thereby providing a means of placing a micro resource analysis technique in a regional context. This method does not attempt to analyze the resources from a specific view or series of views at the micro level.

Evaluating districts The review of regional assessment methods indicated a lack of consensus on the type of evaluative district that could assure a reliable comparative measure between regional zones. A static-sized district was tried, but proved to be inappropriate because of the time constraint and degree of resolution suitable for macro assessment. The scale of such a region suggested that the paved transportation routes can serve as the evaluating districts (cells) because they provide the degree of resolution necessary and possess the following positive characteristics: the grid system of the roadways can be easily identified and transferred with accuracy from various data sources; the roads follow the flow of many landforms, which thereby provide a complementary, natural/man-made edge for the evaluating district; the scenery of such a study region is primarily viewed from the highway corridor.

Evaluative criteria Landform and land-use patterns within the transportation system are evaluated by criteria that seem to have validity according to the findings of the researchers as previously described. The nature of the design elements, such as size, form, and color, associated with the landform and land-use patterns determines the scenic quality of a particular region. Therefore, such design elements are used to measure or rank the landforms and patterns according to the following criteria: *diversity* of the elements or the difference of actual site variables area; *density* of the various types of elements or the coverage of the various site variables; *distribution* of the elements or the relationship of variables that establish a particular pattern; *differentiation* among the elements or the range of differences and contrast of adjoining site variables; *degradation* within the area caused by the presence of negative factors.

Landform description and rank The landforms of the region, as defined next, are ranked according to all the preceding criteria to determine their scenic interest. The highest rank is 5 and the lowest rank 1. The ranking system expresses the composite value of the evaluative criteria as applied to the landform and land use pattern.

Rank 5. *Rock outcrops* (600- 1,400-foot relief): Exposed bedrock or rock sparsely covered by a glacial till. These are the areas of the greatest relief and contain a high degree of ruggedness.

Rank 4. *Terminal moraines* (200- 800-foot relief): Deposits formed at the front of the glacier that are usually curved in plan and several miles wide. They are rolling or hummocky surface drift with basins enclosed among sharp nobs.

Rank 3. *Ground moraines* (20- 100-foot relief): Formed of glacial till that produces a random pattern of small, irregular hills and ponds in various stages of conversion to bogs. Depressions or kettles and drumlins, which are small, elongated parallel hills, are characteristic of the ground moraines.

Rank 2. *Outwash plain* (10- 40-foot relief): Broad plains of sand on the southern border of moraines that are generally flat with many large ponds

Rank 1. *Lakebed plain* (2- 30-foot relief): Flat till plains that are either sand or clay with little vertical relief.

Land-use pattern description and rank The land-use patterns are also ranked according to the five criteria in order to determine the degree of scenic interest. The description and rank of each land-use pattern is as follows:

Rank 5. *Wildland:* Wilderness areas with minimal human impact that may contain one or more of the five forest types found within the region.

Rank 4. *Farmland forest:* Areas with a mixture of farms and forests.

Rank 3. *Continuous forest:* Areas completely covered by coniferous or deciduous trees.
Wetlands: Areas either forested, partially forested, or open, but low and wet.

Rank 2. *Farmland:* Open areas including crop, pasture, and orchard lands with scattered structures.

Rank 1. *Developed land:* Areas where various types of human development have occurred, such as shorelands, cities, towns, and major highway interchanges.

Rank −1. *Extractive land:* Areas where mining has made or is making a high negative impact on the region.

Landscape-type scenic value The combination of a landform and land-use pattern produces a landscape type (landform + land-use pattern = landscape type). The scenic value of each type is determined by multiplying the rank value of the landform and land-use pattern occupying that landform, thereby providing a means of comparing the scenic value of each district that is enclosed by the roadways (landform rank × land-use pattern rank = landscape-type scenic value). A district that contains significant water features that occupy 15 percent of the district or dominate a major portion of the foreground or middleground is given one bonus point, and a district that is adjacent to the Great Lakes is given two.

The landscape-type scenic value matrix (Figure 1) provides the means to evaluate the resources for each district. For example, landscape type B is the product of moraine landform (rank 4) and wildland land-use pattern (rank 5); therefore, its scenic value is 20.

LAND-USE PATTERN TYPE

LANDFORM TYPE	a / b c (a, type value; b, type code; c, scenic order; r*, rank)	Wildland 5*	Varied farm and forest 4*	Continuous forest 3*	Wetlands 3*	Farmland 2*	Developed land 1*	Extractive −1*
Bedrock	5*	25	20	15	15	10	5	−5
		A / I	C / I	F / II	G / II	L / III	T / IV	Z / VI
Moraine	4*	20	16	12	12	8	4	−4
		B / I	E / II	J / III	K / III	S / IV	X / V	Z / VI
Ground moraine	3*	15	12	9	9	6	3	−3
		D / II	I / III	O / IV	P / IV	R / IV	W / V	Z / VI
Outwash plain	2*	10	8	6	6	4	2	−2
		H / III	M / IV	N / IV	Q / IV	U / V	V / V	Y / VI
Old lakebed	2*	10	8	6	6	4	2	−2
		H / III	M / IV	N / IV	Q / IV	U / V	V / V	Y / VI

Figure 1
Landscape type: scenic value matrix.

The landscape types are classified into six scenic orders:

I = 25–20   IV = 5–9
II = 15–19   V = 5–4
III = 10–14   VI = −5– −1

The scenic value of each district was calculated, checked in the field, and recorded. The system proved to be accurate, easy to apply, and capable of determining the scenic quality of a vast region's resources.

Phase 2: Recreation Destinations and Highway Corridor Location

The determination of the best existing scenic-highway corridors employed the scenic values of each district as determined in phase 1; in addition, it required the establishment of travelers' destination and departure points and the location of the major transportation routes that connect such points.

Because the major focus of this project is to determine a scenic highway system that will serve tourists and recreationers in the Upper Great Lakes Basin, the primary destination departure points selected are the national and state parks of the region that contain outstanding water, timber, and geological resources. An extensive historical–cultural survey was also conducted to locate sites that are or have the potential of attracting the leisure traveler.

Scenic-highway characteristics The major routes between traveler attractions were determined by analyzing highway traffic surveys and state-park-user surveys. Generally, such routes were heavily traveled at high speeds and therefore not conducive to the qualities associated with a scenic highway system. According to Norton (1967), in his description of the Washington State Highway Beautification Program, a scenic route should provide diversity of visual experience, contain views that express the image of the region, and present short-loop routes to the traveler as alternatives to the major highway route.

It is proposed by Levin (1967) that the scenic route provide a linkage element to points of interest and pass through regions that contain or have a high potential for adopting land-use regulations and management policies that offer a high degree of land-use stability and permanence of the natural and man-made features.

The U.S. Department of Commerce (1966) states that the scenic route should have sufficient interest to be appreciated in and of itself and should offer ease of access from areas of high user concentration. Also, the route should parallel the basic flow of traffic or desired lines of the traveler, and be based on maximizing the scenic value while minimizing the travel time.

Scenic-corridor value Selection of alternative scenic routes was accomplished by analyzing all roads that ran generally parallel to the main routes and possessed the criteria and qualities associated with a scenic route. The goal of this phase was to determine the two best alternative routes that possessed high regional scenic value and were capable of providing the traveler with a route option that recognized the travel-time factor as secondary to the quality of the scenic resources. The two routes that possessed the highest scenic rate per mile were selected for further micro evaluation.

$$\text{Scenic-corridor value (SCV)} = \frac{\text{district route distance (dd)} \times \text{district landscape value (dlv)}}{\text{route length (rl)}}$$

MICRO ASSESSMENT

Phase 3: Theoretical Basis for a Landscape-Assessment System

Introduction The selection of the best alternative route must be based on a micro analysis that is dependent on the observer's perception of specific scenes within the landscape type that the alternative routes pass through. Therefore, the basis of comparison must consider the physical elements within a scene, their arrangement and effects on the observer. Consequently, it is necessary to present a theoretical framework of visual resource analysis that is based on the arrangement of physical elements or site variables. The key to a

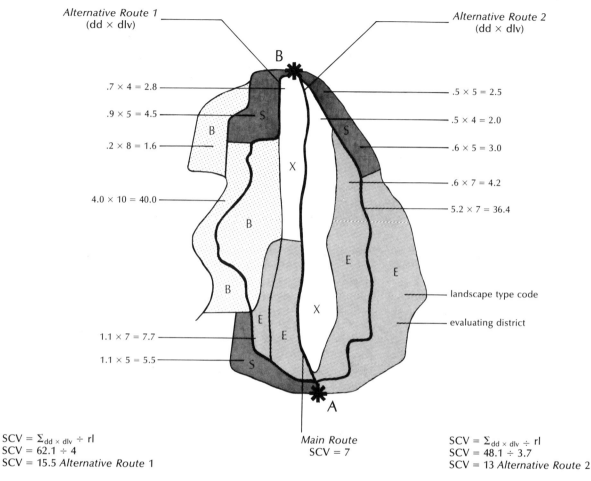

Figure 2
Scenic corridor value calculation example: District landscape value (dlv) is a rank number assigned to each scenic order, with order I having a value of 8 and descending to order VI, which has a value of 3. Bonus points are assigned if water is present in the district; a negative factor point is assigned if the district is on a high-speed road. The highest value that can be assigned to a district is 10 and the lowest value is 2.

unified arrangement or composition is the system of proportion or ratio that is used to guide the distribution of the site variables.

Therefore, a system of proportion is conceptualized for landscape assessment through the presentation of psychological and design data which will provide a foundation for the assessment system. The results of several in-

vestigators in perceptual analysis are integrated by relating their findings to the basic elements of design, whereby the design elements become the vehicle for integrating the conclusions or findings of several landscape-assessment research projects.

The basic principles of visual organization, psychological and physical, were reviewed to determine the relationship between how the observer processes information relative to external stimuli and how the stimuli (site variables) are organized to satisfy the psychological needs of the observer.

Organization of a planned arrangement implies the use of a method that determines a harmonic and dynamic relationship among site variables. Various systems of proportion have been used by designers as a method to achieve a unity of composition. An investigation of the systems used in art, architecture, and urban design is presented here to provide the basic units of measurement for the proposed landscape-assessment system.

Psychological–physical basis of analysis A fundamental thesis of the landscape-assessment technique is that the arrangement of elements has a psychological effect on the mind of the observer; therefore, the form of the composition that is determined by the perceptual relationship of elements is as important as the functional relationships of elements. The functional aspect is concerned with the practical, engineering, or ecological relationship of the elements. Consequently, the analysis technique recognizes that beauty or complete unity of organization is a requirement for man in achieving an optimum balance with his environs. It is based on his unique nature of seeking pleasurable responses from his interpretation of the physical world.

Kepes (1951) suggests that a pleasurable response is dependent on internal and external factors; therefore, it is necessary to consider the physical–psychological processes through which pleasure arises from the perception of site variables.

Internal factors As stated by Hubbard and Kimball (1917), the three physical–psychological information processes through which we obtain knowledge of the environment are sensation, perception, and intellection.

Pleasure is one of the many forms of emotion that accompanies the information processes. The degree of pleasure varies for each process, with sensation being a basic and simple phenomenon, whereas pleasure derived from intellection is more complex and difficult to attain.

Sensation is a process of interpreting and reacting to physical stimulation such as temperature, light, noise, smell, and touch. A sensation will have a pleasant quality if the duration, intensity, and character of the stimulus are favorable to the senses.

Perception is the process by which impressions, created by strong and recognizable sensations, are developed and mentally stored in the form of percepts. A percept is formed by a sensation or a comparison of sensations that impress the senses and are retained by the mind of the observer.

The cause of pleasure, independent of internal conditions that are difficult to control, is the existence of some type of unity. Pleasure in perception is achieved when the observer can recall a clear, pleasant image of the environmental conditions, which is made possible because of the dynamic and memorable arrangement of elements in that unified condition.

External factors Consideration must also be given to the characteristics of the site variables (size, form, and color) to determine which characteristics or combination of characteristics stimulates an effect of pleasure in the mind of the observer. The majority of researchers in visual resource analysis agree that the characteristics of site conditions affect the quality of the scene.

Design element landscape-assessment comparison The site variables that have been identified in various research projects can be related to the three basic design elements that have been the primary factors in the visual arts for centuries. Size, form, and color are the primary building blocks of the designer and can provide a framework for integration and comparison to classify the work of the researchers in landscape-resource assessment. Thereby, a clear understanding of the diverse work is possible through establishment of basic relationships between assessment studies and design elements of the visual artist, designer, and land planner.

Size The greatest area of research activity has related to the design element of size, because of the ease in isolating those determinants that can be measured and quantitatively compared. The *distance* to a landscape feature is considered by many (Sargent, 1967; Litton, 1968; Fines, 1968; Shafer, 1969; Rabinowitz and Coughlin, 1971) as a primary element in determining the interest of a view. Also contributing to the quality of the view is the *area* the view encompasses or the angle of vision, as noted by Appleyard (1963) and Norton (1965).

The perceptual quality of a scene is dependent on the observer's position as related to the particular scene; therefore, the *elevation* of the observer is cited by some researchers (Jacobs and Way, 1969; Litton, 1968; Norton, 1965) as a primary variable in assessing the visual interest of a landscape scene. The essence of a scene is determined by the enclosing agents that contain the view; therefore the *height* of vertical plains (edges) as suggested by some investigators (Appleyard, 1963; Leopold, 1969b; Shafer, 1969; Weddle, 1969) is an element that determines the spatial interest of a scene.

The variety or diversity of a landscape is dependent upon the *number* of man-made and natural forms within a view, as stated by Sargent (1967), Norton (1967), and Weddle (1969) as well as the *number* of changes in the occurrence of forms as suggested by the U.S. De-

partment of Commerce (1966), Rabinowitz and Coughlin (1970), and Hebblethwaite (1970).

The majority of the investigators have focused on the analysis of two or three of the determinants, and only a few (Leopold, 1969b; Sargent, 1967; Shafer, 1969; Norton, 1965) have concerned themselves with the interrelationship of size variables and their effect on determining the quality of the landscape scene. Their basic problem has been the framework of analysis that could measure the relative value of each variable and its role in creating a scene with high visual value.

Form Some researchers (Fines, 1968; Litton, 1968; Laurie, 1970) have applied a geomorphological approach to the assessment of visual resources, thereby implying that landforms have an intrinsic value based on contrast of elevation, vegetative cover, and land-use pattern. Perceptual studies by Kepes (1951) have indicated that man is constantly establishing visual equilibrium with his environs by placing elements in a larger-form context, thus suggesting that the form-creating perceptual phenomenon supports this assessment approach in determining the quality of landscape types that contain either convex, concave, or plain landforms.

Color This is one of the three basic design elements, but because of its complexity in measurement and analysis, it has received very little attention by investigators. It is considered briefly by Litton (1968), Shafer (1969) and Leopold (1969) in their assessment techniques of evaulating a landscape. The Gestalt psychological theory suggests that color as a visual element is much more basic than form when organizing a physical world, and it is only through training that the child loses this color consciousness and relates more to the more subtle aspects of form. The physical planning theory of this study as developed by my research team substantiates the perceptual theory, stressing the importance of the assessment of color in the landscape.

An analysis of the current research effort in landscape assessment within the design element framework suggests a lack of concern for the organization of site variables, with too much emphasis on analyzing isolated variables to evaluate the quality of a view or region. The primary difficulty is the lack of an analysis technique to guide the evaluation of visual resources from an organizational or compositional approach whereby the harmonic relationship of elements or aesthetic unity is considered the dominant factor in analyzing the visual quality of a region. The assessment technique as proposed here is based on the importance of spatial forces that are created by positive, physical objects and a recognition of how man processes this visual information.

Principles of visual organization Perception of the environment is a creative act of interpretation by the observer. It is truly a participatory activity through which man seeks harmony with his environs. According to S. Kaplan (1973b), man develops cognitive maps as a means of processing information that enables him to understand his environs. Kaplan also states that man is always seeking a sense of stability or definiteness which ranges from coherency to uncertainty depending on time, state of mind, complexity, and the capacity of the observer to absorb information. The dependent variable of great importance to the researcher in landscape assessment is "complexity of uses" or the external conditions that the researcher has some controls for measuring and organizing to ensure a sense of coherency or unity.

An understanding of some of the visual organization principles developed by designers to arrange or compose the design elements of size, form, and color is needed in order to relate the concerns of the psychologist to the practice of design and landscape assessment so that they respond to the physical and psychological needs of man.

Kepes (1951), a visual designer, states that, when man is confronted with a complex optical field, he will attempt to reduce it to basic relationships. Two psychological limitations to attention are present: the limited number of optical units one can encompass and the limited duration of time that man can focus on one optical situation. Therefore, the observer's first reaction when responding to such a condition is to organize the greatest number of units (space span) within the shortest time interval (time span). Kepes suggests that the means by which observers organize the information are nearness, similarity, closure, and continuance.

Goldfinger (1941), an architect, believes that the perception and comprehension of visual space are dependent on the degree of enclosure or the relationship of form type to size, the relationship or sequence of visual spaces, and the position of the observer within the space. He also states that lighting, noise, smell, and type of human activity will affect the sensation or perception of space.

Lynch (1960), an urban planner, submits the thesis that man's imageability or legibility of his environs is dependent on the means of visual organization that he employs. The results of his perceptual research in urban areas indicates that man organizes the environs by identifying pathways or circulation routes, site districts or zones, edges or transition zones, landmarks or visual features, and activity zones.

The organizational systems of Kepes, Goldfinger, and Lynch, although developed through different art forms to fulfill different needs, possess compatible means of organization with the major similarity being that *it is the relationship of elements that is most important, and the systems that can harmoniously arrange or compose these elements are fulfilling a significant role.*

Visual organization framework A framework that can successfully relate the principles of design or methods of organization to a comprehensible system that permits an understanding of the principles which have been used by designers throughout the world in various art forms, including the arrangement of landforms, structures, and vegetation, is expressed in Figure 3. The pivotal element in this framework is the organizational method of proportion that is used to relate the two primary principles, which are repetition and contrast, in such a way as to achieve unity and not an environment that is sterile or chaotic.

Systems of proportion The "search for pleasingness" or a proportional system based on the geometry found in nature began with the early Egyptians and continues today. Man has always felt that a ratio, which is the comparison of size, measure, or magnitude, was the key to producing unity in design. A brief historical sketch on the use of proportion in art and

architecture may provide a conceptual basis for the establishment of a proportional system adaptable to visual resource analysis.

The early architecture of Egypt was based on a triangle with two interior angles of 51 degrees 30 minutes. The reverse superimposition of two Egyptian triangles forms a rectangle with a ratio of 1:1:618. This ratio is also known as the "golden mean" and appears frequently in Egyptian and Greek art. It is the structural motif found in plant and animal life as in arrangements of seed pods, sea shells, and cell growth.

The Greek mathematician Pythagoras learned of this ratio in his trips to Egypt and promoted its use in Greek art and architecture; the basic dimensions of the Parthenon relate to the "golden mean." The use of the ratio continued into the Rennaissance; in fact, geometric analysis of many Gothic structures and paintings reveals the use of this proportional system. The Greeks also searched the surface of the human body in the belief that the secret ratio of its form would be the key to all creative arts. An ideal human form evolved through the work of Polyclitus, which was based on the basic measurement of the middle finger. The body, which measured 19 fingers high, could be reduced to the key divisions (elbows, knees, and so on) by the use of this ideal ratio. The dimensions of the nose and head were also used as basic dimensions found in the proportions of their temples and statues.

The Roman architect Vitruvius continued the search. He believed that the navel was the natural central point and key to the ideal ratio. He stated that if a man is placed flat on his back with his head and feet extended and a compass centered at his navel, the fingers and toes of the two hands and feet will touch the circumference of a circle described therefrom; a square is formed by the connection of the four points created by the fingers and toes. The

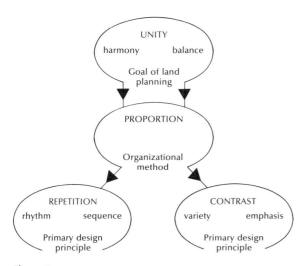

Figure 3
Visual organization framework.

picture of a man in a circle, which was created by Leonardo Da Vinci to represent this theory, has pleased many generations because it seems to offer evidence of the importance of man in the scheme of things.

The belief that the elusive "perfect" human body holds the secret of universal proportional beauty is still present today. The French architect Le Corbusier, founder of modern architecture, presents his method of proportion in Modular I (1954) and II (1958). The basic dimension is 2.26 meters, which is the height of the ideal man with one arm raised. Again the navel was used to mark the starting point for arriving at his three decisive dimensions, which are ground to navel, navel to top of head, and top of head to fingertips. An analysis of this method will indicate that the relationship of these key dimensions follows the traditional concept of perfection in the proportion of the "golden mean."

Le Corbusier was delighted when Einstein wrote a critique on the use of proportion; he stated, "it is a scale of proportions which makes the bad difficult and the good easy." Basically, systems of proportion have been related to architecture, sculpture, and painting, with some adaptation to urban design as it relates to plaza dimensions and the height of enclosing buildings. The initial attempt to use a range of scales relating diverse site variables was made by Leopold (1969b). This work represents a significant effort in seeking a system of organization for site characteristics at a scale beyond a building or urban space.

Phase 4: Micro-Composition Analysis Method

The investigation and development of a proportion system seems like a necessary step in the development of techniques for evaluating our scenic resources. The basis for developing such a system is logical when considering the physical–psychological phenomena of visual organization. The methods of composition or visual organization and systems of proportion that have been developed through the ages are adaptable to the analysis and assessment of the external view.

The thesis for this assessment technique is that the arrangement or disposition of site variables is the primary factor in determining the quality of the scene. The scene cannot be evaluated by merely analyzing the presence of the variables as employed in the macro-geomorphic analysis. The variables must be related to the observer and his position within the landscape type.

Therefore, the micro-composition analysis method was established to evaluate the scene by using the golden mean ratio of 1:1:618 as the basis of measurement. The method analyzes the scene from two basic viewpoints: the composition as viewed by the observer (photo scene) and the composition of the variables as they exist on the site (site–scene).

Photo-scene composition analysis procedure The procedure for evaluating the quality of a landscape scene within the various landscape types is accomplished through the following stages: selection of site variables and landscape scene types; determination of the landscape scene's visual field; development of a proportional frame for photo-scene analysis; establishment of measurement components for landscape photo-scene analysis; a ranking system for the proportional frame's division lines and junctions; formulas for determining the photo-scene compositional value.

Site variables and landscape scene types The macro-geomorphic analysis identified 14 primary landscape types within the Upper Great Lakes Basin, types A, B, C, E, H, I, J, M, P, R, T, U, V, and Z; see the landscape-type scenic-value matrix (Figure 1) to identify the landform types and land-use pattern type that compose the fourteen primary landscape types. The arrangement of the following site variables will determine the value assigned to the landscape scene within the landscape type:

1. Sky
2. Vegetation (trees, shrubs, woodlands, and hedges)
3. Open space (pasture, crop lands, and marshes)
4. Water (lakes, rivers, and streams)
5. Structures (buildings, bridges, utilities, and roads)
6. Topography (slope zones)

The establishment of the key combinations of the six site variables is accomplished by reducing the scene to three basic zones that can provide a framework common to all landscape types. The three zones and their perceptual characteristics are as follows:

1. *Foreground:* the recognition of landscape detail such as leaves, bark, rocks, water texture and sound, and individual building components.
2. *Middleground:* the recognition of vegetation and structure outlines, area limits of open space, and water bodies.
3. *Background:* the recognition of vegetation and structure masses and absence of characteristics such as color, texture, and form.

The five primary scenes that were identified for each landscape type are as follows:

Scene Type	Foreground	Middleground	Background
1	Open space	Vegetation	Water
2	Open space	Water	Vegetation
3	Vegetation	Open space	Water
4	Vegetation	Water	Open space
5	Water	Vegetation	Open space

The sky is regarded as a constant and independent variable that could occupy any position within the three zones. Topography relates very closely to the land-use patterns that are the result of the location of open space, vegetation, and water. Therefore, it is regarded as a dependent variable that is difficult to isolate for measurement, but is recognized by the evaluation of the other site variables.

Visual field of the landscape scene The limits of the visual field were determined according to the speed of an auto traveling on a scenic road at 30 miles per hour. According to Hornbeck et al. (1969), the angle of vision for such a speed covers a horizontal angle of 100 degrees with a focus point of 800 feet and a clear vision field (nonblurred zone due to speed) at 30 feet. This visual data, in addition to an analysis of head movement while driving at a low speed, indicates that the range of vision can cover a zone of 90 degrees perpendicular to the edge of the road.

Therefore, in accordance with this visual data a three-photo panoramic was taken at five viewing stations representing the five landscape scene types within the 14 landscape types. Constraints such as weather, time, and absence of some scene types prevented the optimum coverage, or 60 different viewing stations.

The zone of photo analysis within the panoramic field of vision was determined by selecting the most "interesting scene" within the golden rectangle proportional frame. The most "interesting scene" is defined as a view containing the optimum amount of dynamic equilibrium, which is derived from an asymetrical composition. The rationale for this method of scene selection is based on the theory that perception is a participatory activity in which man is involved in a creative act of visual interpretation by which he selects and arranges the site variables into unified scenes that produce an effect of pleasure.

Proportional frame for photo-scene analysis The landscape scene is analyzed with a proportional frame that has 12 basic orders of division. A more complex breakdown with a larger number of orders was not used because of the nature of viewing a landscape from a scenic road. The observer is reacting to a scene within a limited time–space reference that prevents a detailed visual inspection of small parts within a scene composition.

The orders are all a function of the golden-mean ratio, and the system equally considers the horizontal and vertical division series (see Figure 4). The scene is evaluated from either the H or O series and from either the V and E series and from any combination, but always limited to two series. The determination of what series to use is based on the relation of the scene's compositional lines to either H1 or O2 and to either V1 or E2.

Components of photo-scene analysis The landscape scene is evaluated with the proportional frame in accordance to the degree of similarity between the scene's compositional lines and the proportional division lines of the photo-scene frame. Also, the point of intersection for the horizontal and vertical lines is a point of high visual interest because it relates strongly to both directional lines. The location of a landscape feature, such as a structure, vegetation, or water-body edge, at such a junction will provide a view with a high visual interest. The junctions have a different value because the division lines are of different order. Thus, a hierarchy of junctions or focal points within the composition is established (see Figure 4). The landscape scene is therefore evaluated according to the compatibility of the three proportional frame components within the photo scene: horizontal composition–division lines; vertical composition–division lines; junctions of horizontal and vertical lines.

Ranking systems of composition-division lines and junctions

H Series	O Series
(— — —) Line H1 = 3	(— — —) Line O2 = 3
(— · —) Line H1–O4 = 2	(— · —) Line O2–H3 = 2
(– – –) Line H1–H3 = 1	(– – –) Line O2–O4 = 1
or	or
(· · ·) Line H1–H5 = 1	(· · ·) Line O2–O6 = 1

V Series	E Series
(— — —) Line V1 = 3	(— — —) Line E2 = 3
(— · —) Line V1–E4 = 2	(— · —) Line E2–V3 = 2
(– – –) Line V1–E3 = 1	(– – –) Line E2–V4 = 1
or	or
(· · ·) Line V1–E5 = 1	(· · ·) Line E2–V6 = 1

Junction H–V Series	Junction H–E Series
Junction point A	Junction point E
(1H or 1V) = 1.5	(1H or 2E) = 1.5
Junction point B	Junction point F
(4O or 4E) = 1	(4O or 3V) = 1
Junction point C	Junction point G
(3H or 3V) = .5	(3H or 4E) − .5
or	or
Junction point D	Junction point H
(5H or 5V) = .5	(5H or 6E) = .5

Junction O–V Series	Junction O–E Series
Junction point I	Junction point M
(2O or 1V) = 1.5	(2O or 2E) = 1.5
Junction point J	Junction point N
(3H or 4E) = 1	(3H or 3V) = 1
Junction point K	Junction point O
(4O or 3V) = .5	(4O or 4E) = .5
or	or
Junction point L	Junction point P
(6O or 5V) = .5	(6O or 6E) = .5

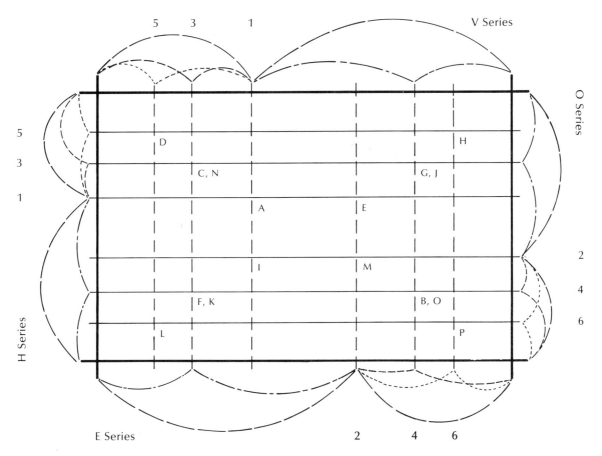

Figure 4
Proportional frame for photo-scene analysis.

Each landscape scene will have a minimum of 3 points assigned because the horizon line will either be near H1 or O2 division lines, which are the initial lines for evaluating all scenes. The maximum a landscape scene can score is 15 points: 6 for horizontal composition, 6 for vertical composition, and 3 for junction points. The junction points are not ranked as high as the division lines because they are similar to both line types; hence, there is an aspect of redundancy to this analysis component.

Landscape scene compositional value formulas

$$CV = H + (E \text{ or } V) + (J_{abc \text{ or } d} \text{ or } J_{efg \text{ or } h})$$
$$= O + (E \text{ or } V) + (J_{ijk \text{ or } l} \text{ or } J_{mno \text{ or } p})$$

where CV = compositional value
H, O, E, V, = proportional division lines
$J_{a \ldots p}$ = junction points

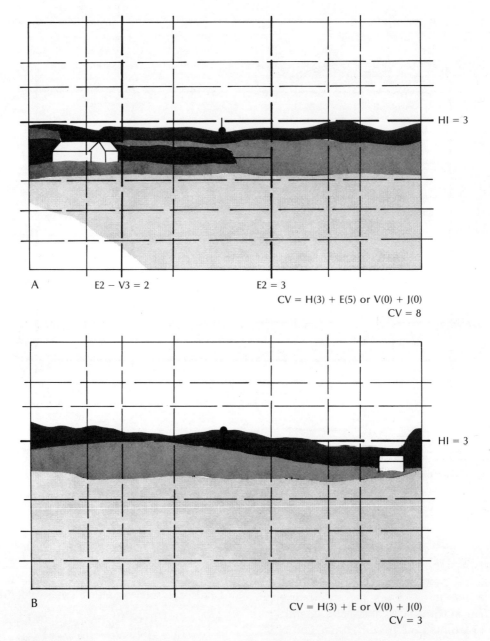

HI = 3

A   E2 – V3 = 2   E2 = 3

CV = H(3) + E(5) or V(0) + J(0)
CV = 8

HI = 3

B   CV = H(3) + E or V(0) + J(0)
CV = 3

Figure 5
Examples of landscape scene compositional value calculations. (A) landscape type E, scenic order II, scene type 1; (B) landscape type C, scenic order I, scene type 1.

RESEARCH IN PROGRESS

Site–scene composition analysis The second basic viewpoint of scene composition analysis is the evaluation of the landscape scene relative to the actual arrangement of site variables. This analysis is being conducted to determine the relationship of the scene as viewed and the scene as it is spatially arranged. If the results of this research phase indicate a high correlation between the two scene aspects, the investigation will provide an interchangeable tool for landscape assessment, thereby producing a reliable method for evaluating the quality of a landscape's scenic resources.

The site–scene analysis method is using the same proportional system used in the photo-scene analysis. The analysis of the site–scene is primarily concerned with the proportional division of the real measurements of the site variables. Preliminary investigations indicate that the proportional analysis of the following relationships is necessary to determine the site–scene compositional value: lineal distance between site variables; height of the edge of the variables lineal distance between variables; elevation of observer–ground plane–horizon; area of each site variable; length of each variable edge.

Scenic-highway corridor selection The selec-

tion of the best of the alternative highway routes as determined by the macro-geomorphic analysis method will be accomplished by evaluating each alternative route through the use of the micro-compositional analysis method (photo-scene and site–scene techniques).

The specific research procedure for analyzing each possible route is in the process of formulation. A segment of this procedure is currently devoted to the analysis of the relationship of the same scene type within different landscape types and the different scene types within the same landscape. The results of such analysis will provide a deeper insight into the interrelationship of the photo-scene and site–scene characteristics.

In conclusion, this landscape-assessment procedure for scenic-highway route selection is only in its first phase of development. This chapter describes the conceptual framework of the assessment, but the model is not yet operational. The refinement of each of the two major levels (the macro-geomorphic and micro-composition analysis) and the testing of the detailed procedures described here are being carried out for at least another year by the research team of the Department of Landscape Architecture at the University of Michigan under the direction of the author of this chapter.

A Landscape Assessment-Optimization Procedure for Electric-Energy Corridor Selection

Bruce H. Murray and Bernard J. Niemann

The environment, of which man is a part, is a complex and interrelated system. There can be little question that man is a powerful agent and the future quality of life and the environment rests with the actions of man. The same powerful role rests with the producers and transporters of energy. In addition to the residual pollution effects of energy production, the individual and collective ability of the energy producers and transporters to direct and effect urban and industrial growth is not fully appreciated by the users and suppliers of energy; and the consequences of uninformed actions are not clearly understood.

It seems apparent that energy producers must interface the users of energy and the users' quality-of-life aspirations into the future energy-need projection curves, and interface with the users or other persons being affected when establishing the factors that should influence the location of energy-production sites and energy-transmission corridors. Since the users are the consumers of electric energy, society has a critical and justifiable role in future energy planning.

A primary responsibility of environmental

Bruce H. Murray is an Associate Professor in the Department of Landscape Architecture at the University of Wisconsin and Associate Director of the Environmental Awareness Center.
Bernard J. Niemann is Chairman of the Department of Landscape Architecture at the University of Wisconsin.

planners (including electric-energy-related planning) is to evaluate the cost–benefit ratio of actions and plans to achieve an optimum solution. In the procedure of predicting or planning, cost (the economic aspect of plan feasibility) exerts a major influence on plan adoption and implementation. Today planners (including energy planners) are being asked to predict costs that exceed consideration of project implementation for the cheapest dollar costs. Society is requiring that social and environmental costs be developed, evaluated, and given their due consideration. The passage of the National Environmental Policy Act (NEPA) requiring the execution and submission of environmental impact statements is one clear and historic example of legislative representatives insisting that the environment, and its constituents, be given equal consideration and appropriate influence.

The present energy crisis could suggest to some that the recent emphasis of environmental concern will diminish and disappear. Given the amount of current and developing environmental legislation (federal, state, and local) and the increasing desire by many facets of society for a life style that includes environments of high quality, the notion of returning to the transmission-location methods of the past is naïve and altogether inappropriate.

The infusion of social and environmental costs into the location planning of transmission systems is no easy task. If the task is to be accomplished, however, one could argue that the energy industry is better equipped to expedite a more objective planning function. The electric-energy industry, or that collective group responsible for the transmission of electric-energy production and supply, is equipped today to do this because it has substantial economic resources, and is conversant with systems and procedures that simulate and predict. Energy-flow prediction, construction

management, customer billing, and accounting are all examples of systems application. These procedures depend upon computing systems and supporting technology to realize the full potential of a more objective and comprehensive planning methodology. At this moment in history the power and usefulness of the computer for transmission planning is just beginning to be recognized.

CONCEPT

The method of determining the critical data inputs that represent social and environmental concerns constitutes an essential aspect of the process and is ultimately achieved through systematic methods.

The first task is to define concisely the nature of the problem, thus focusing all thought and efforts on an explicit problem. A systematic procedure to solve the problem of transmission-corridor selection is reviewed next.

Three hierarchical levels constitute the foundation of the problem-solving method. They are the problem, or the development of electric-energy-corridor-related constraints (for example, location of a transmission system), which is composed of determinant, components, variables, and policy. These three levels are structured as follows: (1) problem (location constraints); (2) determinant (organization of factors to be considered in the location), consisting of components (major parts of the physical and cultural resource, environment), variables (subparts of the physical and cultural resource environment), and data (objective physical measurement of the variables and components); (3) policy (a single determinant or combination of determinants that represent the viewpoint of a segment of the user community). An essential aspect of the process lies in representing the specific characteristics of the region and the natural and cultural characteristics of the particular study area under investigation.

The authors have been engaged in the development of an electric-energy transmission-corridor location process for the Bonneville Power Administration (BPA); this work has been conducted by Landscapes Limited, Madison, Wisconsin. An Earth Resources Technology Satellite (ERTS) image mosaic (1:500,000) was constructed and compared with existing mapping to assist in delineating subregions in the BPA service area. The subdivision of the 300,000-square-mile BPA transmission service area (which consists of the states of Washington, Oregon, Idaho, and Western Montana) was necessary because of the variance in physical environments, ranging from rain forests to deserts. Ultimately, a set of nine models was constructed that represented social, economic, environmental, engineering, and visual considerations pertinent to finding an optimum transmission corridor. The study team considers the use of a study area (area representative of the region under study) when dealing with the potential implementation of a physical network (that is, electric-energy transmission system) in a landscape.

The study area constitutes a spatially defined area wherein the physical properties (vegetation, surface water, land use, transportation networks) are characteristic of the regional landscape in which future transmission systems may be located.

Utilization of a study area is advantageous from the standpoint that physical properties (of the study area) are considered. In some instances, given an adequate budget, more than one study area may be utilized for the purpose of representing the diverse natural and cultural characteristics of a region; the benefit is in developing a methodology based upon the real social, environmental, and economic charac-

teristics of an area. A methodology is then developed to deal with the landscape characteristics pertinent to the area under investigation.

For the purposes of explanation the authors will utilize examples of determinants, components, variables, data, and policies developed in several electric-energy corridor-selection studies.

Generation of Constraints

The initial step in the process involves the development (generation) of a preliminary outline of problems associated with transmission-corridor selection; these aspects are called constraints. The purpose of this step is to develop, from the generation of constraints, a set of determinants that represents various aspects of the problem. The term constraint, or problem, is a designation of negative and positive influences that a potential electric-energy transmission system could have on a variety of natural (for example, surface water, forests, wildlife) and cultural (for example, land uses, roads, recreation areas) systems.

Information pertaining to potential negative and positive influences is elicited from representatives of public and private agencies that possess knowledge of the region under study, as well as any other individuals who possess pertinent knowledge. The method of determining pertinent considerations is achieved by sending questionnaires to individuals or groups with professional interest in the area potentially affected. Another technique is an intergroup constraint-development seminar. The seminar is conducted for the purpose of articulating the scope and intent of the study, and to establish lines of communication with the client and individuals (representing public and private groups) whose knowledge will potentially strengthen the scope and quality of the study. The content of this seminar may include the following objectives:

1. Orientation of the consultant (by interaction with representative area groups and experts) to the nature of the problem to be investigated and to the landscape characteristics of the region.
2. Provision of an opportunity for nonclient participants to declare problems or opportunities pertinent to the problem in question.
3. Declaration of nonclient participant willingness to continue interaction with consultant and client.

Constraints emanating from regional participants are then transposed into appropriate determinants, which represent broad issues to be considered in finding an optimum electric-energy transmission corridor. The questionnaire and seminar process also assists in an initial structuring of components, variables, and data within each determinant.

Determinant

An important aspect of generating determinants comprehensively descriptive of significant aspects of the problem (or opportunity) is to interact with the individuals, groups, and agencies concerned with the transmission-system problem in question in the region affected. Comprehensiveness necessitates a formalized process of professional interaction. For example, in the Bonneville Power Study, a list of federal, state, regional, county, and local groups whose activities are potentially related to electric-energy transmission was prepared. These groups were requested to inform us (through the combination vehicle of a questionnaire and an on-site

intergroup constraint seminar) of factors which should be considered in transmission alignment that represent their particular interests. In addition to the interaction with public and private groups, an intensive information-exchange session was conducted with individuals representing a variety of related divisions in BPA for the purpose of including the significant engineering related aspects of the problem. From this information, 12 determinants were developed, which represented the factors that, to some extent, should affect the location of transmission routes.

As stated previously, the determinant category is the second level utilized in dealing with the problem. Determinants describe the primary aspects of a problem; the comprehensiveness of a program is achieved at the determinant level of organization. In the Bonneville Power Study 12 transmission-system determinants, representing a variety of considerations characteristic of the four-state BPA service area, were developed. The route determinants generated were the following:

1. least disruption to existing urbanized land-use and human settlement.
2. least disruption to agricultural land-use practices.
3. least disruption to the natural systems.
4. least visual impact.
5. least disruption to recreational land uses.
6. maximum utilization of rights-of-way.
7. least financial investment.
8. least impact upon projected human settlement.
9. greatest system reliability.
10. greatest accessibility.
11. least disruption to extractive and storage resources.
12. least disruption to forestry practices.

The determinant model development seminar constitutes an activity reliant upon interaction between the client, public and private agency representation, and the consultant. Several weeks prior to this seminar the content of each determinant is prepared, consisting of relevant components, variables, and data representing the elctric-energy system, and natural and cultural concerns. Activities conducted during the seminar include a review of the determinants, components, variables, and data by the participants from the perspective of individual expertise, education, and knowledge. These aspects are reviewed and appropriate changes and additions are made.

An essential aspect of this procedure is the assignment of professional (resource experts) judgments in the form of numerical weights to each of the components, variables, and data levels. The weights assigned range from 1 to 100; those factors that constitute the greatest incompatibility with the transmission system receive a value of 100, whereas the most compatible factor receives a value of 1. In the context of this process, resource experts are people who represent a body of knowledge and experience about a specific determinant or some part of the determinant organization (that is, a component or variable).

The numbers (or relationships) assigned represent the relative weighting of components, variables that make up components, and data that make up variables within each of the determinants. The obvious key is Table 1; this is a determinant model utilized in the Wisconsin Power and Light (WPL) and Madison Gas and Electric Company (MGE) transmission-corridor location study (Niemann, 1973). The determinant model is similar to determinant 4 in the BPA investigation (Murray and Niemann, 1973). The determinant comprises three components, consisting of 724 "type of potential visual exposure," 725 "potential visual access to facility," and 726 "potential visual screen." In the WPL and MGE application components are 700 numbers, variables are 600 numbers, and data range between 100 and 500 numbers. The number in parentheses is the weight assigned by resource experts to each level. Figure 1 is a lattice organization of Table 1, indicating the organizational hierarchy of the component, variable, and data; reflective weights are included above the various boxes. The number within the rectangle is the data, variable, and component descriptor, and the weight (shown in the upper left corner over the rectangle) is the relative weight, indicative of the compatability of the item with the proposed transmission system. The key to the successful completion of the determinant organization activity depends on the willingness of the participants to represent their objective judgments in each of the determinant models. As described earlier, each determinant requires interaction among diverse disciplines; for this reason all participants must contribute their knowledge based upon a particular expertise, the expert assigns the value based on a particular body of knowledge.

During the month of November 1973, the authors participated in interaction seminars conducted in Portland, Oregon, Boise, Idaho, Missoula, Montana, and Richland, Washington. These seminars were conducted within the BPA service area to facilitate participation of individuals that possess knowledge about one or several aspects of one or more determinants, to assist in developing determinant models representative of each of the five regions that comprise the BPA service area, and to solicit numerical values representative of the relative compatability of an electric-energy system to the various landscape characteristics included in each determinant. During a $2\frac{1}{2}$-week period, about 200 people representing a variety of disciplines (land-use planners, foresters, mining engineers, and the like) participated in the interaction seminars.

At this juncture, comments regarding the selection of participants are appropriate. The selection of individuals to participate in each determinant model development seminar was determined on the basis of the disciplines required to deal substantively with a specific

Table 1
Determinant: Maximization of Compatibility with Potential Visual Exposure

- (5) 724 Type of potential visual exposure
  - (15) 661 Potential exposure to rural land use
    - (26) 110 Rural residential — suburban
    - (15) 111 Rural residential — rural
    - (15) 113 Rural residential — agriculture
    - (10) 114 Rural commercial
    - (10) 115 Rural industrial
    - (24) 117 Rural institutional
  - (30) 662 Potential exposure to recreational and conservational land uses
    - (9) 130 Recreation — state park
    - (5) 131 Recreation — county park
    - (5) 132 Recreation — local park
    - (3) 133 Recreation — local forest
    - (15) 135 Recreation — scientific area
    - (10) 136 Recreation — organized public and private
    - (9) 137 Recreation — public hunting area
    - (9) 138 Recreation — public fishing area
    - (5) 139 Recreation — private hunting area
    - (5) 140 Recreation — private fishing area
    - (3) 141 Recreation — wayside
    - (13) 143 Recreation — historic site
    - (9) 144 Recreation — Poynette Game Farm
  - (25) 663 Potential exposure to water systems being utilized for recreational activities
    - (2) 301 Stream
    - (11) 302 Stream — trout
    - (8) 303 Stream — smallmouth bass
    - (5) 304 Stream — panfish
    - (5) 305 Stream — other game fish
    - (3) 310 River
    - (8) 311 River — smallmouth bass
    - (5) 312 River — panfish
    - (5) 313 River — complex
    - (5) 314 River — other game fish
    - (3) 320 Pond
    - (2) 321 Pond — seasonal
    - (3) 330 Lake
    - (11) 331 Lake — trout
    - (9) 332 Lake — smallmouth bass
    - (5) 333 Lake — panfish
    - (5) 334 Lake — complex
    - (5) 335 Lake — other game fish
  - (10) 664 Unique views
    - (110) 142 John Muir's View
  - (20) 667 Potential exposure to highways
    - (49) 202 Interstate highway
    - (25) 203 Federal highway
    - (20) 204 State highway
    - (5) 205 County highway
    - (1) 206 Local roadway
- (30) 725 Potential visual access to facility
  - 350 Centroid elevation
  - 351 Center east elevation
  - 352 Center south elevation
  - 353 Center west elevation
  - 354 Center north elevation
- (20) 726 Potential visual screen
  - (60) 665 Vegetation height
    - (1) 540 Upland height
    - (1) 541 Hardwoods with conifers
    - (1) 542 Oak hickory
    - (5) 543 Pin cherry
    - (1) 544 White pine
    - (5) 545 Popple with white birch
    - (4) 546 Jack pine
    - (1) 547 Swamp hardwoods
    - (4) 548 White cedar
    - (3) 549 Tamarack
    - (22) 550 Tag alder, willow, dogwood
    - (52) 557 Nonvegetated
  - (40) 666 Vegetation density
    - (4) 554 Vegetation closed
    - (14) 555 Vegetation medium
    - (30) 556 Vegetation open
    - (48) 557 Nonvegetated
    - (4) 125 Agricultural — plantation

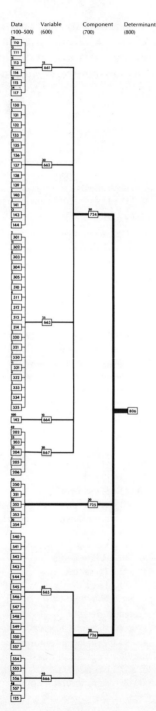

model. For example, in the specific case of the determinant ''maximization of compatibility with potential visual exposure'' (see Table 1), variables include the following:

1. Potential visual exposure to rural land use.
2. Potential visual exposure to recreational and conservational land use.
3. Potential exposure to water systems being utilized for recreational activities.
4. Unique views.
5. Potential exposure to highways.
6. Vegetation height.
7. Vegetation density.

These variables, and the data itemized under each variable, determine the types of expertise required to deal with the model in a complete fashion and appropriate individual participants for this study are thus identified. The expertise, of course, will vary to some degree from one model to another owing to the very different characteristics of the models.

The success of a determinant model development seminar is correlated to the diversity and knowledge of the participants. Each seminar must have input from individuals who can speak to each significant aspect in the model in the context of the area under investigation. The participants are selected on the basis of (1) knowledge of the pertinent area, (2) experience related to one or several aspects of a specific model, and (3) willingness to present knowledge in an objective fashion.

Component The next level of organization is the component level. A component describes the major aspects of the determinant. For example, in the WPL study, in the determinant ''maximization of compatibility with potential

Figure 1
Diagram of corridor determinant: maximization of compatibility with potential visual exposure.

visual exposure," a variety of components, as described earlier and indicated on Table 1, were developed from information obtained from individuals with expertise in this area (Niemann, 1973). Components under this determinant include "type of potential visual exposure," "potential visual access to facility," and "potential visual screen."

The components were derived, as organized in Table 1 and diagrammed in Figure 1, through interaction and consensus by "visual experts," including such disciplines as landscape architects and graphic artists (Niemann, 1973). In review, the group involved with the visual model reasoned that component 724 addresses the problem of what land uses are most incompatible with transmission systems. Component 725 considers topographic form as a means of screening the transmission system. Component 726 addresses the problem of screening the facility with various types of vegetation (Niemann, 1973).

Two other determinants applied in the WPL and MGE application (Niemann, 1973) are described next to indicate the type of components developed. In contrast to the 12 determinant models considered important to reflect the complexity of the BPA service area, seven determinant models were developed in the WPL and MGE study and 10 in the Wisconsin Electric Power study. In addition to the one determinant mentioned previously and the two following, the four other determinants were minimization of disruption to agricultural land-use practices, minimization of disruption to recreational land-use practices, maximization of potential for functional right-of-way sharing, and minimization of financial investment.

In the determinant "maximization of compatibility with urbanized land-uses," four components were developed: greatest compatibility with existing land uses, greatest

compatibility with communication systems, greatest compatibility with proposed land uses, and greatest compatibility with zoned land uses. In the determinant "minimization of disruption to the natural system," three components were utilized: tolerance of vegetation to impact, tolerance of water systems to impact, and potential impact on wildlife.

Variable The variable level is the next level of detail and determinant organization. Using the determinant "maximization of compatibility with potential visual exposure" and the component "type of potential visual exposure," five variables were developed: "potential exposure to recreational and conservational land users," "potential exposure to water systems being utilized for recreational activities," "unique views," "potential exposure to highways," and "potential exposure to rural land uses."

The component represented the variance in land-use compatibility with a transmission system. Surface water systems were included because in Wisconsin surface water is owned by the public and therefore is a pattern of land use or activity.

Data The data level is the last and most specific level of detail within the determinant organization. The data level constitutes an objective list of data under each of the variables. The data level is the level at which the information is collected on a spatial, geographic basis. The intention is to collect the data in an objective format so that the data can be used in a variety of variables. For example, because information was stored on the basis of vegetation type, this information could be used to assist in developing vegetation weight and density in the visual determinant and also in the natural determinant by varying the weights among the vegetation types within each determinant. The weighted relationship among vegetational types differs because screening is a very different problem from that of the capacity of vegetation types to sustain impact from cutting transmission-route openings. An objective data format provides for many uses of the data and allows for future use of the data for other land-use decisions. Examples of data listed under the variable "vegetation height" include upland hardwoods, hardwoods with conifers, oak hickory, pin cherry, white pine, popple with white birch, jack pine, swamp hardwood, white cedar, tamarack, tag alder, willow, dogwood, and nonvegetated.

Data-bank generation After the study area has been selected, the data are collected and interpreted in a spatial format suitable for computer storage in the form of uniform cells. Data are stored on a percentage of cell basis. For example, if a water data type encompasses the entire cell, the value stored is 100. The computer printout examples which follow represent one portion (900 square kilometers; 3,600 one quarter cells) of the total study area for the Wisconsin Power and Light transmission-corridor location study. The 3,600-cell study area is located in Dane and Columbia counties in south central Wisconsin. The source of the power is a fossil-fuel plant located in cell 8105 + 3035 and the terminus is a substation located in cell 8090 + 3250. Each mapped symbol represents $\frac{1}{4}$ square kilometer, with the visually darker cells having greater values and therefore representing the greater

problem. In the process of developing the 20,056-cell data bank, 119 data were collected and 54 additional data were generated, which were used to create 53 variables and 19 components for the 7 determinants.

Example — Visual Determinant Model Development

The determinant "maximization of compatibility with potential visual exposure" utilized in the WPL and MGE application (Niemann, 1973), as described in Table 1 and Figure 1, has been chosen to expand the determinant-development procedure. This determinant was included because the constraint development process revealed (through input from participants) that the visual aspects of transmission towers and public response to them have generated concern for more aesthetic considerations in locating transmission systems to minimize visual impact. The model was structured using group participating techniques (previously described) to identify the land-activity context in which the transmission system may be seen, areas that conceal the tower with topographic features, and vegetation that can act as a screen. This search was accomplished with a program developed for WPL

Figure 2
Potential exposure to rural land uses.

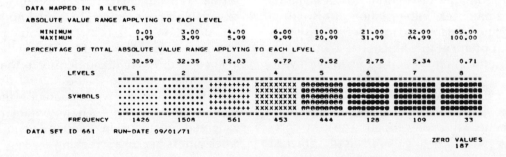

Data Set ID 661
Potential exposure from rural land uses

Phase one, power-transmission-line
corridor-selection study

Columbia power-generating plant
to North Madison substation

15%

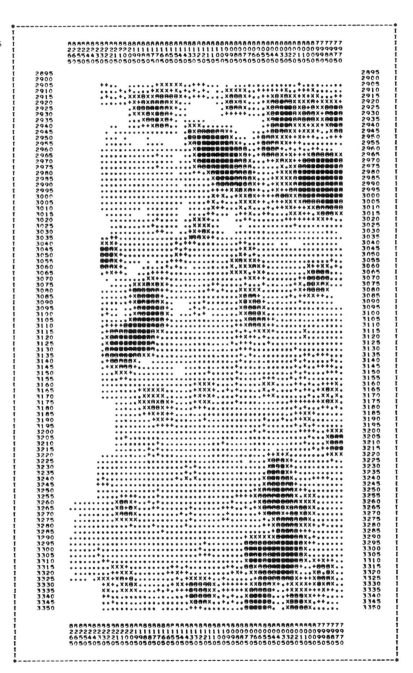

called LUSEARCH, which, based upon described parameters, searches adjoining cells (Niemann, 1973).

To analyze the type of exposure, viewers and the context in which the tower would be seen were identified as five variables. Figure 2 depicts the analysis and output of the variable "potential exposure to rural land uses" (661); the weighting was based on the compatibility of the transmission facility (tower and conductor) and the existing land use (the *darker* the cell, the *less* compatible the transmission system). The consensus of the determinant model development seminar participants was that towers are least offensive in industrial and commerical areas due to the functional characteristics of these areas and associated smoke stacks, parking lots, storage areas, and the like. At the other extreme, transmission towers were more than twice as offensive in residential or institutional areas (see Table 1 and Figure 1). Additionally, the model hypothetically places a tower in each cell and searches visually in a 1-mile radius around the tower, accumulating information about potential viewers (land-use activity types), and selects the most suitable alternative locations on the basis of the land-use activity.

The extent of "potential exposure to recreational and conservational land uses" (662) was a separate variable (Figure 3), based on the consensus of the participants that much of the

Wisconsin environment is used for recreational purposes. This variable considers only those areas that are publicly owned and used for recreational or conservational purposes. As stated previously, the model (LUSEARCH) searched not only at the individual cell, but at adjacent cells as well.

Much of the study area to be traversed by a transmission system is utilized for recreation other than public or quasi-public land recreation. The variable "potential exposure to water systems being used for recreational activities" (663) (Niemann, 1973) took into consideration the water systems that are legally public and are being used for fishing or boating, although they are not labeled as recreational land. The continuum of weights was based upon the type of user and the compatibility of the view of transmission towers by participants in various recreational activities and environments. Figure 4 spatially illustrates this analysis. John Muir's View, the only unique view officially recognized by the Wisconsin Historical Society (664) was the fourth variable based upon uniqueness, historic importance, and existence as a visual resource within the study area. The area encompassed by this view from a highway overlook is shown in Figure 5.

The final variable involved consideration of

Figure 3
Potential exposure to recreational and conservational land uses.

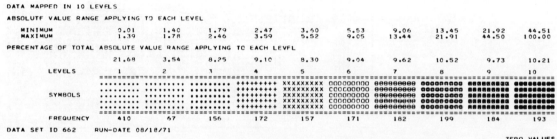

```
DATA MAPPED IN 10 LEVELS
ABSOLUTE VALUE RANGE APPLYING TO EACH LEVEL
       MINIMUM        0.01    1.40    1.79    2.47    3.60    5.53    9.06   13.45   21.92   44.51
       MAXIMUM        1.39    1.78    2.46    3.59    5.52    9.05   13.44   21.91   44.50  100.00
PERCENTAGE OF TOTAL ABSOLUTE VALUE RANGE APPLYING TO EACH LEVEL
                      21.68    3.54    8.25    9.10    8.30    9.04    9.62   10.52    9.73   10.21
       LEVELS           1       2       3       4       5       6       7       8       9      10

       SYMBOLS

       FREQUENCY      410      67     156     172     157     171     182     199     184     193
DATA SET ID 662    RUN-DATE 08/18/71

                                                                              ZERO VALUES
                                                                                  2958
```

Data Set ID 662
Potential exposure from
recreation and conservation
land uses

Phase one, power-transmission-line
corridor-selection study

Columbia power-generating plant
to North Madison substation

30%

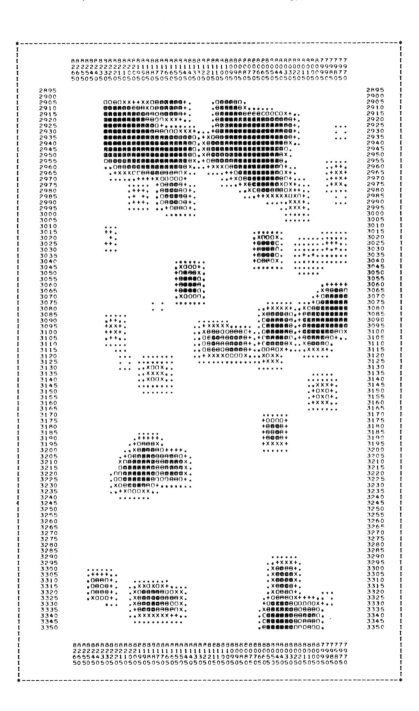

the extent of potential visual exposure to passing motorists. Figure 6 displays the weights and results as applied to varying levels of highway use. The search routine (LUSEARCH) was used to identify the area of potential vision from the highway. The broad bands shown encompass the highways and their gradually diminishing potential for viewing a hypothetical transmission facility adjacent to the highway right-of-way (Niemann, 1973).

The five variables described (see Figure 1 and Table 1) were then combined to form component 724, "type of potential visual exposure" (see Figure 7). It was concluded by the model-weighting participants that the weights reflect the intensity of the potential visual conflict. The higher weights were applied to the recreational considerations (variables 662 and 663) because the consensus was that people seek such areas to get away from other people and the ever-present urban form. Less weight was given to highway uses, because people are still present in great numbers and the highways in question are more functional than scenic. There were no identified scenic highways in the study area.

Having identified the extent of potential exposure, the remaining two components, "potential visual access to facility" (725) and "potential visual screen" (726), search for potential screening by topographic relief and vegetation. Utilizing the stored data on elevations at various points in each cell, an analysis was made of the relative change in elevation, assuming that a hypothetical tower was located in the center of the designated cell. By comparing the centroid elevation of the location of the hypothetical tower with the adjacent edge elevations and the centroid elevations of the adjacent cells, the model identifies areas where topographic features are sufficient to conceal a tower. This selection equation uses the sum of the differences of the adjacent edge and centroid elevations, calculates the potential topographic screen, and spatially displays the output in map format. Figure 8 is the output of this analysis. Once again, the darker symbols indicate the greater incompatibility with a transmission system. The problem in this instance was an absence of topographic screening. The light areas of the map display the Baraboo Bluffs (a large unglaciated geographic formation), stream valleys, and an east–west ridge line about midway on the computer map.

The component "potential visual screen" (726) encompasses two variables: the height of the vegetation and the density of the vegetation. Figure 9 displays the location and potential screening of vegetation based on the average height of the vegetational species present. "Vegetation density" (666) considers vegeta-

Figure 4
Potential exposure to water systems used for recreational activities.

Data Set ID 663
Potential exposure from water
systems used for recreation

Phase one, power-transmission-line
corridor-selection study

Columbia power-generating plant
to North Madison substation

25%

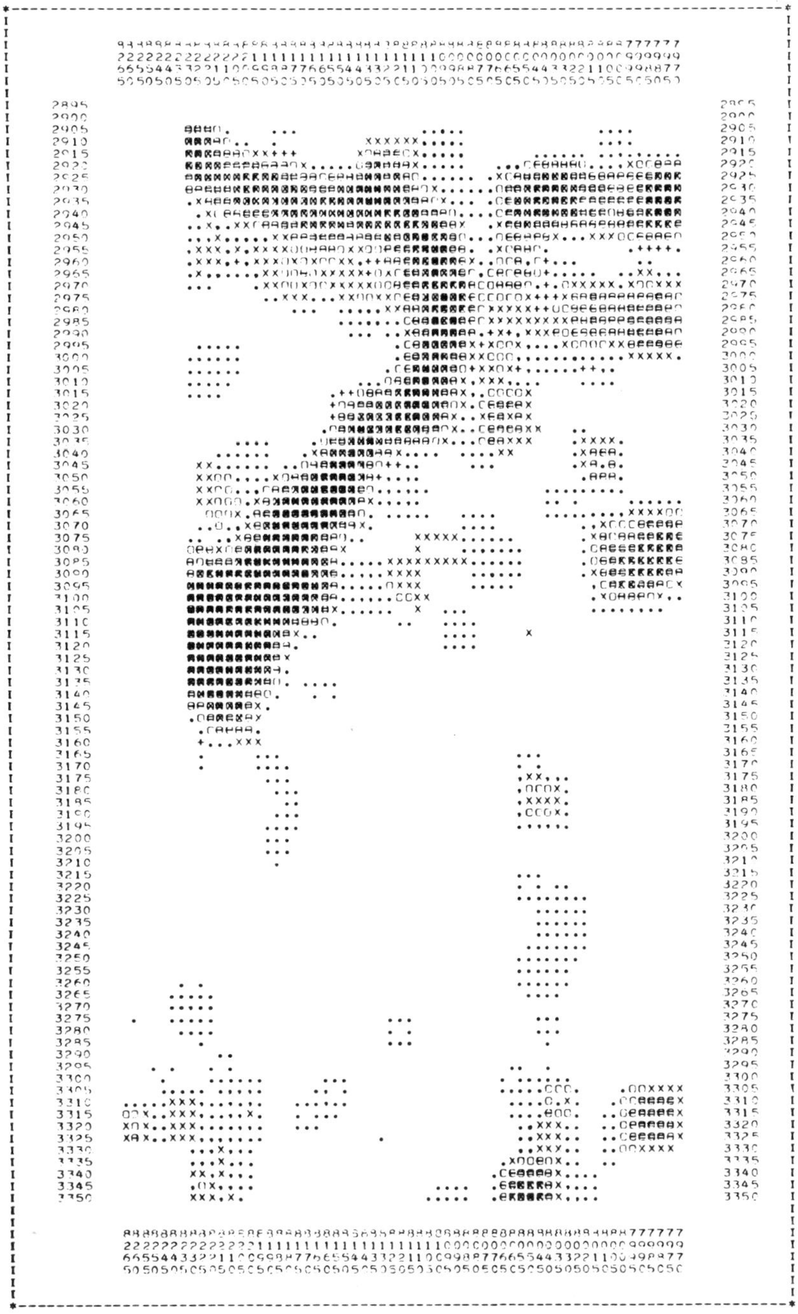

tion (or capacity to see a transmission system behind the vegetation type in question) applied to three categories of vegetational density: open, medium, and closed, plus cultivated plantations. The analysis is displayed in map forms as Figure 10. In combining vegetation height and density, greater importance was given to height as a potential to screen transmission towers. Figure 11 comprises the component "potential visual screen" (776), and it should be noted that the darker area to the south and southeast of the study area presents the greatest visual problems. This area is heavily farmed and includes the Arlington prairie (an area known for farm productivity); hence, the absence of vegetation and its screening potential.

The three components "type of potential visual exposure" (724), "potential visual access to facility" (725), and "potential visual screen" (726) were then combined in the final analysis to the magnitude of influence each has in the determinant "maximization of compatibility with potential visual exposure" (see Figure 12). The determinant name represents the factor concerned with visual awareness or perception of a potential transmission system. The weights applied indicate the reflective importance of the components that comprise the visual factor. The component weights were 50 percent of the total consideration for "extent of the potential exposure" (724), 30 percent for "po-

tential visual access to facility" (725), and 20 percent for "potential visual screen" (726) (Miller and Niemann, 1971). As in the case of the relationship of data to variable manipulation (percentage of cell value times the data weight) and the manipulation of the variable to component weight (percentage of cell value times variable weight), the cell receiving the highest cell score is rescaled to 100, thereby assuring that at each level (variable, component, or determinant) the worst condition is represented. This rescaling or normalization process is necessary to assure that the value assigned at the data, variable, or component level maintains its designated relative influence. Lesser value was assigned to vegetation, because of its nonpermanent characteristic. To generalize, the major recreation areas, the major urban areas, and the interstate highway are each areas that potentially contain the most severe problems from the visual awareness or perception point of view.

As stated before in relation to the BPA conceptual investigation, 12 determinants were developed to represent the BPA service area and seven determinants were developed for the WPL and MGE application; the determinant "maximization of compatibility with potential visual exposure" was elaborated upon. The

Figure 5
John Muir's View.

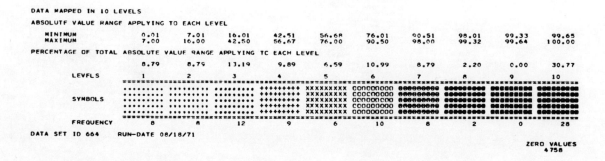

Data Set ID 664
Unique views

Phase one, power-transmission-line
corridor-selection study

Columbia power-generating plant
to North Madison substation

10%

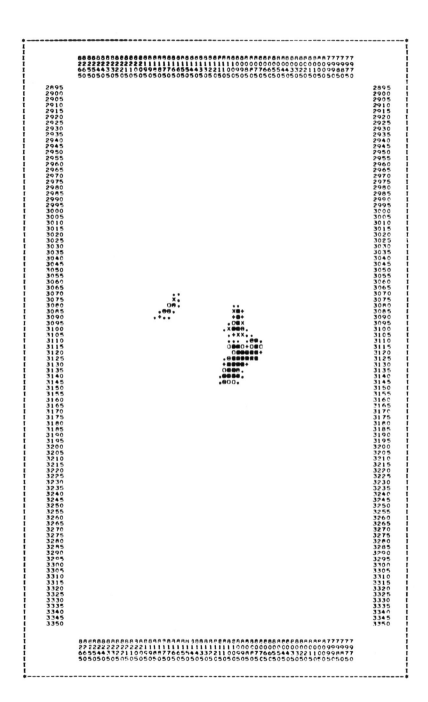

same type of weighting, data manipulation, and mapping was accomplished for the remaining six determinants. The relative combining of the determinants creates the next level — that of policy.

Policy

Policies (the combination of weighted determinants) are derived by reviewing the concerns expressed in the seminars through the questionnaires and interaction with the client and public groups.

The previous discussion described the means by which transmission-corridor location determinants were identified, created, and manipulated. Each determinant, in concept, exerts some influence upon the final corridor selection. At the determinant level, values (or weights) were applied to data, variables, and components by professionals, based upon their education and experience. The question of the importance of any given determinant was *not* part of the determinant development. This procedure of separating the development of the determinant location factor, based on objective expertise, from the location or policy question is an important concept (Miller and Niemann, 1971). It provides a forum for the resource expert to interact with all decision makers to influence the location of the transmission system in question. The resource ex-

pert can maximize the use of his or her education and experience. The policy-level decision remains the responsibility of people at decision-making levels. A similar approach was applied in the Interstate 57 study, an interstate right-of-way corridor-selection study (Miller and Niemann, 1971). Some of the policies were developed by the Wisconsin Highway Commission members. The procedure was one of attempting to approximate the variance in views expressed to them as a result of chairing public hearings on highway location. The same basic procedure was utilized in the WPL and MGE application, in which the consultants (Landscapes Limited) and the clients generated a series of policies together. Altogether, 20 policies were developed by weighting the seven determinants in various combinations.

The establishment of policies to be considered and applied for consideration is obviously an important step. Objective methods of developing representative policies by direct public involvement are essential because of the inherent dynamic characteristics of the machine application. To date the authors have not attempted public interaction involvement at the policy level because of client timidity and inexperience. Public involvement is essential and must become part of policy-scale decisions.

Figure 6
Potential exposure to highways.

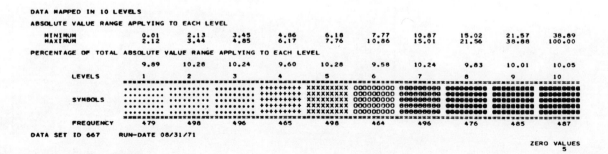

Data Set ID 667
Potential exposure from highways

Phase one, power-transmission-line
corridor-selection study

Columbia power-generating plant
to North Madison substation

20%

Once the policies have been established, determinants are weighted to reflect a specific policy, and a computer optimization route is developed. The program (LU 140) calculates and selects the optimum route based upon the described policy and on a "least-cost" concept. The "least cost" would be when the cells represent the policy of greater cost. As part of the same procedure, probable resource impact affected within the one-cell corridor can be quantified, and sensitivity to other policies can be reviewed. Corridor selection therefore is based upon knowledge of the probable impact before construction. Also, the geographical location of the policy can be considered. The corridor optimization procedure provides for policy development and then objective corridor selection. This assures that personal corridor selection by decision makers is minimized. In addition, corridors selected by others can have input by storing the cell locations and be evaluated and compared with machine-selected corridors on the basis of sensitivity to other policies (agreement or variance) and probable resource impact.

Figure 13 represents a policy of more emphasis upon natural systems. This alternative represents a weighting of emphasis toward determinants that make up the natural landscape and deemphasis of determinants that comprise other concerns, such as cost and human settlement factors. (The darker the cells, the more

inappropriate the location for the transmission corridor.) The visual aspect is included and represents 12 percent of the alternative. The remaining 88 percent is shared in varying proportions by the remaining six determinants. (The large dark band in Figure 13 is an area that comprises an existing 345-kilovolt system which, because of power grid requirements, cannot be paralleled within 1 mile of the centerline.) Figure 14 is the output of the LU 140 program, which, as described, optimizes a route given the calculated or coefficient values of each cell in the policy model. From one known point (power-plant site or substation), optimized corridors can and were run for a series of policies. The development of various policies is only limited by the ability, willingness, or time to develop them. Results have indicated that given enough difference in policy (difference in weighting of the determinants) the transmission or highway route will shift geographical location. Also, and very importantly, at times different policies will concur or overlay each other locationally. This was the case in the WPL and MGE study when sharing existing utility rights-of-way was an emphasized policy. The eventual decision as to which policy to select and, therefore, which corridor location to use remains a human

Figure 7
Type of potential visual exposure.

```
DATA MAPPED IN 10 LEVELS
ABSOLUTE VALUE RANGE APPLYING TO EACH LEVEL
    MINIMUM         0.01    3.15    4.57    5.01    8.16    10.97   14.99   21.06   27.89   40.01
    MAXIMUM         3.14    4.56    5.00    8.15    10.96   14.98   21.05   27.88   40.00   100.00
PERCENTAGE OF TOTAL ABSOLUTE VALUE RANGE APPLYING TO EACH LEVEL
                    10.06   10.13   3.05    17.10   9.69    10.02   9.96    10.06   9.45    10.48
    LEVELS          1       2       3       4       5       6       7       8       9       10
    SYMBOLS
    FREQUENCY       488     491     148     829     470     486     483     488     458     508
DATA SET ID 724    RUN-DATE 09/01/71
                                                                              ZERO VALUES
                                                                                  0
```

Data Set ID 724
Extent of potential visual
exposure

Phase one, power-transmission-line
corridor-selection study

Columbia power-generating plant
to North Madison substation

50%

```
8888888899999999888888888888888888888888888888888888888888888888777777
22222222222222211111111111111111111111100000000000000000000999999
66554433221100998877665544332211009998877665544332211009998877
5050505050505050505050505050505050505050505050505050505050505050

2895                                                                        2895
2900                                                                        2900
2905        8880008888888888888888880BX0X8880X+.........++XX+X0X0X+.        2905
2910        888888888888888888888808BXN008880XXXX8+++++XX+XXX0000+++        2910
2915        88888888888888888880000X+0888888888000X+X8888800X+          2915
...
3350        .+.+.++++......+.+......+X+++08888888888888+.......         3350

8888888899999999888888888888888888888888888888888888888888888888777777
22222222222222211111111111111111111111100000000000000000000999999
66554433221100998877665544332211009998877665544332211009998877
5050505050505050505050505050505050505050505050505050505050505050
```

process, but the policy reasons for the selection are quite visible and open to review.

Comment

As it seemed to the study team, this model has the following characteristics. Structured procedures of problem solving can be accomplished utilizing more traditional modes of information manipulation, such as the two-dimensional overlay method; current and future technology is capable of coping with the quantitative requirements of decision makers and the judicial and legislative process.

It has become increasingly apparent that decisions related to electric-energy-transmission problem solving and similar problems are complex and probably extend beyond the traditional professional limits and expertise. Although the traditional disciplines provide a vital contribution to the process, social and environmental responsibility requires reform. The important concern for economy, system reliability, and public safety must be supplemented by representation of broader social, economic, and environmental inputs provided by competent individuals from a variety of disciplines, and objective techniques must be developed equal to the complexity of the problem.

Figure 8
Potential visual access to facility.

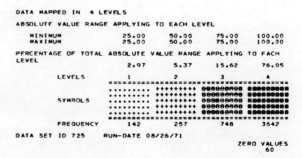

Data Set ID 725
Potential visual access to
facility

Phase one, power-transmission-line
corridor-selection study

Columbia power-generating plant
to North Madison substation

30%

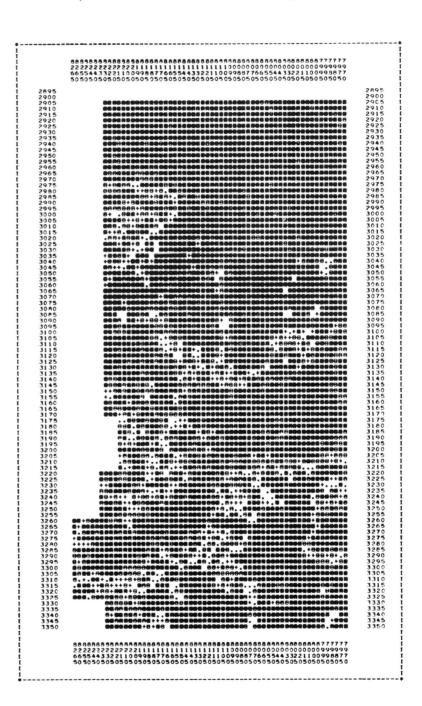

Figure 9
Vegetation height.

```
DATA MAPPED IN 10 LEVELS
ABSOLUTE VALUE RANGE APPLYING TO EACH LEVEL
     MINIMUM        0.01     43.33    55.21    65.68    73.89    80.19    85.65    91.32    96.44    99.22
     MAXIMUM       43.32     55.20    65.67    73.88    80.18    85.64    91.31    96.43    99.21   100.00
PERCENTAGE OF TOTAL ABSOLUTE VALUE RANGE APPLYING TO EACH LEVEL
                    9.99     10.11    10.23     9.88     9.82    10.81    10.44    10.17    10.29     8.29

     LEVELS           1        2        3        4        5        6        7        8        9       10
                   =========================================================================================
     SYMBOLS      ......... ......... ......... +++++++++ XXXXXXXXX CCCCCCCCC 888888888 ......... ......... .........
                   =========================================================================================
     FREQUENCY      484      490      496      479      476      524      506      493      499      402
DATA SET ID 665   RUN-DATE 08/18/71
                                                                                          ZERO VALUES
                                                                                               0
```

Data Set ID 665
Vegetation height

Phase one, power-transmission-line
corridor-selection study

Columbia power-generating plant
to North Madison substation

60%

Figure 10
Vegetation density.

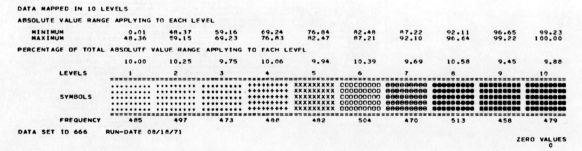

DATA SET ID 666   RUN-DATE 08/18/71

Data Set ID 666
Vegetation density

Phase one, power-transmission-line
corridor-selection study

Columbia power-generating plant
to North Madison substation

40%

Figure 11
Potential visual screen.

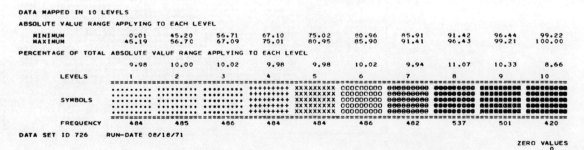

DATA MAPPED IN 10 LEVELS

ABSOLUTE VALUE RANGE APPLYING TO EACH LEVEL

MINIMUM	0.01	45.20	56.71	67.10	75.02	80.96	85.91	91.42	96.44	99.22
MAXIMUM	45.19	56.70	67.09	75.01	80.95	85.90	91.41	96.43	99.21	100.00

PERCENTAGE OF TOTAL ABSOLUTE VALUE RANGE APPLYING TO EACH LEVEL

	9.98	10.00	10.02	9.98	9.98	10.02	9.94	11.07	10.33	8.66
LEVELS	1	2	3	4	5	6	7	8	9	10
FREQUENCY	484	485	486	484	484	486	482	537	501	420

DATA SET ID 726   RUN-DATE 08/18/71

ZERO VALUES
0

Data Set ID 726
Potential visual screen

Phase one, power-transmission-line
corridor-selection study

Columbia power-generating plant
to North Madison substation

20%

Figure 12
Maximization of compatability with potential visual exposure.

```
DATA MAPPED IN 10 LEVELS
ABSOLUTE VALUE RANGE APPLYING TO EACH LEVEL
     MINIMUM        0.01     43.56     50.22     54.24     57.17     59.38     61.32     63.83     68.06     74.78
     MAXIMUM       43.55     50.21     54.23     57.16     59.37     61.31     63.82     68.05     74.77    100.00
PERCENTAGE OF TOTAL ABSOLUTE VALUE RANGE APPLYING TO EACH LEVEL
                   10.09      9.92      9.92      9.94     10.13     10.19      9.86      9.96     10.05      9.94
     LEVELS            1         2         3         4         5         6         7         8         9        10
```

```
     FREQUENCY       487       479       479       480       489       492       476       481       485       480
DATA SET ID 806    RUN-DATE 01/25/72
                                                                                            ZERO VALUES
                                                                                                 0
```

Data Set ID 806
Maximization of compatibility
with potential visual exposure

Phase one, power-transmission-line
corridor-selection study

Columbia power-generating plant
to North Madison substation

Figure 13
Naturalist's viewpoint with all others.

```
DATA MAPPED IN 10 LEVELS
ABSOLUTE VALUE RANGE APPLYING TO EACH LEVEL

    MINIMUM        0.01    20.66    22.49    24.92    28.27    30.26    31.01    35.13    39.72    74.61
    MAXIMUM       20.65    22.48    24.91    28.26    30.25    31.00    35.12    39.71    74.60   100.00

PERCENTAGE OF TOTAL ABSOLUTE VALUE RANGE APPLYING TO EACH LEVEL

                  10.11    10.15     9.96     9.88    10.21     4.62    15.33     9.92     9.76    10.07

        LEVELS      1        2        3        4        5        6        7        8        9       10
               ===========================================================================================
               ......... ,,,,,,,,, ......... +++++++++ XXXXXXXXX OOOOOOOOO 888888888 [illegible] [illegible] [illegible]
               ......... ,,,,,,,,, ......... +++++++++ XXXXXXXXX OOOOOOOOO 888888888 [illegible] [illegible] [illegible]
        SYMBOLS  ......... ,,,,,,,,, ......... +++++++++ XXXXXXXXX OOOOOOOOO 888888888 [illegible] [illegible] [illegible]
               ......... ,,,,,,,,, ......... +++++++++ XXXXXXXXX OOOOOOOOO 888888888 [illegible] [illegible] [illegible]
               ......... ,,,,,,,,, ......... +++++++++ XXXXXXXXX OOOOOOOOO 888888888 [illegible] [illegible] [illegible]
               ===========================================================================================
        FREQUENCY  488      490      481      477      493      223      740      479      471      486

DATA SET ID 906    RUN-DATE 01/08/72

                                                                                            ZERO VALUES
                                                                                                 0
```

Data Set ID 906
Naturalist's viewpoint with all
others

Phase one, power-transmission-line
corridor-selection study

Columbia power-generating plant
to North Madison substation

```
88888888888888888888888888888883888888888888888888888888777777
22222222222222211111111111111111111000000000000000000000999999
665544332211009988776655443322110099887766554433221100998877
50505050505050505050505050505050505050505050505050505050505050
```

2895	2895
2900	2900
2905	2905
2910	2910
2915	2915
2920	2920
2925	2925
2930	2930
2935	2935
2940	2940
2945	2945
2950	2950
2955	2955
2960	2960
2965	2965
2970	2970
2975	2975
2980	2980
2985	2985
2990	2990
2995	2995
3000	3000
3005	3005
3010	3010
3015	3015
3020	3020
3025	3025
3030	3030
3035	3035
3040	3040
3045	3045
3050	3050
3055	3055
3060	3060
3065	3065
3070	3070
3075	3075
3080	3080
3085	3085
3090	3090
3095	3095
3100	3100
3105	3105
3110	3110
3115	3115
3120	3120
3125	3125
3130	3130
3135	3135
3140	3140
3145	3145
3150	3150
3155	3155
3160	3160
3165	3165
3170	3170
3175	3175
3180	3180
3185	3185
3190	3190
3195	3195
3200	3200
3205	3205
3210	3210
3215	3215
3220	3220
3225	3225
3230	3230
3235	3235
3240	3240
3245	3245
3250	3250
3255	3255
3260	3260
3265	3265
3270	3270
3275	3275
3280	3280
3285	3285
3290	3290
3295	3295
3300	3300
3305	3305
3310	3310
3315	3315
3320	3320
3325	3325
3330	3330
3335	3335
3340	3340
3345	3345
3350	3350

```
88888888888888888888888888888888888888888888888888888888777777
22222222222222211111111111111111111000000000000000000000999999
665544332211009988776655443322110099887766554433221100998877
50505050505050505050505050505050505050505050505050505050505050
```

Figure 14
Optimized corridor of naturalist's viewpoint with all others.

DATA MAPPED IN 1 LEVELS

ABSOLUTE VALUE RANGE APPLYING TO EACH LEVEL

MINIMUM	0.10
MAXIMUM	0.10

PERCENTAGE OF TOTAL ABSOLUTE VALUE RANGE APPLYING TO EACH LEVEL

100.00

LEVELS	1
SYMBOLS	▓▓▓▓▓▓▓▓▓
FREQUENCY	57

DATA SET ID 906 RUN-DATE 01/14/72

ZERO VALUES
2505

Data Set ID 906
Naturalist's viewpoint with all
others

Phase one, power-transmission-line
corridor-selection study.

Optimum corridor for power
transmission lines between the
Columbia generating station and
the North Madison substation.

Anomaly sensitivity high

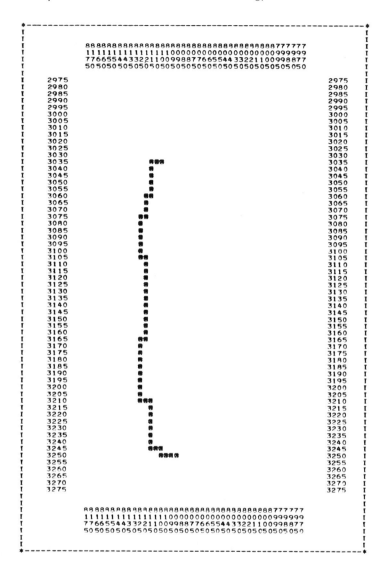

Model for Evaluation of the Visual–Cultural Resources of the Southeastern New England Region

R. Jeffrey Riotte, Julius Gy. Fabos, and
Ervin H. Zube

Until the 1960s, public policy relating to scenic resources, identification, and management manifested itself primarily in the form of national, state, and local parks for recreational uses. The "everyday" nonurban environment was ignored as a scenic resource of value. Most planning programs that included consideration of scenic resources were oriented to recreation and tended to focus on the identification of specific sites for public use.

Since the mid 1960s, however, there has been an increasing concern with scenic values in the landscape as they relate to a broader range of resource issues than recreation alone. Several multibasin, water-resources planning studies have included specific efforts to assess the visual–cultural quality of the regional landscape continuum (for example, the North Atlantic region, the Upper Mississippi River, and the Red, Rainy, and Souris rivers). In addition, under the Water Resource Planning Act of 1965, multipurpose water-resources planning studies have attempted to include data on scenic resources as inputs to the resource-allocation decision process. The data have tended to be most useful in geographic terms; that is, in identifying those sections of the

R. Jeffrey Riotte is a senior planner on the Merrimack Valley Planning Commission, Haverhill, Massachusetts.

Julius Gy. Fabos is an Associate Professor in the Department of Landscape Architecture and Regional Planning at the University of Massachusetts.

Ervin H. Zube is the Director of the Institute for Man and Environment and a Professor in the Department of Landscape Architecture and Regional Planning at the University of Massachusetts.

planning region where certain resource development or management practices should be encouraged or prohibited on the basis of their probable impact on the area's scenic quality.

These studies, as well as recent environmental legislation in a number of states (Vermont and Maine, for example), suggest that there are varying scenic values just as there are varying economic values relating to the surface of the land. They also suggest that the visual and cultural values are significant factors for resource planning and management decisions. There are, however, no accepted inventory procedures, classification, and evaluation criteria that are analogous to those used for the assessment of economic values. Zube (1973a) states that

If this concern [for scenic resources] is to become institutionalized in the setting of policy and in resource planning and management decisions, a generally acceptable vocabulary as well as a set of dimensions and procedures for inventory, classification and evaluation of scenic resources is essential.

This chapter describes a landscape-assessment technique that attempts to go further than classification and evaluation, and results in a set of landscape-management recommendations.

Definitions and Assumptions

Landscape assessment involves more than simply evaluating the scenic aspects of the landscape. Implicit in the analysis is the importance of having access to *use* of the landscape. Therefore, the term *landscape quality* as used in this chapter will subsume both these attributes of scenic (visual) quality and accessibility.

The landscape comprises both natural (mountains, rivers) and man-made components (urban areas, farms) interacting to produce varied cultural landscapes, each with individual identifiable images (Zube et al., 1970).

These various images are the results of man's actions on different landscapes over time. They are also a reflection of the values or lack of values man has placed on the land as a resource to be managed for economic, social, and/or environmental values. Within this frame of reference, it is assumed that the concept of landscape quality, like all other value-laden concepts, is culturally derived and may change over time and space (Zube, 1971a).

Objectives of Landscape Assessment

A number of objectives must be satisfied in any approach to landscape assessment. First, it is important that the entirety of the landscape continuum, from the natural to the man-made and from the coast to the mountains, be included in the landscape-classification procedure. Answering basic questions such as what do we have? where is it? and how much? provide the basis for the classification system. The system must identify landscapes of special value to man as well as differences in the "everyday" landscape. Second, the classification and evaluation systems should be applicable to diverse regions. Relative qualities among various landscapes must be identifiable, and changes in quality as a result of changes in human activity on the landscape should be predictable. Finally, the data generated should have utility for the development of recommendations within the established planning framework for the improvement, maintenance, protection, preservation, development, and/or rehabilitation of landscapes within the area under study.

DESIGN OF THE MODEL

In striving to satisfy the aforementioned objectives, a broad general approach has been developed (Figure 1). It consists of three major components: *classification and identification* of the natural and cultural components of the

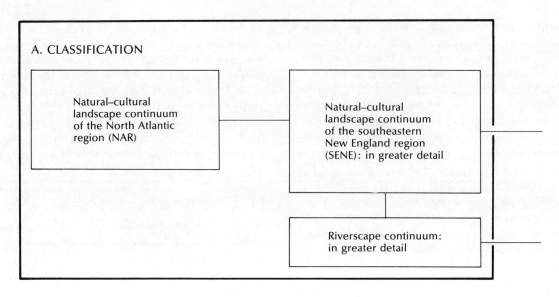

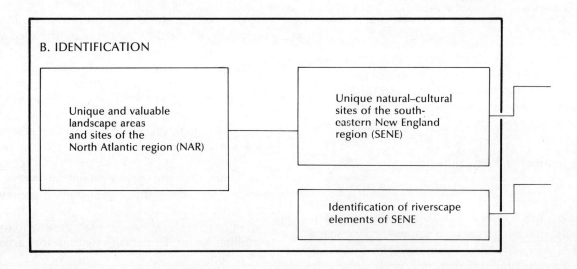

Figure 1
Simplified model for visual–cultural landscape assessment.

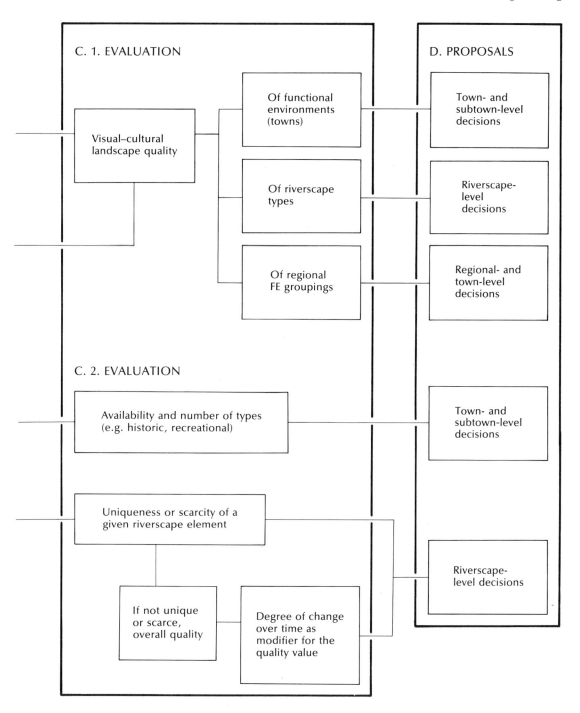

landscapes; *evaluation* or assessment of the relative quality of each of the identified landscape types and areas; *proposals* or development of recommendations for landscape planning and management related to landscape use and quality.

This chapter discusses the application of the model to two regional water-resources planning studies: the North Atlantic Regional Water Resources Study (NAR) and the Southeastern New England Water and Related Land Resources Study (SENE). The latter comprises a small portion of the NAR. The landscape classification systems of both studies explain the evolution of the SENE system as a refinement of the NAR in terms of level of detail and differences in scale. The evaluation variables discussed are those developed at the SENE level of analysis, and proposals or recommendations for action follow that support the evaluative findings.

Relationship between NAR and SENE The NAR study, encompassing 167,000 square miles, included all the major river basins of the United States that drain into the North Atlantic Ocean. The study area extended from North Carolina to the Canadian border and measured approximately 900 miles in length and averaged 200 miles in width. The SENE study area of 4,400 square miles is located within the NAR region and includes the eastern half of Massachusetts, most of Rhode Island, and a small portion of southeastern Connecticut. The smaller area, the larger scale, and the requirement for greater specificity in the SENE study require a more detailed level of inventory and evaluation, as well as the development of recommendations relating to general landscape characteristics and specific sites.

Landscape Classification

NAR landscape classification The NAR regional landscape continuum is conceived as two major systems, the natural and the man-made or the man-manipulated, which is superimposed on the natural system (Zube et al., 1970). Most often the elements of topography, vegetation, and water are associated with the visual image of the natural landscape. Of these, topography or landform is assumed to be the most dominant and the most enduring. This is the most nearly permanent component of the landscape and constitutes basically a fixed supply in terms of both land area and kinds of landform. The landform component, described as being essentially "immutable," comprises the "landscape series" classification. Criteria for distinguishing landform categories or "series" include relative elevation, degree of steepness, and profile configuration. Seven landform series were identified at the NAR scale using these criteria: mountains, steep hills, rolling hills, undulating land, flat land, coastline, and compound landscapes (see Table 1).

Superimposed upon this natural system is the visual manifestation of the presence or absence of man.

This man-made or man-manipulated landscape is one which is more susceptible to change than the landform component of the natural system. Within this man-manipulated system one can identify patterns which have a dominant image that are created as a result of the kind and extent of man's manipulation. These man-manipulated patterns constitute a spectrum which ranges from that landscape which appears to be completely man-made to that which is apparently untouched by man. It includes landscape patterns which generate images of cities, towns, farms, forest, and/or combinations thereof (Zube et al., 1970).

These patterns, which are based more on mutable landscape components (open land, forest lands, developed areas), are the basis for the classification of "landscape units." Criteria for distinguishing various units are areal distribution or percentages of open land, closed (forest) land, land covered with man-made structures, population density, and the distance between towns. Nine regional landscape

Table 1
Landscape Series

Series Name	Description
Mountains	Dominant vertical dimension; at least 2,000 feet of relative elevation between valley floor and ridge line or peak, with a jagged or pointed profile.
Steep hills	High hills rising steeply from the base plane, ranging in height from 800 to 2,000 feet above the adjacent base plane, usually with a strong vertical dimension and a rounded profile.
Rolling hills	Rounded hills with an apparent horizontal dimension ranging in height from 200 to 800 feet, low to moderate slopes, and a rolling profile.
Undulating land	Variation in the horizontal ground plane without identifiable hill forms.
Flat land	Dominant horizontal dimension with little or no variation in the ground plane.
Compound	Combination of any two or more identifiable series of essentially equal visual importance.
Coastline	Dominant water surface and the immediately adjacent strip of land.

units were identified: center city, intermediate city, fringe city, special pattern, town–farm, farm, farm–forest, forest–town, and forest–wildland. The names reflect the dominant visual image imparted by each distinctive landscape unit (see Table 2).

SENE landscape classification The SENE area included three NAR landscape series and four NAR landscape units (see Figure 2). The three landscape series were rolling hills, undulating land, and coastline. No additional criteria were developed to further refine the landscape series *classification* at the SENE level.

The four landscape units found in the SENE area were center city, intermediate city, fringe city, and forest–town. The NAR unit criteria were refined and a new cultural landscape classification, *functional environments* (FEs), was devised. The FE concept was developed to express those visual–cultural characteristics which describe dominant land uses (on a town-by-town basis) and their respective distributions throughout the planning region. An FE was defined as "A general landscape class determined by a prescribed proportion of open, forest, and urban land uses, population distribution and the population density per square mile within that town" (Bartels et al., 1972).

Thus, at the SENE level, five FEs were established: center city, intermediate city, fringe city, forest-town clustered, and forest-town dispersed (see Figure 3). Each FE is characterized in terms of land-use proportions and densities (see Table 3). For example, a forest–town clustered functional environment consists of at least 5 percent open land, at least 60 percent forest land, 0–25 percent developed land, with at least half of the development clustered rather than dispersed, and less than 1,000 people per square mile. The FE classification system provides a means for analyzing environments of similar characteristics.

Coinciding with the development of the five FE types at the town level, more detailed study was focused on the major river corridors (Clifford, 1973). Each of the 14 major river corridors in the region was inventoried and then classified into subsections on the basis of the most prevalent land uses. The corridor was defined as extending approximately ½ mile from each bank of the river. Seven distinct *riverscape functional environments* (RFEs) were identified. In four areas one land use (landscape

LANDSCAPE CONTINUUM (NAR)

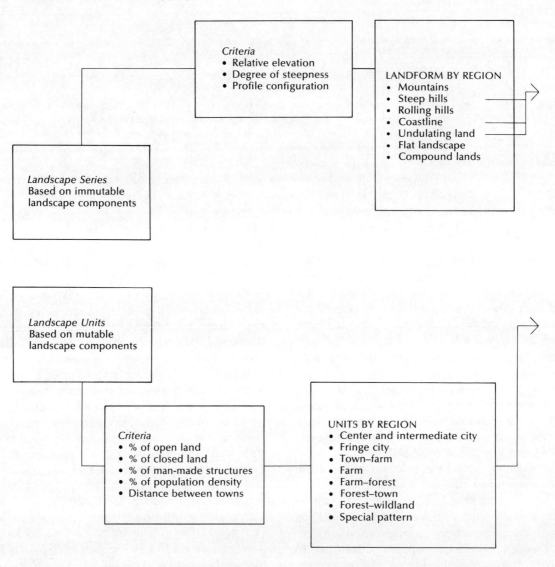

Criteria
- Relative elevation
- Degree of steepness
- Profile configuration

LANDFORM BY REGION
- Mountains
- Steep hills
- Rolling hills
- Coastline
- Undulating land
- Flat landscape
- Compound lands

Landscape Series
Based on immutable
landscape components

Landscape Units
Based on mutable
landscape components

Criteria
- % of open land
- % of closed land
- % of man-made structures
- % of population density
- Distance between towns

UNITS BY REGION
- Center and intermediate city
- Fringe city
- Town–farm
- Farm
- Farm–forest
- Forest–town
- Forest–wildland
- Special pattern

Figure 2
Submodel A: classification (see also Figure 1).

LANDSCAPE CONTINUUM (SENE)

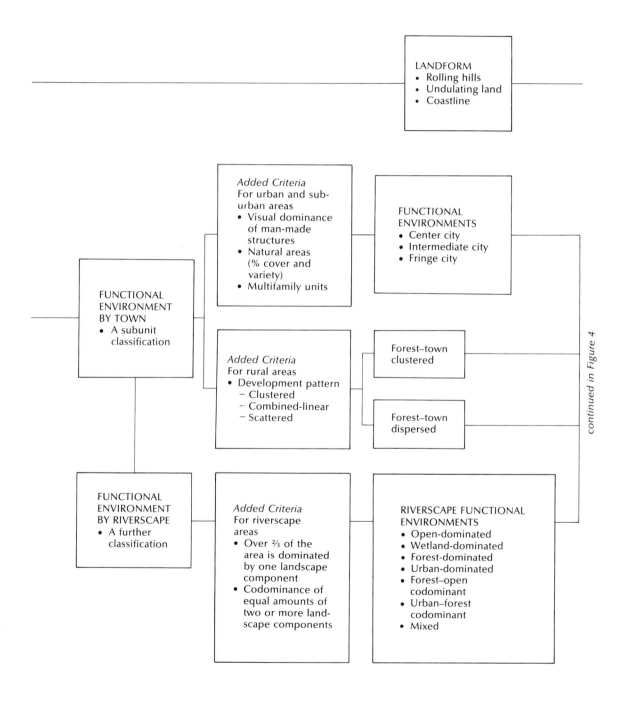

Table 2
Landscape Units

Unit Name	Description
Center city	Typified by the absolute visual dominance of multistory structures, extremes in scale, and a great variety of buildings; open spaces including streets are created and defined by structures; vegetation when it exists is a product of man's manipulation.
Intermediate city	Typified by a codominance of structures and open spaces, mainly streets, and a general horizontal character; structures range primarily from densely distributed single-family dwellings to multistory structures and secondary commercial and small-scale industrial developments.
Fringe city	Typified by a general dominance of open spaces exemplified by streets and the spaces around individual structures (yards). Structures are basically single-family dwellings, but include shopping centers, strip developments, and industrial parks.
Special pattern	Landscapes such as those created by large industrial complexes, harbor and warehouse areas, large areas covered by tank farms, transportation centers such as major airports, and concentrations of heavy industry.
Town–farm	Population density ranges from 50–500 persons per square mile, towns average 2 to 5 miles apart, 20–50 percent of the land is in open-field agriculture and less than 65 percent of the land is in forest and/or woodland.
Farm	50 percent or more of the land is in open-field agriculture, less than 50 percent of the land is in forest and/or woodland, population density varies from less than 50 to 500 persons per square mile, and towns range from 2 to more than 5 miles apart.
Farm–forest	20 to 35 percent of the land is in open-field agriculture, 65–80 percent of the land is in forest and/or woodland, population density varies from less than 50 to 500 persons per square mile, and towns range from 2 to more than 5 miles apart.
Forest–town	65 percent or more of the land is in forest, towns average 2 to 5 miles apart, population density is from 50 to 500 persons per square mile, and less than 20 percent of the land is in open-field agriculture.
Forest–wildland	75 percent or more of the land is in forest or wildland (scrubmarsh and the like), population density is less than 50 persons per square mile, towns average more than 5 miles apart, and less than 20 percent of the land is in open-field agriculture.

component) dominated. In the other three, there were equal amounts of two or more land uses. The seven RFEs were open dominated, wetland dominated, forest dominated, urban dominated, forest–open codominant, urban–forest codominant, and mixed.

Landscape classification summary The approach to landscape classification developed for the NAR study was "broad brush" in scope. It focused on landform or landscape series and land-use pattern or landscape units as the major classification entities. The SENE study

refined parts of this classification system so as to deal with a smaller geographic area and a larger planning scale. The landform classification was used without modification, but the land-use pattern or landscape unit classification was further developed. Landscape units were classified as functional environments. These FEs provided the basis for orienting the landscape inventory to the scale of individual towns within the planning area and also for a more detailed examination of the main stems of the major rivers.

Forest–Town Dispersed FE
(*Linear development along major roadways*)

Forest–Town Clustered FE
(*Houses form a distinct town center*)

Fringe City FE
(*Heavy, single-family-home development throughout town*)

Intermediate City FE
(*Heavily urbanized condition with many multifamily units*)

Center City FE
(*Downtown business–industrial districts*)

Figure 3

Evaluation

Landscape quality within SENE is measured at three levels: town, riverscape or subtown, and multitown or regional (see Figure 4).

Landscape quality at the town level Landscape quality measurements at the town level entail the qualitative assessment of both landform and the functional environment. In terms of landform, it is assumed that greater relative

relief and the relative distribution of landforms enhances landscape quality. Various studies completed in the Department of Landscape Architecture and Regional Planning at the University of Massachusetts seem to confirm the importance of landform as a major input improving relative levels of landscape quality (Burns and Rundell, 1969; Melillo, 1970; Bartels et al., 1972). A more detailed analysis of these studies is discussed in the chapter by Zube et

Table 3
Functional Environment Criteria Used to Classify Towns and Determine Environmental Holding Capacity

FE Criteria	Center City	Intermediate City	Fringe City	Forest–Town Dispersed[a]	Forest–Town Clustered[a]
Max. population density/sq. mile	No limit	10,000	5,000	1,000	1,000
Max. % of developed land	90	80	60	25	25
Min. % of forest and open land	10	20	40	75	75
Min. % of forest land				60	60
Min. % of open land				5	5

[a] Although development patterns were used to divide the forest–towns into dispersed and clustered FEs, for the purpose of determining the environmental holding capacity, only one set of criteria was used.

al. in the perception section. Translating this into categories of elevation change, areas with less than 50 feet of change per square mile are scored low, areas with between 50 and 150 feet of change per square mile are scored medium, and those with over 150 feet of change per square mile are scored high (Bartels et al., 1972). Areas of high, medium, and low relief value were defined and mapped by superimposing a 1-square-mile grid over each town on a U.S. Geological Survey topographic map (1:24,000). Further refinement of landform measurement is currently in progress. The landform measurement system described does not sufficiently express the frequency levels of landform.

Landscape quality at the town level was also influenced by the land-use configurations of each town (FE). It is assumed that greater variety and distribution of land uses also enhance landscape quality. It is also assumed that greater amounts of edge (created by the ad-

jacencies of land uses) as well as increased contrast (brightness, height differentiation, and texture of edges) add to the overall landscape quality of each town. The importance of these variables in influencing levels of landscape quality are further verified in detail in the Bartels et al. (1972) study written at the University of Massachusetts. That volume utilized extensive research gained from earlier studies done primarily by behavioral scientists dealing with variety and distribution concepts as well as edge densities and edge contrast (Berlyne, 1960; Gibson, 1961; Kaplan and Wendt, 1972; Lynch, 1960; Munsinger and Kessen, 1964; Rappaport and Kantor, 1967; Vitz, 1966; Wohlwill, 1968).

Variety of land uses on a town basis was measured again by placing a 1-square-mile grid over 1:62,500 scale maps and determining the number of land uses per unit area. Five general land-use classes (forest, open lands, wetlands, water bodies, and developed land) were in-

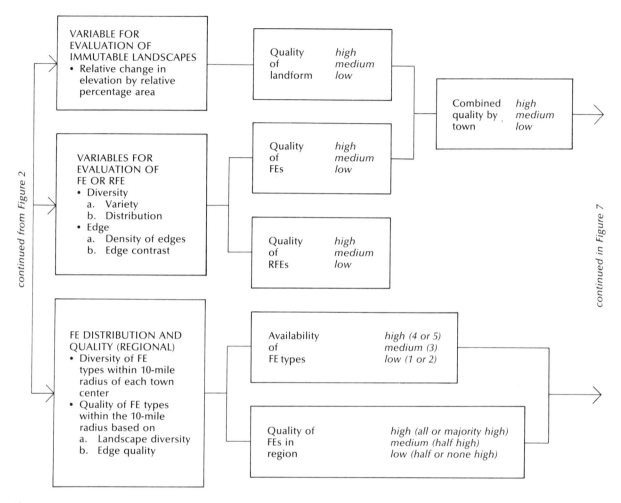

Figure 4
Submodel C-1: evaluation (see also Figure 1).

cluded. The average number of land uses per square mile per town was determined, and towns of the same functional environment were rated high, medium, or low for land-use variety.

Distribution of land-use types throughout the town was visually assessed and rated high, medium, or low. The two variables (variety and distribution) were combined for each town to produce a *diversity index.*

Edge scores were also produced for each town by measuring the total length of edges between land-use types and dividing by the area of the town. The resultant *edge-density* factor is converted into high, medium, or low scores (Bartels et al., 1972). Edge-contrast scores of high, medium, and low were produced on a town basis by adding up all edges and applying weighting factors to those edges that displayed the greatest contrast (for example, a forest–water edge displays greater contrast than a wetland–water edge).

A landscape quality score was developed by adding up diversity and edge. This score, in combination with the previously discussed landform score, produced a *combined landscape quality score* for each town in the SENE region.

Riverscape quality at the subtown level The quality of the riverscape FE is assessed in essentially the same manner, utilizing the same variables, as the town FE (see Figure 4). The major difference is that landform is not included as a qualitative variable under the assumption that the scale of analysis (river corridors) and the general homogeneity of landform along major rivers in SENE renders it insignificant.

Landscape quality at the regional level Landscape quality at the regional or multitown level is a function of both the variety of FE types and the landscape quality scores of the FEs in the region. For example, regions that display little variety of FE types and have low scores for FE quality score low for regional landscape quality. In other words, the homogeneity or diversity of land use across the region is a critical indicator of regional landscape quality.

The variety of FE types is measured in terms of a 10-mile radius from the center of each town. Ten miles appears reasonable in terms of time–distance zones or accessibility, as well as in relation to the overall size of the SENE region. All towns falling within the 10-mile radius of a given town are assessed to determine the multitown or regional FE variety. These data provide an initial basis for recommendations as to which FEs might be altered to increase re-

gional FE variety and/or to accommodate population growth. These data also provide a basis for suggesting *where* population growth can best occur in addition to *how much*.

Similarly, regional recommendations can be made based on the relative quality of FEs. For example, assuming that all variables are essentially equal in a region except for FE landscape quality, the towns with lower landscape quality might be identified for types of development that could enhance land-use diversity and edge diversity (for example, planned unit developments or impoundments).

Landscape–population limitations Functional environment criteria combined with information on soil capabilities were also used for setting theoretical population limits for each town in the SENE region under the assumption that no town would change its FE status. In other words, an upper growth limit was set whereby population increase was limited to maintain the image of the town. In this manner, a rough estimate as to a town's *environmental holding capacity* (population limitations) was determined, with the landscape serving as the independent variable constraining the upper limits of growth.

Under certain circumstances, however, it is desirable for a town to change its present FE status either because of regional issues or because intense growth cannot be avoided. These issues are developed and discussed in detail later in the chapter.

Evaluation summary The approach to landscape evaluation developed in the SENE study focuses on the town, the riverscape, and the multitown region. Towns are analyzed in terms of relative changes in elevation, diversity of land uses, edge densities and contrast, and their landscape–population limitations. River corridors are assessed using the same variables as for towns, but without the landform and the population-limitation inputs. Regions are assessed on the variety of FEs and their relative qualities within the 10-mile-radius multitown region.

Identification of Special-Value Areas and Sites

Identification at the NAR level In addition to the town and riverscape qualities already discussed, specific areas or sites also contribute to our perception of landscape quality. These special-value areas were identified in the NAR study (see Figure 5) by the following criteria: the area is scientifically, historically, or aesthetically significant at the state or regional level; the area has a wilderness quality to it, is remote from roads, and appears to be relatively untouched by man; the area is ecologically fragile and extremely sensitive to the intrusion of man; and the area consists of an unusual combination of ecosystems, landforms, or land-use patterns (Zube et al., 1970).

The application of these criteria resulted in the identification of seven general types of special-value areas: wilderness areas, coastline areas, mountain areas, vegetative areas, areas of high diversity, historical or cultural sites, and unique natural sites.

Identification at the SENE level The last two categories — significant historical or cultural sites and unique natural sites — have been carried forward and utilized in the SENE study. Because of the difference in scale, however, the criteria for defining these unique sites have been further refined. Sites of cultural significance at the SENE town level of analysis include areas with recreational, historic, or educational value; unique natural sites include parks, recreation areas, ecologically fragile areas, wetlands, and unusual vegetative or physiographic sites. At the riverscape level of analysis, specific beach areas, wetlands, mature forest types, and agricultural lands are flagged as de-

serving preservation or protection (Clifford, 1973).

Evaluation of Special-Value Areas and Sites

Availability and quality at town level Special-value natural and cultural sites are identified if they are significant at the town level. However, sites were included only if they were accessible for viewing or physical use. In addition, the numbers of people who can potentially utilize the site and the number of sites available are important in evaluating the contribution of special values to landscape quality on a town basis.

Therefore, a town's *unique-site index* is a function of the number of unique or special-value sites present within a 10-mile radius and of the ratio of the available acres per thousand population. The higher the number of unique sites and the greater the number of acres available per thousand people, the higher the unique-site index and the landscape quality of the town.

Availability and quality at subtown level Unique or unusual sites and areas were also important at the riverscape level of analysis. Those sites deemed as unique or scarce have been identified and mapped (see Figure 5). All other elements — land use areas down to 5 acres in size — are mapped within the river corridor and are evaluated on relative scales, such as most to least, for each of the following variables: fragility, maturity, feature and focal attributes, renewability, internal diversity, and internal contrast. In deriving a combined value for each area, the greatest importance was placed on those areas most resistant to change over time. In other words, the most stable areas, where high landscape quality was associated with elements that were not likely to change rapidly as a result of natural processes,

LANDSCAPE CONTINUUM (NAR)

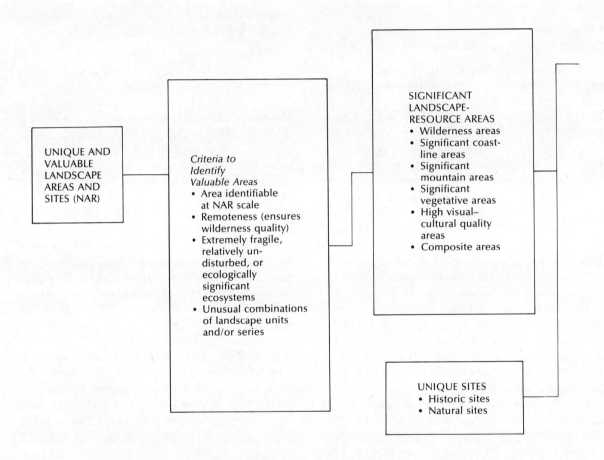

Figure 5
Submodel B: identification of valuable areas and sites (see also Figure 1).

LANDSCAPE CONTINUUM (SENE)

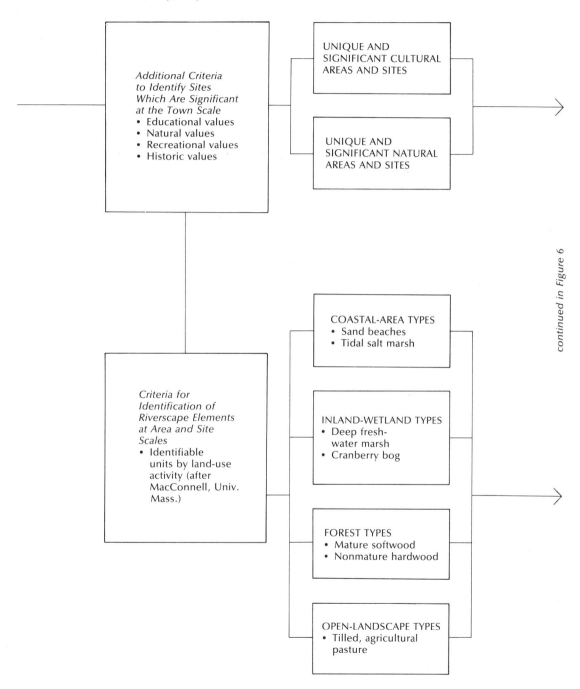

continued in Figure 6

were weighted and ranked highest (see Figure 6).

Planning Proposals

After qualitative evaluations are made on the town, riverscape, and regional levels (Figures 4 and 6), and after all special-value areas and sites are identified (Figure 5), planning proposals are developed for each of the three levels of analysis in terms of landscape preservation, protection, development, or rehabilitation (see Figure 7).

At the town and riverscape levels, recommendations are advanced for the preservation of the highest landscape quality areas. Protection recommendations are directed to the next highest landscape quality areas. Protection recommendations provide for changes in land use, but also provide for carefully delineated land-use controls, which protect critical landscape resources such as shore lines, open land, and ridgelines so that they are accessible — visually and physically. The lowest-quality areas provide opportunities for planning recommendations that use development as a device for enhancing landscape quality. The development of impoundment sites, for example, can introduce diversity into otherwise uniform landscapes. Preservation or protection recommendations including fee simple acquisition are also advanced for all existing unique or special-value natural and cultural sites at both levels.

At the regional level, recommendations relate primarily to the maintenance or change of FEs within towns. With good FE variety and high landscape quality scores, recommendations to maintain existing FEs are advanced. By maintaining these FEs, corresponding environmental holding capacities (population limitations) do not change and land-use patterns are assumed to stabilize. However, for those regions where the variety and quality of FEs is poor, selected FEs are recommended for change (for example, forest town to fringe city), which also automatically revises the environmental-holding-capacity limitations.

SUMMARY

The landscape-assessment model (Figure 1), discussed in this chapter presents an orderly, logical progression of analysis, beginning with an inventory of the study region and followed by the classification of the inventory data and the evaluation of the classification system, which results in a series of planning recommendations. The approach is systematic, workable, and reasonable in terms of time and money requirements. The model attempts to isolate the critical factors that relate directly to evaluating, maintaining, or improving landscape quality. In other words, the general model appears to have potential for fairly broad geographic application.

Another positive aspect of the model is the suggested hierarchy of landscape planning and management recommendations, which are directly related to levels of landscape quality (high quality — preservation, medium quality — protection; and low quality — development or rehabilitation). For example, the evaluation criteria established at the riverscape level state clearly that elements deemed unique or of special value are to be flagged immediately for preservation; all other elements must be analyzed in terms of fragility, maturity, feature and focal attributes, renewability, internal diversity, and internal contrast. Those elements (for example, areas) that score the lowest for the evaluative criteria are subject to recommendations for protection or for development. Most specifically, the model provides a way of relating population growth to landscape quality in explicit terms.

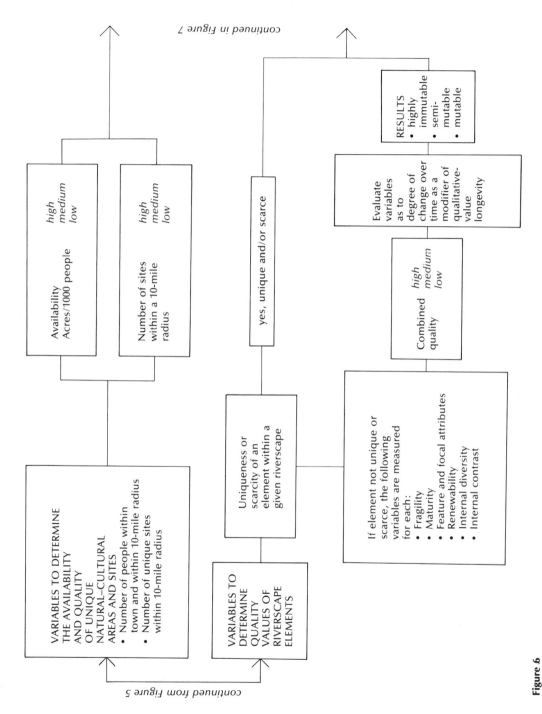

continued in Figure 7

continued from Figure 5

Figure 6
Submodel C-2: evaluation (see also Figure 1).

271

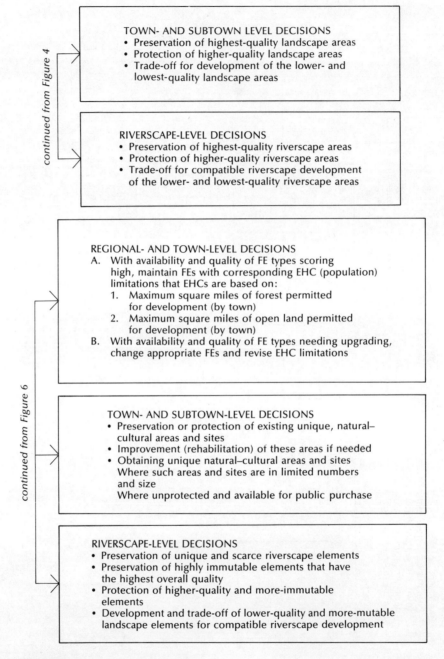

Figure 7
Submodel D: proposals (see also Figure 1).

The model also has the capability to predict changes in quality as a result of changes in human activity on the land (Fabos, 1971). In so doing, the landscape is treated as the independent variable that limits the amount of development permissible based on minimum land-use requirements for each FE. In addition, the model suggests where development should take place to affect landscape quality directly.

The variables used in the model are appropriate to the scale and purpose of the study (Fabos, 1971). They appear to satisfy the study objectives by facilitating recommendations at regional and subregional levels, as well as facilitating specific site recommendations at the local level.

A problem with the model as it presently exists is the complexity arising from the many variables and several levels in the analysis of landscape quality. Even with all these variables, however, the model does not cover all aspects of the landscape-quality spectrum.

The model also requires specific and current data on land use (statistical and spatial) and population density and distribution. These requirements can constrain the model's utility in a number of regions where the requisite data are not available.

In summary, the inventory, classification, and evaluation outlined in this landscape-quality model for southeastern New England represent an attempt to examine a large land area for purposes of developing reasonable planning recommendations for the preservation of high-quality landscapes, for protecting intermediate qualities, and for developing or rehabilitating areas of low quality. It is but one contribution to a comprehensive plan that considers planning interests ranging from the environmental to the economic.

Assessing Landscape Resources: A Proposed Model

Wayne D. Iverson

Our agency, the U.S. Forest Service, is one of many organizations interested in assessing landscape resources so as to be better equipped to place values upon landscape scenes. The values may be expressed as relative values, numerically from 1 to 10 or 0 to 100, or even ultimately in terms of dollars per acre. Without the establishment of numerical or dollar values for scenery, there is a strong likelihood that the value will be underestimated or even ignored. We most definitely recognize that scenery is a valuable resource and have been strongly reminded of it by the public when the results of our land management seemed to indicate that we did not give it a proper value.

There has been strong reluctance in the past to quantify scenic resources, perhaps due to the complexity of the task, which is admittedly much more difficult and time consuming than intuitive judgments aided by arm-waving. Typical of arguments against such quantification (Tennessee Valley Authority, 1938) is "Scenery, like art, is a thing which cannot be classified, tagged, and set apart from all human and other physical contacts and relationships."

Others have come to quite definite conclu-

Wayne D. Iverson is a Regional Landscape Architect for the California Region of the U.S. Department of Agriculture — Forest Service in San Francisco.

274

sions (Dearinger, 1968) that "esthetic and recreational values can be identified, inventoried and used to evaluate a watershed's development potential"; and Leopold (1969b) says "the result of the data collection and analysis indicates that it is possible to set up a list of factors that influence the esthetic nature of a given location." A more conciliatory approach to the problem (Coomber and Biswas, 1973) states that

Beauty, whether it is man-made or natural, can never be accurately measured. There is no reason, however, why it' should not be modeled. By defining the variables associated with an object and a subject's perception of it, a reasonable understanding of aestheticism may be attained.

We have developed a basis for our search for scenic values which is tempered by the premise (Belden and Williams, 1969) that the total composition is more important than its specific parts, and by Litton's (1973) statement:

I recognize that it is not altogether possible to isolate the different components which come together to make up a landscape. Yet it seems essential to try to separate them for the sake of weighting factors and establishing better understanding as to vulnerability sources.

Quantification is dependent upon acceptance of the concept of breaking down a landscape scene to its component parts and studying them separately and collectively to determine if, and how much, they affect the sensitivities of people viewing that scene. Since some degree of visual change is necessary in land-management activities, we are searching for modifications that have the least-negative visual impacts to the majority of those who will view National Forest lands.

We have wrestled with the problem for several years, found some promising avenues to solutions, and feel we are hot on the track of others. In this chapter we shall try to emphasize what appears to be practical for a land-management organization in the field of landscape resource assessment for large land areas, but yet put forth some concepts that might stimulate further research. These large land areas would normally be in the range of 25,000 to 250,000 acres, with an average of 100,000 acres being assessed as one unit. This is not to mean that landscape resource assessment is not or should not be carried out on smaller land units.

The National Forest lands in our region that are being assessed are generally in the mountainous terrain of the Sierra Nevada, Cascade, and Coast ranges of California. In some cases, they are assessed as a part of land-use planning and in others for project planning, such as timber harvesting, road construction, or recreation developments. The areas range from the relatively unmodified and roadless to those which may be heavily modified by roads, utility lines, timber-harvesting activities, recreation developments, and the like. The lands may be viewed in varying degrees by the public from the air, from all types of roads from interstate highways to jeep trails, and from waterways, residences, resorts, campgrounds, and/or hiking trails. The lands are utilized primarily for their capacity to produce water, timber wildlife, forage for livestock, and recreation opportunities.

Taking the basic premise that scenic values result from scenic quality and the market for scenery, we need to know what constitutes scenic quality and its marketability. In this case, scenic quality defines a product of a certain quality and quantity. Quantity is considered since, as suggested (Leopold 1969a), a rare scenic composition often is in greater viewing demand because it occurs infrequently (even though it may be grotesque). The marketability of that product is dependent upon the demand — the numbers and types of existing and potential viewers who wish to view landscapes of the various scenic quality levels. Demand, in turn, is dependent on the location or availability to people of the viewing experiences, whether on-site or through other visual media. We have made a secondary premise that the ability of the landscape to withstand change without long-term impairment of its inherent visual quality is dependent upon its visual variety, the psychological and physical limitations of perception, the land's physical recuperative powers to revegetate itself, the nature and extent of the proposed modification, and actions taken to improve or speed up the land's recuperative powers.

There are numerous ways to set up a visual analysis and assessment model, dependent on the objectives of the study. We have experimented with several of them. We have learned from each study and are continually adding to and readjusting our models to better analyze the data and display them. Two case studies with which we have been associated, the Smith River Highway Visual Analysis, a proj-

ect corridor study, and the Mineral King Visual Analysis, another project-type study, will be discussed.

CASE STUDIES

Smith River Highway Visual Analysis Study

A recent case study is the Smith River Highway Visual Analysis Study (Kunit and Calhoon, 1973), a contracted study by the landscape architectural firm of Royston, Hanamoto, Beck and Abey for a visual analysis of 25 miles of state highway through a scenic canyon in Six Rivers National Forest in Northern California. Since the project involved an existing highway that was proposed for reconstruction to higher standards, there was less need to determine the number and types of people viewing the area than the scenic quality and its ability to

Smith River Highway Analysis Criteria

Natural Sensitivity Criteria	*Visual Attractiveness Criteria*
River flood zone	Number of enclosing sides
Geologic stability	Verticality
Percentage of slope from stream	Valley width
Vegetation size	Visibility of river around landforms
Vegetation density	Vegetation enclosure
Vegetation type	Vegetation size
Soil erosion potential	Surface dimension of river
Recreation use	Vegetation density
Wildlife habitat	Elevation change in river bed
Aspect of slope face	Horizontal distance to nearest shore
	Uniqueness of vegetation
	Texture of surface geology
	Chromatic value of surface geology
	Percentage of time land disturbance is seen
	Divergence from natural line
	Compatibility of resulting surface
	Surface area of landscape disturbance

withstand change without visual quality impairment. The Smith River study team (after macroanalysis to determine the most visually critical sections of the highway through analysis of vegetation, soils, geology, and physiographic spaces), therefore searched out and analyzed two major categories: natural sensitivity of the canyon as a visual resource, and visual attractiveness of the roadway location. Natural sensitivity refers to the relative visual impact potential that a physical phenomenon has in relation to highway construction. Visual attractiveness refers to conditions that combine to form the existing visual impression a driver experiences when traveling this highway, whether positive or negative.

The data were keypunched and stored on the basis of 100- by 100-foot grid cells. The criteria composites were weighted by the contractor's project team and displayed on separate sensitivity and attractiveness computer printouts and comparatively analyzed, along with photomontages of computer perspectives of the proposed highway design, to develop the final recommendations.

Mineral King Visual Analysis

The Mineral King Visual Analysis (Johnson, 1973) is being carried out by our agency as background for an environmental statement. In this study we are working with Elsner and his research staff of the Pacific Southwest Forest and Range Experiment Station on the computer programs and maps. The objective is to evaluate the potential visual impacts of a major winter–summer resort and its alternative transportation developments. Numbers and types of viewers were considered to a greater degree in this study because of the nature of the proposed new development.

Map display of data initially involved three quantifications:

1. Number of times each land unit might be seen from selected viewing points.
2. Variety classes (scenic quality rating).
3. Capability to absorb visual modification.

The first display involved the digitization of 3.1-acre grid cells for the 110,000-acre study area, followed by application of the VIEWIT computer program (Amidon and Elsner, 1968; Elsner, 1971) with sets of scanning points at selected locations on each of the proposed transportation system routes (highway, busway, cog railway, and tramway) and key viewing points for both summer and winter use patterns. The 3.1-acre cell size was chosen on the following criteria: the accuracy of detailed topographic data available, the relative cell size desired, and the mechanical limitations of line printer output maps with $\frac{1}{5}$- by $\frac{1}{6}$-inch character sizes. The computer printout map indicated whether each 3.1-acre grid cell was visible from zero through nine or more times from the scanning points.

The second display was manually developed through analysis of the existing variety of vegetation, landform, rock outcrops, and water bodies. Three classes of scenic quality, A, B, and C, were applied to the scenic continuum on a rather broadbrush approach, initially, in a transparent overlay form.

The third display was also manually developed to indicate the ability of the landscape to absorb modification without scenic quality impairment to the viewer. This involved distance-zone classification to allow for the degree of visual scrutiny to which modifications would be subjected, and ratings of the effectiveness for visual screening of the various types of vegetative cover, combined with ratings of their more detailed variety of texture, color, line, and form (Figure 1). For example, a dense stand of mature white fir would result in a high screening rating but a low rating of mod-

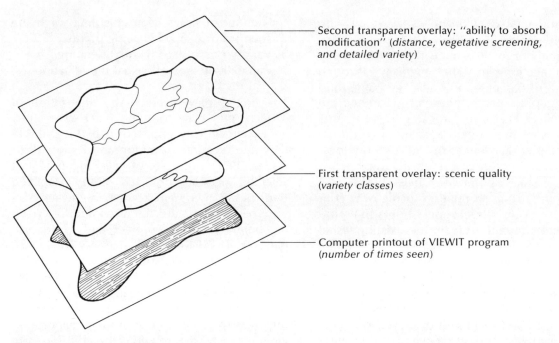

Second transparent overlay: "ability to absorb modification" (*distance, vegetative screening, and detailed variety*)

First transparent overlay: scenic quality (*variety classes*)

Computer printout of VIEWIT program (*number of times seen*)

Figure 1
Initial display — Mineral King Visual Analysis.

ification absorptive capacity for variety due to homogenous line, form, color, and texture characteristics. Thus, its total rating was "*moderate* ability to absorb visual modification as compared to the other areas of the study unit." Landform screening was not considered as it was covered in the first display resulting from the VIEWIT computer program.

Subsequent to this, through the Pacific Southwest Forest and Range Experiment Station we became aware of a computer software package (Travis et al., 1973) that would convert the free-form shapes of "variety classes" and "capability to absorb visual modification" maps into grid-digitized data. This makes possible the compositing of the three separate displays into a single computer output display, rather than having to mix computer line printer output with manually produced transparent overlays. Each of the two maps were digitized

separately and individual computer printouts are being prepared. It was also apparent that the distance-zone classifications could be greatly improved by dropping the foreground, middleground, and background classifications in favor of a computer program to rate distance from scanning points by a weighting system that can be displayed in 10 increments of importance. Distance weights were assigned on the basis of the highest single weight from a combination of scanning points to each grid cell. Cumulative weights would have distorted the system, since they would have given double weighting to the "number of times viewed" factor. For this study it was most appropriate to utilize $\frac{1}{3}$-mile increments and assign the highest weight to the nearest increment. The map will be printed out separately and then combined with the printout map on "ability to absorb modification" to develop a composite.

Another refinement was to add a weighting system to the angle of viewed plane of the grid cells to allow for land surfaces that are seen at acute angles vertically and/or horizontally (Figure 2). Those cells are of less visual magnitude and should be so weighted. This weighting was printed out separately and then combined in the first display computer printout to obtain a composite map that represented the "number of times viewed" printout. The final display of the visual analysis involves a total composite by computer printout of initial displays 1, 2, and 3, which had all been digitized (Figure 3). Thus, one composite computer printout is being developed to delineate the relative degrees of visual sensitivity of the total study unit. The printout display reads in tones of gray developed by character images from a line printer. Types of modification were categorized into linear, free form, and spot-type actions, and were evaluated in terms of their predicted visual impacts in the varying cover types.

PROPOSED MODEL FOR LANDSCAPE-ASSESSMENT QUANTIFICATION

The preceding studies gave us more insight into the organization of future landscape assessments. There are numerous categories and category combinations that could be established. However, the model in Figure 4 is suggested as being applicable to a wide variety of landscape-assessment projects, such as visual-resource input into land-use planning of large tracts of forest lands capable of being controlled by a single owner or agency; rural highway corridors; and timber sale, utility line, fuel break, reservoir development, or recreation development proposals in rural or forested areas, especially where middleground and background zones are visible. The five major components of the proposed model are social sensitivity of the landscape view, landscape scene sensitivity, visual perception sensitivity, modification contrast, contrast reduction potential.

Social Sensitivity of the Landscape View

The essence of a measure of social sensitivity (U.S. Department of Agriculture, 1972, 1973a) is the number of time units (hours, days) a scene is viewed times the factors of the viewer's sen-

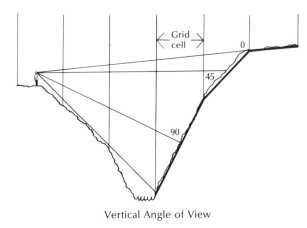

Vertical Angle of View

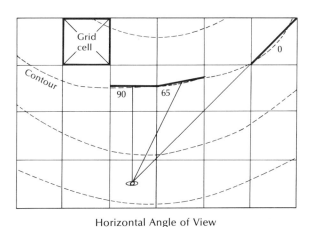

Horizontal Angle of View

Figure 2
Angle of viewed land plane.

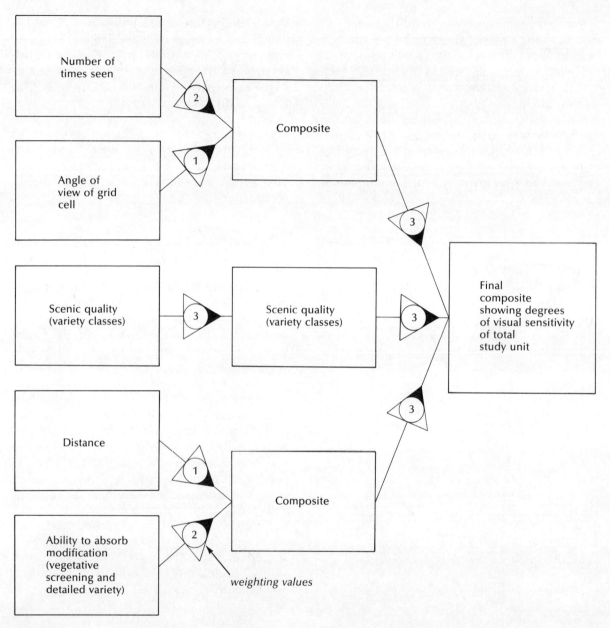

Figure 3
Computer printouts and composite printouts for final display — Mineral King Visual Analysis.

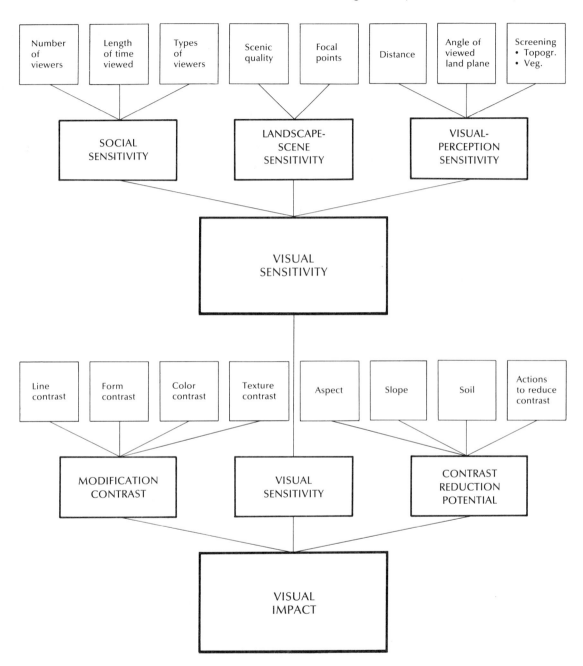

Figure 4
Proposed model for landscape-assessment quantification.

sitivity as determined by background, education, experience, and psychological state while viewing this particular scene. It involves number of viewers, length of viewing time, and types of viewers. The determination of the number of viewers and the length of viewing time does not need further explanation. However, the types-of-viewers category should be more fully discussed.

Types of viewers Our assessment of types of viewers, as we suspect is the case with most studies, is only a broad-brush approach. We do not feel that our knowledge of this complex field is sufficient to claim any expertise.

In this approach we try to estimate whether the people on travel routes through the area or those on occupancy sites in the area are concerned about the scenery. For example, a typical forest highway may have 40 percent recreation traffic, 30 percent service-type through traffic, and 30 percent logging industry traffic. We would assume that most recreation visitors are sensitive to scenery, that some service-type through-traffic viewers are sensitive to scenery, and a few of the people in the logging industry traffic are sensitive to scenery. In this example, we might say that 50 percent of the highway users are sensitive to the scenery.

Research studies in this field are now being conducted by a variety of institutions and numerous individuals. We are awaiting results that will help us to develop a better measure of viewer psychology. We recognize this measure as a vital one. It has been stated (Coomber and Biswas, 1973) that the characteristics of the perceivers may be more important than the content of the landscape.

Landscape Scene Sensitivity

Not only is the existing and potential market for scenery important, but of prime importance is the quality of the product. The scenic quality of a landscape unit has been the subject of numerous studies. Often, and possibly wrongly so, the scenic quality has been considered the *only* measure of value. We consider it to be one of several factors involved in a total landscape-assessment model and one of two factors that must be considered in determining the sensitivity of the landscape scene. Focal points are the second factor.

Scenic quality Most studies in this field deal largely with visual variety in the landscape composition as well as its uniqueness or distinctiveness (Leopold, 1969a,b; Dearinger, 1968; Burke et al., 1968; Belden and Williams, 1969). The theory is that there is a degree of variety which creates the optimum of visual stimulation and pleasure, and that scarcity of a certain type of landscape scene increases its value and thus its sensitivity to modifications.

We have utilized a three-class scenic-quality (visual variety) rating system in recent months (U.S. Department of Agriculture, 1972). Since scenic quality is most certainly a continuum, our three classes are quite arbitrary divisions of that continuum. Until exact measurements are both possible and practical, the following three classes seem adequate: distinctive high-quality landscapes (class A); quality (common to the area) landscapes (class B); monotonous low-quality landscapes (class C). The underlying basis for such classifications is the variety in landforms, vegetation, rock forms, and water forms present in the scene. Not only is variety a factor in scenic quality; it is extremely important in determining the ability of a landscape to absorb modification. Litton (1973) has said "however, a complex surface pattern can also hide and obscure alterations so as to reduce visual vulnerability."

A less scientific approach (Burke et al., 1968) to classification, which we nevertheless find practical to some degree, is high quality = scenes that most visitors would be likely to photograph; quality = scenes that most visitors enjoy but would not photograph; low quality = scenes that no one except an educator, scientist, or land manager would photograph. Many computerized studies refer to these factors of visual quality as attractiveness models. A profusion of research and practical application is taking place in this field.

Focal points A further refinement of landscape scene sensitivity is the analysis of focal points (U.S. Department of Agriculture, 1973a, b). Focal points are the result of the arrangement of visual elements (line, form, color, and texture) into visual dominance principles (contrast, enframement, axis, convergence, and sequence). Whether there is one strong focal point or secondary and tertiary focal points, the landscape has increased visual sensitivity at and adjacent to that focal point. Thus, the focal points of high-quality landscapes are *extremely* sensitive, since a high degree of visual attention is directed toward these areas. A prime example of this would be Bridalveil Falls in Yosemite National Park.

Visual Perception Sensitivity

Possibly due to the nature of our organization — its concerns and its land-managing activities that often create changes in the landscape scene — we are greatly concerned not only in social and scenic quality factors, but also in the actual physical perceptive limitations of the viewer. Just how important are the individual land units that make up a total landscape composition?

There are several factors that we feel are involved in visual perception sensitivity. This category is designed to include pertinent measurable factors that affect the perceptual capabilities of the human eye. The objective of such measures is to determine the visual magnitude without regard to the qualitative visual impact. These measurements would include screening — landform, vegetative or structural; angle of viewed land plane (Holcomb, 1973); and distance. These measurements would show if the land unit were visible and how large an area it would form in the visual field.

From that base it would be possible to measure and analyze contrasts of line, color, texture and form of proposed landscape-modification activities. That measurement, in turn, could allow testing of alternatives to reduce the potential negative contrasts to meet scenic-quality objectives.

All these measurements in visual perception sensitivity lend themselves to computerized systems. The VIEWIT (Amidon and Elsner, 1968; Elsner, 1971) program includes the essential framework for these measurements.

Screening The digitization of topography provides a data bank for three-dimensional models. Once this information is cardpunched or placed on magnetic tape to produce grid cell printout maps, the VIEWIT program tells which cells can be seen from any location on the land surface or above that surface, or from how many cells any cell or object can be seen. It can also accumulate the seen-area data from several viewpoint scans to tell how many times (or what percentage of times) a particular cell is visible. Additionally, the VIEWIT program can be set up to limit both the horizontal and vertical angles of view owing to the presence of nearby vegetation or structures that block the views.

Angle of viewed land plane With the available data stored in the digitized topography, it is also possible to display weightings to the grid cells by the vertical and horizontal angle of visual incident with the land cell plane. Thus, these measurements could apply to a range from a full 90-degree view (such as downhill and across to the opposite canyon wall) to a 0-degree view (or silhouette view) (Figure 2).

As Litton (1973) has stated:

Within whatever landscape we care to consider, a crude axiom may be suggested "the steeper the slope, the greater the potential for visual vulnerability." Several reasons support this — one is perceptual, another is impact scale and repair.

On flat gentle sites, we observe with nearly a level line of sight. As a result, much is hidden by overlapping objects and perspective foreshortening.

Screening is almost automatic. As we observe steeper and steeper slopes rising in front of us we see increasingly more of the slope surface and whatever it supports. Screening is not apt to be effective. Thus the scale of impact tends to grow with it, the scope and difficulty in reestablishing vegetation and soil stability also expand.

Distance It has long been recognized that distance from the observer is important. Near-view and far-view areas were mapped by the U.S. Forest Service — California Region for land-use planning in the early 1960s. After researchers found that the middleground views were often more important than foreground views (since the viewer can see the middleground in relationship to the total scene in quite sharp detail), we began to utilize a suggested (Litton, 1968) three-class distance-rating system: foreground, 0 to $\frac{1}{4}-\frac{1}{2}$ mile; middleground, $\frac{1}{4}-\frac{1}{2}$ to 3–5 miles; background, 3–5 miles to infinity.

In the Mineral King study it became obvious that the three-distance zone system in combination with computer printout maps was less than satisfactory. The number of viewpoints and terrain configuration were such that no background zones existed (those that did exist from certain viewpoints were overridden by middleground distances from other viewpoints on the major public access routes). Thus, there were two zones, and the division between the two gave an artificial map display impression that was not satisfactory.

An output of the program that has recently been added to overcome this is a weighting for the distance of the grid cell to the viewer. The weighting may be displayed in 10 increments of importance. Cumulative weightings of distance from adjacent scanning points could be made, but should be analyzed in each specific case to determine if such weightings duplicate other ratings and thereby distort the total ratings.

Summary of visual perception sensitivity With these measurements, a true measurement of the visual magnitude of each grid cell in the total visual field could be developed from individual or composite viewing points. The visual magnitude would be an expression of visual perception sensitivity. A 1-minute angle of vision might be considered as a basic measure of visual magnitude, as it is the smallest discernible area or object visible with 20-20 vision and without artificial aids under good lighting and background contrast conditions. A 1-minute angle of vision would be 1.5 feet square at a distance of 1 mile, and 15.3 feet square at a distance of 10 miles. At a 10-foot distance it would approximate a $\frac{1}{30}$-inch square, and at 5 feet, a $\frac{1}{60}$-inch square (Figure 5).

For instance, a 40-acre timber clearcut square on a 50 percent slope at 5 degrees above the horizontal line of vision that is 3 miles distant would have a visual magnitude of about $122 \times 293 = 35,746$ units. Converting back for a simulation display of this impact at 10 feet, the measurements would be of a magnitude 4.06 inches by 9.78 inches. There may be value in such visual-magnitude displays for office reference by land-managing decision makers, in addition to comparative graphics showing relationships to scale of landforms and vegetative cover or other reference points. Or, for a more realistic simulation of visual magnitude, the viewer of the graphic simulation display could stand a specific distance from the display.

From a static view, the average human eyes have a binocular coverage of 120 degrees (7,200 minutes) horizontally and 130 degrees (7,800

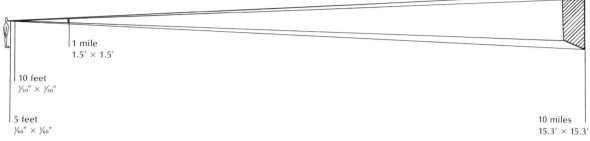

1 mile
1.5′ × 1.5′

10 feet
$\frac{1}{30}''$ × $\frac{1}{30}''$

5 feet
$\frac{1}{60}''$ × $\frac{1}{60}''$

10 miles
15.3′ × 15.3′

DISTANCE
One-minute-square units

Figure 5
Visual magnitude.

minutes) vertically in a modified oval or ellipti-
cal cone of vision. Taking the 1-minute angle of
vision as a standard visual-magnitude measurement, some common reference objects can
be related to this as in the accompanying
table.

Object	Distance (miles)	Approximate Visual Magnitude
Man	4	1
Man	2	2
Man	1	4
Man	$\frac{1}{2}$	8
Man	$\frac{1}{4}$	16
Man	$\frac{1}{8}$ (660 ft)	32
Man	$\frac{1}{16}$ (330 ft)	64
Automobile (front view)	12	1
Automobile (front view)	4	3
Automobile (front view)	2	6
Automobile (front view)	1	12
Automobile (front view)	$\frac{1}{2}$	24
Automobile (front view)	$\frac{1}{4}$	48
Automobile (front view)	$\frac{1}{8}$	96

There should be a term developed to communicate such relative visual magnitudes.
Once it became used and understood, it would
be much easier to describe relative visual mag-

nitude impacts. For lack of any known existing
term, it might be called the smallest expanse of
visual resolution (SEVR).

At this point the landscape assessment could
be terminated. In effect, the foregoing sections
have rated the visual sensitivity of the landscape unit being studied. This provides the
land manager with a comparative rating system
that he can analyze against other values, such
as water, timber, soils, and wildlife in order to
make basic land-use decisions.

Following this, as projects are proposed, the
second phase of landscape assessment can be
applied to determine the visual impact of these
projects on the landscape. This will provide a
portion of the data the land manager can
analyze to determine if the project appears to
be acceptable as proposed, needs to be modified, or should be abandoned.

Modification Contrast

Assuming that all measurements have been
made of visual perception sensitivity and a project has been proposed within that area, the
next logical step is to measure the contrast of
the proposed landscape modifications. The objective of contrast measurement is to deter-

mine the degree of potential deviation from the existing landscape character. It would appear that comparison charts could be developed to convert contrasts to a numerical system. This measurement would not be as precise as the visual perception sensitivity measurement, but it could be greatly improved from the subjective ratings ordinarily made. The measured categories, as developed (U.S. Department of Agriculture, 1973b), could be line contrast (normally edge or silhouette), form contrast, color contrast, texture contrast, effect of distance on contrasts.

Before going into the contrast ratings, it would be desirable as a first step to develop another form of vegetative screening map that would indicate the relative degree of modification impact potential on the land. This would involve a rating of the types of vegetation to determine heights, shapes, densities, and spacing. For example, barren rock has no screening ability, grasslands have minimal screening ability, a scattered stand of young deciduous trees has some seasonal screening ability, and a dense stand of tall conifers has maximum screening ability.

Contrast ratings should apply to landforms, vegetation, water forms and structures. Color and texture contrast have the greatest possibilities for objectivity since comparative charts could be developed for them, line and form contrast would probably have to be judgmental, based on a visual survey of adjacent lines and form patterns without the use of charts.

Line and form contrast Line and form contrast ratings may be less objective than color or texture ratings. The main considerations in these areas would be the relationship to existing lines and forms in the landscape. A timber clearcut in an otherwise unmodified natural scene would have maximum form contrasts if rectangular shapes were applied that ran counter to the landforms. If its edges were crisply defined (line), the line contrast would be strong. A linear development, such as a highway, power-line clearing, penstock or canal, would have high but varying degrees of contrast with natural landscapes, depending on the natural linearity of landforms and water courses and attendant vegetative cover.

Color contrast For projects that involve grading, soil color would be highly important. The degree of contrast with the adjacent visual characteristics would be one of the cumulative measures. Reddish-yellow soil against adjacent blue-green vegetation might form a maximum contrast. If only vegetative removal were involved, only the surface soil color would be measured for contrast of color. If only trees were removed and ground cover remained, the contrast between it and surrounding trees would be measured. To a certain degree, predictions would be involved in such contrast measurements. In many cases there would be examples of similar modifications in the vicinity to strengthen the predictive accuracy.

Textural contrast Textural contrasts could be handled quite similarly to the color contrast ratings. A comparison chart might be utilized. The possibility of optical scanner measurements of photographs or retouched photographs might be worth investigation for color and texture contrast ratings. Rather than trying to account for variations in color and texture as affected by distance, the ratings could be made from nearby. The following section on distance could automatically apply these factors in a composited rating.

Effect of distance on contrasts Distance compensation ratings for contrast are essential. Through retrieval of distance measurements developed in the VIEWIT program, the relative reduction in visual resolution can then be applied to these ratings to account for normal atmospheric conditions encountered in the project area. The net effect will be a decreasing contrast rating as distance increases.

Effect of atmospheric conditions on contrasts The final measurements on modification contrast would thus be rated for line, form, color, and texture contrast as modified by atmospheric conditions.

Contrast Reduction Potential

If all measurements in the four preceding steps have been made and a composited rating has been made (after determining a weighting system for each variable in the step plus a weighting system for each of the four steps), then another step in the measurement of the landscape unit's recovery ability could be made. This added step would be most appropriate if the visual impact was predicted to be high and in need of some measure of the length of time that the impact would exceed acceptable contrast standards. Factors involved could include inherent ability of the land to recover (aspect, slope, and soil fertility), and actions to reduce contrast. These factors are especially pertinent to the forested and rural situations with which we normally deal.

Inherent ability — aspect, slope, and soil fertility Aspect and slope maps are simple to obtain if the VIEWIT program has been utilized since they can be computer-printout byproducts of that system. Aspect and slope combinations create variations in microclimatic conditions that often bear directly on revegetation or natural regeneration potential. Soil fertility is another factor of revegetation potential.

In natural landscape situations, there may be advantages in taking a more direct approach. It is proposed to rate the revegetation potential on the basis of existing vegetative situations, which normally reflect aspects of slope, soil fertility, and a host of more subtle factors and

the effects of the interaction of all these factors.

Action to reduce contrasts Another rating should be applied to account for the actions to be taken to reduce the length of time of the contrasts. For vegetation this could include seeding and planting, fertilization, soil conditioning, and irrigation. Other actions could be rated for structural contrasts not subject to contrast reduction through vegetative means.

The composited rating of all these factors of contrast reduction potential should give a much clearer picture of the time required for contrast to be reduced to acceptable levels. Such knowledge is essential to sound decision making.

Weighting Systems of the Proposed Model

The model for quantitative assessment of landscape resource as presented would be successful only if the weighting system between the model component parts is established in a balanced manner. Dependent upon the user's biases, the model could overemphasize or underemphasize a factor. One of the best guarantees against such imbalance would be to set up a representative team to determine variable factors and the weights of these factors, or to utilize the Delphi technique. In the absence of such a possibility, the suggestion of Coomber and Biswas (1973) may have some validity:

The variables incorporated in all aesthetic measure models were, as stated earlier, given equal weight. Without knowledge of the explanatory power of each variable, however, there seems little justification for altering their quality.

However, it would seem that this would be acceptable only if the variables were carefully designed to approximate equal values or composited values.

SUMMARY

There appears to be a definite need for landscape-assessment models so as to have a sound basis for developing visual-resource data for both land-use and project planning. The current emphasis on land-use planning at all levels of government provides an ideal opportunity to include scenic values in the data for decisions on land-use allocations. Requirements of P.L. 91-190, The National Environmental Policy Act, have brought about the need to analytically evaluate the scenic values and assess potential negative impacts on those values for projects.

Our visual analysis studies to date have indicated that there are possible approaches to a more objective assessment of the landscape. Data storage, retrieval, analysis, and display of scenic values can be greatly aided through the use of computers. Certain parts of landscape assessment lend themselves to distance and angle measurements, which can be manipulated to provide numerous combinations of information rapidly. The computer, however, must be treated as one more tool, which is dependent upon the input and instructions of the landscape-assessment team. Parts of this model were largely based on the VIEWIT computer program developed by Elsner and Amidon of the Forest Service Pacific Southwest Forest and Range Experiment Station; its add-on subroutines were developed as it was utilized in various visual studies.

Based on our experience in visual-resource studies, we found that there seemed to be value in regrouping the factors that were measured or rated. As yet we have not developed any firm basis for weighting the composite values of each group or of setting dollar values on the visual resource, but we feel that a step has been made in that direction.

There appears to be a need to evaluate the sensitivity of the viewers based on a measure of viewer days combined with the type of viewers, and then to separately measure their physical perceptive capacities of the landscape being assessed. These ratings, in combination with the ratings of the inherent scenic value and sensitivity of the landscape, would create a relative measure of the sensitivity of the visual resources of that landscape. The value of the visual resource of the landscape can then be determined comparative to the land's values for other uses.

A measure of the relative visual impact of a proposed modification of the visual resource can then be made by analyzing the degree to which it will positively or negatively contrast with the existing landscape character. As a further step, if it is determined that the visual impact will be higher than acceptable, another measure can be taken to determine the relative duration of the negative impact if the landscape is left to its own recovery devices and if specific actions are taken to speed up the recovery. The system would have greatest application on large-scale landscapes in rural or forested areas under single land ownership.

Assessing Visual–Cultural Values of Inland Wetlands in Massachusetts

Richard C. Smardon

This chapter addresses itself to the problem that land-use decisions affecting inland wetlands are being made without consideration of many important inland wetland values. This is true in Massachusetts (Commonwealth of Massachusetts, June 6, 1966) and throughout the United States, as evidenced by the rapid disappearance of many valuable wetland areas (Niering, 1970).

The problem is not new, but is as old as the negative attitude that many of our European ancestors displayed toward wetlands. The "bog-swamp" mythology can be traced to Europe, where people thought pixies, heathens, and strange mythical creatures lived in wetlands (Jorgensen, 1971). The bog-swamp

Richard C. Smardon is an Associate Planner with the Executive Office of Environmental Affairs of the Commonwealth of Massachusetts and a professional staff member of the Center for Environmental Policy Studies in the Institute for Man and Environment at the University of Massachusetts.

This work was supported by the U.S. Department of the Interior, Office of Water Resources Research, as authorized under the Water Resources Act of 1964 (P.L. 88-379), Joseph Larson, Chief Investigator. Julius Gy. Fabos and Walter Cudnohufsky were coinvestigators, and Richard Smardon was the research assistant on the landscape planning subproject. Tirath R. Gupta assisted in the review of the economic evaluation section. Much of the conceptual model framework development and comprehensive detailed review of this paper is due to the efforts of Dr. Fabos, for which the author is deeply indebted.

mythology was brought across the Atlantic and intensified with more stories of wolves, wild dogs, crop-destroying hordes of crows, and quicksand (Williams, 1971). The industrial revolution changed man's attitude toward wetlands from fear to indifference. Wetlands were commonly believed to be wastelands good for nothing except causing disease and mosquitoes (Odum, 1963:122). During the last decade, centuries of bog-swamp mythology, ignorance, prejudice, and trouble associated with wetlands have been slightly reversed by the efforts of enlightened environmentalists.

To deal with the increasingly recognized values of wetlands in connection with land-use decisions, the Commonwealth of Massachusetts pioneered wetland legislation with the Hatch Act (Commonwealth of Massachusetts, 1966) and the Inland Wetlands Protection Act (Commonwealth of Massachusetts, 1968). Both these acts and a few others are included in the umbrella-like Wetland Protection Act (Commonwealth of Massachusetts, 1971). Many other states have drafted wetland protection legislation since 1966, the time of the initial Massachusetts Hatch Act.

A multidisciplinary inland wetlands research project started at the University of Massachusetts soon after the Inland Wetlands Act became law in Massachusetts. The objective of the research project's organizer, Joseph S. Larson, was to create a tool that would help decision makers reach better land-use decisions concerning inland wetlands. Larson assembled a multidisciplinary team to formulate the decision-making tool and to investigate the many different types of inland wetland resource values. This interdisciplinary study included a wildlife biology subproject, which assessed the wildlife values; an aerial photogrammetry subproject, which provided the wetland resource data; a hydrogeology subproject, which assessed the water supply and quality; a resource economics subproject,

which assessed the economic value of each major wetland resource; and a landscape planning subproject.

The landscape planning subproject specifically addresses the issues of how to conceptually develop an overall model and how to incorporate the visual–cultural resource values of wetlands into the decision-making process. This has not yet been done comprehensively in any state under any legislation.

This chapter details how the landscape planning subproject of the inland wetlands research team articulated the visual–cultural values of inland wetlands and designed a multistage assessment model to measure these values.

Study Objectives

The major study objectives were the following:

1. To identify, analyze, and classify inland wetland types and surrounding landscape types that are important for discerning and identifying different types of visual–cultural values.
2. To identify the major visual–cultural values that can be attributed to inland wetlands in Massachusetts and design an assessment model to estimate those values.
3. To design the inland wetlands assessment model for visual–cultural values as a module submodel in a larger inland wetlands assessment model that includes other inland wetland values.
4. To ensure that the inland wetlands assessment model for visual–cultural values has utility at all decision-making levels and scales.

Definition of Critical Terms

There are certain terms that are used throughout the chapter which should be understood at this point. The following is a list of those terms and their respective definitions.

Resources "Resources are entities which are useful and finite. They are like money held in the bank; they are available for human use, but scarcity dictates that some mechanism be established defining the objectives of use and the allocation of resources according to those objectives. Planning processes are one type of response to defining objectives and allocating resources" (Fabos, 1973:1).

Visual–cultural Visual–cultural refers to the visual landscape portion of the physical environment. "It consists of natural entities such as soil, trees, landform, water and various cultural entities or artifacts such as farms, recreational developments and housing. These entities or artifacts have various perceptual attributes and characteristics" (Fabos, 1973:2).

Wetlands Wetlands in this chapter are freshwater wetlands. Freshwater inland wetlands include marshes, swamps, meadows, and bogs by themselves, adjacent to, or part of streams, rivers, lakes, ponds, and reservoirs. They can be generally characterized as having a year round surface or above-surface water level with submergent, surface, and emergent aquatic vegetation or herbaceae and woody vegetation resistant to frequent flooding.

Visual–cultural wetland resources These are the finite natural resources available for human use that are perceived, found within, or associated with wetland areas. Examples of human use that treat wetlands as a visual–cultural resource are outdoor classroom use for natural history, canoeing, or hiking.

Visual–cultural wetland values "Values are defined by human individuals and groups. The reason for segregating visual–cultural resource values for separate study is that they have received relatively little attention by the American decision-making process. A basic premise of this paper is that articulation and definition of visual–cultural [wetland] values, even if through primitive quantitative techniques, will increase societies' favoring more explicit consideration of these values in individual and group decision-making processes" (Fabos, 1973:2).

Landscape resource variables "Landscape resource variables represent a given quantity and quality of a resource [for example, visual contrast or wildlife productivity] that may have a number of different values" (Fabos, 1973:2). For instance, landform contrast may vary from high, owing to a 1,000-foot-high mountain situated adjacent to a wetland, to low, owing to no perceptual height difference of any landforms adjacent to a wetland. "The quantity (height difference) and quality all represent different values. They vary and yet they are still quantifiable within the metric; hence the term landscape resource variable" (Fabos, 1973:2).

Landscape dimension This is the metric unit or measurement process used to rate a given landscape resource variable. In the case of landform contrast, the two landscape dimensions are relative relief measured in feet, and ratio of relative relief to wetland width, a pure number.

Measurement "A process which estimates the magnitude of a visual–cultural wetland value at a given point in time. The measurement of the value of the landscape resource variable or the measurement of several attributes (parameters) of a landscape resource variable is directed toward defining physical units useful in considering collective human values" (Fabos, 1973:3).

Rating "This refers to the process which orders [visual–cultural] values of a landscape resource variable in a hierarchy [from high value to low value] in respect to a larger geographic area" (Fabos, 1973:3).

Assessment "The process which combines the measurements and ratings of all landscape variables" (Fabos, 1973:3).

The remainder of this chapter presents the development of the visual–cultural submodel. But first we include a brief discussion of the overall framework of the inland wetlands assessment model of which the visual–cultural submodel is a part. Then the visual–cultural submodel itself will be discussed and broken down into its various parts. First, the identification and classification of inland wetlands and their landscape context will be discussed. Second, the visual–cultural resource values of inland wetlands will be evaluated by various levels of quantitative and qualitative rating and ranking systems. The final part is the economic valuation of the resource benefits measured by the second part of the submodel. In the conclusion we discuss possible uses or applications of the submodel and future research needs.

INLAND WETLAND
ASSESSMENT MODEL

The visual–cultural assessment submodel developed as an integral part of the overall inland wetland assessment model (Figure 1). This was done to ensure that all the different subproject efforts would culminate into an effective interdisciplinary tool for assessing wetland resource values.

The inland wetland assessment model has three major parts: classification, natural cultural resource evaluation, and economic valuation. The classification part of the assessment model necessitated a separate classification for each of the three subprojects: wildlife, visual–cultural, and hydrogeologic. The second part, the natural cultural resource evaluation section of the model, has three different levels, which constitute an eliminative system in that a wetland is "eliminated" from further deliberation or analysis if the wetland has a high value or scores high within any given

level of evaluation. A wetland receiving a high value early in the evaluation process may require top priority for preservation or protection and is accordingly "eliminated" from further evaluation.

Level 1 evaluates a given wetland for a possible single outstanding natural or cultural value (for example, is it a major flyway and feeding area for large numbers of migratory waterfowl?). If a single outstanding value is not found, the wetland area is assessed at level 2, which evaluates a wetland for several possible values simultaneously (for example, water-supply quantity and quality; wildlife-habitat quality and quantity; visual diversity and contrast) by rating the natural attributes and characteristics of the wetland area. If the combined value of the natural attributes is not substantial, the wetlands cultural attributes (for example, accessibility or proximity to urban areas) are then evaluated in level 3. In each evaluation level the wetlands can be ranked from most to least valuable for wildlife, visual–cultural, and water-resource values. The third major part of the assessment model deals with the economic evaluation of the combined values of each of the three subprojects: wildlife, visual–cultural, and hydrogeologic. In addition, it assesses the flood storage value of the wetlands. This assessment model can be used with or without the economic evaluation by the decision maker, who has the option of using any combination of levels and resource factors, depending on the types of wetland values with which he is concerned.

VISUAL–CULTURAL
SUBMODEL FRAMEWORK

The visual–cultural submodel (Figure 2) as part of the wetland assessment model has two basic parts: the wetland and landscape context classification system and the visual–cultural resource evaluation. The visual–cultural sub-model evaluation is also a three-level eliminative process. This study is described in detail by Smardon (1972).

Level 1 evaluates a given wetland for a possible single outstanding value (for example, an outstanding natural area for nature education). If outstanding values are not present, the wetland is further evaluated in level 2. At this level, visual, recreational, and educational values (landform contrast, land-use diversity, associated water body size, etc.) are rated by the attributes and characteristics of the wetland and its surroundings. If the combined value is not substantial, the wetlands cultural variables (educational proximity, physical accessibility, and ambient quality) may be evaluated in level 3, and rated from the most to the least valuable. The following sections will describe in more detail the visual–cultural classification and evaluation systems of the visual–cultural wetland assessment submodel.

Visual–Cultural Classification Systems

A two-part inland wetland classification system (see Figure 2) was developed as part of the visual–cultural assessment submodel. One classification system served to differentiate the interior landscapes of inland wetlands themselves. The second classification system was needed to identify and differentiate the many different possible landscape contexts within which wetlands are found.

Identifying and classifying inland wetland types Previous wetland classification systems existed (Shaw and Fredline, 1956; U.S. Department of the Interior, Fish and Wildlife Service, 1954a; Lacate, 1969), which used the criteria of water level, vegetation, and soils to differentiate wetland types.

MacConnell and Garvin's wetland classification system was used to identify and map inland wetlands in the Commonwealth of Massachusetts in 1952. This system (1956) was slightly revised by MacConnell and is presently being used to identify and map wetlands in Massachusetts, utilizing 1971–1972 photos (MacConnell, 1971). The utility of this wetland classification system (existing as mapped data from 1951–1952 and 1971–1972) and its similarity with other existing wetland classification systems (Shaw and Fredline, 1956; U.S. Department of the Interior, Fish and Wildlife Service, 1954a) made it acceptable for adaptation to the visual–cultural wetland submodel.

This inland wetland classification system then was tested in the field. The wetland types tested included open freshwater, deep fresh marsh, shallow fresh marsh, fresh meadow, shrub swamp, wooded swamp, and bog. These wetland types are shown in Figures 3 through 9, respectively.

Identifying and classifying surrounding landscape contexts Wetlands cannot be separated from their surrounding physical landscape. To evaluate the visual–cultural values of inland wetlands that were dependent on the immediately surrounding landscape, it was important to be able to accurately identify and classify the immediate landscape surroundings. There are two components or parts of the surrounding landscape context: first, the land use, and second, the landforms underlying the land use.

Land use The continuum of cultural or man-affected land use can be classified from center city to forest wilderness. A number of descriptive systems were reviewed that classified the cultural characteristics of the landscape (Zube et al., 1970; Olin et al., 1971; Lewis et al., 1969). MacConnell's land-use and vegetative types were used to identify and classify the surrounding vegetation and land use of the

CLASSIFICATION
SYSTEMS

NATURAL–CULTURAL

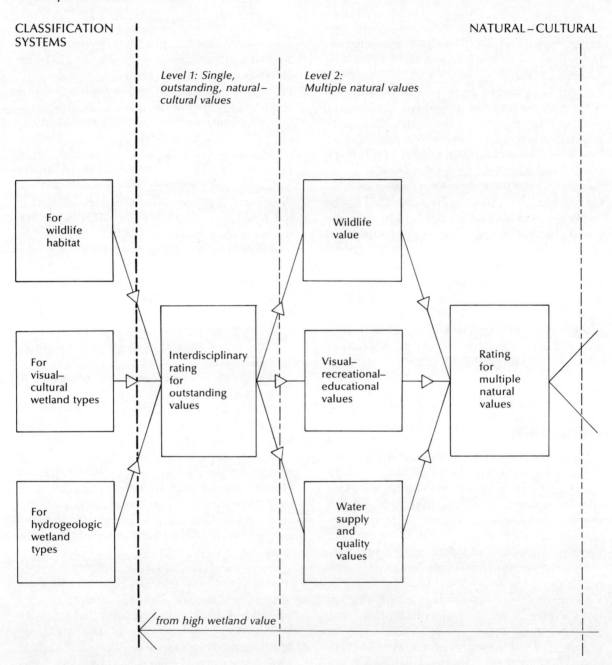

Figure 1
Inland wetland assessment model.

RESOURCE EVALUATION

ECONOMIC VALUATION

Level 3: Multiple cultural values

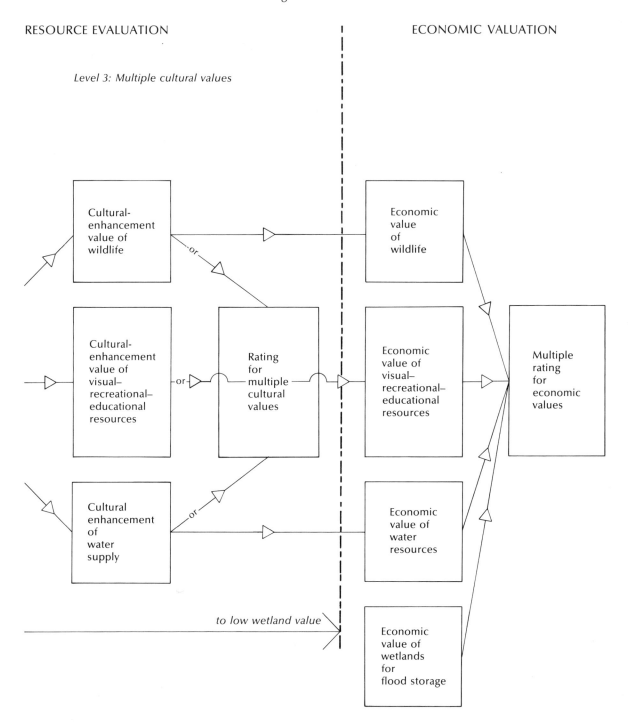

CLASSIFICATION

*Level 1: Single,
outstanding values*

EVALUATION

Level 2: Multiple visual–recreational–

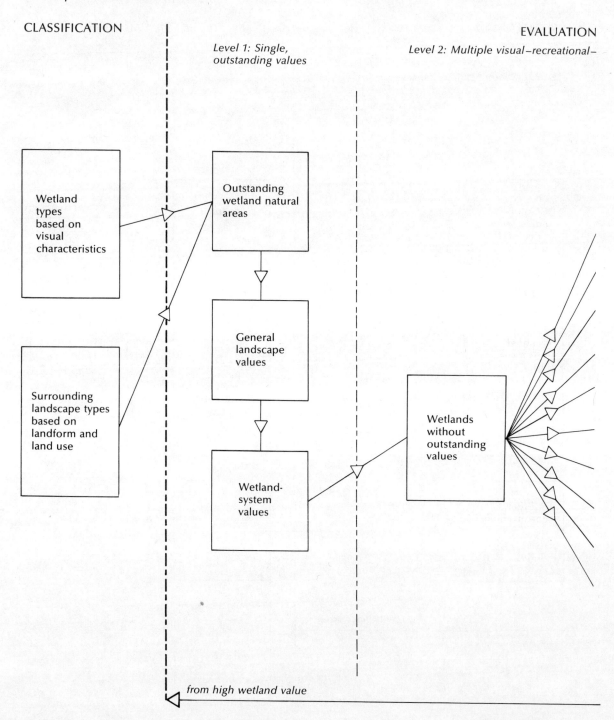

Figure 2
Visual–cultural wetlands assessment submodel.

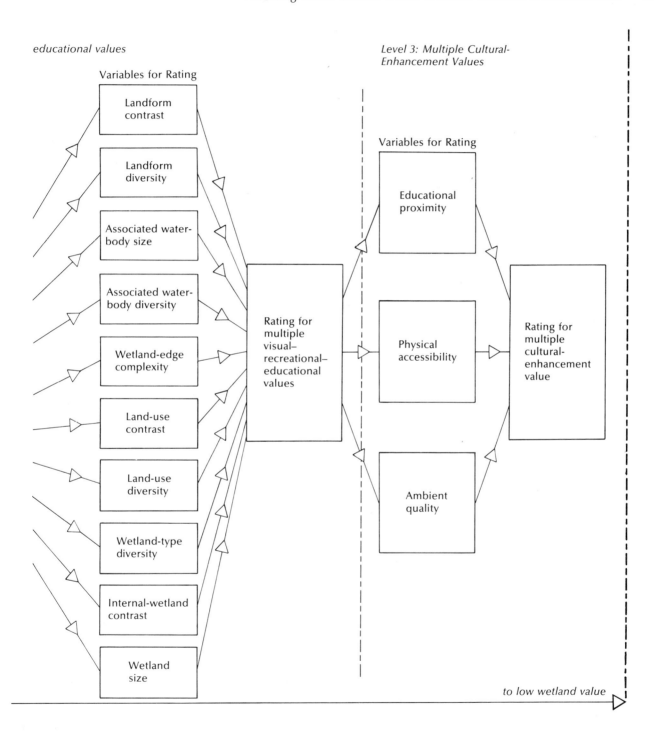

Figure 3
**Typical cross section and examples of open freshwater. Definition: water less than
10 feet deep bordered by emergent vegetation: pondweed, naiads, wild celery,
water lilies. Photos by R. C. Smardon, cross section by C. H. Greene.**

landscape, the same system that was utilized for identifying and classifying inland wetland types (MacConnell and Garvin, 1956; MacConnell, 1971).

Landforms Little has been done in Massachusetts to identify and describe distinct landform types in the same detail or universality as has been done for the land-use landscape. Physiographic divisions for Massachusetts have been suggested (Fennemen, 1938; Beaumont, 1956; U.S. Department of the Interior, Fish and Wildlife Service, 1954a) that use the gross continuous pattern of similar landforms. Rather than devise a site scale classification system for landforms, the general physiographic regions were defined within Massachusetts for areas with similar geomorphological characteristics. The visual–cultural subproject together with

the wildlife and geology subprojects used criteria such as topography, surficial geology, bedrock geology, and drainage patterns to define physiographic regions for Massachusetts (see Figure 10).

Description of fieldwork and results of visual–cultural classification systems Sample study areas were chosen within Massachusetts that were representative of inland wetland types and surrounding landscape types occurring within the state. The study areas were selected to cover all eight physiographic regions shown in Figure 10. The study area within each physiographic region was selected to represent as much as possible of the vegetative/land-use landscape continuum, ranging from highly urbanized to forest–wilderness within the given physiographic region. Anywhere from

Figure 4
**Typical cross section and examples of deep fresh marsh. Definition: soil covered
with 6 inches to 3 feet of water. Cattails, reeds, bulrushes, spike rushes, wild rice.
Photos by R. C. Smardon and F. C. Golet, cross section by C. H. Greene.**

one to five U.S. Geological Survey quadrangle
map areas were picked out within the physiographic region to best represent all wetland
types occurring within the region. Each study

area included all the wetland types, as well as
large complexes of wetlands and small isolated
wetlands (Figure 10).

The actual study procedure consisted of

Figure 5
Typical cross section and examples of shallow fresh marsh.
Definition: soil waterlogged during growing season; often
covered with 6 or more inches of water. Grasses, bulrushes, spike rushes, cattails, arrowhead, smartweed, pickerelweed.
Photos by R. C. Smardon and F. C. Golet, cross section by
C. H. Greene.

documentation of individual wetland attributes and characteristics using field sheets and photography (see Smardon, 1972). Study area results indicated that MacConnell's aerial photogrammetric land-use and vegetative- cover maps, as well as the wetland types and surrounding land-use types, were accurate and usable for the general assessment of visual–cultural values. A more refined classification system for wetlands was desirable at the time

Figure 6
Typical cross section and examples of fresh meadow. Definition: without standing water during growing season; waterlogged to within a few inches of surface. Grasses, sedges, rushes, broadleaf plants. Photos by R. C. Smardon and F. C. Golet, cross section by C. H. Greene.

the study was done (Golet, 1973). No suitable set of detailed landform types existed in mapped form for the purpose of visual–cultural evaluation.

Visual–Cultural Evaluation

The results of the classification indicated that different kinds of visual–cultural values could be related to wetlands, or wetlands and their

landscape contexts. Three potential visual–cultural values were identified:

1. That inland wetlands themselves have educational and scientific values as outstanding natural areas.
2. That inland wetlands and their landscape contexts have visual, recreational, and educational value at a given site, because of the attributes of the wetland, surrounding land-

Figure 7
Typical cross section and examples of shrub swamp. Definition: soil waterlogged; often covered with 1 or more feet of water. Photos by F. C. Golet, cross sections by C. H. Greene.

form, water bodies, and surrounding vegetation and land use.

3. That large inland wetland complexes have visual–cultural values not found in small individual wetland sites.

The following evaluation section of the submodel defines the visual–cultural values indicated and includes methodologies for the measurement of these values. The process used here is the same as discussed earlier under the inland wetland assessment model, that is, a three-level eliminative model.

Level 1: Individual outstanding values (Figure 2) Certain wetlands may have a single natural visual or cultural value that merits top priority

Figure 8
Typical cross section and examples of wooded swamp. Definition: soil water-logged; often covered with 1 foot of water. Along sluggish streams, shallow lake basins, and flat uplands. Photos by F. C. Golet, cross sections by C. H. Greene.

for preservation or protection. These single outstanding attributes in most cases were jointly identified and defined by all the sub-projects within an interdisciplinary framework (Figure 1).

It was concluded that certain unique wetland resources should not be assessed quantita-tively. It was also concluded and widely ac-cepted by the entire interdisciplinary team that there could be no monetary value attached to outstanding wetland resources, and that their greatest value to society is their present natural state. It was therefore proposed to use similar social norms to preserve outstanding wetlands as were used to create national parks, wildlife refuges, and wilderness areas.

The purpose of level 1 is therefore to flag those wetland areas that are outstanding either

by virtue of a single attribute or a number of attributes. There are three types of values evaluated in level 1:

1. Outstanding wetland natural areas (such as an endangered-species habitat).
2. General landscape values (for instance, a scarce wetland type within a region).
3. Wetland system value (for example, several significant wetlands interconnected with rivers and lakes).

The first and third values cannot be readily separated into subproject areas and really draw on all subproject research areas. The second value represents primarily a visual–cultural value.

Outstanding wetland natural areas are de-

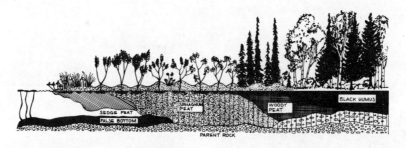

Figure 9
Typical cross section and examples of bogs. Definition: soil waterlogged, spongy
covering of mosses. Heath shrubs, sphagnum, sedges. Photos by F. C. Golet, cross
section redrawn from R. L. Smith (1966:184).

fined as wetland areas with high or outstanding visual, educational, or scientific value. Previous attempts to deal with this type of value in assessment literature have resulted in the concept of "uniqueness" (Leopold, 1969a) or "being unique" (U.S. Department of the Interior, National Park Service, 1954b). The similar concept of "outstanding areas" corresponds closely with the concept of nationally significant natural areas used by the National Park Service (1954b). The only difference is that wetland natural areas can be "outstanding" in a statewide or regional context. "Natural areas" as defined in the literature are "areas where at present natural processes predominate and are not significantly influenced by either deliber-

ate manipulation or interference by man" (Maryland State Planning Department 1968:1).

Criteria for the identification of outstanding natural wetland areas were derived from professional judgment and other existing criteria (U.S. Department of the Interior, National Park Service, 1954b; Natural Areas Criteria Committee, 1972) for identifying outstanding natural areas. The following criteria used to identify outstanding wetland natural areas were developed by Smardon (1972), Golet (1972), and Heeley (1973). The wetland could qualify if any one of the criteria applied. If two or more criteria applied, it would strengthen the qualification of the wetland as an outstanding natural area:

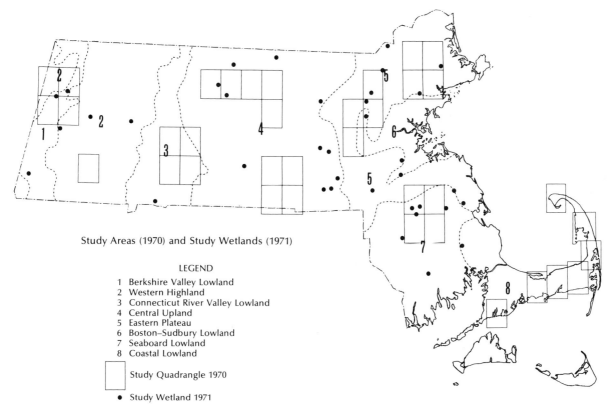

Study Areas (1970) and Study Wetlands (1971)

LEGEND
1 Berkshire Valley Lowland
2 Western Highland
3 Connecticut River Valley Lowland
4 Central Upland
5 Eastern Plateau
6 Boston–Sudbury Lowland
7 Seaboard Lowland
8 Coastal Lowland

☐ Study Quadrangle 1970

● Study Wetland 1971

Figure 10
Physiographic regions of Massachusetts.

1. The presence of rare, restricted, endemic, or relict flora or fauna (for example, the rare red-shouldered hawk).
2. The presence of flora of unusually high visual quality and infrequent occurrence (for example, the American lotus).
3. The presence of wetland flora or fauna at or very near the limits of their range (for example, the white-throated sparrow).
4. The juxtaposition, in sequence, of several serial stages of hydrarch succession (for example, an ideal upland bog).
5. High production of native waterfowl species (for example, an important breeding ground for wood ducks).

6. Use by great numbers of migrating water-fowl, shorebirds, marsh, and wading birds (for example, Sudbury–Concord River marshes).
7. The availability of reliable scientific information concerning the geological or biological history of the wetland (for example, Hawley Bog in West Hawley, Massachusetts).
8. The presence of outstanding or uncommon geomorphological features within or associated with a wetland (for example, Coskata Pond on Nantucket formed behind a cuspate bar).
9. The known presence of outstanding archaeological evidence or information (for

example, American Indian dugout canoe found in Hockomock Swamp).

General landscape values There are two general wetland landscape values. One is the value of a wetland type that is relatively scarce within a specific geographic or physiographic region in Massachusetts (see Figure 10). Scanning of the aerial photogrammetric land-use and vegetative-cover maps of the state produced several relatively scarce wetland types within physiographic regions (Table 1).

The second general landscape value is that of visual contrast. Visual contrast is produced by a wetland providing openness in a predominantly forested landscape with little physical relief (the seaboard lowlands in Figure 10), or providing both forest and openness in a predominantly urban landscape (the Boston–Sudbury basin). Visual contrast is provided in the landscape by keeping or introducing landscape types that contrast in height or texture

with the general surrounding landscape. Table 2 is a summary of the outstanding wetland types that provide visual contrast to the various geographic or physiographic regions.

Wetland system value constitutes the third type of outstanding value identified. Wetland systems are combinations of wetlands, rivers, streams, lakes, and ponds. Because of their size and interconnectedness, large wetland systems have many conservation and open-space values, which include the following:

1. Oxygen production by green plants in swamps, bogs, and lakes where the green plants are not oxidized because of the presence of oxygen-free sediments (Deevey, 1969; Cole, 1970).

Table 1
Scarce Wetlands Within Specific Geographic Regions of Massachusetts

Physiographic Region	Scarce Wetland Type
Western highlands	Seasonally flooded flats Deep fresh marsh Shallow fresh marsh Fresh meadow
Berkshire valley lowland	Seasonally flooded flats Bogs
Connecticut valley lowland	Seasonally flooded flats Bogs
Central upland	Seasonally flooded flats
Eastern plateau	Seasonally flooded flats Bogs
Boston–Sudbury basin	Bogs
Seaboard lowland	Seasonally flooded flats
Coastal plain	Seasonally flooded flats Wooded swamp

Table 2
Wetlands With Outstanding Visual Contrast Within Specific Geographic Regions of Massachusetts

Physiographic Region	Wetland Types
Western highlands	Deep fresh marsh Shallow fresh marsh Seasonally flooded flats Fresh meadow Bogs
Berkshire valley lowland	All types
Connecticut valley lowland	All types
Central upland	Deep fresh marsh Shallow fresh marsh Seasonally flooded flats Fresh meadow Bogs
Boston–Sudbury basin	All types
Seaboard lowland	Deep fresh marsh Shallow fresh marsh Seasonally flooded flats Fresh meadow Bogs
Coastal plain	All types

2. Maintenance of pond, lake, and reservoir water quality by the nutrient storage and siltation action of marshes (Commonwealth of Massachusetts, 1967; Threinen and Engelbert, 1966).
3. Prevention of flood damage through physical retardation and storage of peak sream and river storm flow (Niering, 1970; Commonwealth of Massachusetts, 1971; U.S. Department of Agriculture, Soil Conservation Service, 1964; U.S. Army, Corps of Engineers, 1971; Wadleigh, 1963, 1965).
4. Structuring urban development by providing open-space linkages; giving visible form to towns to improve their perceptual identity; serving as buffers or wedges between incompatible land uses or different areas of development; and by defining and separating towns, cities, and metropolitan areas (U.S. Department of Agriculture, Economic Research Service, 1968; Lynch, 1960; Central Massachusetts Regional Planning District, 1967).

Because of the open-space values that a large system has, all wetlands within the system should be protected if the wetland system values are to be kept. The criteria developed for identifying large wetland systems within a New England landscape context are the following:

1. The wetland should be connected to another wetland by a large river or stream of at least 15 miles navigable length; or
2. A wetland must be connected to another wetland by a lake, pond, or reservoir of over 200 acres in area; or
3. The wetland should constitute a continuous 1,000 acres in size.

If a wetland does not meet any of the criteria for individual outstanding values in level 1; it is then further evaluated in level 2.

Level 2: Multiple visual, recreational, and educational values of inland wetlands (Figure 2) The purpose of level 2 is to evaluate the large bulk of wetland areas that may not have a single outstanding visual, recreational, or educational characteristic. However, several attributes together may result in a wetland with high visual, recreational, or educational value. Level 2 is more quantitative and more complex than level 1.

This portion of the model is developed on the premise that values of the wetland benefit both recreational and educational uses. Primary recreational uses of wetlands are fishing, hunting, bird watching, and nature study. Other recreational uses of wetlands include hiking, photography, canoeing, boating, and skating. Recreational uses of areas adjoining the wetland could include camping and picnicking; recreational activities involving movement include utilizing trails and roads adjacent to wetlands by walking, cycling, horseback riding, cross-country skiing and pleasure driving. Educational uses of wetlands include use as outdoor educational and scientific laboratories.

Obviously, there is a great overlap among the visual–recreational–educational attributes of a wetland. For example, a wetland has recreational value for canoeing, visual value for the scenery experienced while canoeing, and educational value for the species of fauna and flora that can be seen and identified while canoeing.

Key attributes were used to derive *variables*, which indicate differences in the visual, recreational, and educational quality of inland wetland sites. The two significant visual variables selected and substantiated were *visual contrast*, which can be attributed to the variables of landform contrast, water-body size or length, surrounding land-use contrast, and internal wetland contrast, and *visual diversity*, which can be attributed to the variables of landform diversity, wetland-edge complexity, and wetland-type diversity.

The *recreational carrying capacity* of wetlands was also estimated. It, too, can be attributed to the variables of landform diversity and wetland-edge *complexity,* but in addition water-body size or length are equally important. Opportunity for *recreational diversity* and *educational diversity* of wetlands can be attributed to the variables of landform diversity, water-body diversity, surrounding land-use diversity, wetland-edge complexity, and wetland-type diversity. As a result of this rationale, the following resource variables were identified and measured (also see Figure 2):

1. *Landform contrast* is the amount of visual edge manifested in the form of object dominance or spatial enclosure of the wetland in reference to a given landform.
2. *Landform diversity* is the variety of shape and/or mode of origin of landforms surrounding, adjacent to, or part of a wetland.
3. *Wetland-edge complexity* is the degree of irregularity of the physical boundary of the wetland where it meets a landform or vegetated edge.
4. *Associated water-body size* is the area of any lake, pond, or reservoir, or the length of a river or stream, that borders, goes through, or is part of a wetland.
5. *Diversity of associated water bodies* is the number of different types of water features surrounding or comprising the given wetland.
6. *Surrounding land-use contrast* is the amount of contrast generated by the difference in vegetative and structural height and texture between the wetland and the adjacent land use or uses.
7. *Surrounding land-use diversity* is the amount of contrast generated by the dif-

ferent vegetative and compatible land uses bordering a wetland.

8. *Wetland-type diversity* is the number or variety of different wetland types or microlandscapes within the wetland itself.
9. *Internal wetland contrast* is the amount of contrast generated within a wetland by differences in vegetative and water height and texture.
10. *Wetland size* is the gross area of the continuous wetland area.

A measuring and rating procedure was developed on a scale from 1 to 5, with 5 the highest and 1 the lowest. A simplified version of some sample variables (landform contrast, wetland-edge complexity, and wetland-type diversity) are shown in Figure 11; a detailed procedure and description is found in the report of Smardon (1972).

The measurement and rating procedure that determined the proposed values of each variable was substantiated from research results of behavioral scientists. Sources include the following: *literature on visual qualities and values* (Rodgers, 1970; Lynch, 1971; Eliot and Baxter, 1893; Errington, 1957; Jorgensen, 1971; Johansson, 1967; Leopold, L., 1969b); *wetland recreation* (Errington, 1957; Larson and Foster, 1955; Commonwealth of Massachusetts, June 6, 1967; Strong, 1965; Shaw and Fredline, 1956); *educational values of wetlands* (Niering, 1970; Odum, 1971; Wharton, 1970; U.S. Department of the Interior, Fish and Wildlife Service, Bureau of Sport Fisheries, 1962; Randall and Brainerd, undated); *visual and recreational preference studies, primarily visual* (Albert, 1969; Burns and Rundell, 1969; Melillo, 1970; Halverson, 1970; Morisawa, 1971; Craik, 1971; Kaplan and Wendt, 1972; Shafer et al., 1969; Wohlwill, 1968; Zube, 1971b); *primarily recreation-oriented* (Hendee et al., 1968; Hendee and Harris, 1970; Reid, L., 1964; Shafer, 1968; Shafer and Mietz, 1969); *behavioral studies* (Gratzer and McDowell, 1971; Bond and Oulette, 1968; Bond and Whittaker, 1971; Burch, 1965; Driver, 1972; Gibson, 1950, 1961; Lucas, 1963, 1970, 1971; Morton and Stark, 1971; McKechnie, 1969; Newby, 1971a; Prohansky et al., 1970; Roenigk and Cole, 1968; Shafer and Thompson, 1968; Stankey, 1971; Stone and Taves, 1958; Thomas, 1968; Van Doren, 1967; Wagar, 1966); *attitude studies* (Babeu et al., 1965; Larson and Foster, 1955; Kates, 1966–1967; Lowenthal, 1966; White, 1966); *professional evaluation or assessment systems* (Fines, 1968; Murray, 1969; Skinner, 1968; Trueman, 1949; Hart and Graham, 1967; Kiemstedt, 1968; Leopold, L., 1969, 1969b; Lewis, 1964a, 1969; Vedenin and Miroschnichenko, 1971; Williams and Beldon, 1969; Wilson et al., 1970; Dearinger, 1968; Litton, 1968; Allison and Leighton, 1971; Hills, 1966; Hills et al., 1970; U.S. Department of Agriculture, Soil Conservation Service, 1964, 1966, 1972; Toth, 1968, 1971; Handley et al., 1969; Chubb et al., 1967; Richards and McKay, 1970; Shafer and Mietz, 1970; Zube et al., 1970); *ecological studies* (Allen, 1954; Dasmann, 1964, 1968; Elton, 1958; Leopold, A., 1933; Lime and Stankey, 1971; Niering, 1966, 1970; Odum, 1963, 1971; Oosting, 1956; Pimentel, 1961; Pimlott, 1969; Reid, G., 1961; Taylor, 1956; and Trippan, 1958). Various other planning reports and documents by federal, state, and local planning agencies were reviewed in developing the value measurement and rating procedure.

Weighting the visual-resource variables After each variable is rated, the score is adjusted by use of significance coefficients based on two criteria, immutability and multiple value. Immutability is the degree of permanence. The landscape attributes that are more

permanent are more valuable for visual–cultural values because they are less likely to be changed naturally or by man's actions. Immutability in the landscape attribute means long-term benefits without extra efforts, such as maintenance, to sustain visual, recreational, and educational quality (Fabos, 1971). Immutability was rated on a scale from 1 to 3 where 1 represented high mutability (vegetation) and 3 represented immutability (landform) (see Table 3).

Table 3

Natural Resource Variable	Landform (3)	Water Body (2)	Vegetation (1)	Visual (1)	Recreation (1)	Education (1)	Significance Coefficient	Highest Possible Rating	Highest Possible Total Score
Landform contrast	×			×			3	5	15
Landform diversity	×				×	×	6	5	30
Associated water-body size		×			×		2	5	10
Associated water-body diversity		×		×	×	×	6	5	30
Wetland-edge complexity	×			×	×	×	9	5	45
Land-use contrast			×	×			1	5	5
Land-use diversity			×	×	×		2	5	10
Wetland-type diversity			×	×	×	×	3	5	15
Internal wetland contrast			×	×			1	5	5
Wetland size			×		×		1	5	5

Total 170

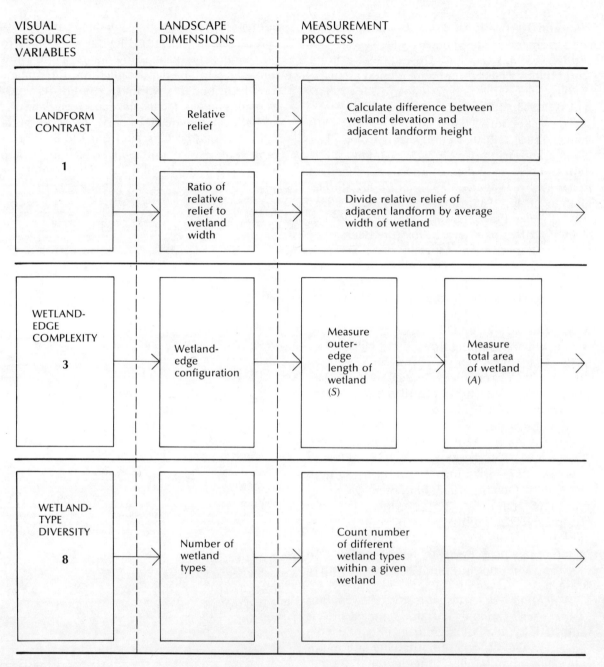

Figure 11
Samples of measuring and rating procedures for visual, recreational, and educational resource variables.

RATING
PROCEDURE

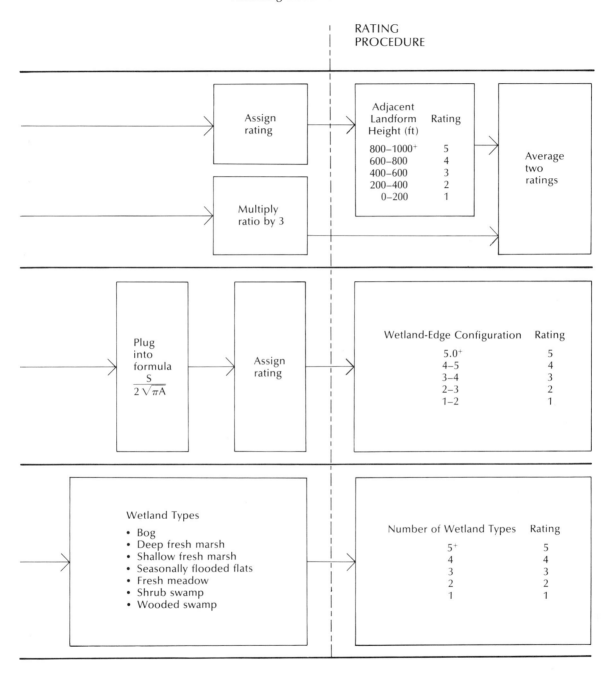

The other criterion, multiple value, compensates for the fact that some variables have multiple use values (visual, recreational, and educational), whereas other variables are significant for only one use value. The significance coefficients for visual resource variables are calculated by multiplying the number of use values (visual, recreational, and educational) that the given variable pertains to by the immutability number (see Table 3).

The overall visual resource value is computed with the following algebraic formula:

$$\sum_{t=1}^{m=1...11} (rv_m)sc_m = x$$

where rv = visual-resource variable
sc = significance coefficient
m = number of visual-resource variables
x = visual-resource value

Higher scores indicate greater visual, recreational, and educational value. Thus, evaluation level 2, the visual-resource evaluation system, can be used to rate inland wetlands from the highest to the lowest values. If a wetland did not receive a high enough score to be eliminated from further analysis, the evaluation process continues to level 3.

Level 3: Multiple cultural enhancement values of inland wetlands (Figure 2) The purpose of level 3 was to acknowledge the man-made or cultural attributes, both positive and negative, of wetlands. A cultural attribute may increase the visual–cultural value to society (for example, greater accessibility). At the same time pollution may decrease the visual–cultural values of a wetland.

Cultural enhancement variables and corresponding landscape dimensions Cultural variables are what Lewis terms "extrinsic" (Lewis, 1969), which can be defined as "man-made changes, adaptations, and additions to the

natural resources" (Lewis et al., 1969:23). Thus, cultural variables are concerned with the existence or nonexistence of man-made effects, which can both add to and detract from the natural resource value. The cultural enhancement variables are briefly defined as follows:

1. *Educational proximity* is the nearness of elementary schools, high schools, and colleges to a wetland area.
2. *Physical accessibility* is the degree of accessibility to a wetland by trail or road, and accessibility within the wetland by boat, trail, or road.
3. *Ambient quality* is the physical condition of the wetland as indicated by the lack of water pollution, air pollution, high noise levels, and visual misfits or noncompatible land uses.

Figure 12 summarizes the measurement and rating processes of the cultural enhancement variables. The rating scales are the same as level 2 (see Figure 11).

Weighting the cultural enhancement variables The cultural variables are weighted by using significance coefficients or multipliers. The criterion used was the relative importance of the variable to visual, recreational, and educational quality. A summary of the significance coefficients, the maximum points possible per variable, and the total number of points possible from level 3 evaluation can be seen in Table 4.

A wetland's rank in relation to other wetlands may change from the rank received in level 2 owing to the ratings given in level 3. Its rank may increase or decrease.

A wetland's score after a level 3 evaluation is the cultural enhancement value of the wetland site for visual, recreational, and educational quality. This can be expressed algebraically as

$$\sum_{t=1}^{n=1...3} (cv_n)sc_n = y$$

where cv = cultural enhancement
variable
sc = significance coefficient
n = number of cultural variables
y = cultural enhancement value

When a wetland is ranked with other wetlands after level 3 evaluation, it can be ranked on its cultural enhancement value (y) alone or ranked with both scores from the visual, recreational, educational resource value and the cultural enhancement value $(x + y)$ to *yield the total visual–cultural resource value (z)*. Furthermore, the visual–cultural resource values can be expressed in dollars if an economic evaluation is conducted as developed by members of our economics subproject. A short summary of their submodel is presented next (also see Figure 1).

ECONOMIC VALUATION

The inland wetland assessment model described earlier (Figure 1) shows the evaluation of three separate resource values of wetlands, wildlife-habitat, visual–cultural, and water-resource values. Each separate study developed a submodel to assess the qualities of all wetlands in the state of Massachusetts. The submodels did not evaluate, however, the economic value to society of any of these resources. The landscape planner may rank a highly rated wetland for visual–cultural value as number 10 among 130 wetlands. But, what does one tell a decision maker who needs to translate ratings into monetary values? He may use the economic valuation submodel developed by our resource economists.

The economics subproject of the wetland

Table 4

Cultural Resource Variable	Visual (1)	Recreational (1)	Educational (1)	Significance Coefficient	Highest Possible Rating	Highest Possible Total Score
Educational proximity			×	1	5	5
Physical accessibility	×	×	×	3	5	15
Ambient quality	×	×	×	3	5	15
						—
						35

study developed techniques to estimate visual–cultural, wildlife-habitat, and water-supply values of wetlands. In addition, benefits to society resulting from flood control by preserving wetlands were included (Gupta, 1973). We describe here only the technique used to obtain values for the visual–cultural wetland resources (Gupta and Foster, 1973).

The basis for the economic valuation of visual–cultural values was provided by data on land purchases made by Conservation Commissions in Massachusetts during the fiscal year 1972. The open-space value was assumed to correlate visual, recreational, and educational values in evaluation level 2. Particular attention was paid to open-space lands for nonactive recreation, the purchase of which was made with the aid of a subsidy of 50 percent of the price through the "Self-Help" program utilizing state funds.

Data were collected from 29 municipalities which received "Self-Help" assistance from the Division of Conservation Services, Massachusetts Department of Natural Resources, to ac-

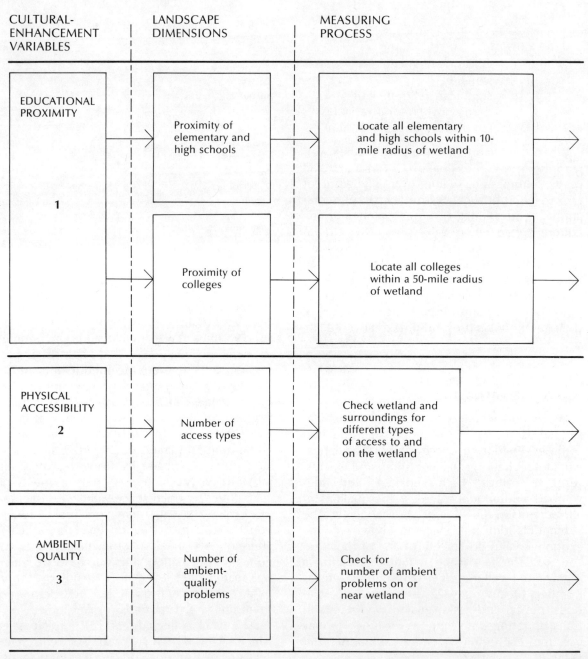

Figure 12
Measuring and rating procedures for cultural enhancement variables.

RATING
PROCEDURE

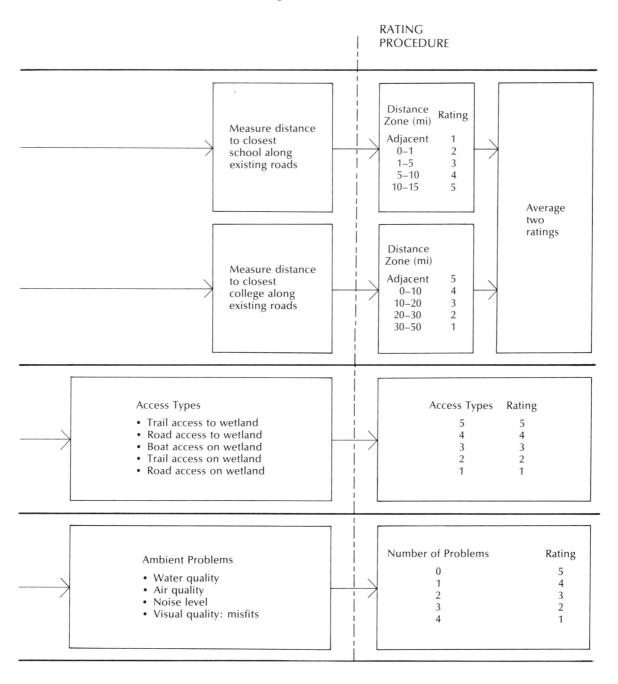

quire 42 parcels of open-space lands totaling 1,516 acres. The average price was $1,608 per acre.

The range of the five highest prices of land purchased was from $3,684 to $5,769 per acre. Based on these results, the resource economists estimated what they considered to be a fair maximum price that society had agreed to pay for high-quality open-space land, which was $5,000 per acre. If 5.375 percent is used as the capitalization rate of interest, the public cost of acquiring visual–cultural benefits on such lands was calculated to be approximately $270 per year per acre. If 7 percent is used as the capitalization rate, the figure would change from $270 to $350 per acre per year. Based on the assumption of maximum willingness, $270 was accepted as an economic value measure of the annual productivity per acre of visual–cultural values of high-quality wetlands as assessed by the visual–cultural evaluation. This economic figure was correlated with the high-quality visual–cultural values assessed by our submodel.

Similar values for wildlife-habitat, water-supply, and flood-control benefits were also derived by the economics subproject. Table 5 summarizes the results in terms of high, medium, and low values of benefits per acre of wetlands per year.

These benefits were then translated through computer analysis into capitalized values for different types of wetlands, and were capitalized over a number of years using two different rates of interest. A summary of the results is presented in Table 6.

The figures in the last two columns imply that, given a rate of interest, society is supposedly better off purchasing and preserving a wetland for its accrued benefits as long as its price is less than or equal to the respective figures in the table.

Table 5
Monetary Equivalents of High, Medium, and Low Values of Annual Benefits of Wetland Preservation (Gupta, 1973:153)

Type and Nature of Benefits	Dollar Values of Benefits Per Acre of Wetlands		
	High	Medium	Low[a]
Wildlife	70	35	10
Visual–Cultural	270	135	30
Water supply	2,800	1,400	400
Flood control	80	40	10

[a] It may be noted that the dollar figures of low benefits bear no proportionate relationship to the high figures.

Table 6
Summary of the Computer Analysis Showing the Nature of Benefits from Preserved Wetlands and Their Capitalized Values per Acre, Massachusetts, 1972 (Gupta, 1973:175)

Nature of Benefits				Capitalized Value of Wetland Benefits per Acre at:	
Wildlife	Visual–Cultural	Water Supply	Flood Control	5.375%[a] ($)	7%[a] ($)
High	High	High	High	59,000	46,000
High	High	Medium	High	33,800	26,000
High	High	Low	High	15,200	11,700
High	High	None	High	7,800	6,000
Medium	Medium	None	Medium	3,900	3,000
Low	Low	None	None	700	500
High	Low	None	None	1,800	1,400
Low	High	None	Low	5,300	4,100
Low	Low	None	High	2,200	1,700
Low	Low	High	Low	53,000	40,700
Low	Low	Low	Low	8,300	6,400

[a] Figures in the last two columns have been rounded to the nearest $100.

POTENTIAL UTILITY OF
THE VISUAL–CULTURAL SUBMODEL

In this section we discuss the third study objective, which is *to ensure that the visual–cultural wetlands assessment submodel has utility at all decision-making levels and scales.* Illustrating the utility of the submodel can be done by showing who can use it, how they can use it, and the tasks that it can be used for.

At the site scale, an inland wetland could be rated by a wetland owner, whether a private individual, conservation commission, state agency, or federal agency, to see if the individual wetland achieves a high, middle, or low score for visual–cultural values. The score may indicate the desirability of preserving or protecting the wetland, developing the wetland for multiple or single use, or trading off the wetland for another use. Ideally, the wetland score for visual–cultural values as well as other values, such as water supply and wildlife habitat, could serve as a preliminary assessment for the wetland owner of the degree of difficulty he might expect from the Department of Natural Resources or a local conservation commission in obtaining a permit to alter the wetland.

At the town scale, the ideal user would be town or city conservation commissions in Massachusetts or Connecticut, or town selectmen, planning boards, and city–town planners in other New England states. Conservation commissions in Massachusetts and their parallels in other states could use the visual–cultural submodel to rate various wetlands within their respective towns or cities. The rated wetlands could then be ranked to help determine which wetlands should be acquired first, utilizing money from the "Self-Help" state program, or the equivalent, and/or federal Bureau of Outdoor Recreation programs. The visual–cultural

resource value could be translated into the economic worth of the wetland by using the economic valuation. This would help to indicate whether the land is worth preserving solely for its visual–cultural values for a certain acquisition price. A combined economic valuation, including water-supply, wildlife-habitat and flood-control, values might indicate to the Conservation Commission that the purchase price is more than worth the combined values of the wetland.

At the regional scale, regional planning agencies in Massachusetts, development commissions in Vermont, and comparable agencies in other New England states would be ideal users. In Massachusetts regional planning agencies could utilize the visual–cultural submodel to rate and rank wetlands on a regional basis to indicate priorities for preservation of wetlands, especially regional wetland systems. In Vermont, the visual–cultural submodel could be used to help countywide development commissions to make decisions concerning developer's proposed uses or changes of Vermont wetlands. In Massachusetts regional planning agencies could provide needed technical assistance to town or city conservation commissions to better utilize and understand the visual–cultural assessment submodel and/or the larger inland wetlands assessment model.

At the state scale, state planning agencies in all the New England states could use the visual–cultural submodel or the larger inland wetlands assessment model to rate inland wetlands on a statewide scale. This could indicate preservation priorities for wetlands with visual–cultural values of statewide significance, water-supply values, wildlife-habitat values, wetlands with single "outstanding" values for educational and scientific use, and even wetlands for flood-control purposes as outlined in the economic valuation. The economic valuation would indicate whether the wetlands would be worth purchasing with state funds.

Interstate users would be primarily federal agencies, such as the National Park Service, Corps of Engineers, and the New England River Basins Commission. The National Park Service could use the visual–cultural and wildlife-habitat submodels, and the larger inland wetlands model, to rate wetland areas in New England. With some alteration the submodels could probably be used on a national scale for rating wetlands. The assessment systems could be utilized to indicate wetland areas of extremely high natural value or "outstanding" wetlands that would merit national status for preservation. The New England River Basins Commission and the Corps of Engineers could utilize the visual–cultural, wildlife-habitat, and water-supply submodels, and especially the economic valuation of flood-control benefits of wetlands, to rate wetland systems on an interstate river basin scale.

This partial listing of possible users and the possible uses of the visual–cultural submodel or the overall inland wetlands assessment model merely indicates the value of a comprehensive wetland assessment system. There are many more probable uses of the system at many different scales.

The visual–cultural submodel is an assessment system for measuring the visual–cultural values of inland wetlands, and is an integral part of the overall inland wetlands assessment model that could help to facilitate better wetland-use decision making. It is needed now. Land-use allocation questions concerning wetlands are in the news every day and confront many decision-making bodies on many political levels and geographic scales.

It should be realized, however, that the system as a whole has not been thoroughly tested through actual use. Evaluation level 2 has been extensively pretested in the field to determine if there is a good point spread between rating scores and to see if the variables account for reasonable differences in visual–cultural value. Level 2 sample ratings were also compared with expert panel ratings of the same wetlands. Evaluation levels 1 and 3 have not been developed to the same degree.

To improve the model, research is proposed in three areas. First, the design of the model should be modified in such a way that the average conservation commission member could use it. Then, through the use of the model, additional necessary changes and modifications should be made to improve the submodel.

Second, the validity of the submodel should be improved through behavioral studies and by testing each variable and criterion, as well as the overall structure of the submodel. Probable new additional variables should be developed to improve the value rating procedure.

Third, assessment systems for evaluating the visual–cultural values of the larger surrounding landscapes of wetland environment might be developed. Many of the variables and assessment principles used in this study are central to visual–cultural values for many other types of environments.

In short, much more research is needed in assessment systems to enable better environmental resource decisions to be made.

Visual and Cultural Components of the Landscape Resource Assessment Model of the METLAND Study

Julius Gy. Fabos, William G. Hendrix,
and Christopher M. Greene

This chapter is a summary of several quantitative assessment models that have attempted to estimate the value of certain visual–cultural landscape resources within the Boston metropolitan region. Before describing the thesis and objective of the METLAND study for which these models were developed, the terms "landscape resource" and "visual–cultural landscape resource" need to be defined operationally.

Landscape resources, for the purpose of the study, are observable entities and artifacts of the landscape (for example, water, trees, soil, wildlife, landscape diversity) each of which can provide man with a range of utility values. Natural resource specialists often distinguish between flow resources, that is, renewable resources, such as water or trees, and stock resources, such as aggregate and coal. The MET-

Julius Gy. Fabos is an Associate Professor in the Department of Landscape Architecture and Regional Planning at the University of Massachusetts.

William G. Hendrix is a graduate student in forestry at the University of Massachusetts.

Christopher M. Greene is an American landscape architect working in England.

Model for Metropolitan Landscape Planning (METLAND), a study enjoying the joint support of the Massachusetts Agricultural Experiment Station, the Pinchot Institute of Environmental Forestry — U.S. Department of Agriculture Forest Service, and the U.S. Department of Interior, Office of Water Resources Research, 1971–1976. The study area is the Boston metropolitan region.

LAND study is concerned with both these natural resource types.

In addition, the study has identified visual–cultural characteristics of the landscape as a third major landscape resource type termed *visual–cultural landscape resources*. These resources are defined as the results of several environmental activities (natural and man-influenced) normally present in the landscape, which have proven value to society (for example, visual contrast or the presence of tree cover). They are *intrinsic* aspects of the physical environment whose value varies with the type and intensity of the uses of the land.

This chapter will briefly introduce the overall landscape resource model developed by the METLAND study. Its major emphasis however is on those models which assess perceived values of visual–cultural landscape resources.

The major hypothesis of the METLAND study is that the process of post-World War II metropolitanization has resulted in a loss in value of several landscape resources. Use of the landscape necessarily involves altering it, so that providing a growing population with numerous social benefits in the form of housing, commerce, employment, and recreation often lessens or sometimes even eliminates the value of existing landscape resources. Trees are cut down, open fields are subdivided for suburban homes, and wetlands are filled to provide for shopping areas or industries. It is the contention of this study that the satisfaction of these human needs has resulted in an *inordinate* amount of landscape resource value loss, which could have been at least partially averted through wise land-use allocation practices and through sound management decisions.

The objective of the study, therefore, has been to develop a quantitative system that will measure the effect of metropolitanization on visual–cultural landscape resource values. Once we are able to estimate this resource value change with some accuracy, it should be possible to design predictive models that will have utility in allocating land uses so that loss in existing resource value can be minimized. The assessment model presented here represents only the first phase of the larger study, which will deal with additional landscape resources and develop a planning aid for the making of land-use allocation decisions within metropolitan regions.

It is also important to state what the study does not attempt to do. This is not intended to be basic research into human behavior or natural science. The study rather interprets the results of other researchers, such as environmental psychologists and ecologists, and, based on those results, makes assumptions about human behavior and natural resource values. From this synthesis of previous research, the study has proceeded to develop a quantitative methodology that estimates the value of a given landscape resource in a given area at a given point in time. In one instance only, for the visual land-use compatibility resource variable, a primary testing procedure was designed to acquire data about people's attitudes and human behavior. This testing was deemed necessary since a review of pertinent literature did not produce research results useful for the assessment model.

The remainder of this chapter is organized into three parts. The first part briefly introduces the overall landscape resource assessment model (Fabos, 1973). The second part deals in greater detail with the visual–cultural submodels (Fabos, 1973; Greene, 1972; Hendrix, 1973). In the third part we discuss the limitations and potential utility of the study.

LANDSCAPE RESOURCE ASSESSMENT MODEL

The value of a given landscape resource to a society is greatly influenced by three factors: the availability of the landscape resource in question, the inherent attributes or characteristics of that resource, and the society's previous and present uses of and attitudes toward that resource. For the purpose of this study, therefore, the significance of a resource variable was determined by analyzing it in terms of its availability, attributes, and uses. Thus, abundant resources having little utility to society were not considered to be significant enough for inclusion in this type of study. For example, to the pioneer of New England in the eighteenth century, forests were not perceived as an important resource because of their great abundance and the nuisance they presented when land was being cleared for farming and defense. On the other hand, water in metropolitan areas today is becoming scarce, its quality tends to decrease, and its use continues to increase both in type and quantity. An additional criterion for selecting resource variables for this study was the availability of the data and research results that are necessary for assessing a landscape resource.

Initially, 25 landscape resources variables were analyzed in terms of these factors and criteria. The following seven were eventually selected for the pilot study, phase I of the METLAND model: ground and surface water quantity; water quality; wildlife productivity (open land, woodland, and wetland); agricultural productivity; visual land-use complexity (based on visual land-use diversity and visual land-use contrast); visual land-use compatibility; and tree cover. The last three variables have been identified under the visual–cultural resource category, which is the focus of this paper. At present, two additional variables, flood hazards and environmental noise, are being studied.

The use of a landscape resource can be analyzed from at least two points of view. One kind of analysis was mentioned earlier in reference to the use of trees in the eighteenth century and water in modern cities. The emphasis here was on either the attitude toward a given landscape resource or on the demand for a given landscape resource. A second type of analysis is concerned with all the different types of land uses to which land can be put (for example, farming or highway) and whether they affect positively or negatively the value of a landscape resource variable (for example, water supply or quality).

In a metropolitan region, such as that surrounding Boston, land uses range from wildlife preserves in a wetland area to the office–shopping facilities contained in the Prudential complex. The effects of these land uses and all other possible land uses between these two extremes may be considerably different for each of the nine landscape resource variables listed previously.

To analyze the land use and landscape resource interaction, a workable land-use classification system is needed. Of the several known land-use classification systems, MacConnell's technique (1971) was selected for this study. The availability and validity of this system were major considerations in its selection. In addition, the MacConnell system has already been used to map the various land uses of the Boston metropolitan region (which includes the METLAND study area) from 1952 and 1971 air photos. This system is based on six general land-use categories within which 126 land-use types are identified. The six general categories, with examples, are agricultural or open land (pastures, orchards), forest lands (softwood forests), wetlands (shrub swamps, deep marshes), mining or waste-disposal areas (dumps, filter beds), urban lands (light industrial areas, urban residential), and outdoor recreation facilities (playgrounds, golf courses). The study could not use all 126 land-use types. Therefore, 54 land uses, which were considered to be the most appropriate, were adopted (Fabos, 1973:42).

Conceptual framework of the model The

evaluation of the attributes of a given land-scape resource (for example, high value for water quality), the analysis of land uses with respect to the landscape resource variable in question (for example, the influence of land coverage in the form of buildings or parking lots on water runoff or water rechargeability), and the interaction between these two (for example, the negative effect of decreased water rechargeability that results from erecting buildings and parking lots on the given land use) *provide a landscape resource value for any given parcel of land.* This process also constitutes the conceptual framework of the landscape resource model (see Figure 1).

If it is assumed that the value of a given landscape resource at a given time for a given parcel (area) can be assessed, it is then possible to ascertain the values of that parcel both before and after urbanization. The value difference between the two time frames thus becomes the resource value change resulting from urbanization in the study area. If this assessment of resource value change due to metropolitanization is substantiated, a predictive

model can be designed to show possible landscape resource value changes that would occur under potential land uses. The hypothetical allocation of land uses through simulation modeling would identify those landscape resources and land-use interactions that would either minimize landscape resource value loss or maximize its benefits. The present landscape resource assessment model is not able to perform all these tasks, but it is intended that succeeding phases of the study will be able to optimize landscape resource values by indicating the most appropriate directions for land-use allocation.

Methodological framework of the model At the time of the first phase of this study (1971–1973), adequate computer hardware was not available to assess the resource value change occurring in large metropolitan landscapes. Although computerized grid methods (SYMAP and others) were adaptable to the computers at the University of Massachusetts, they were found to be unsuitable for this study since specific data were required at a small scale responsive to irregularly shaped land areas. Instead, a limited number of $\frac{1}{25}$-square-kilometer parcels (about 11 acres) were analyzed in great detail in each of the three towns (Burlington, Wilmington, and Tewksbury) in the Boston metropolitan area. Resultant resource value changes for each town were then statistically tested for significance. (At present, the METLAND team is adapting the assessment model for computer graphics using map digitizers and plotters.) In addition to analyzing parcels of uniform size throughout the study area, three other elements of the assessment methodology were standardized: the dimensions of the landscape resource variables, the dimensions of change in resource value, and the coefficients representing popular attitudes toward the landscape resources.

Dimensions of landscape resource varia-

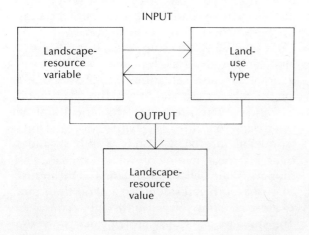

Figure 1
Conceptual framework of the model for landscape-resource assessment.

bles All resource values for each variable were uniformly expressed on a relative scale ranging from 0 to 100, where 0 constituted the lowest possible and 100 the highest possible resource value in the study area.

Dimensions of change of resource value All resource value changes for each variable were expressed on a relative scale ranging from −100 to +100, since an initial resource value of 100 (highest value) could be fully lost by a new land-use allocation to constitute a resource value change of −100, and vice versa.

Coefficients to represent attitudes of people It was seen that the various landscape resources studied might potentially represent varied values to society or decision makers. Water supply, for example, may be considered more significant than tree cover, or vice versa. In addition, social attitudes such as these change over time. Perceived values are often modified through the influence of interest groups, increased education, and other factors. An assessment model, therefore, should be able to express changing and varying values. For this reason, a survey technique was developed to deal with these values. The results and the criticism of the survey are detailed in the first study report (Fabos, 1973:83–90).

General Model

The general model constitutes an assessment of the composite resource value change of all landscape resource variables distributed geographically within and between towns. The conceptual model used to develop submodels for each landscape resource variable constitutes the basis for this general model. The principal difference is that the land-use effect is assessed against all landscape resource variables and results in a composite landscape resource value (see Figure 2).

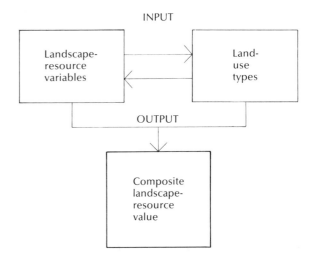

Figure 2
Conceptual framework of the general model.

A simplified step-by-step description and a diagram of the general model (see Figure 3) are as follows:

1. Determine landscape resource variables (1 to *n* in number) to be measured and rated.
2. Obtain the mean change in value of each resource variable occurring between two points in time. (The study used the years 1952 and 1971 since aerial photogrammetric data were available. The first date, 1952, coincides with the completion of Route 128 around Boston, which contributed to the rapid urbanization of nearby communities.)
3. Compute the average composite change in value of all resource variables in each cell. (Weighting of variables can be applied here if coefficients have been obtained.) Contour or other graphic mapping techniques can be applied to demonstrate visually the degree of change occurring.

When the overall resource value change per township is calculated by obtaining the mean

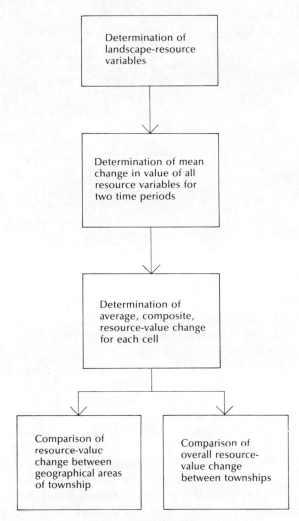

Determination of
landscape-resource
variables

Determination of mean
change in value of all
resource variables for
two time periods

Determination of
average, composite,
resource-value change
for each cell

Comparison of
resource-value
change between
geographical areas
of township

Comparison of
overall resource-
value change
between townships

Figure 3
Model of overall resource-value change.

resource value change for all resource variables of all parcels assessed within a town, comparisons can be made among towns.

VISUAL–CULTURAL SUBMODELS

There are several levels of importance at which resources may be regarded as they apply

to human beings (Maslow, 1970:97). Some resources are essential to one's survival (food, air, water); others are merely conducive to one's psychological well-being (visual and cultural amenities). When the essential resources of a given area have been exhausted, the need is often met through importation. Boston's water supply, for instance, is presently imported from Quabbin Reservoir, 80 miles away. Although the technology exists for such operations, the wisdom or necessity of these procedures is open to question. For example, had the water resources of Boston been managed differently or had future needs been better anticipated, it is possible that this water importation (which costs four times more than local water; Gupta, 1972) might have been unnecessary. If, because of the significant rise in population, importation was deemed necessary, management on a limited scale might have resulted in a great savings in money to the region.

It is the assumption of this study that visual-resource values can likewise be managed and preserved. Although it is possible to "import" them (that is, create them, as in Constitution Plaza in Hartford or the Golden Gate development of San Francisco), the cost of "importation" is significantly higher than the cost of maintaining previously existing visual resources. It is, therefore, reasonable and necessary to assess these so-called nonessential resources in the same way that the more essential resources are assessed.

A second assumption is based on the belief that it is possible that visual–cultural values can be reasonably defined. That is, through research, principles of human behavior and human need can be identified and *quantified*. Such research results could be the basis of visual and cultural value scales that could be translated into landscape-assessment models — valuable tools for the landscape-planning process. Unfortunately, the science of environmental psychology is not as advanced as many of the physical sciences, such as botany, which has defined a number of universally accepted principles regarding the behavior or natural processes of plants. Despite the absence of well-defined principles for visual–cultural value needs at this time, there are numerous studies available on behavior patterns. These can be roughly divided into two categories: those related to the biological bases of human behavior, and those related to the influence of human experience and learning on behavior. This portion of the study, therefore, has proceeded on the premise that these two types of behavior patterns exist and that together they determine the visual–cultural values and needs of people. Values that seem to be generated by behavior relating to inherent biological behavioral mechanisms are called here *generic preference values*. Those relating to acquired behavioral mechanisms are referred to as *individual preference values*.

The METLAND team reviewed and interpreted the literature and research findings on this subject. As a result, four visual–cultural variables were suggested initially for assessment. The two visual variables were visual landscape complexity (a generic preference variable) and visual land-use compatibility (a variable based on individual preference). The two cultural variables were environmental noise (a generic preference variable) and tree cover (a variable based on individual preference).

Visual Land-Use Complexity Variable

Several behavioral studies have concluded that a complex environment will stimulate most individuals and affect the actions of most animals (Berlyne, 1963; Day, 1967; Munsinger and Kessen, 1964; Terwilliger, 1963; and Vitz, 1966). Wohlwill (1968) cited similar results when using slides of landscape scenes scaled for relative complexity. In addition to the findings of psychologists, several environmental designers have correlated high complexity and great diversity with positive visual quality. Diversity has been an intricate part of ecological theory (Margalef, 1971). However, laboratory experiments have also demonstrated that complexity becomes undesirable when increased above a certain level of tolerance. Leuba (1955) describes this phenomenon in terms of "optimal stimulation levels."

From the interpretation of these study results it can be concluded that, in the landscape, maximum visual landscape complexity is desirable. In other words, complex land areas (those which consist of several land uses, views, or perceivable edges) contribute more to the visual quality of a landscape than those areas which are very simple (having a single land-use type, similar views, or few perceivable edges). The next obvious question is: Can a landscape be so complex that an individual's processing capacity is surpassed? It is believed that such complexity in the landscape is very unlikely. However, certain land uses can occasionally provide stimulation above an individual's tolerance level. A strip development, for instance, on rainy nights, with its many signs, under heavy traffic conditions may surpass the information processing capacity of many people.

Further study into the landscape complexity variable indicated that two aspects of complexity are measurable. The first aspect is based on the fact that each distinct land use provides a different and specific perceptual experience (Mussinger and Kessen, 1964; Terwilliger, 1963; Rapoport and Hawkes, 1970; Pyron, 1972).This aspect of visual landscape complexity is developed under the visual land-use diversity subvariable. The second aspect of complexity is based on the degree of visual contrast that can be perceived between land uses (Thomas, 1968; Noton and Stark, 1971; Gratzer and McDowell, 1971; Kiemstedt, 1967; Shafer, 1969) and is developed under the visual land-use contrast subvariable.

Visual land-use diversity subvariable To assess the value of visual landscape diversity as a result of land use, a metric of variability in the landscape was needed. To find an appropriate method of quantifying diversity or variability, several research approaches were reviewed. Several researchers have borrowed the concept of "bits" from information theory as conceived by Shannon and Weaver (1949). Pyron's (1972) application of this concept to large-scale chunks of the environment was the most pertinent to the needs of this study. Pyron speaks of being "embedded" in a three-or-more acre area of the environment which has a "character of its own." He further asserts that it is "the different character of the various embedding areas seen in sequence which determines the amount of diversity in the sector." Therefore, to measure quantitatively the visual diversity of

land-use types, Pyron's basic concept was adopted. The metric used involved the calculation of the amount of information available at the "land-use-type" scale within each cell (parcel of land) of $\frac{1}{25}$ square kilometer. It was hypothesized that the visual diversity of land-use types in a given cell increases as the number of different land-use types increases, and as the area of each land-use type approaches equivalent size. The first parameter simply states that the more land-use types found in a given area, the greater the visual diversity. This parameter is illustrated in Figure 4. The second parameter is a modifier which states that the visual-diversity value decreases as the sizes of the land uses occurring within a cell vary. This parameter is adopted from the "entropy" concept developed in thermodynamics (Shannon and Weaver, 1949) and utilized in information theory. In essence, the individual's chance of receiving information from each part of the whole increases as the parts become equal. Thus, as the sizes of land uses within a cell or a given area approach equality, the individual has a greater opportunity of experiencing each land-use type. Maximum entropy is reached when all land

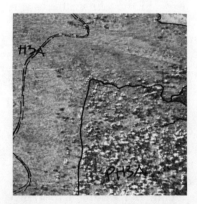
Low degree of land-use diversity

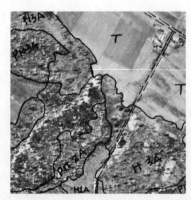
Medium degree of land-use diversity

High degree of land-use diversity

Figure 4
Land-use patterns illustrating varying degrees of land-use diversity.

uses in the cell are of equal size. For example, the diversity values of parcels A and B in Figure 5 would be higher than the values of parcels C and D. In Figure 6 a simplified version of the visual land-use diversity submodel is shown. It presents the step-by-step procedure for the measurement of visual diversity. Greene (1972) and Fabos (1973) explain this procedure more fully.

Visual land-use contrast subvariable Visual contrast constitutes the second subvariable of visual land-use complexity, and refers to the degree of contrast that can be perceived between land uses. Gibson (1961) suggested that the most important aspect of visual stimulation arises from changes in the characteristics of light. In the environment, perceivable edges provide those changes. Two aspects of visual edges seem to be pertinent to this subvariable. One is the amount of transition at a boundary

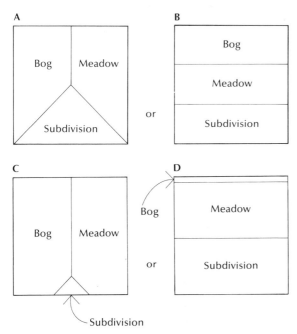

Figure 5
Diversity values of land parcels.

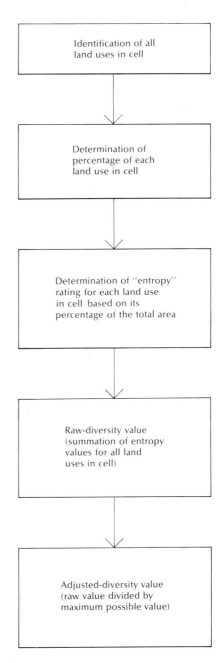

Figure 6
Visual land-use diversity submodel.

in a visual array. (This describes the quality of difference between the visual characteristics of adjacent land uses.) The second is the presence or absence of transitions in the array. (This deals with the quantity of areas of contrast as measurable by boundary or edge length.) Figure 7 illustrates these two aspects of contrast.

The importance of edges in the environment has been studied from several viewpoints. Each suggests the importance of quality and quantity of contrast. The ecological concept of increased species variety and density of community interfaces (ecotones) has been long established (Odum, 1971). Numerous experiments with eye movement have discovered that when people look at something their eyes fix on the edges that are apparent in the views (Thomas, 1968; Noton and Stark, 1971; Gratzer and McDowell, 1971). Landscape-preference studies have also revealed positive relationships between the amount of edge in the landscape and perceived quality (Shafer, 1969; Burns and Rundell, 1969). Other research work indicates that people not only notice edges, but also actively seek them in their movement through the landscape. In an aerial survey of the distribution of visitors to various Dutch recreation areas, de Jonge (1967–1968) found that the "border zones" (such as the edges between forest and open land) attracted the largest concentrations of people. Similar studies by Kiemstedt (1967) concluded that the visual–recreational values of edges were significantly higher than inner areas of a given land use. Kiemstedt's planning model rates edge areas (forest–open land and water edges) nearly twice as high as his three other variables — relief, land use, and climate — combined. In the United States, measurement of contrast and edge for landscape assessment and description has been proposed by several landscape architects and planners (Litton, 1968,

Zube et al., 1970; Lynch, 1960; Bartels et al., 1972).

These research results and planning norms suggest that visual land-use contrast would be a significant variable for inclusion in a landscape-assessment model. The two aspects of Gibson's theory (the amount and quality of contrast) suggest that a quantitative measurement of visual contrast can be designed. The rating of this subvariable, therefore, is based on this premise. The degree of contrast is seen to depend on the visual characteristics of each of two adjacent landscape types (quality of contrast), and the length of the edge between the two types (quantity of contrast). For example, if a water body abuts a pasture for 50 feet, the quality of contrast (due to height) is less than if the water body abutted a forest edge of 50 feet. Also, a water–forest edge of 50 feet has less value than one of 500 feet (if only because there is more chance of encountering it).

In the rating of contrast used in the model, three types of contrast between land uses were employed: relative height, relative texture, and relative naturalness. The procedure for evaluating contrast by measuring contrast quality and length of edge are discussed in the research report by Fabos (1973). A simplified step-by-step explanation and model is found in Figure 8.

Visual land-use compatibility variable The second variable that is primarily concerned with visual resources is the visual land-use compatibility variable. This variable is considered to relate to *acquired* behavior, and is thus regarded here as being based on individual human preference rather than generic human preferences. Important to this variable is the notion of "appreciability." The major question is: Are there characteristics of land use A that impair an individual's *ability* to *appreciate* an adjacent land use B? For instance, the visual land-use complexity rating discussed pre-

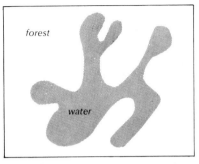

Land-use pattern illustrating high
contrast due to length of edge

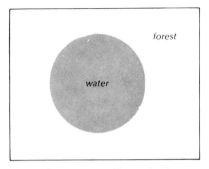

Land-use pattern illustrating low
contrast due to length of edge

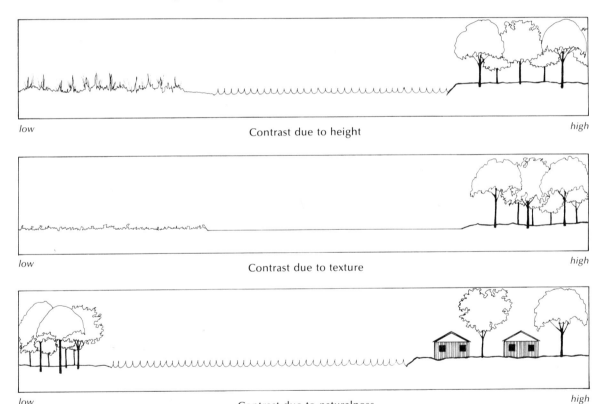

Figure 7
Land-use contrast.

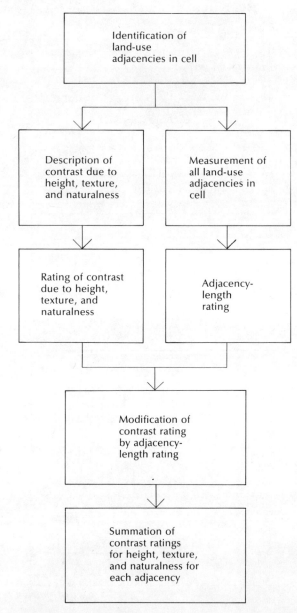

Figure 8
Visual land-use contrast submodel.

viously may conclude that a residential land use adjacent to a junkyard land use is visually complex and therefore deserving of a high rating. However, from the visual land-use compatibility point of view, such a land-use combination may receive a very low rating. People (usually) react negatively to the type of complexity represented by a junkyard abutting their homes.

The literature reviewed in this area supported, in part, this notion of appreciability, which is often in conflict with visual land-use complexity values. The most significant evidence of visual compatibility values, however, comes from the numerous land-use control and zoning ordinances. These controls usually result in the segregation of land uses to separate areas of the town, implying that certain land uses are more compatible than others. This implication obviously does not suggest that these responses represent only visual values. Indeed, one's attitudes toward or perceptions of the landscape are a result of all the senses, an accumulation of all experiences, and perceptions of social norms and contextual conditions (Hendrix, 1973). According to Hall, "Everything that man is and does is associated with the experience of space. His sense of space is a synthesis of many inputs: visual, auditory, kinesthetic, olfactory and thermal, and each is molded and patterned by his culture" (Hall, 1966).

Land-use controls are influenced, therefore, by numerous factors, which in great part seem to be expressed in the form of visual–cultural land-use relationships. A more specific example is the current interest in historic-district zoning in many cities. The major goal of historic-district zoning is to exclude activities, or land uses, that are not compatible with the visual and cultural character of the district (Miner, 1969). The driving force of the conservation movement in this country seems also to stem from the conflict arising between incompatible uses of the landscape, such as the proposed reservoir for water and hydroelectric power for the city of San Francisco in Yosemite National Park (Udall, 1963). These efforts, however, are not particularly significant until they become politically relevant social issues (Caldwell, 1971). The recent passage of the National Environmental Policy Act of 1970, the Highway Beautification Act of 1965, the 1965 White House Conference on Natural Beauty, and several other federal and state actions suggest that environmental quality, proper land use, and land use compatibility have indeed become significant social issues. The problem remains as to how these social values can be assessed and translated into landscape and land-use planning? The land-use complexity variable, in great part, was supported by experimental work and preference studies. Unfortunately, similar studies are not, to date, available for the visual land-use compatibility variable.

Initially, the METLAND study developed a metric for the assessment of visual land-use compatibility by estimating people's perception of the relationships between land uses (Greene, 1972; Fabos, 1973). The review of literature and the personal judgments of the METLAND team were the basis of the estimates. However, this first attempt was less than satisfactory owing to its subjective nature. For this reason, a direct testing procedure was developed to learn more about visual land-use compatibility (Hendrix, 1973:8–52). This process included the identification of general land-use classes that are representative of land-use types exhibiting similar visual–cultural characteristics, and the development of a testing procedure. The test results were then transferred to a visual land-use compatibility matrix. Finally, a submodel was designed to assess visual land-use compatibility.

Land uses for testing The 126 land-use types classified by MacConnell (1972) would produce 7,875 possible different adjacencies. Among the majority of these land-use pairs, the question of visual land-use compatibility would be very insignificant (for example, two mature hardwood forest types, one 40 feet and the other 30 feet in height). To reduce the land-use types to a manageable number, a pilot survey was applied to a group of 10 designers, planners, and resource managers. They were asked to sort 126 cards, each describing a land use, into nine categories ranging from most manmade to most natural, according to visual characteristics. Examination of the data received from this survey identified 11 distinct groups consisting of land uses with very similar visual characteristics. The 11 land-use categories identified for further consideration were water bodies, wetlands, forests, agricultural lands, recreation–park lands, low-density residential areas, medium-density residential areas, high-density residential areas, transportation routes, commercial areas, and industrial areas. Figure 9 illustrates these 11 land uses.

Testing procedure Five groups of 10 persons each (designers, planners, realtors, conservationists, and nonprofessionals) were selected for testing. If differences were to occur among groups, this type of stratification would be likely to reveal it. Since several of these groups do not regularly use land-use terminology, black-and-white photographic prints were selected as an acceptable means of representing environmental stimuli. To control the variance in photographic quality, three different examples of each land use were photographed, and the examples were distributed within each of the five groups. Other variables controlled in the photography were light quality, time of day and year, topographic relief, amount of foreground, horizon line, and viewer's position. Each photograph represented only one land-use type.

The entire survey was administered by one person to ensure a continuity of procedure. The first step involved the familiarization of the participants with all the photographs. Then one of the photographs was placed on his or her left. The remaining photographs were then presented in a predetermined random order on the right. The participants in all cases were asked to respond to the question, ''If the two land uses represented by the photographs you are observing were adjacent to one another, how would the land use on the right affect the *visual quality* of the land use represented by the photograph on the left?'' The procedure was repeated until all 11 photographs had appeared on the left and had been compared

Figure 9
Land-use types used for testing.

with the other 10 photographs. This made a total of 110 observations. The responses were recorded on the following scale: -3, -2, -1, 0, $+1$, $+2$, $+3$, where -3 represented the most negative effect and $+3$ represented the most positive effect; no effect was represented by 0. The responses thus recorded the degree of enhancement or detraction.

For each of the 110 observations a two-way analysis of variance was conducted to examine the difference between groups and between photo sets. This analysis showed a relatively high level of overall agreement. With some observations involving wetlands, however, there was little agreement between the five groups. The extent-of-agreement matrix showed that of the 55 adjacencies only two exhibit no agreement, 20 exhibit moderate agreement, and 23 high agreement among respondents. In only a very few cases was significant variance found between photo sets.

To improve the results, larger samples and more sophisticated testing procedures will be needed. The results (see Figure 10), nonetheless, further support the study's interpretation of the literature connected with various land-use controls, which in the past has substantiated the visual land-use compatibility variable. For instance, the test results show that industrial and commercial uses are incompatible with most other use categories, while among wetlands, forest, agricultural lands, and recreation uses, the degree of compatibility is high. Figure 11 illustrates these examples of land-use relationships. Obviously, proper planning and design could eliminate many of these perceived incompatibilities. It is equally obvious, however, that those planning and design devices are not sufficiently communicated to the people, at least not to those who were tested for this study. The idea of the segregation of uses, including visual segregation, seems to be an inherent part of this culture (a

thesis strongly supported by Toll, 1969). The values expressed in the matrix and used in the visual land-use compatibility assessment model, if valid, represent an interpretation of existing cultural norms. These norms seem to favor buffer zones between the incompatible land uses, rather than overall integrated design, which may be more acceptable in Europe as demonstrated by the numerous new town design approaches there (Strong, 1971).

The submodel in Figure 12 is a simplified version of the visual land-use compatibility submodel.

Noise Variable

To justify an investigation of noise, it must first be established that noise is a cultural landscape resource variable. Noise is defined here to be "cultural" for two reasons: high environmental noise levels have become increasingly characteristic of our contemporary culture in the last two decades, and these noise levels are negatively affecting the environmental quality of many areas. Since most Americans live in metropolitan areas, it is in those "landscapes" that noise becomes an important consideration. Noise, or lack of noise, is defined as a "resource." Environments with low noise levels are sought by many people in the same way that they seek wooded sites, locations with views, or water. Furthermore, the noise-level value of any location is subject to human influence in the same manner as the value of any other landscape resource considered in the METLAND study.

It was stated earlier that some variables are generated by behavior which relates to inherent biological mechanisms. These variables we have called generic preference variables. "There is no question that high levels of sound or noise have become an insidious form of environmental degradation which threatens

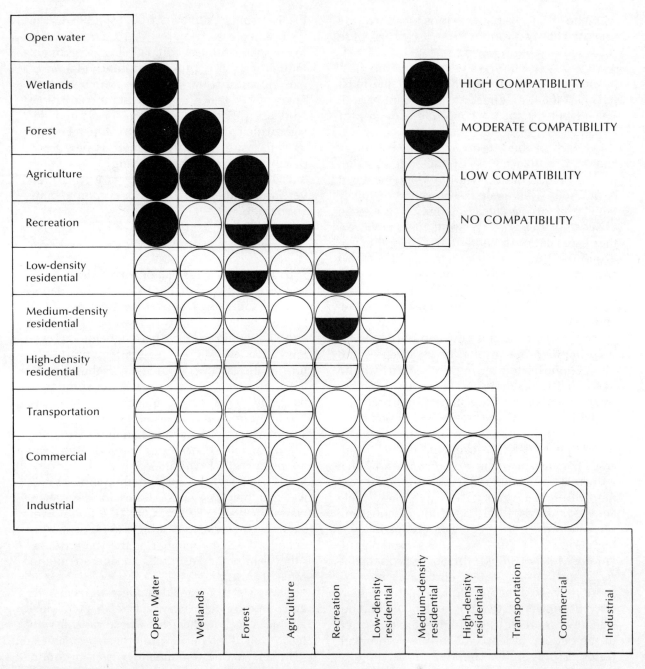

Figure 10
Land-use compatibility matrix.

both man's physical health and his psychological well-being" (Caswell, 1973). For this reason, the noise variable is classified as an appropriate generic preference variable to be dealt with under this assessment of cultural values.

The initial investigation of the noise variable (Caswell, 1973) suggests that, in keeping with all other METLAND variables, it can be studied as a function of land use. To date, most of the research work reviewed by Caswell deals with specific measurements of noise at specific locations. However, the synthesis of a sufficient number of measurements has been undertaken in order to make a relatively accurate correlation between various land uses and the noise levels they generate. For instance, the noise level of a given highway can be estimated from such information as highway size, speed, traffic count, and type of vehicles. This type of information provides a *noise-generating index* for each land use. Noise attenuation is a function of vegetation, man-made elements in the landscape, topographical barriers, wind, and temperature, among other parameters. This second type of information results in an *attenuation index* of each land use. From these two sets of information, the determination of the effect of one land use upon an adjacent land use is possible. The development of this model is planned in order that, based on specific land-use information, noise contour maps can be produced for the metropolitan landscape, or any part of it, at any given point in time. Location measurements or spot checking could then be used to refine the contours.

The initial noise submodel (Figure 13) is now being developed in such a manner that it can be a part of the general landscape resource assessment model.

Tree-Cover Variable

The justification of the tree-cover variable as a cultural landscape resource variable has been

intriguing to the METLAND team for two reasons. First, it is easy to demonstrate that the social acceptance of the value of "trees" is a cultural axiom in the United States. For example, a major Japanese automobile manufacturer offered, in a recent advertising campaign, to plant one tree on Forest Service land for every test drive of their auto, a Datsun. This gimmick was clearly based on the belief that Americans value trees. The second intriguing aspect of this variable is that a changing behavioral pattern, influenced by learning and human experience, can be demonstrated here. Literature clearly indicates that in the eighteenth century trees were regarded as a nuisance despite their intrinsic value for lumber. In colonial times, villages and surrounding farms were largely stripped and cleared of trees because major vegetation was an impediment to farming and because trees were considered to offer concealment and protection for attacking Indians (Zube, 1971b). The relocation of farms to the Great Plains and the end of warfare with the Indians, coupled with the influence in the mid-nineteenth century of Romanticism greatly changed this value construct. Trees and natural landscapes began to be seen as functionally and aesthetically valuable (Jackson, 1970). The METLAND study accepts the idea that contemporary society values trees highly. The design of a submodel to measure the changes in the value of trees in the metropolitan landscape is therefore appropriate.

The substantiation of the tree-cover variable has been derived from three different types of sources: scientific findings, literature indicating man's desire for trees in the landscape, and prevalent planning norms. Numerous scientific investigations during the past decade (Bates, 1962; Embleton, 1963; Federer, 1969; Cooperative Extension Service of Massachusetts, 1971; Olgyay, 1963; Heideman, 1971; Reinhart, 1971) support the value of trees in terms of air-pollution reduction, noise reduction, improvement of water quality, oxygen generation, humidity control, provision of microclimatic amelioration, provision of privacy, and prevention of erosion and flooding. Each study concludes or implies that the more trees in the metropolitan landscape the better.

Human-preference literature similarly supports the concept that more trees result in a better environment. A survey of attitudes of people toward the METLAND landscape resource values was conducted (Fabos, 1973). The 226 respondents from the townships of Burlington, Wilmington, and Tewksbury within the Boston metropolitan region rated the value of tree cover as the highest of all METLAND variables. Peterson (1967), in his study of people's preference for the visual appearance of residential neighborhoods, found that trees were perceived to significantly increase the quality of the neighborhoods.

A third type of substantiation has been drawn from planning norms. A number of planning and design studies propose the planting of trees or the protection of tree-covered areas for the purposes of recreation, screening of visual misfits, and so on. The noted "Plan for the Valleys" in Maryland (McHarg, 1969) specified that "Valley walls in forest cover . . . should be developed in such a manner as to perpetuate their present wooded aspect." The visual and cultural appendix of Zube et al. to the North Atlantic Regional Water Resources Study (1970) went a step further and proposed comprehensive reforestation programs for every major metropolitan area in the Northeast. Jacobs and Way (1969) studied the tree-

Figure 11
Land-use relationships: (A) high compatibility and high agreement among respondents; (B) low compatibility and low agreement among respondents; (C) no compatibility and high agreement among respondents.

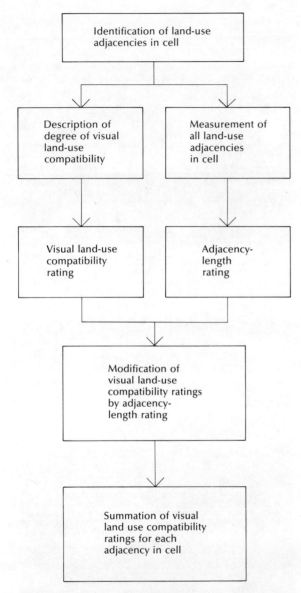

Figure 12
Visual land-use compatibility submodel.

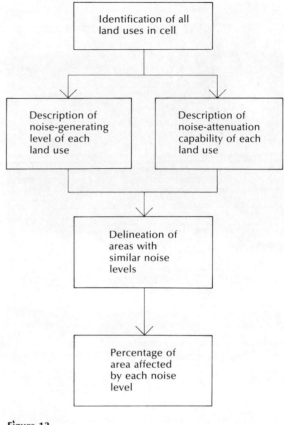

Figure 13
Noise submodel.

covered landscape from the aspect of absorptivity. They concluded that forested landscapes can absorb a greater amount of de-

velopment without visual change when compared with open landscapes.

From the point of view of the tree-cover variable, the METLAND study concluded that the amount of tree cover within the metropolitan landscape is directly proportional to the value of that landscape. If this argument is true, the tree-cover value can then be measured against three parameters: height (suggesting that taller, older trees are more beneficial); density (suggesting that more trees per acre is more beneficial); and finally, percentage of total area covered (suggesting that the more area covered by trees, the greater the benefit derived from that area). The tree-cover submodel in Figure 14 shows the simplified step-by-step procedure that has been applied to the three towns of Burlington, Wilmington, and

Tewksbury within the Boston metropolitan region.

Application of the Visual–Cultural Submodels

To date, three of the four visual–cultural variables have been applied to the three towns of Burlington, Wilmington, and Tewksbury. These communities are located between Route 128 and Route 495 in the Boston metropolitan area. These highways have generated considerable metropolitan growth during the past two decades. For this reason, the assessment models have been applied at two points in time: 1952 (the beginning of the impact of Route 128) and 1971. It was hypothesized that metropolitanization has a negative effect on visual–cultural landscape resources. Because of time constraints, a statistical procedure based on a 2 percent sample of the total numbers of cells was conducted in the initial application of the submodels. (The noise variable has not yet been applied since the detailed submodel has not been completed at this time.)

The initial results specify that both negative and positive value changes accrued from urbanization (see Table 1). These results indicate that the reallocation of land use through metropolitan expansion is negatively correlated with all variables with the exception of visual contrast in Burlington (where the most growth occurred), visual diversity in Wilmington, and both visual diversity and visual contrast in Tewksbury. However, it should also be noted that each time the value derived from visual diversity or contrast increased, the value of visual compatibility decreased. This relationship would tend to vitiate the few positive changes observed.

The estimated resource-value losses when

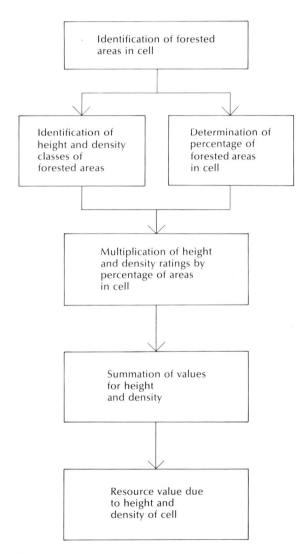

Figure 14
Tree-cover submodel.

Table 1
Summary Result of the Initial Application of Visual–Cultural Submodels

	Burlington		Wilmington		Tewksbury	
	Mean Resource Value Change	*Significance (H_0 hypothesis can be rejected at $\alpha = .05$)*	*Mean Resource Value Change*	*Significance (H_0 hypothesis can be rejected at $\alpha = .05$)*	*Mean Resource Value Change*	*Significance (H_0 hypothesis can be rejected at $\alpha = .05$)*
Land-use diversity (visual)	−2.42	$\alpha > .05$	+2.00	$\alpha > .05$	+9.55	$\alpha < .05$
Land-use contrast (visual)	+2.50	$\alpha > .05$	−1.70	$\alpha > .05$	+5.33	$\alpha < .05$
Intercompatibility (visual)	−6.46	$\alpha < .05$	−5.13	$\alpha < .05$	−12.60	$\alpha < .05$
Tree cover	−16.45	$\alpha < .05$	−11.49	$\alpha < .05$	−5.38	$\alpha > .05$

closely analyzed are more significant than they appear in Table 1. For instance, a 10-point loss does not seem to be too large on a scale of 0 to 100. However, the initial resource values at any place are seldom +100 in value. If the initial value is 50 and a 10-point loss occurs, the percentage loss of a given resource is 20 percent or twice as great within that township. Furthermore, when the geographic distribution of resource value changes is analyzed, the visual–cultural loss is often very dramatic. Combined losses in Burlington at highway intersections and related urban areas decreased by as much as 20 points.

Perceived benefits of the model as seen by the METLAND team The quantitative demonstration of metropolitan landscape-resource-value loss is analogous to water-pollution measurement and techniques. A 20-point loss in landscape resource value is similar to the change of a river from a natural B quality water to a C or D quality water. The value of these types of measurements is negligible in standard cost–benefit analysis since they are based on an

arbitrary scale. What may be useful, however, is the fact that this information can be applied to the design of planning models capable of predicting potential losses on some sort of consistent, objective scale. (Water resource planners already have this capability.) Landscape-planning models are needed to demonstrate the probable impact of alternative land-use allocation and management practices. If predictive models can be designed, it would be possible to select those alternatives which minimize landscape resource value loss resulting from metropolitanization. We are working toward this objective of building landscape-planning models to perform this task.

Limitations and deficiencies of the study To date, the availability of basic research has been limited. Environmental psychology (which ideally would provide basic research support for the visual variables) is a relatively new specialization of psychology and, therefore, little documentation has been produced. Often, we made inferences from research works that may have been only partially relevant. It is also possible that we have distorted the research results of those few studies which have been produced.

The analysis of visual quality proceeded on the proposition that there is a component of human preference which results from generic factors, common to every human being. It also acknowledged that a major factor in what people prefer results from learning and experience, which is different for each individual. The creation of a dichotomy between the generic and individual was made to try to isolate some aspect of preference patterns that would be amenable to objective measurement. Generic responses would be much easier to quantify and generalize about. The problem is that this remains a hypothesis. The development of the measurement systems for complexity in this study have not dealt with the validity of the original hypothesis; the research team has merely extended it to test its utility as a tool. The relative significance of individual preferences and, most important, the dynamics between individual and generic preference patterns within a person remain to be investigated. Furthermore, the variables selected to measure visual–cultural values, in some instances, may duplicate one another, or they may be found to be inappropriate as visual–cultural value indicators.

The appropriateness of the variables should be studied from the point of view of "scale." The assessment technique used here deals with intermediate land scale, yet some of the variables we included may actually be more suited to a micro or site scale level. The data obtained from aerial photography may not accurately represent the value of a resource as it is perceived from the ground. Neither the visual impact of landform nor the importance of the mutability of landscape resources has been considered. Values attributed to an immutable landscape resource, such as a coastline, are more significant than those derived from a mutable resource, such as the edge formed by a forest and an open field. (The value of the former may prevail for centuries; the value of the latter may disappear within a decade or two through natural processes, unless it is maintained by man.) Similarly, a mutable value of a resource can be permanently eliminated by man, whereas the misuse of an immutable visual landscape may eventually be reclaimed. Visual–cultural assessment techniques should deal with this value modifier.

These are only some of our self-criticisms. It is not our objective to provide our readers with an exhaustive list. Rather, we propose to solicit constructive criticisms and suggestions for the improvement of future phases of the study.

Selected Bibliography

Abbey, E. (1970) *Desert Solitaire*. New York: Simon and Schuster.

Acking, C.-A., and G. J. Sorte (1973) "How Do We Verbalize What We See?" *Landscape Architecture 64:*470–475.

Albert, J. C. (1969) "A Study of Visual Recognition in the New England Rural Landscape." Master's thesis. Amherst, Mass.: University of Massachusetts.

Alexander, C. (1964) *Notes on the Synthesis of Form.* Cambridge, Mass.: Harvard University Press.

Allen, D. L. (1954) *Our Wildlife Legacy*. New York: Funk & Wagnalls Company.

Allison, R. C., and R. S. Leighton (1971) "Evaluating Forest Campground Sites." University of New Hampshire. Cooperative Extension Service Extension Folder 64. Durham, N.H.: University of New Hampshire.

Amidon, E. L., and G. H. Elsner (1968) "Delineating Landscape View Areas — A Computer Approach." U.S. Department of Agriculture Forest Service Research Note PSW-180.

Appleyard, D. (1963) "View from the Road: A Highway Redesigned for the Drama of Driving." *Architectural Forum 119* (Oct.): 75–77.

————, K. H. Craik, M. Klapp, and A. Kreimer (1973) *The Berkeley Environmental Simulation Laboratory: Its Use in Environmental Impact Assessment.* Berkeley, Calif.: Institute of Urban and Regional Development, University of California.

————, K. Lynch, and J. R. Meyer (1964) *The View from the Road.* Cambridge, Mass.: MIT Press.

Ardrey, R. (1970) *The Social Contract*. New York: Atheneum Publishers.

Arensberg, C. M. (1955) "American Communities."

American Anthropologist 57(Dec.): 1143–1162.

Babeu, R. G., A. D. Rhodes, W. P. MacConnel, and J. H. Foster (1965) "Forest Owner Characteristics and Attitudes in Berkshire County, Massachusetts." Amherst, Mass.: Massachusetts Agricultural Experiment Station.

Barron, F. (1952) "Personality, Style, and Perceptual Choice." *Journal of Personality 20:*385–401.

—— (1953) "Complexity–Simplicity as a Personality Dimension." *Journal of Abnormal and Social Psychology 48:*163–172.

——, and G. S. Welsh (1952) "Artistic Perception as a Factor in Personality Style: Its Measurement by a Figure-Preference Test." *Journal of Psychology 33:*199–203.

Bartels, J., et al. (1972) "A Visual Classification and Landscape Evaluation System for the Southeast New England Region." Master's terminal project. Amherst, Mass.: University of Massachusetts.

Barton, T. A., et al. (1969) "An Aesthetic Evaluation, Souris–Red Rainy River Basins." Ames, Iowa: Iowa State University.

Barzini, L. (1965) *The Italians.* New York: Bantam Books, Inc.

Bates, M. (1962) "Purpose of the Suburban Forest: Man and Nature," pp. 22–34 in Waggoner and Ovington (eds.), *Proceedings of the Lockwood Conference on the Suburban Forest and Ecology.* Storrs, Conn.: Connecticut Agricultural Experiment Station.

Beaumont, A. B. (1956) *Classification of Soils in Massachusetts.* Washington, D.C.: Government Printing Office.

Beck, R. (1967) "Spatial Meaning and the Properties of the Environment," pp. 18–29 in D. Lowenthal (ed.), *Environmental Perception and Behavior.* Chicago: University of Chicago, Department of Geography, Research Paper 109.

Belden, W. M., and H. G. Williams (1969) *Phase III: Appalachia Recreation and Cultural Resources Study.* Albany, N.Y.: State of New York, Office of Planning Coordination.

Berlyne, D. E. (1960) *Conflict, Arousal and Curiosity.* New York: McGraw-Hill Book Company.

—— (1963) "Complexity and Incongruity Variables as Determinants of Exploratory Choice and Evaluative Ratings." *Canadian Journal of Psychology 22*(3):274–289.

—— (1971) *Aesthetics and Psychobiology.* New York: Appleton-Century-Crofts.

——, and K. B. Madsen (eds.) (1973) *Pleasure, Reward, Preference.* New York: Academic Press, Inc.

Blake, P. (1964) *God's Own Junkyard.* New York: Holt, Rinehart and Winston, Inc.

Block, J. (1961) *The Q-Sort Method in Personality Assessment and Psychiatric Research.* Springfield, Ill.: Charles C Thomas, Publisher.

Blodgett, H. W., and B. Sculley (eds.) (1965) Walt Whitman, *Leaves of Grass.* New York: New York University Press.

Bond, R. S., and G. J. Oulette (1968) "Characteristics of Campers in Massachusetts." Amherst, Mass.: Massachusetts Agricultural Experiment Station.

——, and J. C. Whittaker (1971) "Hunter–Fisherman Characteristics: Factors in Wildlife Management and Policy Decisions." Paper given in Forest Recreation Symposium at State University of New York, College of Forestry, Syracuse, N.Y., Oct. 12–14. Upper Darby, Pa.: Northeastern Forest Experiment Station, Forest Service, U.S. Department of Agriculture.

Bosselman, F., and D. Callies (1971) *The Quiet Revolution in Land Use Control.* Prepared for the Council on Environmental Quality. Washington, D.C.: Government Printing Office.

Boyce, D. E., N. D. Day, and C. McDonald (1970) *Metropolitan Plan Making: An Analysis of Experience with the Preparation and Evaluation of Alternative Land Use and Transportation Plans.* Philadelphia: Regional Science Research Institute.

Boyle, T. J. (1971) *Inventory of Vermont Scenery.* Burlington, Vt.: Office of T. J. Boyle.

Brown, M. (1968) "Landscape Survey and Analysis for Urban Development." *Planning Outlook 4* Spring: 44–53.

Brubaker, S. (1972) *To Live on Earth.* Baltimore: The Johns Hopkins Press.

Brunswik, E. (1943) "Organic Achievement and Environmental Probability." *Psychological Review 50:*255–272.

—— (1956) *Perception and the Representative Design of Psychological Experiments,* 2nd ed. Berkeley, Calif.: University of California Press.

Burch, W. R., Jr. (1965) "The Playworld of Camping: Research into the Social Meaning of Outdoor Recreation." *American Journal of Sociology 70:*604–612.

Burke, H. D., G. H. Lewis, and H. R. Orr (1968) "A

Method for Classifying Scenery from a Roadway." U.S. Forest Service, Park Practice Development, Guideline 3/68.

Burns, W. T., and D. D. Rundell (1969) "A Test of Visual Preferences in a Rural New England Landscape." Amherst, Mass.: University of Massachusetts terminal project report.

Caldwell, L. K. (1971) *Environment: A Challenge to Modern Society.* Garden City, N.Y.: Doubleday & Company, Inc.

Calhoun, J. B. (1971) "Space and Strategy of Life," pp. 329–387 in A. H. Esser (ed.), *Behavior and Environment.* New York: Plenum Publishing Corporation.

Calvin, J. S., J. A. Dearinger, and M. E. Curten (1972) "An Attempt at Assessing Preferences for Natural Landscapes." *Environment and Behavior* 4:447–470.

Carritt, E. F. (1932) *What Is Beauty? A First Introduction to the Subject and to Modern Theories.* New York: Oxford University Press, Inc.

Caswell, S. (1973) "Review and Explanation of Progress Made to Date with Respect to the METLAND Noise Variable." Amherst, Mass.: University of Massachusetts, Department of Landscape Architecture. Unpublished report.

Central Massachusetts Regional Planning District (1967) "The Nature of Open Space," pp. 7–8 in Chap. II of *Open Space and Recreation.* Worcester, Mass.

Chapin, S. (1965) *Urban Land Use Planning.* Urbana, Ill.: University of Illinois Press.

Chapman, J. D. (1969) *Resources and Man.* San Francisco: National Academy of Sciences–National Research Council and W. H. Freeman and Company, Publishers.

Child, I. L., and S. Iwao (1968) "Personality and Aesthetic Sensitivity: Extension of Findings to a Younger Age and to Different Cultures." *Journal of Personality and Social Psychology* 8:308–312.

Chubb, M., et al. (1967) "Outdoor Recreation Planning in Michigan by a Systems Analysis Approach, Part III: The Practical Application of Program RECSYS and SYMAP." Technical Report 12. Lansing, Mich.: Recreation Research and Planning, Michigan Department of Conservation.

Cicchetti, C. J., and A. M. Freeman (1971) "Consumer Surplus and Option Value in the Estimation of Benefits." Washington, D.C.: Resources for the Future, Inc. (mimeographed).

Clark, K. (1961) *Landscape into Art.* Boston: The Beacon Press, Inc.

——— (1969) *Civilization.* New York: Harper & Row, Inc.

Clark, S. B. K. (1968) "Landscape Survey and Analysis on a National Basis." *Planning Outlook* 4(Spring): 15–19.

Clawson, M. (1971) *Suburban Land Conversion in the United States: An Economic and Governmental Process.* Published for Resources for the Future, Inc. Baltimore: The Johns Hopkins Press.

Clifford, C. W. (1973) "Natural Quality Change and Its Relationship to Visual Landscape Quality Along the Main Stem Rivers of the Southeastern New England Region." Master's thesis. Amherst, Mass.: University of Massachusetts.

Clynes, M. (1969) "Toward a Theory of Man: Precision of Essentic Form in Living Communications," Chap. 10 in N. Leibovic and J. C. Eccles (eds.), *Information Processing in the Nervous System.* New York: Springer-Verlag New York, Inc.

——— (1970) "Emotion Communication in the Living Moment." Reprint of a paper presented at the Symposium, Biocybernetics of the Dynamic Communication of Emotions and Qualities. Chicago: American Association for the Advancement of Science.

Cole, L. C. (1970) "Are We Running Out of Oxygen?" *Catalyst for Environmental Quality 1* (1):2–4.

Cole, T. (1835) "Essay on American Scenery." *American Monthly Magazine 1:*1–35.

Committee on Water Quality Criteria (1968) *The Report.* Washington, D.C.: Government Printing Office.

Commonwealth of Massachusetts (1966) *An Act Relating to the Protection of Flood Plains.* Chap. 131, Sec. 40, G.L., Dec. 20. Boston.

Commonwealth of Massachusetts (1967) *Report of the Department of Natural Resources Relative to the Inland Wetlands and Flood Plains of the Commonwealth with Respect to Their Location, Ownership, and Value for Purposes of Recreation, Wildlife, and Conservation of Natural Resources and the Other Matters Related Thereto.* Senate Report 1273, June 6. Boston.

Commonwealth of Massachusetts (1968) *An Act Providing for the Protection of the Inland Wetlands of the Commonwealth.* Chap. 131, Sec. 40A, G.L., June 26. Boston.

Commonwealth of Massachusetts (1971) *An Act Permanently Protecting the Coastal Marshes and Inland Wetlands of the Commonwealth*. Senate Bill 1439, May. Boston.

Conservation Foundation, The (1972) *National Parks for the Future*. Washington, D.C.: The Foundation.

Coomber, N. H., and A. K. Biswas (1973) *Evaluation of Environmental Intangibles*. Bronxville, N.Y.: Genera Press.

Cooper, C. C. (1965) *Some Social Implications of House and Site Plan Design at Easter Hill Village: A Case Study*. Berkeley, Calif.: Institute of Urban and Regional Development, Center for Planning and Development Research, University of California.

Cooperative Extension Service (1971) "Trees and Forests in an Urbanizing Environment." Amherst, Mass.: Experiment Station Bulletin.

Coughlin, R. E., and K. A. Goldstein (1970) "The Extent of Agreement Among Observers on Environmental Attractiveness." Philadelphia: Regional Science Research Institute Discussion Paper 37.

Council on Environmental Quality (1970) *Environmental Quality*. Washington, D.C.: Government Printing Office.

Cox, P. T., A. L. Haught, and E. H. Zube (1972) "Visual Quality Constraints in Regional Land Use Changes." *Growth and Change 3* (2):9–15.

Craik, K. H. (1968) "The Comprehension of the Everyday Physical Environment." *Journal of the American Institute of Planners 34*:29–37.

——— (1969) "Human Responsiveness to Landscape: An Environmental Psychological Perspective," pp. 168–193 in K. Coates and K. Moffett (eds.), *Response to Environment*. Student publication of the School of Design, vol. 18. Raleigh, N.C.: North Carolina State University.

——— (1970a) "Environmental Psychology," pp. 1–22 in K. H. Craik et al. (eds.), *New Directions in Psychology*, Vol. 4. New York: Holt, Rinehart and Winston, Inc.

——— (1970b) "A System of Landscape Dimensions: Appraisal of Its Objectivity and Illustration of Its Scientific Application." Report to Resources for the Future, Inc. Berkeley, Calif.: Institute of Personality Assessment and Research, University of California.

——— (1971) "The Assessment of Places," pp. 40–62 in P. McReynolds (ed.), *Advances in Psychological Assessment*, Vol. 2. Palo Alto, Calif.: Science and Behavior.

——— (1972a) "Appraising the Objectivity of Landscape Dimensions," pp. 292–346 in J. V. Krutilla (ed.), *Natural Environments: Studies in Theoretical and Applied Analysis*. Baltimore: The Johns Hopkins Press.

——— (1972b) "Psychological Factors in Landscape Appraisal." *Environment and Behavior 4*:255–266.

——— (1973) "Environmental Psychology," pp. 402–422 in P. H. Mussen and M. R. Rosenzweig (eds.), *Annual Review of Psychology*, Vol. 24. Palo Alto, Calif.: Annual Reviews, Inc.

Craik, K. J. W. (1943) *The Nature of Explanation*. New York: Cambridge University Press (paperback edition, 1967).

Crutchfield, R. S., D. G. Woodworth, and R. E. Albrecht (1958) "Perceptual Performance and the Effective Person." Technical Report WADC-TN-58-60, ASTIA Document AD 151 039. Lackland Air Force Base, Tex.: Personnel Laboratory, Wright Development Center.

Cullen, G. (1961) *Townscape*. New York: Van Nostrand Reinhold Company.

Darling, F. F., and N. Eichhorn (1967) *Man and Nature in the National Parks*. Washington, D.C.: The Conservation Foundation.

———, and J. P. Milton (eds.) (1966) *Future Environments of North America*. Garden City, N.Y.: Doubleday & Company, Inc.

Dasmann, R. F. (1964) *African Game Ranching*. New York: Macmillan Publishing Co., Inc.

——— (1968) *A Different Kind of Country*. New York: Macmillan Publishing Co., Inc.

Day, H. (1967) "Evaluations of Subjective Complexity, Pleasingness and Interestingness for a Series of Random Polygons Varying in Complexity." *Perception and Psychophysics 2*:281–286.

Dearinger, J. A. (1968) "Esthetic and Recreation Potential of Small Naturalistic Streams Near Urban Areas." Research Report 13. Lexington, Ky.: University of Kentucky, Water Resources Institute.

Deevey, E. S. (1969) "In Defense of Mud." *Bulletin of the Ecological Society of America 51*(1):5–8.

de Jonge, D. (1967–1968) "Applied Hodology." *Landscape 17*(2):10–11.

Douglas, W. O. (1960) *My Wilderness: The Pacific West*. Garden City, N.Y.: Doubleday & Company, Inc.

——— (1961) "Wilderness and Human Rights," pp.

5–15 in D. Brower (ed.), *Wilderness: America's Living Heritage*. San Francisco: Sierra Club.

——— (1965) *A Wilderness Bill of Rights*. Boston: Little, Brown and Company.

Doxiadis, C. A. (1966) *Emergence and Growth of an Urban Region: The Developing Urban Detroit Area*. Detroit: Detroit Edison Company.

Driver, B. L. (1972) "Potential Contributions of Psychology to Recreation Resource Management," pp. 233–244 in J. F. Wohlwill and D. H. Carson (eds.), *Behavioral Science and the Problems of Our Environment*. Washington, D.C.: American Psychological Association.

Dubos, R. (1968) *So Human an Animal*. New York: Charles Scribner's Sons.

Eckbo, Dean, Austin and Williams, Inc. (1970) "State of Hawaii Land Use Districts and Regulations Review." Honolulu: Hawaii Land Use Commission, Department of Planning and Economic Development.

Economic Research Service (1968) "Open Space: Its Use and Preservation." U.S. Department of Agriculture Miscellaneous Publication 1121. Washington, D.C.: Government Printing Office.

Economist, The (1973) "The Phony Oil Crisis" *The Economist 248*(July 7):19–23.

Edward, A. L. (1957) *Techniques of Attitude Scale Construction*. New York: Appleton-Century-Crofts.

Edwards and Kelcey, Inc. (1972) *Highway Planning Studies, Vol. 4: General Findings and Applications*. Minneapolis.

Eibl-Eibesfeldt, I. (1971) "Transcultural Patterns of Ritualized Contact Behavior," pp. 236–246 in A. H. Esser (ed.), *Behavior and Environment*. New York: Plenum Publishing Corporation.

Eliot, C. W. (1902) *Charles Eliot, Landscape Architect*. Boston: Houghton Mifflin Company.

Eliovson, S. (1971) *Gardening the Japanese Way*. London: George G. Harrap & Company Limited.

Eliot, C. and S. Baxter (1893) *Boston Metropolitan Park Report*. House Document 150. Boston: Metropolitan Park Commissioners.

Elsner, G. H. (1971) "Computing Visible Areas from Proposed Recreation Developments." U.S. Department of Agriculture, Forest Service Research Note PSW-246.

Elton, C. (1958) *The Ecology of Invasions by Animals and Plants*. London: Methuen & Company Ltd.

Embleton, T. F. W. (1963) "Sound Propagation in Homogeneous Deciduous and Evergreen Woods." *Journal of the Acoustical Society of America 35*(July):1119–1125.

Errington, P. L. (1957) *Of Men and Marshes*. Ames, Iowa: Iowa State University Press.

Fabos, J. G. (1969) *The Great Meadows of the Connecticut River*. Amherst, Mass.: Department of Landscape Architecture and Regional Planning, University of Massachusetts.

——— (1971) "An Analysis of Environmental Quality Ranking Systems," pp. 40–55 in *Recreation Symposium Proceedings*. Syracuse, N.Y.: U.S. Department of Agriculture.

——— (1973) "Model for Landscape Resource Assessment: Part I of the Metropolitan Landscape Planning Model (METLAND)," College of Food and Natural Resources Research Bulletin 602. Amherst, Mass.: University of Massachusetts.

———, G. T. Milde, and V. M. Weinmeyer (1968) *Frederick Law Olmsted, Sr. Founder of Landscape Architecture in America*. Amherst, Mass.: University of Massachusetts Press.

Fairbrother, N. (1970) *New Lives, New Landscapes*. New York: Alfred A. Knopf, Inc.

Federer, C. A. (1969) "Reduction of Summer City Temperatures by Trees." Upper Darby, Pa: Northeastern Forest Experiment Station, Forest Service, U. S. Department of Agriculture.

Fein, A. (1967) *Landscape into Cityscape*. Ithaca, N.Y.: Cornell University Press.

Fennemen, N. M. (1938) *Physiography of Eastern United States*. New York: McGraw-Hill Book Company.

Fines, K. D. (1968) *Landscape Evaluation: A Research Project in East Sussex*. Elmsford, N.Y.: Pergamon Press, Inc.

Flannery, K. V. (1965) "The Ecology of Early Food Production in Mesopotamia." *Science 147*:1247–1256.

Flexner, J. (1962) *That Wilder Image*. Boston: Little, Brown and Company.

Gibson, J. J. (1946) "Perception of Distance and Space in the Open Air." Reprinted, pp. 415–431 in D. C. Beardslee and M. Wertheimer (eds.), *Readings in Perception* (1958). New York: Van Nostrand Reinhold Company.

——— (1950) "Perception of Visual Surfaces." *American Journal of Psychology 63*:367–384.

——— (1959) "Perception as a function of Stimulation," in S. Koch (ed.), *Psychology: A Study of a*

Science, Vol. 1. New York: McGraw-Hill Book Company.

———— (1960) "The Concept of the Stimulus in Psychology." *American Psychologist* 15:694–703.

———— (1961) "Ecological Optics." *Vision Research* 1:253–262.

Gilpin, W. (1792) *Three Essays: On Picturesque Beauty; On Picturesque Travel; and On Landscape Painting*. London: R. Blamire.

Glacken, C. H. (1967) *Traces on the Rhodian Shore: Nature and Culture in Western Thought from Ancient Times to the End of the Eighteenth Century*. Berkeley, Calif.: University of California Press.

Goldfinger, E. (1941) "The Sensation of Space." *Architecture Review* 90:148–151.

Golet, F. C. (1972) "Classification and Evaluation of Freshwater Wetlands as Wildlife Habitat in the Glaciated Northeast." Ph.D. dissertation. Amherst, Mass.: University of Massachusetts; and pp. 257–279 in Vol. 30 of the Annual Northeast Fish and Wildlife Conference, Mt. Snow, Vt. (1973).

Gombrich, E. H. (1966) "The Renaissance Theory of Art and the Rise of Landscape," pp. 107–121 in *Norm and Form: Studies in the Art of the Renaissance*. London: The Phaidon Press Ltd.

Gottman, J. (1961) *Megalopolis, the Urbanized Northeastern Seaboard of the United States*. Cambridge, Mass.: MIT Press.

Gough, H. G., and A. B. Heilbrun, Jr. (1965) *The Adjective Check List Manual*. Palo Alto, Calif.: Consulting Psychologists Press.

Graham, A. (1973) *The Gardeners of Eden*. London: George Allen & Unwin Ltd.

Gratzer, M. A., and R. D. McDowell (1971) "Adaptation of an Eye Movement Recorder to Esthetic Environment Mensuration." Research Report 36. Storrs, Conn.: Agricultural Experiment Station, College of Agriculture and Natural Resources, University of Connecticut.

Greenbie, B. B. (1971) "Sentics and Biocybernetics in the Search for an Optimum Human Habitat." Symposium on Sentics, Brain Function, and the Sources of Human Values. Paper presented at the Annual Meeting of the American Association for the Advancement of Science, Philadelphia.

———— (1972) "Essentic Form: Bridging the Gap Between Fact and Feeling." Unpublished manuscript.

————, R. W. Tuthill, and M. A. Brown (1973) "Contrasting Cognitive Maps of City Neighborhoods by Diverse Segments of the Population." Manuscript submitted for publication.

Greene, C. H. (1972) "The Aesthetic-Cultural Submodels of the Metropolitan Landscape Planning Model (METLAND)." Unpublished Master's thesis. Amherst, Mass.: University of Massachusetts.

Griswold, A. W. (1948) *Farming and Democracy*. New York: Harcourt Brace Jovanovich, Inc.

Gupta, T. R. (1972) "A Multivariate Model for Public Management of Freshwater Wetlands." Ph.D. dissertation, Amherst, Mass.: University of Massachusetts.

———— (1973) "Economic Criteria for Decisions on Preservation and Alteration of Natural Resources with Special Reference to Freshwater Wetlands in Massachusetts." Ph.D. dissertation. Amherst, Mass.: University of Massachusetts.

————, and J. H. Foster (1973) "Valuation of Visual-Cultural Benefits from Freshwater Wetlands in Massachusetts." *Journal of the Northeastern Agricultural Economics Council* 2(1):262–273.

Hackett, B. (1971) *Landscape Planning*. Newcastle-Upon-Tyne, England: Oriel Press.

Hall, E. T. (1966) *The Hidden Dimension*. Garden City, N.Y.: Doubleday & Company, Inc.

Halprin, L. (1965) "Motation." *Progressive Architecture* 46:126–133.

Halverson, C. C. (1970) "Scenic Quality in the Landscape: A Testing Format of Human Perceptual Values." Master's thesis. Amherst, Mass.: University of Massachusetts.

Handley, R. B., J. R. Jordan, and W. Patterson (1969) "An Environmental Quality Rating System," Bureau of Outdoor Recreation, Northeast Regional Staff.

Hart, W. J., and W. W. Graham (1967) "How to Rate and Rank Landscape." *Landscape Architecture* 57(Jan.):120–122.

Haskell, E. (1971) *Managing the Environment: Nine States Look for New Answers*. Washington, D.C.: Woodrow Wilson International Center for Scholars, Smithsonian Institution.

Hays, S. P. (1959) *Conservation and the Gospel of Efficiency*. Cambridge, Mass.: Harvard University Press.

Hebblethwaite, R. (1970) "Landscape Assessment: Qualitative Zones of Visual Influence with

Quantitative Assessment." National Countryside Classification Structure Seminar Proceedings (England, Dec.).

Heeley, R. W. (1973) "Hydrogeology of Wetlands in Massachusetts." Master's thesis. Amherst, Mass.: University of Massachusetts.

Heideman, M. L. (1971) "Human Benefits Attributable to Forests." Report to Northeast Experiment Station, Upper Darby, Pa.

Hendee, J. C., and R. Harris (1970) "Foresters' Perception of Wilderness — User Attitudes and Preferences." *Journal of Forestry* 68(Dec.): 759–762.

————, W. R. Catton, Jr., L. D. Marlow, and C. F. Brockman (1968) "Wilderness Users in the Pacific Northwest — Their Characteristics, Values, and Management Preferences." U.S. Forest Service Research Paper PNW-61. Portland, Ore.: Pacific Northwest Forest and Range Experiment Station.

Hendrix, W. (1973) "The Visual Land Use Compatibility Component of the Model for Landscape Resource Assessment." Unpublished Master's thesis. Amherst, Mass.: University of Massachusetts.

Hepburn, R. W. (1968) "Aesthetic Appreciation of Nature," in H. Osborne (ed.), *Aesthetics in the Modern World.* London: Thames and Hudson.

Heyman, M. (1964) "Space and Behavior: A Selected Bibliography." *Landscape* 13:4–10.

Hilgard, E. R. (1950) "The Role of Learning in Perception," pp. 95–120 in R. R. Blake and G. V. Ramsey (eds.), *Perception: An Approach to Personality.* New York: The Ronald Press Company.

Hills, G. A. (1966) "Ranking the Recreational Potential of Land Units by Gradient Analysis: A Physiographic Classification of Land for Recreational Use." *Proceedings, National Meeting on Land Capability Classification for Outdoor Recreation.* Ottawa: Feb. 23–24.

————, D. V. Love, and D. S. Lacate (1970) "Developing a Better Environment; Ecological Land Use Planning in Ontario — A Study of Methodology in Development of Regional Plans." Toronto: Ontario Economic Council.

Hofstadter, R. (1955) *The Age of Reform.* New York: Alfred A. Knopf, Inc.

———— (1965) *The Paranoid Style in American Politics.* New York: Alfred A. Knopf, Inc.

Holcomb, D. B. (1973) "Scenery Management Guides — Six Rivers National Forest." U.S. Department of Agriculture — Forest Service, California Region, unpublished booklet.

Hole, W. V., and A. Miller (1966) "Children's Play on Housing Estates." *Architects' Journal* 143:1529–1533, 1535–1536.

Hornbeck, P., et al. (1968) *Highway Aesthetics: Functional Criteria for Planning and Design.* Cambridge, Mass.: Harvard University, Department of Landscape Architecture.

———— (1969) Comprehensive Highway Planning: A Study of Qualitative Factors in Rural Highway Location Methodology. Washington, D.C.: U.S. Department of Transportation.

Hough, E. (1922) "The President's Forest." *Saturday Evening Post* 196.

Howard, R. B., F. C. Mlynarski, and C. G. Sauer, Jr. (1972) "A Comparative Analysis of Affective Responses to Real and Represented Environments," *Edra III, Proceedings of the Third Environmental Design Association Conference,* Los Angeles, Calif.

Hubbard, H. V., and T. Kimball (1917) *An Introduction to the Study of Landscape Design.* New York: Macmillan Publishing Co., Inc.

Hussey, C. (1927) *The Picturesque: Studies in a Point of View.* London: Putnam's & Company Ltd.

Huxley, A. (1954) *The Doors of Perception.* London: Chatto and Windus.

Ise, J. (1961) *Our National Park Policy, A Critical History.* Baltimore: The Johns Hopkins Press.

Ittelson, W. H. (1962) "Perception and Transactional Psychology," pp. 660–704 in S. Koch (ed.), *Psychology: A Study of a Science,* Vol. 4. New York: McGraw-Hill Book Company.

———— (1973) "Environment Perception and Contemporary Perceptual Theory," pp. 1–19 in W. H. Ittleson (ed.), *Environment and Cognition.* New York: Seminar Press.

Iverson, W. D. (1971) "Scenic Quality Inventory — A Proposed Rating System." U.S. Department of Agriculture — Forest Service, California Region, unpublished paper.

Jackson, J. B. (1970) "Several American Landscapes," in E. H. Zube (ed.), *Selected Writings of J. B. Jackson.* Amherst, Mass.: University of Massachusetts Press.

———— (1972) *American Space.* New York: W. W. Norton & Company, Inc.

Jacobs, P. (1973) *The Landscape Image: A Comparative Study of Existing Analysis Methods.* Indian and Northern Affairs, Parks Canada, and Université de Montreal.

———, and D. Way (1969) *Visual Analysis of Landscape Development.* Cambridge, Mass.: Department of Landscape Architecture, Graduate School of Design, Harvard University.

James, H. (1941) *Romance of the National Parks.* New York: Macmillan Publishing Co., Inc.

James, W. (1902) *Varieties of Religious Experience.* New York: Random House, Inc. (Modern Library reprint).

Johansson, W. I. (1967) "Geologic Features as Recreational Assets," in O. C. Farquar (ed.), *Economic Geology in Massachusetts.* Amherst, Mass.: University of Massachusetts Graduate School.

Johns, E. (1960) "Langstone Rock: An Experiment in the Art of Landscape Description." *Geography* 45:176–182.

Johnson, C. G. (1973) "Mineral King Visual Analysis." U.S. Department of Agriculture — Forest Service, California Region, unpublished report.

Johnson, H. A., and J. R. Russel (1967) "Economics of Natural Beauty." Paper presented at the 22nd annual meeting, Soil Conservation Society of America, Aug. 12–16, Des Moines, Iowa.

Johnson, R. U. (1968) "Aesthetics and Conservation." *Century* 1910:637–638; reprinted in R. Nash (ed.), *The American Environment: Readings in the History of Conservation.* Reading, Mass.: Addison-Wesley Publishing Company, Inc.

Jorgensen, N. (1971) *A Guide to New England's Landscape.* Barre, Mass.: Barre Publishers.

Josephy, A. M., Jr. (1973) "Agony of the Northern Plains." *Audubon* 75(July):68–101.

Kaplan, R. (1972) "The Dimensions of the Visual Environment: Methodological Considerations," in W. J. Mitchell (ed.), *Environmental Design: Research and Practice.* Proceedings of the Environmental Design Research Association Conference Three, Los Angeles, Calif.

——— (1973a) "Predictors of Environmental Preference: Designers and 'Clients'," pp. 265–274 in W. F. E. Preiser (ed.), *Environmental Design Research.* Stroudsburg, Pa.: Dowden, Hutchinson & Ross, Inc.

——— (1973b) "Some Psychological Benefits of Gardening." *Environment and Behavior* 5:145–162.

——— (1974) "A strategy for dimensional analyses." Appendix to Mautz, R. K., and R. Kaplan, "Residential modification as a mode of self-expression." Pp. 66–68 of Part 9 in D. H. Carson (ed.), *Man–Environment Interactions: Evaluations and Applications.* Environmental Design Research Association, Inc.

Kaplan, S. (1972) "The Challenge of Environmental Psychology: A Proposal for a New Functionalism." *American Psychologist* 27:140–143.

——— (1973a) "Cognitive Maps in Perception and Thought," pp. 63–78 in R. M. Downs and S. Stea (eds.), *Image and Environment: Cognitive Mapping and Spatial Behavior.* Chicago: Aldine–Atherton, Inc.

——— (1973b) "Cognitive Maps, Human Needs and the Designed Environment," pp. 275–283 in W. F. E. Preiser (ed.), *Environmental Design Research.* Stroudsburg, Pa.: Dowden, Hutchinson & Ross, Inc.

———, and J. S. Wendt (1972) "Preference and the Visual Environment: Complexity and Some Alternatives," in W. J. Mitchell (ed.), *Environmental Design: Research and Practice.* Proceedings of the Environmental Design Research Association Conference Three, Los Angeles, Calif.

———, R. Kaplan, and J. S. Wendt (1972) "Rated Preference and Complexity for Natural and Urban Visual Material." *Perception and Psychophysics* 12:354–356.

Kates, R. W. (1966–1967) "The Pursuit of Beauty in The Environment." *Landscape* 16(2):21–24.

——— (1967) "The Perception of Storm Hazard on the Shores of Megalopolis," pp. 60–74 in D. Lowenthal (ed.), Environmental Perception and Behavior, Research Paper 109. Chicago: University of Chicago, Department of Geography.

———, and J. F. Wohlwill (eds.) (1966) "Man's Response to the Physical Environment." *Journal of Social Issues* 22.

Kepes, G. (1951) *Language of Vision.* New York: Theobald.

Kiemstedt, H. (1967) *Zur Bewertung der Landschaft für die Erholung.* Stuttgart: Eugen Ulmer Verlag K. G.

——— (1968) "The Evaluation of the Natural Components of the Landscape for Leisure." Paper presented at the Congress of International Federation of Landscape Architects, June.

———— (1971) *Harzlandschaft und Freizeit*. Berlin: Institute für Landschaftsbau und Gartenbunst der Technischen Universität.

Kilgore, B. M. (1969) "Wilderness and the Self-Interest of Man," in W. Schwartz (ed.), *Voices for the Wilderness*. New York: Ballantine Books, Inc.

Klausner, S. Z. (1971) *On Man in His Environment*. San Francisco: Jossey-Bass, Inc., Publishers.

Klingender, F. (1971) *Animals in Art and Thought to the End of the Middle Ages*. Cambridge, Mass.: MIT Press.

Kluckhohn, C., and H. A. Murray (1950) "Personality Formation: The Determinants," pp. 35–50 in C. Kluckhohn and H. A. Murray (eds.), *Personality in Nature, Culture and Society*, New York: Alfred A. Knopf, Inc.

Kluckhohn, F. R., and F. L. Strodtbeck (1961) *Variations in Value Orientations*. New York: Harper & Row, Inc.

Knight, H. (1967) "The Use of 'Good' in Aesthetic Judgments," pp. 147–160 in W. Elton (ed.), *Aesthetics and Language*. Oxford: Blackwell Scientific Publications Ltd.

Knight, R. P. (1808) *An Analytical Inquiry into the Principles of Taste*, 4th ed. London: T. Payne.

Koestler, A. (1969) *The Act of Creation*. New York: Macmillan Publishing Co., Inc.

Kojima, M., and J. A. Wagar (1972) "Computer-Generated Drawings of Ground Form and Vegetation." *Journal of Forestry* May:282–285.

Kragh, G. (1968) "The Practice of Landscape Planning." *Planning Outlook* 4(Spring):74–78.

Krasnowiecki, J. Z. (1965) "Planned Unit Development: A Challenge to Established Theory and Practice of Land Use Control." *University of Pennsylvania Law Review* 114(1):47–97.

Krutilla, J. V. (1967) "Conservation Reconsidered." *American Economic Review* 57:777–786.

Kuhn, T. S. (1962) *The Structure of Scientific Revolutions*. Chicago: University of Chicago Press.

Kulik, J. A., W. R. Revelle, and C.-L. C. Kulik (1970) "Scale Construction by Hierarchical Cluster Analysis." University of Michigan, unpublished paper.

Kunit, E. R., and K. S. Calhoon (1973) "Smith River Highway Visual Analysis Study." Royston, Hanamoto, Beck, and Abey for U.S. Forest Service, Contract 39-4402.

La Barre, W. (1954) *The Human Animal*. Chicago: University of Chicago Press.

———— (1970) *'The Ghost Dance'* Garden City, N.Y.: Doubleday & Company, Inc.

Lacate, D. S. (1969) "Guidelines for Bio-physical Land Classification," in *Canada Land Inventory*. Ottawa: Department of Regional Economic Expansion.

Land Use Consultants (1971) "A Planning Classification of Scottish Landscape Resources." Battleby, Perth: Countryside Commission for Scotland.

Langer, S. K. (1967, 1972) *Mind: an Essay on Human Feeling*, Vols. I and II. Baltimore: The Johns Hopkins Press.

Lansing, J. B., and R. W. Marans (1969) "Evaluation of Neighborhood Quality." *Journal of American Institute of Planners* 35:195–199.

————, R. W. Marans, and R. B. Zehner (1970) *Planned Residential Environments*. Ann Arbor, Mich.: University of Michigan Institute of Social Research.

Larson, J. S., and C. H. W. Foster (1955) *Massachusetts Marshes . . . and Their Owners*. Boston: Wildlife Conservation, Inc.

Laurie, I. (1970) *Landscape Evaluation Research Project*. Manchester, England: University of Manchester.

Leckart, B. T., and P. Bakan (1965) "Complexity Judgements of Photographs and Looking Time." *Perceptual and Motor Skills* 21:16–18.

Le Corbusier (1954) *The Modulor*. Cambridge, Mass.: Harvard University Press.

———— (1958) *Modulor 2, 1955*. Cambridge, Mass.: Harvard University Press.

Lee, S. E. (1964) *A History of Asian Art*. New York: Harry N. Abrams, Inc.

Leopold, A. (1924) *A Plea for Wilderness Hunting Grounds*. Madison, Wis.: Leopold Papers.

———— (1925a) "Conserving the Covered Wagon." *Sunset* 54:21.

———— (1925b) "The Last Stand of the Wilderness." *American Forests and Forest Life* 31:599–604.

———— (1933) *Game Management*. New York: Charles Scribner's Sons.

———— (1945) "The Green Lagoons." *American Forests* 51:376–377,414.

———— (1949) *A Sand County Almanac*. New York: Oxford University Press, Inc.

Leopold, L. B. (1969a) "Quantitative Comparison of Some Aesthetic Factors Among Rivers." Geological Survey Circular 620, Washington, D.C.

—— (1969b) "Landscape Esthetics." *Natural History Magazine 78:*4,36–45.

——, and M. O. Marchand (1968) "On the Quantitative Inventory of the Riverscape." *Water Resources Research 4*(4):709–717.

Leuba, C. (1955) "Toward Some Integration of Learning Theories: The Concept of Optimal Stimulation." *Psychological Reports 1:*27–33.

Levin, D. R. (1967) "Scenic Corridors." Highway Research Record 166:14–21.

Lewis, P. F., D. Lowenthal, and Y. F. Tuan (1973) "Visual Blight in America." Association of American Geographers, Resource Paper 23.

Lewis, P. H. (1964a) "Quality Corridors in Wisconsin." *Landscape Architecture Quarterly 54*(2): 100–108.

—— (1964b) *The Outdoor Recreation Plan* (Wisconsin Development Series). Madison, Wis.: Wisconsin Department of Resource Development.

Lewis, P. H. Jr., and associates (1969) Upper Mississippi River Comprehensive Basin Study, Appendix B: Aesthetic and Cultural Values. Madison, Wis.

Lime, D. W., and G. H. Stankey (1971) "Carrying Capacity Maintaining Outdoor Recreation Quality." Paper given in the Forest Recreation Symposium of the State University of New York, College of Forestry, Syracuse, N.Y., Oct. 12–14. Upper Darby, Pa.: Northeastern Forest Experiment Station, Forest Service. U.S. Department of Agriculture.

Lindsay, C. M. (1969) "Option Demand and Consumer's Surplus." *Quarterly Journal of Economics 83:*344–346.

Lingoes, J. C. (1972) "A General Survey of the Guttman-Lingoes Nonmetric Program Series," pp. 52–68 in R. N. Shepard, A. K. Romney, and S. B. Nerlove (eds.), *Multidimensional Scaling,* Vol. 1. New York: Seminar Press.

Linton, D. (1968) "The Assessment of Scenery as a Natural Resource." *Scottish Geographical Magazine 84*(3):219–238.

Little, C. E. (1969) *Challenge of the Land.* Elmsford, N.Y.: Pergamon Press, Inc.

Litton, R. B. (1968) "Forest Landscape Description and Inventories; a Basis for Land Planning and Design." U.S. Department of Agriculture, Forest Service Research Paper PSW-49. Berkeley, Calif.: Pacific Southwest Forest and Range Experiment Station, U.S. Department of Agriculture, — Forest Service.

—— (1972) "Aesthetic Dimensions of the Landscape," pp. 262–291 in J. V. Krutilla (ed.), *Natural Environments: Studies in Theoretical and Applied Analysis.* Baltimore: The Johns Hopkins Press.

—— (1973) "Visual Vulnerability of Forest Landscapes." Proceedings of U.S. Forest Service Recreation Research Applications Workshop, June 19–21, Northern Michigan University, Marquette, Mich.

——, and R. H. Twiss (1967) "The Forest Landscape: Some Elements of Visual Analysis," pp. 212–214 in *Proceedings of the Society of American Foresters,* 1966. Washington, D.C.: Society of American Foresters.

Lowenthal, D. (1962) "Not Every Prospect Pleases: What Is Our Criterion for Beauty?" *Landscape 12:*19–23.

—— (1964) "Images of Nature in America." *Columbia University Forum 7:*34–40.

—— (1966) "Assumptions Behind the Public Attitudes," in H. Jarrett (ed.), Environmental Quality in a Growing Economy. Resources for the Future, Inc. Baltimore: The Johns Hopkins Press.

—— (1968) "The American Scene." *Geographical Review 58:*61–88.

——, and H. C. Prince (1964) "The English Landscape." *Geographical Review 54:*309–346.

——, and H. C. Prince (1965) "English Landscape Tastes." *Geographical Review 55:*186–222.

——, and M. Riel (1972) "The Nature of Perceived and Imagined Environments." *Environment and Behavior 4:*189–207.

——, et al. (1967) "An Analysis of Environmental Perception." Interim Report. Washington, D.C.: Resources for the Future, Inc.

Lucas, R. C. (1963) "Wilderness Perception and Use: The Example of the Boundary Waters Canoe Area." *Natural Resources Journal 3:*394–411.

—— (1970) "User Evaluation of Campgrounds on Two Michigan National Forests." U.S. Department of Agriculture, Forest Service Research Paper NC-44. North Central Forest Experiment Station.

—— (1971) "Hikers and Other Trail Users." Forest Recreation Symposium Proceedings. Upper Darby, Pa.: Northeastern Forest Experiment Station, Forest Service, U.S. Department of Agriculture.

Lynch, K. (1960) *The Image of the City.* Cambridge, Mass.: Harvard University Press and MIT Press.

——— (1971) "A Design Concept: The Openness of Open Spaces for Human Needs," in *Open Spaces for Human Needs,* prepared by Marcou, O'Leary, and Associates. Washington, D.C.: Open Space Institute.

———, and M. Rivkin (1959) "A Walk Around the Block." *Landscape* 8:24–34.

MacConnell, W. P. (1971) *Remote Sensing Twenty Years of Change in the Human Environment in Massachusetts, 1952–1972.* Amherst, Mass.: University of Massachusetts, College of Agriculture Cooperative Extension Service.

———, and L. E. Garvin (1956) "Cover Mapping a State from Aerial Photographs." *Photogrammetric Engineering* 22(Sept.):702–707.

MacDonald, M. (1967) "Some Distinctive Features of Arguments Used in Criticism of the Arts," pp. 114–130 in W. Elton (ed.), *Aesthetics and Language.* Oxford: Blackwell Scientific Publications Ltd.

Mace, R. L., and W. J. Wicker (1969) "Do Single Family Homes Pay Their Way." Washington, D.C.: Urban Land Institute.

MacKaye, B. (1962) *The New Exploration: A Philosophy of Regional Planning.* Urbana, Ill.: University of Illinois Press.

Mackworth, N. H., and A. J. Morandi (1967) "The Gage Selects Informative Details Within Pictures." *Perception and Psychophysics* 2(11):547–552.

MacLean, P. D. (1970) "The Triune Brain, Emotion and Scientific Bias," in F. O. Schmitt (ed.), *The Neuroscience: Second Study Program.* New York: Rockefeller University.

——— (1973) "The Brain's Generation Gap: Some Human Implications." *ZYGON/Journal of Religion and Science* 8(2):113–127.

———, T. J. Boag, and D. Campbell (1973) *A Triune Concept of the Brain and Behavior.* Toronto: University of Toronto Press.

Magoon, E. (1852) *The Home Book of the Picturesque.* New York.

Manwaring, E. (1925) *Italian Landscape in Eighteenth Century England.* New York: Oxford University Press, Inc.

Margalef, R. (1971) *Perspectives in Ecological Theory,* as quoted in E. P. Odum, *Fundamentals of Ecology.* Philadelphia: Saunders, 3rd ed.

Margolis, J. (1965) *The Language of Art and Art Criticism: Analysis Questions in Aesthetics.* Detroit: Wayne State University.

Marsh, G. P. (1864) *Man and Nature,* D. Lowenthal (ed.). Cambridge, Mass.: Harvard University Press, 1965.

Marsh, P. (ed.) (1955) *The Prose of Philip Freneau.* New Brunswick, N.J.: Scarecrow Press.

Marx, L. (1964) *The Machine in the Garden: Technology and the Pastoral Ideal in America.* New York: Oxford University Press, Inc.

Maryland State Planning Department (1968) *Catalog of Natural Areas in Maryland.* Publication 148. Baltimore, Md.: State of Maryland.

Maslow, A. H. (1970) *Motivation and Personality.* New York: Harper & Row, Inc.

McBride, G. A., and M. Clawson (1970) "Negotiation and Land Conversion." *Journal of the American Institute of Planners* 37(1):22–29.

McCarthy, M. M., R. A. Boots, and B. J. Niemann (1973) "Remote Sensing of Infra-Red Imagery: Critical Data for Land-Use Decision-Making." *Landscape Architecture* (Jan.):133–142.

McClelland, D. C. (1961) *The Achieving Society.* New York: Van Nostrand Reinhold Company.

McHarg, I. (1969) *Design with Nature.* Garden City, N.Y.: Doubleday & Company, Inc.

McKechnie, G. E. (1969) "The Environmental Response Inventory: Preliminary Development." Unpublished report of the Institute of Personality Assessment. Berkeley, Calif.: University of California.

——— (1972) "A Study of Environmental Life Styles." Ph.D. dissertation, Berkeley, Calif.: University of California.

McNeill, W. H. (1963) *The Rise of the West.* Chicago: University of Chicago Press.

Medhurst, F. (1968) "A Method of Regional Landscape Analysis." *Planning Outlook* 4(Spring):61–69.

Melillo, S. T. (1970) "Visual Preferences of Landscape Features." Master's thesis. Amherst, Mass.: University of Massachusetts.

Menchik, M. D. (1971) "Residential Environmental Preferences and Choice: Some Preliminary Empirical Results Relevant to Urban Form." Discussion Paper 46. Philadelphia: Regional Science Research Institute.

Metwally, A. A., and J. L. Wright (1973) "The Dallas Ecological Study." A report to the Dallas Department of Planning and Urban Development. Madison, Wis.: Landscapes Limited.

Miller, A. H., and B. J. Niemann (1971) "An Interstate Corridor Selection Process, the Application of Computer Technology to Highway Location Dynamics." Phase I Report to the State of Wisconsin Department of Transportation. Madison, Wis.: University of Wisconsin.

Miller, G. (1956) "The Magical Number Seven, Plus or Minus Two: Some Limits on Our Capacity for Processing Information." *Psychological Review* 63:80–97.

Miner, J. (1969) *The Preservation of Historic and Cultural Resources*. New York: American Society of Planning Officials.

Morisawa, M. (1971) "Evaluating Riverscapes," in D. R. Coates (ed.), *Environmental Geomorphology, Proceedings: First Annual Symposium*. Binghamton, N.Y.: State University of New York.

Morris, D. (1967) *The Naked Ape*. New York: McGraw-Hill Book Company.

Morton, D., and L. Stark (1971) "Eye Movements and Visual Perception." *Scientific American* 224(6).

Munsinger, H., and W. Kessen (1964) "Uncertainty, Structure and Preference," *Psychological Monographs: General and Applied*, Vol. 78.

Murie, M. (1972) "Evaluation of Natural Environments," pp. 43–53 in W. A. Thomas (ed.), *Indicators of Environmental Quality*. New York: Plenum Publishing Corporation.

Murray, A. C. (ed.) (1967) *Symposium: Methods of Landscape Analysis*. London: Landscape Research Group.

——— (1969) *The West Highlands of Scotland; the seaboard from Kintyre to Cape Wrath*. London: Collins, 2nd ed.

Murray, B. H., and B. J. Niemann, Jr. (1972) "Environmentally Planned Transmission Systems." *AWARE*, Community Performance Publications, Inc., Issue 21.

———, and B. J. Niemann, Jr. (1973) "Permits Methodology." A report to Bonneville Power Administration. Madison, Wis.: Landscapes Limited.

———, A. Tsao, and I. Fahmy (1973) "Transmission Alignment Decision-Making: An Environmental Approach." A report to Wisconsin Electric Power Company. Madison, Wis.: University of Wisconsin.

Murray, H. A. (1943) *Thematic Apperception Test: Pictures and Manual*. Cambridge, Mass.: Harvard University Press.

Nairn, I. (1965) *The American Landscape: A Critical View*. New York: Random House, Inc.

Nash, R. (1973) *Wilderness and the American Mind*, rev. ed. New Haven, Conn.: Yale University Press.

Natural Areas Criteria Committee of the New England Botanical Club, Inc. (1972) "Guidelines and Criteria for the Evaluation of Natural Areas." A report prepared for the New England Natural Resources Center. Amherst, Mass.

Neisser, U. (1967) *Cognitive Psychology*. New York: Appleton-Century-Crofts.

——— (1968) "The Processes of Vision." *Scientific American* 219:204–214.

Neutze, M. (1968) *The Suburban Apartment Boom*. Baltimore: The Johns Hopkins Press.

Newby, F. L. (1971a) "Understanding the Visual Resource." Paper given at the Forest Recreation Symposium at the State University of New York, College of Forestry, Syracuse, N.Y., Oct. 12–14. Upper Darby, Pa.: Northeastern Forest Experiment Station, Forest Service, U.S. Department of Agriculture.

——— (1971b) "Perceptual Assessment of Forested Roadside Landscapes." Ph.D. dissertation, Ann Arbor, Mich.: University of Michigan.

Newman, O. (1972) *Defensible Space*. New York: Macmillan Publishing Co., Inc.

Newton, E. (1950) *The Meaning of Beauty*. New York: Whittlesey House.

Newton, N. T. (1971) *Design on the Land, the Development of Landscape Architecture*. Cambridge, Mass.: Harvard University Press.

New York Times, The (1972) "Subsidized Housing Increases in the Suburbs, While Inner Cities Are Avoided, Alarming Many Officials." Jan. 24:15.

Niemann, B. J. (1973) "Environmental Decision Alignment Process." Madison, Wis.: Madison Gas & Electric Company and Wisconsin Power & Light Company.

Niering, W. A. (1966) *The Life of the Marsh*. New York: McGraw-Hill Book Company.

——— (1970) "The Ecology of Wetlands in Urban Areas," in B. F. Thompson (ed.), *Preserving Our Freshwater Wetlands*. New London, Conn.: Connecticut College Bulletin.

Nieswand, G. H., C. W. Stillman, and A. J. Esser (1972) "Inventory of Estuarine Site Development Lagoon Systems." New Brunswick, N.J.: New Jersey Water Resources Research Institute.

———, C. W. Stillman, and A. J. Esser (1973) "Survey of Estuarine Site Development Lagoon Home Owners." New Brunswick, N.J.: New Jersey Water Resources Research Institute.

Northrup, F. S. C. (1947) *The Meeting of East and West.* New York: Macmillan Publishing Co., Inc.

Norton, T. J. (1967) "Decision Making Techniques for Identifying Aesthetically Superior Highway Environments." Highway Research Record 182: 5–8.

Noton, D. and L. Stark (1971) "Eye Movements and Visual Perception." *Scientific American* 224(6):34–43.

Nowlis, V. (1965) "Research with the Mood Adjective Checklist," in S. S. Tomkins and C. E. Izard (eds.), *Affect, Cognition and Personality.* New York: Springer-Verlag New York, Inc.

Odum, E. P. (1963) *Ecology.* New York: Holt, Rinehart and Winston, Inc.

——— (1969) "Air–Land–Water = An Ecological Whole." *Journal of Soil and Water Conservation* 24(1):4.

——— (1971) *Fundamentals of Ecology,* 3rd ed. Philadelphia: W. B. Saunders Company.

Olgyay, V. (1963) *Design with Climate.* Princeton, N.J.: Princeton University Press.

Olin, P. et al. (1971) "Vermont Scenery Classification and Analysis." Prepared for Planning Department, State of Vermont. Amherst, Mass.: Research Planning and Design Associates, Inc., unpublished.

Olmsted, F. L. (1865) "The Yosemite Valley and the Mariposa Big Trees." Reprinted in *Landscape Architecture* 43(1952):20–23.

Olmsted, F. L., Jr., and T. Kimball (eds.) (1970) *Frederick Law Olmsted, Landscape Architect, 1822–1903.* New York: Benjamin Blom, Inc.

Oosting, H. J. (1956) *The Study of Plant Communities.* San Francisco: W. H. Freeman and Company, Publishers.

Osborne, H. (1970) *The Art of Appreciation.* New York: Oxford University Press, Inc.

Osgood, C. E., G. Suci, and P. H. Tannenbaum (1957) *The Measurement of Meaning.* Urbana, Ill.: University of Illinois Press.

Outdoor Recreation Resources Review Commission (1962) *Outdoor Recreation for America: A Report to the President and to the Congress by the OFFFC.* Washington, D.C.: Government Printing Office.

Parr, A. E. (1965) "City and Psyche." *Yale Review* 55:71–85.

——— (1967) "The Child in the City: Urbanity and the Urban Scene." *Landscape 16:*3–5.

Peters, R. (1973) "Cognitive Maps in Wolves and Men." in W. F. E. Preiser (ed.), *Environmental Design Research,* Vol. 2. Stroudsburg, Pa.: Dowden, Hutchinson & Ross, Inc.

Peterson, G. L. (1967) "A Model of Preference: Quantitative Analysis of the Perception of the Visual Appearance of Residential Neighborhoods." *Journal of Regional Science 7*(1):19–31.

———, and E. S. Neumann (1969) "Modeling and Predicting Human Responses to the Visual Recreation Environment." *Journal of Leisure Research 1:*219–237.

Pfeiffer, J. E. (1969) *The Emergence of Man.* New York: Harper & Row, Inc.

Pimentel, D. (1961) "Species Diversity and Insect Population Outbreaks." *Annals of the Entomology Society of America 54:*76–86.

Pimlott, D. H. (1969) "The Value of Diversity." Paper presented in the Thirty-fourth North American Wildlife Conference, Washington, D.C.

Postman, N., and C. Weingartner (1969) *Teaching as a Subversive Activity.* New York: Delacorte Press.

President's Council on Recreation and Natural Beauty (1968) *From Sea to Shining Sea.* Washington, D.C.: Government Printing Office.

Prohansky, H. M., W. H. Ittleson, and L. G. Rivilin (1970) "Freedom of Choice and Behavior in a Physical Setting," in H. M. Prohansky, W. H. Ittleson, and L. G. Rivilin (eds.), *Environmental Psychology: Man and His Physical Setting.* New York: Holt, Rinehart and Winston, Inc.

Public Land Law Review Commission (1970) *One Third of the Nation's Land.* Washington, D.C.: Government Printing Office.

Pyron, B. (1971) "Form and Space Diversity in Human Habitats: Perceptual Responses." *Environment and Behavior 3:*382–411.

——— (1972) "Form and Diversity in Human Habitats: Judgmental and Attitude Responses." *Environment and Behavior 4:*87–120.

Rabinowitz, C. B., and R. E. Coughlin (1970) "Analysis of Landscape Characteristics Relevant to Preference." Paper 38. Philadelphia: Regional Science Research Institute.

———, and R. E. Coughlin (1971) "Some Experiments in Quantitative Measurement of Landscape Quality." Paper 43. Philadelphia: Regional Science Research Institute.

Randall, W. E., and J. W. Brainerd (undated)

"Educational Values of Wetlands in Massachusetts." Massachusetts Wetlands Committee Fact Sheet 5. Boston: Wildlife Conservation, Inc.

Rapoport, A. (1971) "Designing for Complexity." *Architectural Association Quarterly 3*(Winter): 29–33.

———, and R. Hawkes (1970) "The Perception of Urban Complexity." *Journal of the American Institute of Planners 36:*106–111.

———, and R. E. Kantor (1967) "Complexity and Ambiguity in Environmental Design." *Journal of the American Institute of Planners 33:*210–221.

Rawls, J. (1971) *A Theory of Justice.* Cambridge, Mass.: Harvard University Press.

Redfield, M. P. (ed.) (1962) *Human Nature and the Study of Society: The Papers of Robert Redfield,* Vol. I, pp. 231–253. Chicago: University of Chicago Press.

Reid, G. (1961) *Ecology of Inland Waters and Estuaries.* New York: Van Nostrand Reinhold Company.

Reid, L. M. (1964) *Outdoor Recreation Preferences: A Nationwide Study of User Desires,* reprinted by the B. J. Press.

Reilly, W. K. (ed.) (1973) *The Use of Land.* New York: Thomas Y. Crowell Company.

Reinhart, K. G. (1970) "What's New in Forest Influences on the Environment." Upper Darby, Pa: Northeastern Forest Experiment Station, Forest Service, U.S. Department of Agriculture.

Reischauer, E. O., and J. K. Fairbank (1960) *East Asia: The Great Tradition.* Boston: Houghton Mifflin Company.

Richards, J. H., and D. McKay (1970) "Land Capability for Outdoor Recreation," in E. A. Christiansen (ed.), *Physical Environment, Saskatoon, Canada.* Ottawa: Saskatchewan Research Council in cooperation with the National Research Council of Canada.

Rodgers, W. E. (1970) "Design Criteria for the Visual Resources Formed or Altered During the Construction of Major Highways." Master's thesis. Amherst, Mass.: University of Massachusetts.

Roenigk, W. P., and G. L. Cole (1968) "A Profile of Delaware Campers." Bulletin 370. Newark, Del.: University of Delaware, Agricultural Experiment Station.

Roosevelt, T. (1926) *The Works of Theodore Roosevelt,* National edition. New York: Charles Scribner's Sons.

Rose, S. W. (1966) *A Notation/Simulation Process for Composers of Space.* Lincoln, Neb.: University of Nebraska.

Rotter, J. B. (1966) "Generalized Expectancies for Internal Versus External Control of Reinforcement." *Psychological Mongraphs 80*(609): entire issue.

Rudofsky, B. (1964) *Streets for People.* Garden City, N.Y.: Doubleday & Company, Inc.

Saarinen, T. F. (1969) "Perception of Environment." Resource Paper 5. Washington, D.C.: Association of American Geographers.

Samuel, A. L. (1959) "Some Studies in Machine Learning Using the Game of Checkers." *IBM Journal of Research and Development 3:*211–229.

Sanoff, H. (1969) "Visual Attributes of the Physical Environment," pp. 37–62 in G. J. Coates and K. M. Moffett (eds.), *Response to Environment.* Raleigh, N.C.: School of Design, North Carolina State University.

Sargent, F. O. (1967) "Scenery Classification." Report 18. Burlington, Vt.: Vermont Agricultural Experiment Station.

Sauer, C. O. (1956) "The Agency of Man on the Earth," pp. 49–69 in W. L. Thomas (ed.), *Man's Role in Changing the Face of the Earth.* Chicago: University of Chicago Press.

Sax, J. (1971) *Defending the Environment.* New York: Alfred A. Knopf, Inc.

Scheffey, A. J. W. (1969) *Conservation Commissions in Massachusetts.* Washington, D.C.: The Conservation Foundation.

Schubert, G. A. (1960) *The Public Interest.* New York.: The Free Press.

Seaton, R. W., and J. B. Collins (1972) "Validity and Reliability of Ratings of Simulated Buildings." *Edra III, Proceedings of the Third Environmental Design Research Association Conference,* Los Angeles, Calif.

Shafer, E. L., Jr. (1967) "Forest Aesthetics — A Focal Point in Multiple-Use Management and Research." *Proceedings 14 IUFRO Congress.* Paper 7, Sec. 26, Munich.

——— (1968) "The Demand for Water-Oriented Outdoor Recreation." *Parks and Recreation 3*(2):23–24, 57.

——— (1969) "Perception of Natural Environments." *Environment and Behavior 1:*71–82.

———, and H. D. Burke (1965) "Preferences for Outdoor Recreation Facilities in Four State Parks." *Journal of Forestry 63:*512–518.

———, and J. Mietz (1969) "Aesthetic and Emotional Experience Rate High with Northeast Wilderness Hikers." *Environment and Behavior* 1(2):187–197.

——, and J. Mietz (1970) "It Seems Possible to Quantify Scenic Beauty in Photographs." U.S. Department of Agriculture Forest Service Research Paper NE-162. Upper Darby, Pa.: Northeastern Forest Experiment Station, Forest Service, U.S. Department of Agriculture.

——, and T. A. Richards (1971) "Take the Mountain to Mohammed." Upper Darby, Pa.: Northeastern Forest Experiment Station, Forest Service, U.S. Department of Agriculture.

——, and T. A. Richards (1974) "A Comparison of Viewer Reactions to Outdoor Scenes and Photographs of Those Scenes." U.S. Department of Agriculture Forest Service Research Paper NE-302. Upper Darby, Pa.: Northeastern Forest Experiment Station, Forest Service, U.S. Department of Agriculture.

——, and R. C. Thompson (1968) "Models that Describe Use of Adirondack Campgrounds." *Forest Science* 14(Dec.):383–391.

——, and M. Tooby (1973) "Landscape Preferences: An International Replication." *Journal of Leisure Research,* 5(3):60–65.

——, R. C. Thompson, R. Discenze, and J. F. Hamilton, Jr. (1966) "A Systems Analysis That Describes Use Intensities of Adirondack Campgrounds." Unpublished report. Upper Darby, Pa.: Northeastern Forest Experiment Station.

——, J. F. Hamilton, Jr., and E. A. Schmidt (1969) "Natural Landscape Preferences: A Predictive Model." *Journal of Leisure Research* 1:1–19.

Shannon, C. E., and W. Weaver (1949) *The Mathematical Theory of Communication.* Urbana, Ill.: University of Illinois Press.

Shaw, S. P., and C. G. Fredline (1956) "Wetlands of the United States." Circular 39, U.S. Department of the Interior, Fish and Wildlife Service. Washington, D.C.: Government Printing Office.

Shepard, P. (1967) *Man in the Landscape.* New York: Alfred A. Knopf, Inc.

Skinner, D. N. (1968) "Landscape Survey with Special Reference to Recreation and Tourism in Scotland." *Planning Outlook* 4(Spring):37–43.

Smardon, R. C. (1972) "Assessing Visual–Cultural Values of Inland Wetlands in Massachusetts."
Master's thesis. Amherst, Mass.: University of Massachusetts.

—— (1973) "Visual-Cultural Values of Wetlands," in J. S. Larson (ed.), *A Guide to Important Characteristics and Values of Freshwater Wetlands in the Northeast.* Publication 31. Amherst, Mass.: University of Massachusetts, Water Resources Research Center.

Sneath, P. H. A., and R. R. Sokal (1973) *Numerical Taxonomy: The Principles of Numerical Classification.* San Francisco: W. H. Freeman and Company, Publishers.

Soil Conservation Service (1966) "U.S.D.A. Guide to Making Appraisals of Potentials for Outdoor Recreation Developments." Hyattsville, Md.: U.S. Department of Agriculture, Soil Conservation Service.

—— (1972) "Environmental Quality Study," Amherst, Mass.: Soil Conservation Service, Massachusetts State Office, working draft.

Sonnenfeld, J. (1966) "Variable Values in Space and Landscape: An Inquiry into the Nature of Environmental Necessity." *Journal of Social Issues* 22:71–82.

—— (1967) "Environmental Perception and Adaptation Level in the Arctic," pp. 43–59 in D. Lowenthall (ed.), *Environmental Perception and Behavior,* Research Paper 109. Chicago: University of Chicago, Department of Geography.

—— (1969) "Equivalence and Distortion of the Perceptual Environment." *Environment and Behavior* 1:82–100.

Spoehr, A. (1956) "Cultural Differences in the Interpretation of Natural Resources," in W. L. Thomas, Jr. (ed.), *Man's Role in Changing the Face of the Earth.* Chicago: University of Chicago Press.

Spreiregen, P. D. (1965) *Urban Design: The Architecture of Cities and Towns.* New York: McGraw-Hill Book Company.

Stainbrook, E. (1969) "Human Needs and the Natural Environment," pp. 1–6 in Bureau of Sport Fisheries and Wildlife, U.S. Department of the Interior, *Man and Nature in the City,* Washington, D.C.: Government Printing Office.

Stankey, G. H. (1971) "The Perception of Wilderness Recreation Carrying Capacity: A Geographic Study in Natural Resource Management." Ph.D. dissertation. E. Lansing, Mich.: Michigan State University.

Stea, D. (1969) "Environmental Perception and Cognition: Toward a Model for Mental Maps," pp. 63–76 in Student Publication of the School of Design, Vol. 18. Raleigh, N.C.: North Carolina State University.

Stegner, W. (1969) *The Sound of Mountain Water.* Garden City, N.Y.: Doubleday & Company, Inc.

Steinitz and Rogers Associates and Enviromedia, Inc. (1970) *Natural Resource Protection Study.* Cambridge, Mass., and Minneapolis.

Stillman, C. W. (1966) "The Issues in the Storm King Controversy." Black Rock Forest Papers 27. Cornwall, N.Y.: Harvard Black Rock Forest.

——— (1972) "Reflections on Environmental Education." *Teachers College Record* 74(Dec.):195–200.

Stone, G. P., and M. J. Taves (1958) "Camping in the Wildnerness," pp. 290–305 in E. Larrabee and R. Meyerson (eds.), *Massachusetts Leisure.* New York: The Free Press.

Strom, S. (1973) "The Influence of Trees on the Appraised Value of Unimproved Residential Land." Master's thesis. Amherst, Mass.: University of Massachusetts.

Strong, A. L. (1965) *Open Space for Urban America.* Urban Renewal Administration Department of Housing and Urban Development. Washington, D.C.: Government Printing Office.

——— (1971) *Planned Urban Environments: Sweden, Finland, Israel, Netherlands, France.* Baltimore: The Johns Hopkins Press.

Suttles, G. D. (1968) *The Social Order of the Slum: Ethnicity and Territory in the Inner City.* Chicago: University of Chicago Press.

——— (1972) *The Social Construction of Communities.* Chicago: University of Chicago Press.

Tahoe Regional Planning Agency (1971) "Scenic Analyses of the Lake Tahoe Region." South Lake Tahoe, Calif.

Tandy, C. R. V. (1968) "The Future of the Landscape Plan." *Planning Outlook* 4(Spring): 79–88.

Taylor, W. P. (1956) *The Deer of North America.* Harrisburg, Pa.: Stackpole Books; and Washington, D.C.: The Wildlife Management Institute.

Tennessee Valley Authority (1938) *The Scenic Resources of the Tennessee Valley.* Washington, D.C.: Government Printing Office.

Terwilliger, R. R. (1963) "Pattern Complexity and Affective Arousal." *Perceptual and Motor Skills* 17:386–395.

Thiel, P. (1961) "A Sequence-Experience Notation for Architectural and Urban Space." *Town Planning Review* 32:33–52.

Thomas, E. L. (1968) "Movements of the Eye; with Biographical Sketch." *Scientific American* 219:12.

Thomas, W. L., Jr. (1956) *Man's Role in Changing the Face of the Earth.* Chicago: University of Chicago Press.

Thoreau, Henry David (1862) "Walking," in *Excursions.* New York: Corinth Books, 1962.

Thornbrough, G. (1973) "Scenic Resources of the Upper Great Lakes Basin." Master's thesis. Ann Arbor, Mich.: University of Michigan.

Threinen, C. W., and L. E. Engelbert (1966) *The Significance of Marshes in Lake Water Quality Maintenance.* Madison, Wis.: Wisconsin Conservation Department.

Toll, S. I. (1969) *Zoned American.* New York: Grossman Publishers.

Tombaugh, L. W. (1970) "Option and Existence Value of Outstanding Natural Environments." Paper written for the National Science Foundation (mimeographed).

Toth, R. E. (1968) "Criteria for Evaluating the Valuable Natural Resources of the TIRAC Region." Stroudsburg, Pa.: Tocks Island Regional Advisory Council consulting report.

——— (1971) "Criteria for Land Planning and Design." *Landscape Architecture* 62(1):43–48.

Travis, M., G. Elsner, and M. Kourtz (1973) "A Computer Software Package to Convert Digitized Geographic Boundary and Contour Data to a Uniform Grid Structure." Information Report FFX-44. Ottawa: Forest Fire Research Institute.

Trippan, R. E. (1958) *Wildlife Management.* New York: McGraw-Hill Book Company.

Trueman, A. E. (1949) *Geology and Scenery in England and Wales.* Baltimore: Pelican Books.

Tryon, R. C., and D. W. Bailey (1970) *Cluster Analysis.* New York: McGraw-Hill Book Company.

Tuan, Y. F. (1961) "Topophilia or Sudden Encounter with the Landscape." *Landscape* 11(Fall):29–32.

——— (1967) "Attitudes Toward Environment: Themes and Approaches," pp. 4–17 in D. Lowenthal (ed.), *Environmental Perception and Behavior.* Research Paper 109. Chicago: University of Chicago, Department of Geography.

——— (1971) "Man and Nature." Resource Paper

360 *Selected Bibliography*

10. Washington, D.C.: Association of American Geographers.

—— (1973) "Ambiguity in Attitudes Towards Environment." *Annals of the Association of American Geographers* 63(4):411–423.

Tunnard, C., and B. Pushkarev (1963) *Man Made America: Chaos or Control?* New Haven, Conn.: Yale University Press.

Twiss, R. H. (1965) "Regional Landscape Design: A Systematic Approach to Research and Education." Paper presented to the National Conference on Instruction in Landscape Architecture, Harvard University.

——, and R. B. Litton (1966) "Resource Use in the Regional Landscape." *Natural Resources Journal* 6:76–81.

——, and R. B. Litton (1968) "Research on Forest Environmental Design." Seattle, Wash. *Proceedings, Society of American Foresters.*

Udall, S. L. (1963) *The Quiet Crisis.* New York: Holt, Rinehart and Winston, Inc.

U.S. Army Corps of Engineers (1971) *Charles River Study*, Appendix D: Hydrology and Hydraulics; Appendix H: Flood Management Plan Formulation. Waltham, Mass.: New England Division, preliminary draft.

U.S. Department of Agriculture (1964) "Recreation Memorandum 3, Supplement 3." Staff publication. Hyattsville, Md.: Soil Conservation Service.

—— (1966) "Guide to Making Appraisals of Potentials for Outdoor Recreation." Staff publication. Hyattsville, Md.: Soil Conservation Service, June.

—— (1968a) *Forest Service Manual, Title 2400 — Timber Management.* Portland, Ore.: Forest Service, Region 6, Suppl. 63.

—— (1968b) "Delineating Landscape View Areas . . . A Computer Approach." Research Note PSW-180. Berkeley; Calif.: Forest Service.

—— (1971) *Forest Landscape Management.* Missoula, Mont.: Forest Service, Northern Region.

—— (1972) *The Visual Management System.* Portland, Ore.: Forest Service, Northwest Region.

—— (1973a) *Visual Resource Management Guides — Visual Quality Standard Determination and Application.* San Francisco: Forest Service, California Region.

—— (1973b) *National Forest Landscape Management*, Vol. 1. Washington, D.C.: Government Printing Office.

U.S. Department of Commerce (1966) *A Proposed Program for Scenic Roads and Parkways.* Washington, D.C.: Government Printing Office.

U.S. Department of the Interior (1941) *A Study of the Park and Recreation Problem of the United States.* Washington, D.C.: Government Printing Office.

—— (1954a) *Wetlands Inventory of Massachusetts.* Boston: Fish and Wildlife Service, Office of River Basin Studies, Region V.

—— (1954b) *Parks for America.* Washington, D.C.: Government Printing Office.

—— (1962) "The Value of Wetlands to Modern Society," in *Proceedings of the MAR Conference*, Nov. 12–16. IUCN Publication (new series) 3. Washington, D.C.: Government Printing Office.

—— (1966a) *NPS Criteria for Parklands.* Washington, D.C.: Government Printing Office.

—— (1966b) *Trails for America.* Washington, D.C.: Government Printing Office.

—— (1967) *Surface Mining and Our Environment.* Washington, D.C.: Government Printing Office.

—— (1968) *Administrative Policies for Natural Areas of the National Park Service: Recreation Areas of the National Park Service.* Washington, D.C.: Government Printing Office.

Van Doren, C. S. (1967) "An Interaction Travel Model for Projecting Attendance of Campers at Michigan State Parks: A Study in Recreation Geography." Ph.D. dissertation. East Lansing, Mich.: Michigan State University.

Vedenin, Y. A., and M. M. Miroschnichenko (1971) "Evaluation of the Natural Environment for Recreational Purposes." *Ekistics* 31(184):223–226.

Vermont Central Planning Office (1966) *Vermont Scenery Preservation.* Montpelier, Vt.

Vitz, P. C. (1966) "Preference for Different Amounts of Visual Complexity." *Behavioral Science* 11:105–114.

Wadleigh, R. S. (1963) "Effects of Swamp Storage on Flood Peaks." Paper presented at the 1963 Annual Meeting of the North Atlantic Section of the American Society of Agricultural Engineers, Portland, Ore.

—— (1965) "Effects of Swamp Storage upon Storm Peak Flows." Master's thesis. Amherst, Mass.: University of Massachusetts.

Wagar, J. A. (1966) "Quality in Outdoor Recreation." *Trends in Parks and Recreation* 3(3):9–12.

Walker, E. L. (1964) "Psychological Complexity as a Basis for a Theory of Motivation and Choice," pp. 47–95 in D. Levine (ed.), *Nebraska Symposium on Motivation*. Lincoln, Neb.: University of Nebraska Press.

———— (1970) "Complexity and Preferences in Animals and Men." *Annals of the New York Academy of Science* 169:619–652.

Water Resources Council (1970) *Standards for Planning Water and Land Resources*. Washington, D.C.: The Council.

Watts, M. T. (1957) *Reading the Landscape: An Adventure in Ecology*. New York: Macmillan Publishing Co., Inc.

Weaver, W. (1960) "The Disparagement of Statistical Evidence." *Science* 132:1859.

Webb, E. J., D. T. Campbell, R. D. Schwartz, and L. Sechrest (1966) *Unobtrusive Measures: Nonreactive Research in the Social Sciences*. Chicago: Rand McNally & Company.

Webster's New Collegiate Dictionary (1953) Springfield, Mass.: G. & C. Merriam Company.

Weddle, A. E. (1969) "Techniques in Landscape Planning." Town Planning Institute Journal (London, England) Nov.:387–391.

———— (1970) "The Approach to Landscape in the South Hampshire Plan." National Countryside Classification Structure Seminar Proceedings, Dec.

Weitenkampf, F. (1945) "Early American Landscape Prints." *Art Quarterly* 8(1):40–67.

Wharton, C. H. (1970) *The Southern River Swamp — A Multi-use Environment*. Atlanta, Ga.: Bureau of Business and Economic Research, School of Business Administration, Georgia State University.

White, G. F. (1966) "Formation and Role of Public Attitudes," in H. Jarrett (ed.), *Environmental Quality in a Growing Economy*. Resources for the Future, Inc. Baltimore: The Johns Hopkins Press.

White, M., and L. White (1962) *The Intellectual Versus the City: From Thomas Jefferson to Frank Lloyd Wright*. Cambridge, Mass.: Harvard University and MIT Press.

Whyte, W. H. (1964) *Cluster Development*. New York: American Conservation Association.

———— (1970) *Last Landscape*. Garden City, N.Y.: Doubleday & Company, Inc.

Wildavsky, A. (1967) "Aesthetic Power or the Triumph of the Sensitive Minority over the Vulgar Mass: A Political Analysis of the New Economics." *Daedalus* 96:1115–1128.

Wildland Research Center (1962) *Wilderness and Recreation — A Report on Resources, Values, and Problems*. Washington, D.C.: Outdoor Recreation Resources Review Commission.

Williams, E. (1971) "History of the Hockomock," in E. Williams et al., *Hockomock: Wonder Wetland*. Boston: Massachusetts Audubon Society and Department of Natural Resources, Commonwealth of Massachusetts.

Williams, H. G., and W. M. Belden (1969) *Appalachia Recreation and Cultural Resources Study*. Syracuse, N.Y.: State University, College of Forestry at Syracuse University.

Willis, N. P. (1840) *American Scenery*. 2 vols. London: G. Virtue.

Wilson, S. O., D. J. Beevers, B. Fullen, and N. Pierson (1970) *Potential Recreation and Open Space Areas in New York State*. N.Y.S. SCORP Technical Paper 6. Albany, N.Y.: New York State Office of Parks and Recreation.

Winkel, G. H. (1968) *Response to the Roadside Environment*. San Francisco: Arthur D. Little, Inc.

Wohlwill, J. F. (1968) "Amount of Stimulus Exploration and Preference as Differential Functions of Stimulus Complexity." *Perception and Psychophysics* 4:307–312.

———— (1971) "Developmental Evidence of the Difference Between Specific and Diverse Exploration." Paper presented at Symposium on Preference and Interest as Function of Stimulus Complexity, SRCD, Minneapolis, April.

———— (1973a) "Factors in the Differential Response to the Natural and the Man-Made Environments." Paper presented at the Symposium on Affective Response to the Outdoor Environment held at the American Psychological Association Meeting, Montreal.

———— (1973b) "The Environment Is Not in the Head," pp. 166–181 in W. F. E. Preiser, *Environmental Design Research*, Vol. 2. Stroudsburg, Pa.: Dowden, Hutchinson & Ross, Inc.

Woodbury, C. (1966) "The Role of the Regional Planner in Preserving Habitats and Scenic Values," in F. F. Darling and J. P. Milton (eds.), *Future Environments of North America*. Garden City, N.Y.: Doubleday & Company, Inc.

Wordsworth, W. (1835) *Guide to the Lakes*. New York: Oxford University Press, Inc., 1970.

Wyckoff, J. B. (1969) "Rural to Urban Land Conversion and Environmental Quality." *Massachusetts Heritage* 7(4):1–3.

Zajonc, R. B. (1968) "Attitudinal Effects of Mere Exposure." *Journal of Personality and Social Psychology Monography Supplement* 9(2):1–27.

Zube, E. H. (1963) *Taconite and the Landscape.* Madison, Wis.: Wisconsin Department of Resource Development.

——— (1970) "Evaluating the Visual and Cultural Landscape." *Journal of Soil and Water Conservation* 25:137–141.

——— (1971a) "Environmental Quality Elements of a Water and Related Land Resources Plan." Consultants' report. Prepared for the New England River Basins Commission.

——— (1971b) "Visual Landscape Dimensions for Design and Planning Decisions." Paper prepared for Resources for the Future Multidisciplinary Workshop on Research in Wildlife and Scenic Resources. Missoula, Mont. Aug. 4–5.

——— (1973a) "Scenery as a Natural Resource: Implications of Public Policy and Problems of Definition, Description and Evaluation." *Landscape Architecture* 63(Jan.):126–132.

——— (1973b) "Rating Everyday Rural Landscapes of the Northeastern U.S." *Landscape Architecture* 63:370–375.

———, and C. A. Carlozzi (1967) "An Inventory and Interpretation — Selected Resources of the Island of Nantucket." Cooperative Extension Service Publication 4. Amherst, Mass.: University of Massachusetts.

———, et al. (1970) *North Atlantic Regional Water Resources Study:* Appendix N, Visual and Cultural Environment. Amherst, Mass.: Research Planning and Design Associates, Inc.

———, T. W. Anderson, and D. G. Pitt (1973) "Measuring the Landscape: Perceptual Responses and Physical Dimensions." *Landscape Research News (England)* 1(6):4–5.

———, D. G. Pitt, and T. W. Anderson (1974) "Perception and Measurement of Scenic Resources in the Southern Connecticut River Valley." Amherst, Mass.: University of Massachusetts, Institute for Man and Environment.

INDEX

363